The Queerness of Home

The
QUEERNESS
of HOME

Gender, Sexuality, and the Politics of Domesticity after World War II

STEPHEN VIDER

The University of Chicago Press
Chicago and London

The University of Chicago Press, Chicago 60637
The University of Chicago Press, Ltd., London
© 2021 by Stephen Vider
Published 2021
Printed and bound by CPI Group (UK) Ltd, Croydon, CR0 4YY

30 29 28 27 26 25 24 23 22 21   1 2 3 4 5

ISBN-13: 978-0-226-80819-2 (cloth)
ISBN-13: 978-0-226-80836-9 (paper)
ISBN-13: 978-0-226-80822-2 (e-book)
DOI: https://doi.org/10.7208/chicago/9780226808222.001.0001

Publication of this book has been supported by the Hull
Memorial Publication Fund of Cornell University.

Library of Congress Cataloging-in-Publication Data

Names: Vider, Stephen, author.
Title: The queerness of home : gender, sexuality, and the politics
of domesticity after World War II / Stephen Vider.
Description: Chicago : University of Chicago Press, 2021. |
Includes bibliographical references and index.
Identifiers: LCCN 2021007617 | ISBN 9780226808192 (cloth) | ISBN
9780226808369 (paperback) | ISBN 9780226808222 (ebook)
Subjects: LCSH: Sexual minorities—Social conditions. | Domestic relations. |
Sexual minorities—Legal status, laws, etc. | Sexual minorities' families.
Classification: LCC HQ73 .V53 2021 | DDC 306.76—dc23
LC record available at https://lccn.loc.gov/2021007617

♾ This paper meets the requirements of
ANSI/NISO Z39.48-1992 (Permanence of Paper).

CONTENTS

CONTENTS

INTRODUCTION
The Politics and Performance of Home

"I'm Marie, and I'm HIV positive. Welcome to my home. I would like to, sort of, let you see how it is living with a person that's HIV positive. We can go through the house and we can see what is and is not different from before. People tend to have misinformation or a misconception that people who are HIV positive should not be touched, talked to, or visited even, so please, welcome, and come in."

These words begin "Being at Home with HIV," a core sequence of the 1990 documentary *We Care: A Video for Care Providers of People Affected by AIDS*. The film was produced by WAVE (Women's AIDS Video Enterprise), a multiracial media collective based in Brooklyn. Marie is a fifty-year-old African American woman who lives in Brooklyn with her twenty-two-year-old son, her three-year-old granddaughter, and her partner. The sequence is intimate and unguarded: Marie greets the filmmakers at the door, and the camera follows her closely as she gives a tour of the apartment room by room. The camera pans across two purple couches in the living room as Marie explains, "It's the same as it's always been. I need a new carpet, but that's another story." A microphone is clipped to Marie's blue dress, and the cord trails behind her.[1]

Marie emphasizes again and again how little has changed since she was diagnosed. She still cooks everyone's meals, and she doesn't use separate pots, pans, or dishes. "I tend to not let nobody use my glass," she admits, "because I've always been that way. My glass is my glass, and my cup is my cup." In the kitchen, she keeps her AZT in a high cabinet, but she always kept her medications and vitamins out of children's reach. In the bedroom, the camera pans again—stuffed animals on the bed, a tabletop fan at the window, a jewelry box open on the dresser—and zooms in on Marie (fig. I.1). "I can't see where no one would get anything by sitting here, sleeping here with me, or walking in this room. . . . Living with a person with the virus does not mean totally uprooting your lifestyle."

The sequence was filmed using a VHS camcorder by Alexandra Juhasz,

FIGURE I.1.   In the 1990 video *We Care*, Marie gives a tour of the apartment she shares with her partner, children, and grandchildren to show "how it is living with a person that's HIV positive." The video, filmed by Alexandra Juhasz, ends in Marie's bedroom. Video still from *We Care: A Video for Care Providers of People Affected by AIDS* (1990), courtesy of Alexandra Juhasz.

the founder of WAVE, with another collective member, Marie's partner, Sharon Penceal, joining her behind the camera. Camcorders had become commercially available in the early 1980s and were largely targeted to middle- and upper-middle-class parents to record birthdays, holidays, vacations, and other family events. Activists quickly recognized the potential of the camcorder, too, to record and circulate stories and voices ignored by the mainstream media. Beginning in the late 1980s, AIDS activists began using camcorders to record demonstrations and promote empowerment for people with HIV/AIDS—still they rarely ventured into people's homes. "Being at Home with HIV" was a radical departure, reorienting the camera to the everyday.[2]

For Marie, opening her home to the camera was not without risk. In the 1980s and 1990s, people living with HIV/AIDS faced open hostility, discrimination, fear, and apathy. Disclosing that you were living with the virus could come with consequences ranging from loss of job to loss of home or family. Marie and the filmmakers refused that stigma by bringing the camera and the audience into her home, challenging dominant, often dehumanizing media representations of people with HIV/AIDS. Women of color, in particular, were often overlooked in mainstream discussions of HIV/AIDS—it would be another three years before the Centers for Disease Control would even update its definition of HIV/AIDS to account for women's symptoms.[3] Marie's home and all its objects—the couches, the carpet, the dishes in the china cabinet, the flowers on the table, the brass pans hanging in the kitchen, the toothbrushes, the stuffed animals—made HIV/AIDS ordinary and made people with HIV/AIDS more familiar—a part of the family. "Being at home with HIV" meant belonging, and belonging meant deserving care. Marie framed her revelation of home as educational—to let the audience see "how it is living with a person that's HIV positive"—but it was also a political act: a means of claiming community.

Home has long been privileged in American life as a central site of intimate affiliation, a protected sphere where romance, marriage, and the family were imagined to find their deepest expression. For Americans during the decades after World War II, homemaking—the performance of domesticity—was also increasingly understood as both an expression and measure of communal and national belonging. The reality of domestic life varied widely, but the dominant script was clear enough: government officials, mental health experts, and popular media all depicted the white, marital, reproductive, suburban home as a unique source of personal and national stability. Those who deviated from the ideal were in turn imagined and frequently treated as outsiders from the home, the family, and mainstream American society. Those norms shifted in the 1960s and 1970s, as feminist writers and activists challenged the male breadwinner/female homemaker ideal, and an emerging social and sexual counterculture challenged the constraints of marriage and the model of the nuclear family. Still, the home largely remained a protected, sentimentalized space for personal expression, family life, romantic and sexual intimacy, and communal connection.[4]

Lesbian, gay, bisexual, transgender, and queer people did not simply reproduce or reject such ideals but rather elaborated new domestic styles and intimacies as a primary means of negotiating their relationship to postwar sexual and gender norms and the nation. This book traces these alternative forms of home life, both to reveal the place of the home in LGBTQ history and to rethink the persistent power of domesticity in shaping American culture and politics. From the start of the modern LGBTQ rights movement in the 1950s through the emergence of the HIV/AIDS epidemic in the 1980s, LGBTQ activists mobilized home as a site of creative tension between integration and resistance: they adapted, challenged, and reshaped domestic conventions at the same time they reaffirmed the home as a privileged site of intimate, communal, and national belonging.[5]

The arc of LGBTQ history I trace in this book turns on the changing social and political stakes of privacy in the United States. In the 1950s, early

LGBTQ activists largely looked to the home as a zone of privacy, a space that provided relative protection from the surveillance of neighbors and the state. Yet by the 1990s, LGBTQ activists increasingly came to see the state as an ally in protecting the everyday practices, privileges, and rights that domestic space was presumed to secure. LGBTQ activists no longer viewed the home as a haven *from* the state, but rather a haven protected *by* the state.

The 1970s was a key pivot in this shift, as LGBTQ activists worked at once to remake domestic norms and achieve wider acceptance and support for LGBTQ people. While the 1970s is often remembered for a new flourishing of public queer cultures—particularly in cities like New York and San Francisco—LGBTQ activists also turned increasingly to domestic space as a site of political, cultural, and economic contestation and possibility. Alongside feminists, New Left activists, and other countercultural radicals, LGBTQ activists increasingly questioned the gender, sexual, and spatial conventions of the American home and family: they experimented with novel forms of household formation; they questioned architectural practices; they worked to disentangle domesticity from capitalist consumption; and they developed new modes of community care and support, centered in home and housing. Through these varied efforts, LGBTQ activists wrestled with their relationship to the state, their communities, and the wider American public, aiming not only to remake their own lives but to remake how Americans more broadly understood domesticity.

The history of queer homemaking has been, and remains, largely absent in histories of LGBTQ life, culture, and politics, and histories of home and family. Scholars tracing the history of the American family and home, for one, have tended to reaffirm the heterosexuality of the household—particularly in studies of the Cold War. Elaine Tyler May, for example, in her classic 1988 book, *Homeward Bound*, notes the Cold War oppression of gay men, but does not explore how gay men may have used domestic space to build lives and communities of their own.[6]

Scholars of LGBTQ history, meanwhile, have largely prioritized public and commercial spaces over private ones as the major sites of LGBTQ community and political formation. In his foundational 1983 book, *Sexual Politics, Sexual Communities*, John D'Emilio, for example, situates the emergence of gay and lesbian bars as the most important precondition for the development of gay social and political identities in the decades after World War II.[7] Many of the groundbreaking works that followed, including George Chauncey's *Gay New York* and Nan Alamilla Boyd's study of San Francisco, *Wide Open Town*, similarly stress the importance of public and commercial spaces—not only bars but also cafes, nightclubs, theaters, bathhouses, parks, beaches, public restrooms, and the street itself—as sites of queer social and sexual connection.[8]

Discussions of domestic space have been far less frequent and more fleeting. Chauncey's *Gay New York*, for example, briefly touches on the role of rooming houses, residential hotels, and YMCAs in enabling many working-class men, from the 1900s to the 1940s, the independence necessary to pursue sexual contacts outside the bounds of marriage. Middle-class white men, at the same time, increasingly set up homes in the city's expanding number of apartment houses, where they could pursue same-sex relationships and host friends with even greater privacy.[9] Several historians have also observed that apartment and house parties were an important venue for gay men and lesbians to socialize in many US cities.[10] These discussions, however, only hint at the range of ways LGBTQ people have made use of domestic space and the many meanings those homes have held for understandings of identity, sexuality, kinship, and community.

The limited attention to domestic space in United States LGBTQ history stems, in part, from the emergence of LGBTQ studies out of the gay liberation movement of the 1970s. The politics of gay liberation were, at their core, a politics of visibility. Taking a cue from radical feminism, the Black Power movement, and 1960s counterculture, gay liberation activists prioritized authentic self-presentation—"coming out"—as central to the larger political goals of increased acceptance and sexual freedom.[11] This new emphasis on visibility brought with it an implicit rejection of privacy, consolidated in the popular slogan "Out of the closets, into the streets." The idea and image of the "closet" first emerged in the 1960s but ascended in usage in the 1970s. It was, first and foremost, a metaphor for personal secrecy and revelation, but quickly became shorthand to describe what activists imagined as a more repressed mode of LGBTQ life before gay liberation. Historians of LGBTQ politics and culture since the 1970s have remained indebted to the paradigms embedded in the image and language of "coming out of the closet"—from invisibility to visibility, from isolation to community, from private to public—even as they have questioned such neat narratives.[12]

Since the 1990s, scholars in queer theory and queer studies have also tended to align domesticity with assimilation. In their 1998 essay, "Sex in Public," Lauren Berlant and Michael Warner critiqued the increasing privatization of American sexual and political life through the idealization and prioritization of heteronormative modes of intimacy—principally the romantic couple and the family. Berlant and Warner aimed to expose the hegemonic practices and unquestioned privileges of heterosexual culture—"a tacit but central organizing index of social membership"—and imagined instead the expansion of a queer world or counterpublic that enabled and sustained modes of intimacy "that bear no necessary relation to domestic space, to kinship, to the couple form, to property, or to the nation." Berlant and Warner wrote, alongside other activists and scholars, in response to the growing erosion of public queer social and sexual cultures, both spaces of radical sexual expression and the unconventional relationships they made possible. They pointed, as principal example, to New York City's new zoning code, passed in 1995 under the Giuliani administration, effectively shutting down the majority of the city's adult entertainment businesses. At the same time, a growing number of lesbian and gay legal advocates, as well as gay pundits, had begun pushing for the recognition of same-sex marriages, as a means of protecting the rights of lesbian and gay couples and families and more broadly drawing lesbians and gay men into the "mainstream" of American culture. The movement for same-sex marriage had spurred resistance from the start, but Berlant and Warner's essay helped to crystallize a queer critique of marriage as inherently heteronormative—a point Warner would amplify in his 1999 book, *The Trouble with Normal*.[13]

Lisa Duggan echoed many of these points in her 2002 essay on what she called a "new homonormativity"—"a politics that does not contest dominant heteronormative assumptions and institutions, but upholds and sustains them, while promising the possibility of a demobilized gay constituency and a privatized, depoliticized gay culture anchored in domesticity and consumption." Duggan reframed the growing push for same-sex marriage as a cultural extension of neoliberalism—government policies, spearheaded by conservative and liberal administrations alike, to privatize industry and trade as well as many services and institutions once operated by the state, ranging from schools to prisons. Pointing especially to an influential cohort of libertarian/conservative gay writers and pundits, like one-time *New Republic* editor Andrew Sullivan, Duggan argued that advocates for same-sex marriage aimed to marginalize radical queer voices and instead privatize gay politics and culture within the constrained field of the family. As Duggan summarized, "There is no vision of a collective, democratic public culture or of an ongoing engagement with contentious, cantankerous queer politics. Instead we have been administered a kind of political sedative—we get marriage and the military then we go home and cook dinner, forever." Duggan's term "homonormativity" has since been adopted widely by historians and queer studies scholars to critique the ways the LGBTQ rights movement and LGBTQ culture have accepted, and perpetuated, a model of mainstream approval predicated on adopting conventional white middle-class norms of social respectability. Yet scholars have also tended to use Duggan's term uncritically and out of historical context, taking the link between domesticity and normativity for granted.[14]

This book aims instead to uncover the queerness of home. Home, I argue, has been a crucial though contradictory space in LGBTQ life and politics—a site of constraint and a site of self-expression, a site of isolation and a site of deep connection, a site of secrecy and a site of recognition. This history not only disrupts now-standard narratives of LGBTQ history but also alters understandings of the meanings and functions of domestic space in American culture more broadly, revealing the home for its perverse contradictions as a normative structure.

This book complements a growing body of scholarship that has begun to bridge LGBTQ history and histories of the family and marriage in the decades after World War II. Heather Murray has investigated how lesbians and gay men shaped and were shaped by relationships with their families of origin. Daniel Rivers has traced how gay fathers and lesbian mothers navigated heteronormative social and legal pressures and came to advocate for their rights as parents. And Lauren Gutterman has shown how women explored and expressed desire for other women within the confines of heterosexual marriage. These works have all demonstrated that postwar marriage and family were more flexible, and more queer, than historians have previously acknowledged.[15] Here, I specifically take up domesticity as a broader category of social formation, to investigate the workings of home for both its material reality and its cultural and political meanings—that is, both as a mode of social performance and a form of cultural citizenship.[16]

DOMESTICITY AS PERFORMANCE

Scholarship on the history of home life in the nineteenth and twentieth centuries has tended to frame domesticity primarily as an ideology: a system of fixed social ideals about how everyday home life should be organized. I understand domesticity differently, as a flexible and ongoing act of social performance. It is the embodied and performative practice of making home: through the everyday acts of creating, maintaining, and being at home, individuals make continuous claims to the control of space over time. They designate a space as their own, separate from the wider world, while defining simultaneously that space's insiders and outsiders—who belongs, who does not, and in what ways: family, household, friends, workers, neighbors, strangers. I use the term "domesticity," then, in a capacious sense to capture the multiple ways people make home and, in turn, make themselves—how they create space (building, decorating, renovating), how they use and maintain that space (cooking, eating, sleeping, cleaning, throwing parties), and how those spaces and practices shape, support, and constrain their identities and relationships. By framing domesticity in terms of performance, I do not mean to deny the power of domestic ideals and ideologies—all acts of homemaking are structured by personal and cultural ideals, as well as by social and economic possibilities and limits. Rather, I focus on the dynamic ways that individuals understand and navigate those ideals.

This reframing of domesticity draws on several major sociological, anthropological, and phenomenological discussions of everyday life in terms of performance and embodiment. Sociologist Erving Goffman was among the first theorists to reread everyday life in theatrical terms: for Goffman, individuals convey their identities, affiliations, and values through an ongoing series of social performances.[17] Judith Butler extends this theatrical reading of everyday life to reframe gender as "an identity instituted through a *stylized repetition of acts.*" For Butler, gender is a kind of script, one that preexists the actor but requires interpretation. The body, in turn, is "not merely matter but a continual and incessant *materializing* of possibilities." Those possibilities are culturally restricted, yet they may also be expanded through their daily and ongoing reenactment.[18]

I frame domestic norms similarly as a script: socially determined yet individually enacted; predetermined yet open to interpretation, improvisation, revision, and failure. Like gender, the idea of home projects stability yet is constantly made and remade through imperfect, and sometimes subversive, repetition. Framing domesticity as performance, rather than an ideology, draws attention both to the script and the interpretation: both the cultural norms and hierarchies that structure everyday home life, as well as the diverse ways individual subjects materialize those structures for themselves. As anthropologist Mary Douglas writes, "The home is the realization of ideas"—it is the materialization in space of personal and cultural ideas about what life should look like. For Douglas, home is defined ultimately not by any specific function but by its regularity—the regularity of its furnishings, its people, and its daily rhythms.[19] Domestic objects might likewise be understood in Robin Bernstein's terms as "scriptive things," objects that call us as users to perform in line with previous performances. A scriptive thing, Bernstein writes, "broadly structures a performance while simultaneously allowing for resistance and unleashing original, live variations that may not be individually predictable."[20]

Lizabeth Cohen provides a useful example in her discussion of working-class homes at the turn of the twentieth century. Reformers noted that the presence of a "parlor"—a room designed chiefly for entertaining guests—frequently indicated the adoption of some middle-class values. At the same time, Cohen notes, the parlor doubled as a bedroom in many houses. Many families also purchased a table and chairs for the dining room, yet used it primarily for sewing and ironing. Working-class families, in other words, knew what a "proper" home was supposed to look like, but didn't (and often couldn't) always follow its rules.[21] Framing domesticity as performance, in this sense, reveals how domestic conventions, spaces, and objects both assimilate subjects and provide a potential means of resistance and revision.

My framing of domesticity also connects with scholarship on the "everyday." Michel de Certeau's influential study, *The Practice of Everyday Life*, directed cultural analysis away from governing social and political institutions to the daily "ways of operating," "doing things," and "making do" by which individual subjects navigate, resist, and reclaim power. De Certeau and his collaborators, Luce Giard and Pierre Mayol, presented daily acts, such as walking in a city, reading, shopping, and cooking, as personally and culturally revealing moments of navigation and negotiation—strategies and tactics by which subjects compose and recompose culture for themselves.[22] As anthropologist Martin Manalansan elaborates, a focus on the everyday or quotidian "unveils the veneer of the ordinary and the commonplace to lay bare the intricate and difficult hybrid negotiations and struggles between hegemonic social forces and voices from below." Domestic space is a privileged space for these kinds of everyday negotiations of power and culture because it is understood to provide relative freedom and control. In Manalansan's study of queer Filipino immigrants in New York City, he gives a vignette about Alden, a middle-aged gay man who has lived in a studio apartment in Greenwich Village since the early 1970s. On the one hand, Alden embraced the opportunity to decorate the apartment as he wished—with "loud curtains and throw pillows" and a nude portrait by photographer Herb Ritts. "I would not even think of putting that up back home; my mother would upbraid me," Alden reflected. At the same time, Alden devoted one corner of the room to photographs of his family back in the Philippines and antique religious icons and statues inherited from his great-grandmother. Alden called this his "guilt corner"—a reminder of his life "back home"—that is, at home with his family of origin. Alden used the everyday space and objects of home to perform and work through his identities—to materialize and navigate competing social identifications and bonds. Such navigations and negotiations of identity, culture, and power within and around domestic space are not, of course, unique to queer people, but they are particularly charged, precisely because dominant ideologies of home and family have tended to rely on restrictive constructions of gender and sexuality, despite divergences from the script.[23]

To understand domesticity as performance is also to reframe its privacy as mediated, managed, and unstable. Since the late eighteenth century, the home has typically been imagined as a private space, whose walls guarantee sanctuary from the public world of labor and politics, as well as surveillance by one's neighbors and the state.[24] But domestic space is not naturally or imminently private; rather it is a stage of performance, variably private and public. Scholar Susan Gal has described the public-private divide not as a simple binary but a fractal distinction: the public-private divide reproduces itself within itself. Gal gives the example of an American middle-class home: from the outside, the street and yard are public, but the interior of the house is private. But once you enter the house, the living room is now public, though the rest of the house, or even a whispered conversation between the hosts, remains private.[25] Home should not be understood as a sealed private space, but rather a portal to the public. Architecture itself plays a crucial role in managing privacy: in the 1950s, for example, homes were increasingly designed with a second bathroom, in part to keep visitors out of more private spaces.[26] The home enables intimacy and restricts it at once.

A resident's capacity to manage the privacy of the home is, nevertheless, conditional. As historian Sarah Igo notes, "Owning a home, making a comfortable living, and conforming to dominant norms of respectability all decidedly increased one's chances of evading society's gaze." Poor people, people of color, and single people have all tended to have less guarantee of privacy.[27] People receiving public assistance, for example, have long been subject to surveillance by the state. In the 1960s, many cities and states practiced "midnight raids" to ensure that single women on welfare were eligible—if a woman was found to be living with a man, her benefits could be revoked under the assumption that he should be the one to support her.[28] Privacy as a right and resource is unevenly distributed.

Attending to domesticity's multiple and malleable enactments challenges a tendency to treat the home reductively as either a site of constraint or agency. Since the 1970s, scholars in history, American Studies, and literature have tended to treat the home principally as a site of social conservatism and cultural imperialism—a view echoed in Duggan's dismissal of domesticity as an anchor of homonormativity. This critique has its roots in 1960s and 1970s feminist writings on domesticity, housework, marriage, and family as sites of women's oppression, starting with Betty Friedan's *The Feminine Mystique*.[29] Other scholars have countered that view, recuperating home as a site of resistance. bell hooks, for example, evokes the subversive potential of homemaking in her account of African American women's historical relationship to domestic space. "Historically," hooks writes, "African-American people believed that the construction of a homeplace, however fragile and tenuous (the slave hut, the wooden shack), had a radical political dimension. . . . Black women resisted by making homes where all black people could strive to be subjects, not objects . . . where black people could affirm one another and by so doing heal many of the wounds inflicted by racist domination."[30] Within the cultures of plantation slavery and domestic service, homeplace emerged as an arena within which women could resist, and help others resist, daily experiences of oppression, by marking out a territory under their own control, by affirming that they had social lives apart from their lives as slaves and servants. More recently, Susan Fraiman has worked to wrest home away from its normative associations by attending to forms of "extreme" domesticity—as Fraiman writes, "the deviant flip side of the domestic ideal," for example, a community living underground in Manhattan.[31]

This book aims to correct for the ways scholars have either condemned domesticity as a site of oppression and conformity or romanticized it as a site of freedom. The underlying perversity of home, I argue, is that it operates simultaneously as a site of agency and constraint: the romance of home as a site of self-expression, intimacy, and autonomy depends on the constraints it imposes. The home, as Douglas observes, inspires sentimental affection as often as resentment. It seduces and holds us with promises of intimacy and stability, while exerting "tyranny" over its inhabitants.[32]

I take the history of LGBTQ home life as a primary arena to explore domesticity's contradictions as a space of normativity and antinormativity. For LGBTQ people, home was the critical site of contact with the conventions of the American family and the gender, sexual, racial, and class norms they consolidated. By centering subjects long imagined as home's outsiders, a history of LGBTQ domesticity makes uniquely visible the home's operations and meanings. Radical innovations betray the circuits of power that enable and constrain them: renovation reveals the home's wiring.

To uncover this history, I have developed a method of research and reading that emphasizes what I call the domestic archive—objects, images, relationships, and affects that compose everyday home life—ordinary, repeated, private, ephemeral, and overlooked. This includes personal photographs, diaries, letters, and home movies. It also means reading organizational and case records for their everyday details. As much as objects and spaces themselves, the domestic archive should be understood in terms of the feelings it carries and evokes. That is to say, the domestic archive is not only a material archive but also, in Ann Cvetkovich's phrase, an archive of feelings—an archive of grief, loss, trauma, isolation, as well as intimacy, community, joy, love, and resilience.[33] Connecting these sources enables a deeper understanding of the complex ways popular representations, social scientific knowledge, cultural ideals, and political discourses circulate and inform everyday practices and experiences.

A HISTORY OF DOMESTIC CITIZENSHIP

The role of home as a stage of selfhood, kinship, and community is not exclusive to LGBTQ people, yet it has been uniquely fraught—at once emancipatory and exclusionary. Since the 1940s, the presumed privacy of home has made it particularly important for many LGBTQ people as a space to safely, and often secretly, express their identities and build social and sexual connections, beyond the gaze of disapproving neighbors, employers, family members, and the police. At the same time, the state has recurrently privileged a narrow vision of domesticity—the heterosexual, reproductive, breadwinner-homemaker household—as a key measure of cultural inclusion, marking LGBTQ people as outsiders. I describe this measure of inclusion and exclusion as "domestic citizenship"—the rights, responsibilities, and recognition that stem from the performance of normative domestic scripts.

My use of the term "domestic citizenship" builds on scholarly conceptions of cultural citizenship. Broader in scope than legal citizenship status, cultural citizenship emphasizes the everyday practices through which individuals negotiate their relationship to each other and to the nation—how they navigate the cultural norms, social categories, and legal policies that together shape what Barbara Welke calls the "borders of belonging."[34] Teresa Anne Murphy has previously used the term to describe how late eighteenth- and nineteenth-century women writers made claims for the political significance of domestic practices, centered on motherhood and marriage. For the writers and editors whose work Murphy explores, domesticity functioned as a differentiated form of cultural citizenship, emphasizing women's role in social reproduction, distinct from formal political rights.[35] Yet the American public and the state grew only more invested in domesticity in the decades after the Civil War. For women as well as men, the reproductive, heterosexual home was increasingly privileged as a prerequisite for social rights, economic opportunity, and national belonging.

The American idealization of the home can be traced back to late eighteenth- and early nineteenth-century New England. In private letters, diaries, published books, and periodicals, white Christian men and women of an emerging middle class increasingly sentimentalized and celebrated the home as a "sanctuary" and "refuge." That idealization was rooted in a gendered discourse of separate spheres, which divided the world into a pri-

vate domestic sphere—the domain of women—and the public commercial sphere—the domain of men.[36] Women writers and reformers rarely
contested this divide. Rather they expanded women's role in American
politics by rooting it in terms of domesticity. Early feminist thinkers like
Judith Sargent Murray argued that women's primary political role was in-
direct: as Republican mothers, elite white women gained civic influence
through marriage and motherhood, tempering their husband's views and
raising virtuous sons to lead the nation.[37] Even as women became more
active in benevolent societies and social movements, including abolition
and temperance, they founded their work on traditional ideals of women's
sphere, aiming to "domesticate" politics and the larger social world.[38] They
expanded the boundaries of women's domestic citizenship at the same
time they reaffirmed its primacy.

　　With the transformation of the United States in the nineteenth century—territorial expansion, urbanization, and increasing immigration—
middle-class domestic ideals amassed new meaning as a site of cultural
integration. As Nayan Shah puts it, "In the prevailing nineteenth-century
ideology, respectable domesticity enabled the proper moral and biological
cultivation of citizen-subjects necessary for American public life to flour-
ish."[39] Through social work and social reform movements, for working-
class immigrants as well as African Americans, the well-managed marital
home took center stage as the foundation of social order.[40] Social workers
also increasingly coordinated with the state to police and reform households that deviated from the marital norm. In San Francisco, white social
workers targeted what Shah calls the "queer domesticity" of Chinese immigrants. An 1885 investigation of Chinatown, for example, revealed hundreds
of Chinese women living independently of men. Many resided in neighboring apartments and shared responsibility for childcare. These alternative family and care networks nevertheless troubled white social workers,
doctors, and city officials, who ranked their homes, as one report put it,
in a "middle stratum between family life and prostitution." Christian mis-
sionaries, in turn, took up a practice of home visits to encourage proper
domestic life, with an emphasis on cleanliness.[41]

　　Normative ideals of domesticity grew still more entrenched in shaping
perceptions and regulations of citizenship after World War I, with the rise of
homeownership as a social and economic ideal. In the 1910s and 1920s, the
National Association of Real Estate Boards, founded in 1908, encouraged
"Own Your Own Home" campaigns in cities nationwide, reframing homeownership as a man's duty to his family, his community, and the nation.
A 1923 ad in the *Pittsburgh Courier*, for example, lauded homeownership
as the "bed-rock of useful citizenship"—fostering "thrift," "independence,"

and "love" while ensuring the stability of the nation.[42] Those ideals were buttressed further during the Great Depression, as the federal government took on a vastly expanded role in homeownership and housing. To stem a foreclosure crisis, President Roosevelt launched a series of programs that dramatically reshaped the housing and mortgage markets—most centrally, the Federal Housing Administration—making it possible, and often cheaper, for many people to purchase homes of their own rather than rent. The GI Bill of 1944 built on many of these reforms, providing no-down-payment, low-interest loans for veterans. The FHA and GI Bill made home-ownership a benefit of good citizenship.[43]

At the same time, the FHA and GI Bill lent new power to existing social norms and forms of discrimination. FHA and Veterans Administration underwriting guidelines determined that some houses and neighborhoods were greater risks than others, funneling loans toward the construction and purchase of single-family suburban homes. FHA guidelines simultaneously supported redlining, to keep neighborhoods economically and racially uniform, under the belief that socially or economically mixed neighborhoods were less stable. In practice, those guidelines made it exceedingly difficult for African Americans to qualify for mortgages.[44]

Federal incentives and regulations simultaneously reinforced dominant sexual and gender scripts—privileging the married, heterosexual, reproductive family, led by a male wage earner. Early FHA underwriting manuals noted, for example, that men with "domestic obligations" were more "dependable," especially when their wives were "efficient in household economy," and encouraged them to take their debts seriously. By 1947, the FHA *Underwriting Manual* included still more explicit entries on "Family Life and Relationship." The manual noted that while a newly married man presented some risk, he was nonetheless a good bet: "The mortgagor who is married and has a family generally evidences more stability than a mortgagor who is single because, among other things, he has responsibilities holding him to his obligations." The mortgagor was assumed to be male: FHA loans largely excluded women, who were seen as greater credit risks. The GI Bill similarly privileged married male veterans—granting more benefits for those who married than those who were single. It also specifically excluded men who had received undesirable discharges for homosexuality. These investments dovetailed with growing concerns and relief aimed at transients or the "unattached"—people without stable homes or families—often linked, as Margot Canaday has shown, with sexual perversity. Suburban communities were engineered as white, middle-class "family" spaces, meaning that most people of color, single people, and sexual and gender minorities still made their homes in the cities.[45]

Cultural norms about what constituted good households and neighborhoods similarly shaped federal investment in affordable housing. The federal government first began supporting subsidized, below-market-rate housing in the 1930s, through the Public Works Administration, and expanded its programs after World War II with the National Housing Act of 1949. Working in conjunction with local and state governments, the Public Housing Authority directly targeted poor housing conditions and housing shortages in urban areas after World War II—encouraging the demolition of older tenement buildings and the construction of new federally subsidized housing developments to take their place. They, too, sought to keep new developments racially uniform and guided builders to give preference in applications to veterans, those with stable employment, and two-parent families. They specifically excluded unmarried mothers.[46]

The privileging of married couples in federal housing policy mirrored and reinforced the larger political and cultural prioritization of the marital household in the years after World War II. In the late 1940s and 1950s, Americans married younger and had more children than they had in the decade before the war. The cause was not only postwar prosperity—marriage and fertility rates largely looked the same across class and race lines. Rather, as Elaine Tyler May argues, marriage, family, and home gained renewed meaning as stabilizing forces in an insecure world, both in the aftermath of World War II and amid an escalating Cold War with the Soviet Union. Marriage would tame the unruly forces and desires unleashed by World War II, returning men and women to their "traditional," complementary roles of breadwinner and homemaker. Women, in particular, were charged with helping veterans readjust to "normal" life through marriage and childbirth. The rising sexual liberalism of the years before and during the war was itself contained: psychological experts stressed the importance of sexual attraction and satisfaction, so long as they were restricted to marriage. More largely, the federal government elevated suburban domestic prosperity as evidence of democracy's success and its superiority to Communism. But that success was always, in fact, engineered. Even the tax code was revised in 1948 to privilege married couples over single people: by filing jointly, husbands and wives could be taxed at a lower rate than if they had filed individually.[47]

These political, cultural, and economic shifts lent renewed power to the heterosexual household by midcentury. They also worked to consolidate a vastly expanded model of domestic citizenship. For women in the nineteenth century, domestic citizenship was a voluntary means of participating in American society through the home. By the mid-twentieth century, domestic citizenship had evolved into a form of entitlement and obligation—the benefits and duties associated with normative, heterosexual homemaking.

The pursuit, performance, and representation of domesticity as a site of citizenship also connected the home to an emerging discourse of "belonging." "Belonging"—a sense of connection and cohesion—was a keyword of postwar America, extending from ideals of family "togetherness," civic participation, suburban "neighborliness," and national character, to anxieties about alienation and conformity. Jewish American psychologist Abraham Maslow went so far as to elevate the need for belonging—for love, affection, and group affiliation—to a primary psychological imperative. Such discourses frequently overlapped with ideas about social and psychological normality, sometimes discussed as the average but more often as the ideal. Belonging implied similarity and consensus in behavior and values. The home lay at the center of these frameworks of belonging, at multiple, nested levels—intimate, communal, and national. Social inclusion, within the family, the community, and the nation, all depended on performing domesticity correctly, that is, following the scripts of the white, middle-class, heterosexual home. Not everyone had the option or resources to follow that script. Those who did may or may not have followed it perfectly. Nevertheless, there were social benefits for espousing and hewing close to heteronormative ideals.[48]

Those ideals were defined as much by outsiders as insiders. Gay men, in particular, were persistently represented in popular culture as foils to the heterosexual home, through a pair of contradictory figures: the pedophile and the decorator. The specter of the male homosexual pedophile haunted postwar American culture, threatening to corrupt boys and young men and disrupt their "normal" development toward heterosexuality. An emblematic narrative of the period, Sid Davis's 1961 educational film *Boys Beware* found an older man in sunglasses befriending a bright-eyed teenage boy through fishing trips and miniature golf, only to bring him back to his shadowy apartment complex for "payment."[49] The image of the pedophile coexisted with a still more widely circulated image, the effeminate male decorator, a figure who appeared in magazines, popular films, fiction, and psychology textbooks. The decorator, too, was an outsider to the breadwinner-homemaker household, but one who reaffirmed its primacy. His passion for decoration and domesticity, coupled with his effeminate mannerisms, essentially confirmed postwar gender roles by comparison—his gender deviance, whether marked for humor or consternation, assured audiences that home was essentially a feminine domain. Real men left the bulk of domestic management to their wives.[50]

Lesbians, too, were frequently represented in popular culture as foils and threats to the heterosexual household. One popular image was the working-class masculine "butch," whose gender presentation marked her sexual deviance and rejection of feminine norms. But lesbian desire could also pose a danger from within: as Lauren Gutterman has shown, postwar psychological experts, journalists, and filmmakers persistently represented the white lesbian wife as a "hidden threat" to marriage and the family. Sexual frigidity, rejection of motherhood and housework, and dominance over her husband were diagnosed alternately as causes and symptoms of a deeper psychological disruption. The goal of these alarmist accounts was not, however, to cast the lesbian wife out of the home but to cure her and restore the heterosexual family ideal.[51]

Transgender people were represented less frequently in popular media, but when they were, they were generally accepted or dismissed based on their ability to conform to dominant norms of white manhood and womanhood. Domesticity was again a central script. Former GI Christine Jorgensen, for example, was widely interviewed and discussed in the mainstream media in the 1950s when she became one of the first Americans to undergo gender-affirming surgery. As Emily Skidmore has shown, Jorgensen herself and the media emphasized her normative, middle-class respectability: when Jorgensen's autobiography appeared in the magazine *American Weekly*, it included several images of Jorgensen at home, learning "kitchen tricks" from her mother. Transgender people of color, while often covered in the mainstream and black press, were much more rarely accepted for their gender presentation once their histories were uncovered. Jorgensen's middle-class domesticity affirmed the authenticity of her gender; for people of color, their bodies already criminalized, publicity largely led to pathologization.[52]

QUEERING DOMESTIC CITIZENSHIP

The reality of LGBTQ domestic life was far more complex and varied than popular representations revealed. LGBTQ people who chose and had the resources to create homes of their own—whether alone, with lovers, or with friends—necessarily fell short of mainstream domestic ideals, but they did not altogether discard them. Rather, an expanding number of LGBTQ people, in their activism, their artistic work, and their everyday lives, adapted, contested, and reformed the terms of domestic citizenship: they experimented with household forms; denaturalized the gender, sexual, and social norms of postwar domesticity; and asserted a right to create home spaces that affirmed their identities, relationships, and desires. Contrary to restrictive, normative visions of the American home, LGBTQ people revalued domestic space as a critical site of queer social connection and reform and, increasingly, made public claims to the emotional, material, and political significance of their private lives.

Home emerged early in the modern LGBTQ rights movement as a key fulcrum of integration. One of the country's earliest gay rights groups, the Mattachine Society, was founded in 1951, by Community Party member Harry Hay. Hay positioned gay people as a minority, akin to African Americans and Jews, but he was pushed out of the organization in 1953 for fear his radical politics would tarnish the group's reputation. Quickly after, the group moved to affirm their commitment to normative American values: they established a new set of aims and principles advocating for the eventual integration of the "well-adjusted homosexual" into society. This included contributing to larger "community endeavors" rather than retreating into "an invert society of their own." Gay people would also need to adjust their behavior to broader social standards "compatible with recognized institutions of a moral and civilized society with respect for the sanctity of home, church, and state." The resolution explicitly linked the outward show of normative domesticity with larger social obligations to religion and the law. Much like their heterosexual peers, some Mattachine leaders looked to the home to contain their sexuality.[53]

Not everyone within the early movement agreed: within a few months, Jim Kepner wrote to a friend to complain that too many Mattachine members supported resolutions like these only for fear of "offending anyone." Soon after, he published an essay in the new homophile magazine ONE under the title, "The Importance of Being Different." Kepner defined gay people as "natural rebels" and criticized those who feared the "specter of non-conformity, and the red tag that goes with it these days." These kind of people, Kepner wrote, "would bend backwards with dishonest but popular slogans about 'upholding the law,' 'sanctity of home, church and state,' 'loyalty to the American way of life,' and such, even though they may admit in private that they don't mean a word of it." For Kepner, the model of citizenship the Mattachine Society called for amounted to hypocrisy and invisibility.[54]

In practice, however, an attachment to home did not translate into simple conformity. At the same time the Mattachine Society was resolving to uphold "the sanctity of home, church, and state," writer and professor Samuel Steward was hosting regular sex parties at his apartment in Chicago. Steward documented those parties and other sexual liaisons using one of the earliest Polaroid cameras. Steward had been sexually active with other men since he was a teenager and had long kept meticulous records of his erotic life, but the Polaroid camera allowed him to record, and recall, his sexual relationships with new detail. Some pictured men wearing prop

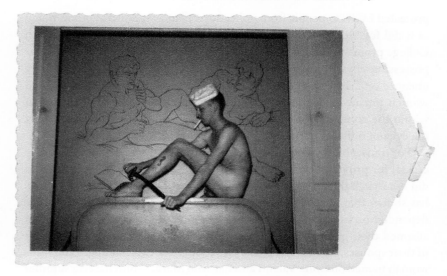

FIGURE I.2. In the early 1950s, Samuel Steward regularly photographed friends and lovers at his apartment in Chicago. This Polaroid (c. 1954) captures a sailor sitting naked on the headboard of Steward's Murphy bed, here lowered to reveal an erotic mural that was otherwise hidden. Courtesy of the Estate of Samuel Steward and Antinous Press.

leather jackets, caps, or sailor's uniforms—though Steward photographed a fair number of actual sailors, too. One photograph captured a mural Steward had painted on the wall behind his Murphy bed: the bed folded down to reveal a painting of two naked muscular men, lying beside each other, one about to light a cigarette. The mural not only suggested the sorts of bodies and sex acts that attracted Steward. It also framed and inspired the sexual activities that took place in his apartment. In the photograph, a young man in a sailor's cap sits naked on the metal headboard, leaning against the wall, with a cigarette in his mouth. In the black and white photographic frame, he becomes a physical extension of the mural—sexual fantasy made real made fantasy again (fig. I.2).[55]

The image is emblematic of the ways home provided many LGBTQ people space both to imagine and realize their desires and identities. At the time, same-sex sexual acts were a crime under many state sodomy laws, though only selectively enforced. Steward's home state of Illinois, for example, would not repeal its sodomy laws until 1961, making it the first state to do so. Possessing photographs or magazines deemed pornographic or obscene was also a criminal offense. But while LGBTQ people were routinely arrested in public spaces under charges of vagrancy, lewdness, public indecency, or solicitation, cultural beliefs and practices of privacy largely protected LGBTQ people from police surveillance or arrest at home, much as it did for Steward.[56] Tragic cases like that of Newton Arvin—a Smith College professor who was arrested at his home on obscenity charges for possessing physique magazines—made headlines but remained relatively uncommon.[57] Lauren Gutterman has similarly shown how many married women pursued relationships with other women not in urban bars but within the confines of their suburban homes and communities, escaping the eye not only of the police but also their husbands.[58]

For transgender people, the relative privacy of home could be similarly crucial for providing space to explore and perform gender identities that did not match those they were socially assigned. Robert Hill, for example, has shown that in the 1950s, 1960s, and 1970s, many transgender people depended on home as a space where they could safely wear clothes that affirmed their gender identities—often with the knowledge and support of their spouses.[59] In the late 1950s, one couple—a Cuban émigré and trans woman named Susanna Valenti and her wife Marie—purchased a summer home in the Catskills, dubbed "Casa Susanna," where they hosted regular retreats for trans women—most, though not all, middle-class professionals (fig. I.3). Susanna regularly documented those summers in the community magazine *Transvestia*, describing in one early column "the incessant chatter of people who had let down all barriers and could be entirely themselves without restraint." *Transvestia*'s editor and founder, Virginia Prince, reflected following her first visit that the retreat was different from the house parties readers more often attended: "Whereas an evening 'party' at someone's house is an occasion to dress up, it's special, and it's only going to last about 4 hours and then all the finery comes off and Cinderella goes back to mopping floors—here it was life and living because it WENT ON for two days and a night (just as you always wanted it to)."[60] Casa Susanna, and other home spaces, provided many trans women unique opportunities for self-expression and social connection at a time when visibility could be dangerous.

This was not only true for trans people in the middle class. Building a sense of home and community was also a key goal of STAR House, a shelter for homeless transgender youth founded in 1969 by two trans women of color, Sylvia Rivera and Marsha P. Johnson. The house was an outgrowth of STAR (Street Transvestite Action Revolutionaries), one of the first transgender activist groups in the country, and while it lasted for only a few years, the house formalized the kind of care networks that many trans women had long created for one another.[61] Two years earlier, photographer Danny Lyon met a group of young black and Latinx trans women who lived in neighboring rooms in Galveston, Texas. The women Lyon photographed

FIGURE I.3. Lily (left) was a regular visitor at Casa Susanna, a summer retreat for trans women founded by Susanna Valenti in the Catskills, New York. Lily emigrated from China to New York in the 1960s and appeared on the cover of the early transgender magazine *Transvestia* in December 1967. This photograph is attributed to Andrea Susan, another regular guest at Casa Susanna. [Photo shoot], 1964.1969. Chromogenic print. Sheet: 8.4 × 10.8 cm (3 5/16 × 4 1/4 in.) Art Gallery of Ontario. Purchase, with funds generously donated by Martha LA McCain, 2015 2014/724.

had come to Galveston from other poor towns and cities in the South, and some depended on sex work to get by. They also developed a sense of family. In one photograph, a young woman named Pumpkin Renee is pictured dancing in her pajamas, in her friend Theresa's bedroom, "Every day began with a dance," Pumpkin said, "that hardly ever stopped" (fig. I.4). Lyon followed them to a local bar, too—Pumpkin Renee still in her pajamas—but their intimacy was expressed most at home. In another portrait, Lyon photographed the mirror in Theresa's room, capturing Theresa and two friends on the bed, unaware, it seems, of the camera. In another, Connie is pictured at home with her boyfriend Lloyd, both sitting in the corner, smiling for the camera—their apartment decorated with floral curtains, a large landscape, and a small portrait of Jesus Christ (fig. I.5).[62] Home space provided a stage to realize and perform a sense of self and a sense of kinship, mediated by larger norms of race, class, gender, and sexuality but not restricted by them.

FIGURE I.4. Photographer Danny Lyon visited Galveston, Texas, in September 1967 and met a small community of trans women, including Pumpkin Renee (front) and Theresa, seen here. "Pumpkin and Theresa, in Theresa's room, 'Every day began with a dance that hardly ever stopped,'" Galveston, Texas, 1967. © Danny Lyon/Magnum Photos.

FIGURE I.5. Danny Lyon, "Connie and Lloyd at Home," Galveston, Texas, 1967. © Danny Lyon/Magnum Photos.

PLAN OF THE BOOK

The book is organized into three sections: Integrations, Revolutions, and Reforms. Each section moves forward in time while focusing on a different strategy of social and political engagement, to explore how LGBTQ activists positioned domesticity in relationship to the norms of domestic citizenship. These strategies should not be understood as discrete but rather layered or sedimented: the revolutionary domestic forms of the 1970s, for example, built on, and rested in tension with, earlier strategies of integration. Each chapter, in turn, focuses on a different mode of domestic performance—marriage, cooking, family, architecture, shelter, caregiving—to explore the material ways LGBTQ people used domestic space to forge new modes of intimacy and community.

The first section, "Integrations," looks at the contested politics of LGBTQ home life in the 1950s and 1960s, as early gay and lesbian activists and their followers sought to make a place for LGBTQ people in the Cold War domestic order. Mobilizing the privacy of home enabled many LGBTQ people to build romantic, sexual, social, and political connections, largely out of view of the state, yet the need for privacy also limited the range of legal reforms activists could advocate for and achieve. Chapter 1 analyzes discussions and practices of "homosexual marriage" during the 1950s and early 1960s to explore how gay men and lesbians variously understood and adapted psychological discourses around adjustment to validate and encourage long-term same-sex romantic relationships. Yet gay men and lesbian writers diverged in the degree to which they prioritized homosexual marriage as a form of adjustment: by the early 1960s, gay male writers in particular grew especially prescriptive, at the same time feminist writers grew more critical of marriage as a social institution. Chapter 2 examines Lou Rand Hogan's 1965 *Gay Cookbook* to consider the place of camp domesticity and culinary cosmopolitanism as they were practiced in everyday domestic life and circulated in the expanding gay consumer market. Camp style and humor transformed the home into a space for connection, while subverting conventional gender codes attached to domesticity and consumption.

The second section, "Revolutions," moves to the rise of gay liberation and lesbian feminism in the late 1960s and early 1970s, to examine how LGBTQ people came to challenge, more publicly and more directly, the conventional gender, sexual, familial, and stylistic conventions of the breadwinner-homemaker household. In effect, LGBTQ activists mobilized domestic space to reject the conventional terms of domestic citizenship.

The first chapter in this section, chapter 3, considers how gay male activists drew inspiration from the counterculture, the women's movement, and lesbian feminism to form gay male communes as a major strategy of sexual and gender liberation. Communes provided members the opportunity to enact theories of gay liberation in their everyday lives, facilitating social bonds across race and class while challenging norms of masculine gender performance and the heterosexual household. Chapter 4 turns to the built environment, demonstrating how lesbian feminists targeted domesticity as a key form of social and sexual oppression. To explore this history, the chapter focuses on the life and work of architect Noel Phyllis Birkby. An active participant in lesbian social and political circles in New York City, Birkby traveled throughout the United States in the 1970s, asking women to describe and draw their environmental fantasies—their ideal living spaces—what Birkby called "woman-identified architecture." The designs that emerged were strikingly communal, emphasizing social and sexual freedom, revealing how lesbian feminist theory opened new possibilities for rebuilding the home and women's social and sexual identities at once.

The final section, "Reforms," explores how LGBTQ activists adapted frameworks of domestic citizenship in later activism to address inequalities in housing and health care. Beginning in the late 1970s, LGBTQ activists increasingly saw the state as an ally and framed appeals for funding and support by articulating their status and rights as worthy domestic citizens. Chapter 5 looks at the history of efforts to address homelessness among LGBTQ young people, from the 1960s to the early 1980s, amid shifting cultural and legislative discourses about runaway youth and homelessness, as well as emergent understandings of transgender identity. LGBTQ shelter activism across the United States struggled to reconcile the communal ideals of early LGBTQ liberation activism with psychological frameworks of normative development, as well as material demands for funding and space. Although activists began by creating alternative domestic spaces, in the end shelters largely reaffirmed values of individual agency, privacy, and productive citizenship. Chapter 6 examines how LGBTQ activists mobilized home as a space of care and community for people with HIV/AIDS in the 1980s and 1990s. It focuses on two pioneering and influential programs of Gay Men's Health Crisis: "buddy" programs, which assigned volunteer caregivers to people with AIDS, and *Living With AIDS*, a public access television program that represented caretaking, home, and family in everyday life for people with HIV/AIDS. The intimacy of AIDS caregiving programs led LGBTQ activists to redefine conceptions of communal belonging to encompass a multiracial, cross-class, and cross-gender coalition.

I specifically do not argue here for an essential or singular mode of "queer domesticity" in opposition to a hegemonic norm. I instead high-light how performances of domesticity, advocacy for home and shelter, and beliefs about privacy and citizenship were shaped by the intersecting iden-tities and relative social, economic, and cultural capital of various LGBTQ people, in relationship to each other, to their communities, and to the state. While the home is not innately freeing, people of various identities and backgrounds have found emancipatory potential within the constraints.

To develop this point, I place side by side the experiences and activism of gay men, lesbians, bisexual men and women, and transgender people, of various race and class backgrounds. The first section focuses particularly on white middle-class gay men and lesbians, to understand how domes-tic citizenship was shaped by dominant constructions of class and race. Their relative privilege amplified their sense of injustice at being excluded, their desires stigmatized and criminalized. To be marked as "deviant" was a form of class and race dislocation. The second and third sections turn more to experiences of people of color and transgender people, both as those groups were given more space and greater leadership roles within LGBTQ activism and as LGBTQ activists reorganized their efforts to respond to intersectional and reinforcing modes of oppression.

Understanding why, how, and when LGBTQ people turned to domes-tic space—and what they hoped domesticity could give them—provides a new genealogy of LGBTQ liberation and rights in the United States. It is a private counterhistory of LGBTQ politics—a history that unfolded along-side and underneath more public forms of LGBTQ social and political ac-tivism but was no less central. At the same time, it is a queer counterhistory of American domesticity—the history of home from the perspective of its supposed outsiders.

My interest in mapping these counterhistories is shaped, in part, by ongoing debates about the political significance of same-sex marriage rec-ognition. Queer critics of the same-sex marriage movement often position marriage and domesticity as a retreat from the more radical politics of gay liberation and HIV/AIDS activism. This book reveals that the debate over domesticity—its meanings, its uses, and its limits—has been central to LGBTQ politics since the emergence of the modern LGBTQ rights move-ment. What unifies the history of LGBTQ domesticity is not its inherent conservatism or radical potential, but rather its ongoing significance as a zone of contact and conflict with the social scripts of everyday life.

ONE

INTEGRATIONS

CHAPTER ONE

"Something of a Merit Badge": Lesbian and Gay Marriage and Romantic Adjustment

James Kam and Mario Firpo met in San Francisco in 1945: as Kam later recalled, he and Firpo literally "bumped into each other" while both were running to catch a streetcar. The two men began living together three years later, in the house Firpo owned on Union Avenue, and they stayed together another eight years until Firpo died in 1956 at age forty-two. In his final will, Firpo left the house to Kam, then fifty-five years old, but Firpo's family contested the claim on the basis of an earlier conflicting will. The case reached the San Francisco Superior Court in 1958. When Kam was called to testify, the lawyer for Firpo's family pressed him to describe the nature of his relationship with Firpo. Kam repeatedly used the word "friendship," but the attorney pushed for clarification: "Anything more?" Kam's own attorney stepped in and requested they go off the record. When they returned, Kam offered this reply, "Complete homosexual marriage. Is that more clear to you?" He explained further, "There were no papers, no law, no nothing. It was just a complete question of decency between two men. He trusted me and I trusted him blindfoldedly. . . . It was a complete, voluntary, beautiful life."[1]

Kam's appeal to the language and ideals of marriage—trust, consent, and fulfillment—to describe a long-term same-sex relationship came under unusual duress, but it was not in itself exceptional. Gay men and lesbians of the 1950s and 1960s routinely used the word "marriage" to describe long-term same-sex relationships. Even in the absence of legal recognition, the rhetoric of marriage held significance for many same-sex couples as a means of understanding and structuring their romantic and sexual lives. Such relationships were not unprecedented, but they took on particular visibility in the postwar period, as the state and culture at large newly prioritized and idealized a model of companionate heterosexual marriage, with the husband-father as the primary breadwinner.[2]

This prioritization of marriage particularly shaped the emerging "homophile" movement, a network of organizations and activists dedicated to improving the legal and social positions of gay men and lesbians—although how this would best be achieved was an ongoing source of debate.[3] Early activists particularly highlighted the question of "homosexual marriages": Were they possible? Were they desirable? And what should they look like? What was at stake was not merely the possibility of long-term gay relationships but the capacity of gay men and lesbians to achieve happiness, emotional stability, and social integration—grouped at the time under the broad, often ambiguous psychological concept of "adjustment." The framework of adjustment—a distinctly American conception of mental health, with roots in social reform, social hygiene, and psychoanalysis—gained wide circulation during World War II and the immediate postwar years. Disregarding definitions of "well adjusted" as always heterosexual, homophile activists frequently invoked the adjustment of the homosexual as a major goal of the movement: to help the individual to adapt to the environment—to make the best of his or her situation.

Within this context, homophile writers and their readers increasingly privileged the capacity for romantic commitment as a sign of mental health in its own right. This new measure—what I call romantic adjustment—provided a language and structure for normalizing same-sex relationships and supporting self-acceptance, by placing gay men and lesbians in greater harmony with prevailing social and sexual ideals of romantic domesticity. Both lesbian and gay activists highlighted homosexual marriage as an alternative to "immature" forms of sexual expression, including anonymous sexual encounters and short-term relationships. As Donald Webster Cory and John P. LeRoy explained in their 1963 book, *The Homosexual and His Society*, "Two men or two women who strive to spend the rest of their lives together feel the stigma against their homosexuality would be mitigated—at least in their own eyes—if their relationship resembled a regular marriage."[4] For homophile writers and readers, homosexual marriage offered an aspirational model for citizenship. Greater domestic stability, they argued, would ensure greater personal fulfillment and a greater sense of belonging.

Cory and LeRoy's caveat, "at least in their own eyes," also suggests the major limitation of extralegal homosexual marriage: fear of social disapproval or legal sanction meant that long-term same-sex relationships largely needed to be kept private. The early homophile movement prioritized privacy in two ways: first as a legal right, in particular, freedom from unlawful search and seizure and police surveillance; and second, as a social strategy, restricting disclosure of sexual identity or practices as a pragmatic response to stigmatization. Privacy was understood as protective.[5]

These claims to privacy were rooted in expectations about racial and class privilege. Since the nineteenth century, the expansion of an American middle class has depended on social and legal constructions of privacy, with the home privileged as a space shielded from public view. This model of domestic privacy has nevertheless been persistently denied to poor and working-class people and people of color: as Nayan Shah and others have shown, the homes of single people, poor and working-class people, people of color, and interracial couples and families have typically proven more permeable—more subject to surveillance by police, the state, and social workers.[6] For the predominantly white leaders and followers of the homophile movement, threats to domestic privacy were experienced as forms of class and race dislocation—a loss of social status.[7] Homophile writers and readers presented homosexual marriage as one way to combat this status loss: advocates for homosexual marriage promised greater respectability through social and sexual containment.[8] If homophile activists could not eliminate laws and social prejudice against gay men and lesbians, marital domesticity could at least make gay people more mature and less visible. Gay men and lesbians of color also, of course, formed long-term relationships and even held wedding celebrations, but their voices were rarely heard in homophile circles.

At the same time, gay men and lesbians diverged in the degree to which they prioritized homosexual marriage as a form of adjustment. From the 1950s into the early 1960s, gay male activists grew increasingly prescriptive in recommending marriage as the healthiest form of same-sex relationship, and one with the greater potential for advancing the political goals of gay integration and toleration. Lesbian activists, meanwhile, increasingly articulated a feminist critique of marriage as a restrictive social institution. Homosexual marriage ultimately proved more appealing to gay male activists than lesbian activists because gay men could more easily imagine the constraints of marriage as a means of consolidating white middle-class social privilege.

In looking back to practices of and discourses around homosexual marriage in the postwar period, I aim specifically to show the extent and diversity of debate around homosexual marriage among homophile activists, and to understand the social and political pathways it both opened and closed.[9] I also aim to understand how homosexual marriages of the 1950s might alter our understanding of marriage in the postwar period and its reverberations today. Homosexual marriage mattered to homophile activists—and particularly men—because it promised to reconcile the demands and entitlements of middle-class life with the presumed deviancy of same-sex desire. This vision of domestic citizenship through extralegal homosexual marriage might be understood as a precursor to what Lisa Duggan has popularly termed "homonormativity."[10] At the time, Duggan was responding to the rise of neoliberal gay advocacy groups and writers, and the growing push for state and federal recognition of same-sex marriage. With same-sex marriage now legally recognized, if not uncontested, nationwide, homosexual marriages of the 1950s and 1960s provide a case study for examining an inherent dilemma of domestic citizenship: the constant demand to make domestic life public—to perform privacy.

DEFINING HOMOSEXUAL MARRIAGE

It is impossible to say how many men and women formed "homosexual marriages" in the 1950s and early 1960s, but two surveys of gay and lesbian life from the period suggest that long-term same-sex relationships were relatively common. From 1960 to 1961, the ONE Institute, founded in 1955 as the educational branch of the Los Angeles homophile organization ONE, Inc., circulated a questionnaire to its national mailing list of several thousand men and women, as well as readers of the *Mattachine Review*. It eventually tabulated results from 388 male respondents, with a median age of 34.8. In the words of the survey, 113 of those respondents were currently "homosexually married." The average length of those relationships was 4.9 years—meaning most of them had been started in the mid-1950s. Overall, roughly 40 percent of the respondents reported being involved in one or more homosexual marriages at some point—amounting to 278 long-term relationships, with an average length of 3.8 years, though 97 lasted more than 5 years, and 16 more than 15 years. "Homosexually married" was not defined but tapped into vernacular understandings of homosexual relationships as serious emotional commitments parallel to heterosexual marriages, even if they were not legally recognized.[11]

A similar, smaller survey, conducted in 1959 by the lesbian homophile group the Daughters of Bilitis, did not use the word "marriage" but also found that the majority of participants who responded (100 gay men, 157 lesbians) had been in same-sex relationships lasting longer than a year, with somewhat longer relationships on average for women. One crucial difference was in rates of heterosexual marriage: only 15 percent of men had ever been legally married versus 27 percent of women, reflecting, the survey analyzers surmised, "the greater social pressure on women to marry."[12] These surveys cannot be taken to give a definitive sample of gay men and lesbians of the period, but they do reflect the political base the homophile movement sought to consolidate: participants in both surveys had higher incomes and more education than average. The Daughters of Bilitis survey also noted that nearly all participants were white. The ONE survey did not ask about race at all, likely because the researchers simply assumed most men on their mailing lists were white.

Sometimes, homosexual marriages were marked with wedding ceremonies. In 1963, for example, Jody Shotwell reported in the lesbian homophile magazine *The Ladder* on a "gay wedding" in Philadelphia between two young women—one dressed in a "white shirt and a black knitted vest," the other in a kelly-green dress with rhinestones—with a butch "best man" and bridesmaids with their hair in beehives. The ceremony, held at a "private home on a quiet street," was officiated by the male manager of a local gay bar. All that seemed unusual to Shotwell was that the participants were women: she noted matter-of-factly that she had "of course, heard of gay weddings, but in most cases the couples were men."[13] Some gay weddings may have been staged as camp. Reporter Jess Stearn recounted one lavish New York wedding where one groom appeared in drag.[14] But most, like the one Shotwell attended, appear to have been quite earnest as expressions of commitment.[15]

Gay and lesbian wedding ceremonies were nevertheless exceptional. More often, sharing a home itself was understood by gay men and lesbians as the primary means for a couple to demonstrate their commitment. Helen Branson described the process in her memoir about the gay bar she operated in Hollywood in the 1950s: "When these boys join forces and set up housekeeping, they are said to be married . . . and they behave similar to a heterosexually married couple."[16] A gay lexicon within the report *Homosexuality and Citizenship in Florida*, produced in the early 1960s by a Florida investigative committee, similarly defined "gay marriage" as "mutual agreements between homosexuals of either sex to live together and observe the normal code of ethics concerning marital fidelity."[17]

Even those who had yet to find a long-term romantic partner tended to view such a relationship as an important goal. From the late 1950s to the early 1960s, the homophile magazine *ONE* received many letters—some published, some not—by men expressing their loneliness and their desire for a romantic partner. One young man with the initials B. C. explained that he had begun exploring "gay life" two years earlier but had so far found it "extremely lonesome and difficult." While he rejected heterosexual marriage as impossible, he lamented his inability to find what he called a "life partner." "I don't want a Greek God," he explained, "I want someone who will love me as I will love him, with whom it is possible to be sincere, with whom I have something in common, and with whom I can enjoy the simple things of life—a relationship in which we can find a home and live together."[18]

In adopting the framework of marriage, gay and lesbian couples also worked to adapt its gendered scripts. For lesbian couples, household responsibilities often divided along traditionally masculine and feminine lines, mirroring broader "butch" and "femme" roles and style within the relationship. Buddy Kent, a popular drag king in Greenwich Village in the 1950s, explained in a 1983 interview, "The femme felt that she would emasculate her dyke if she had her doing some cooking or anything. . . . The only time a butch did cook was if she was like from an old big Italian family where she was really a terrific cook, but then it was never talked about. And eventually that butch tried to teach her wife how to cook, so she would know it." Those roles extended to entertaining, too. "If they had a party," Kent explained further, "the butch greeted you at the door, she took your coats. The femme sat you down and offered you food, and then the butch got you your drink." For Kent and her friends, it was "just the thing to do. Nobody even talked about it or thought about it."[19]

Couples who followed butch/femme roles did more than mimic heterosexual marriages. Rather, butch/femme roles provided a language and structure for adapting and negotiating the conventional norms of marriage at a moment when few other models for long-term romantic relationships existed. Even lesbian couples who did not embrace, or outright rejected, strict butch/femme roles often fell back into the gendered conventions of the breadwinner-homemaker household. In the early 1960s, Suzanne Prosin, a graduate student in sociology at San Fernando Valley State College, conducted a study of twenty lesbian couples, from a range of race and class backgrounds. Prosin visited and interviewed participants in their homes and found that all couples differentiated household responsibilities to some degree along butch and femme lines, even when partners attested there was no difference between them. In some couples, for example, Prosin observed, "One partner did do more of the domestic tasks, although it was often explained in terms of, 'she does them better than I; or I just don't, so by default they go to her.'"[20]

Gay male couples, too, sometimes divided responsibilities along conventional "male" and "female" lines—one partner doing more of the household work, even when both had jobs. Some even referred to each other, and were known among friends, as "husband" and "wife." Those terms, however, were typically used with a wink of camp humor, playing with rather than reproducing the gendered scripts of heterosexual marriage.[21] Just as often, gay male couples seem to have resisted identifying with conventional male and female roles, stressing overlapping interests and shared responsibilities. Bar owner Helen Branson explained that the men in the couples she knew rarely assumed conventionally masculine or feminine roles: "They both work. Each may assume certain duties in the house according to his particular talents. One may be a better cook than the other, but believe me, they both can cook. One may supervise the decorating but they both wield the paint brush. They share the expense of the house. Possibly one assumes the task of food shopping, but this depends on who has the car and the time for it."[22] Branson's insistence that household responsibilities were divided simply according to talent and convenience reflected, in part, a discomfort with male effeminacy or "swishing." For gay male couples— especially in the middle class—acceptance as "normal" still depended on outwardly adhering to the norms of masculinity.[23]

Homosexual marriages were not without risk of public disapproval. In 1957, a pair of gay men in Philadelphia staged a wedding ceremony in an apartment with a small group of friends. As photographs from the evening reveal, the grooms and their guests all wore dark suits and white shirts, with flowers pinned to their lapels. One of the friends performed the ceremony, and afterwards, the two grooms kissed—a moment captured in a snapshot (figs. 1.1, 1.2, 1.3). The grooms, however, never saw their photographs. The drugstore where they brought the negatives refused to distribute images they considered obscene. Only decades later were they discovered by an employee's daughter.[24] It may be surprising that a gay couple would drop off their photographs for development in the first place, but for gay and lesbian couples of the 1950s, living together would not have meant keeping the relationship perfectly secret. Rather, homosexual marriage entailed an ongoing negotiation of privacy, determining how and with whom to share their relationship.

The relative privacy of shared domestic space could itself provide an important foundation for romantic intimacy as well as friendship. A series of small photograph albums from a lesbian couple who lived in Philadelphia in the early 1950s reveal time spent together at home, playing with their dog, celebrating holidays with friends—most of them men. In style, the couple seem to have largely followed the conventions of butch/femme fashion: in most photographs, the taller of the two women appears with a short haircut wearing a jacket, collared shirt, and men's pants; her partner appears in a day dress with her hair curled (fig. 1.4). Their house itself appears carefully decorated, with floral wallpapers and window treatments, but in most photographs, the curtains and blinds are closed to preserve privacy. One album of their photographs also documents the wedding of two gay men held in a basement, exposed pipes decorated with streamers (fig. 1.5).[25]

In the late 1940s, H. Lee Fuller, a doctor at the Pottenger Sanatorium and Clinic for tuberculosis in Monrovia, California, met a man named Frank Leach, a manager at a local plant nursery. On a postcard from the

FIGURES 1.1, 1.2, 1.3. In the 1950s and 1960s, homosexual marriages were sometimes marked with weddings like this one, held at an apartment in Philadelphia in 1957. The grooms never saw these images: the drugstore where they dropped off their film for development refused to distribute photographs they deemed "obscene." Courtesy of ONE Archives at the USC Libraries.

FIGURE 1.4. Photograph from the albums of a Philadelphia lesbian couple, c. 1953, Human Sexuality Collection, Rare and Manuscript Collections, Cornell University Library.

restaurant Lucca in Los Angeles—likely where they first met—Fuller wrote his name, home number, and times he could be reached, and below it, the phone number for the clinic: "If you *have* to—Monrovia 156 mornings— Say it's a personal call." Fuller and Leach moved in together soon after, in the home Fuller shared with his mother, Haidee, on the grounds of the Pottenger Sanatorium. Leach documented their life together in a surviving photograph album—starting with the Lucca postcard. Some pictures depict their travels together and nights out on the town: Fuller and Leach

FIGURE 1.5. Photograph of gay wedding reception from the albums of a Philadelphia lesbian couple, c. 1953, Human Sexuality Collection, Rare and Manuscript Collections, Cornell University Library.

posing together behind a paper moon, in a photo booth, and at popular restaurants. But the majority depicted their domestic life: sitting before a decorated Christmas tree, posing with their dog, pulling a turkey out of the oven, and hosting parties for friends and family (figs. 1.6 and 1.7). In one photograph, Fuller peers inside through a screen door, as though to announce he has just gotten home.[26]

Fuller and Leach's relationship also demonstrates the dangers that faced gay men in public. In December 1950, some time after Leach and Fuller met but before they moved in together, Leach met a twenty-two-year-old ex-Marine and gas station attendant named Elmer Martin at a local bar and brought him back to his house. Martin assaulted him, stealing $30 and $200 worth of suits and pants. Brutally injured, Leach called Fuller, who helped to get him to a local hospital, where he received 100 stitches and spent the next few weeks recovering. Martin was arrested but found not guilty: although Martin admitted to the crime, Leach, the jury found, had made "improper advances," essentially reframing the assault as self-defense.[27] The assault, and the trial that followed, demonstrated not only the risk of violence that many LGBTQ people faced in pursuing sex, but also the antipathy of the courts and the public. Leach and Fuller's shared domestic life, by contrast, provided a space of greater privacy and control—one, it seems, largely removed from the more public world of gay bars. In 1957, they moved with Fuller's mother to a house overlooking the Monrovia canyons, where they lived together another sixteen years until Leach died on April 1, 1973. Leach's obituary noted he was survived "by his close friends, Haidee Fuller and H. Lee Fuller of Monrovia with whom he made his home." Fuller died a few weeks later.[28]

Haidee Fuller's apparent acceptance of her son's relationship with his partner was not as unusual as it may seem: despite social stigma, some parents did accept their children's partners as they might a heterosexual son-

FIGURE 1.6. Frank Leach (left) and H. Lee Fuller met at a restaurant in Los Angeles and moved in together in Monrovia, California, in the early 1950s. Here they are pictured with their dog, c. 1953. Lee Fuller Photograph Album, Human Sexuality Collection, Rare and Manuscript Collections, Cornell University Library.

FIGURE 1.7. Leach and Fuller's photograph album shows that they regularly hosted friends and family at their home, including this holiday celebration, c. 1953. Lee Fuller Photograph Album, Human Sexuality Collection, Rare and Manuscript Collections, Cornell University Library.

or daughter-in-law. Barbara Grier, later a contributor to *The Ladder*, met her longtime partner, Helen Bennett, in 1951 when she was eighteen years old; Bennett was sixteen years older and married to a man. Bennett divorced soon after, and in 1954, the couple moved to Kansas City, Missouri, to be closer to Bennett's family. Grier later reflected, "Her parents accept me as a permanent part of the family, even introduce me as a daughter." Still, Grier conceded, "It wasn't always like this," reminding readers that being open and gaining acceptance from parents was a process.[29]

Before his death in 1956, Mario Firpo's relationship with James Kam produced a range of responses even within Firpo's family. Kam had immigrated to the United States from the Netherlands in the 1920s, leaving his family behind. Firpo, by contrast, was the child and grandchild of Italian immigrants, raised in San Francisco, where most of his family remained. By the time he met Kam, his mother had died and he was living with his father.[30] In the deposition from the case contesting Firpo's will, Kam recounted the relative ease they had, for years, sharing their home with Firpo's father, Salvatore. He referred to him as "Papa." "He liked me," Kam recalled. "He liked our relationship. He liked our friends." When Firpo's health began to fail, Kam expected he would continue to live with Salvatore, but that arrangement seems to have been challenged by Firpo's younger brother, Alfred, who contested that Kam had any right to the apartment.[31]

Kam's sexuality was undoubtedly the subtext. In 1943, a few years before he met Firpo, Kam was working as a butler in Carmel Valley when he was arrested and convicted on a charge of "sex perversion." He was sentenced to six months in the county jail and three years on probation, on the condition of receiving psychiatric care. The conviction still dogged him a decade later: in 1954, Kam's application for naturalization as a US citizen was denied because of a "lack of moral character." By the time Kam came to court, he and his lawyer likely felt he had little to lose by calling his relationship, on the record, a "homosexual marriage."[32]

Most gay and lesbian couples nevertheless worked hard to conceal their relationships from parents and other family members—a unique threat, since family could not easily be turned away at the door. In the early 1960s, University of Chicago graduate student Nancy Achilles spent three months interviewing patrons at a San Francisco bar, and several men discussed the challenges of concealing their relationships from their families. One interview participant who had been with his lover for six years explained, "If two guys are going to try to live together, they have to be on their toes every minute. Even the simplest questions, ones you'd never think about, are hard to answer. Explaining things to people, and parents especially—you have to make up names of girls you're going out with, and explain why you're both paying for the car together, and why you only have one bedroom—things like that." The subject went on to share a story about two gay men he knew who married two lesbians: both the gay couple and the lesbian couple moved into the same house in a small town and bought matching dressers. "When parents or anybody came to visit, all they had to do was run a set of drawers up the stairs, and they were all set." The story could have been a tall tale, but it evokes the ways domestic cohabitation placed additional stress on gay men and lesbians to monitor their presentation across a variety of settings and for various audiences—as well as the pressure many gay men and lesbians felt to enter heterosexual marriages to please their families.[33]

Long-term same-sex commitments could also be a challenge in the workplace. The British anthropologist Colin Turnbull moved to New York in 1959 to take a position as curator of African ethnology at the American Museum of Natural History. Within a few months, he met Joseph Towles, a young African American man from Knoxville, Tennessee, who would be his partner for decades. The two men quickly came to regard themselves as married, marking their "wedding anniversary" to the day they met at Mais Oui, a gay bar on the Upper West Side not far from the museum. Turnbull appears to have been fearless initially about Towles visiting him at the museum and contributing to a range of projects. But Turnbull and Towles's relationship would soon enough draw the ire of another longtime curator at the museum, an archaeologist from Mississippi named James A. Ford. Fueled as much by homophobia as racism, Ford repeatedly targeted Turnbull and Towles and eventually wrote a letter to the museum's direc- tor recommending that he fire Turnbull. As Ford's letter put it, "Judging by all available evidence, [Turnbull] is a practicing homosexual, and most of the Museum personnel as well as many anthropologists are aware of it. His private life might be more easily ignored if he did not insist on bringing his young friend to Departmental parties, to Museum hall openings, and hav- ing him work as a volunteer." The ploy backfired, and Ford was dismissed from the museum; Turnbull remained there until 1969, though his rela- tionship with Towles remained a source of tension.[34] Unlike Turnbull and Towles, most gay and lesbian couples likely regarded their relationships as "private" affairs and kept them secret from their employers.

Private letters and published accounts of homosexual marriage also rarely mention encounters with the police or a perceived threat of arrest. Rather, homosexual marriages, conflated with cohabitation, were more often discussed as a means of ensuring privacy. For many couples, be- ing married and sharing a home typically meant turning away from more public forms of queer life, especially bars where the threat of arrest and public exposure was higher. Indeed, gay men and lesbians in the 1950s and 1960s were far more likely to be arrested under disorderly conduct or cross-dressing laws than for private consensual sex—although the risk was undoubtedly greater for people of color.[35] In April 1953, the *Philadelphia Tribune* reported on the arrest of two African American women, twenty-one-year-old Elsie Holmes and thirty-five-year-old Naomi "Duke" Garry, both dressed in suits, after police raided a North Philadelphia home and discovered nearly fifty guests gathered to witness their wedding. The police learned of the ceremony from an engraved invitation, but the two women claimed the event was only a "'gimmick' for a 'pay-and-eat' party."[36] Such an arrest, however, appears to have been exceptional and was a response to the "disorder" of the ceremony, not cohabitation.

Long-term partners, of course, also faced challenges within their relationships. On July 8, 1948, San Francisco architect Jack Hillmer met photographer Roy Flamm in the bar of the St. Francis Hotel—by the 1950s, their men-only bar, the Oak Room, would become a well-known pickup spot for gay men. Hillmer soon moved into Flamm's home in Pacific Heights, which Flamm shared with his mother, and in July 1952, they purchased a home together near Buena Vista Park. They lived there together—along with both of their mothers—for the next decade. But in early 1962, they had a major fight, and Hillmer and his mother moved out. In the aftermath, both men struggled to settle financially and, despite Flamm's fears of their relationship becoming public, took the case to court. The documents from the case—including a long list from Flamm to Hillmer's lawyer of gifts they had received as a couple—amount to an early legal case of same-sex divorce.[37]

Regardless of formal consequences or the length of the relationships, living with a same-sex partner in the 1950s and 1960s was a courageous act, one that defied social conventions, however loudly or discreetly the couple declared their relationship. Without the possibility of legal recognition, most gay and lesbian couples ultimately came and stayed together out of a sense of romantic and sexual connection. At the same time, how they structured and understood their relationships, and how homophile activists discussed and mobilized them, were shaped by broader political and cultural discourses.

PSYCHOLOGY AND THE MEANINGS OF ADJUSTMENT

For many homophile activists, writers, and their followers, the most influential discourse for understanding and promoting homosexual marriage was psychology. In the decade after World War II, Americans increasingly looked to the home as a site of personal comfort and security, and to marriage as a cornerstone of national stability. It was also understood as the primary path to adulthood. While the specific roles of husband and wife, father and mother, were an ongoing source of debate, the importance of marriage as a social institution was rarely questioned.[38]

Gay men and lesbians were hardly exceptions. Psychoanalyst Albert Ellis, a frequent contributor to the *Mattachine Review* (though not entirely sympathetic to its aims), remarked, with some surprise, that homosexual men seemed as driven by conventional middle-class romantic and sexual values as many heterosexual men and women—especially in judging their own promiscuity. He concluded that while homosexuals may "outwardly decry" heterosexual culture, "they are actually doing their best to uphold it, and to carry almost all its (often quite irrational) traditions over to their own sex mores and ideologies."[39] What Ellis failed to acknowledge was the role of psychology itself in constructing and perpetuating romantic and sexual values and ideals.

The expanding influence of mental health clinicians owed, in large part, to a major shift in the field: from an emphasis on severe mental disturbance to one on "mental hygiene." Even "normal" men and women, it was now understood, might develop neuroses as the result of environmental stressors.[40] The goal of the therapist was to help the patient to adapt and achieve greater balance and maturity. The key term was adjustment. The concept of "adjustment," as it was understood in the 1940s and 1950s, was most frequently linked to psychodynamic theory. As Freud's American translator and popularizer A. A. Brill explained in his introduction to *Totem and Taboo* in 1918, neurotic symptoms resulted from an individual's failure to adapt or adjust to his or her environment—an inability to adequately resolve a conflict between internal, "primitive," and "infantile" demands, and external reality.[41] It is important to note that Freud did not have a single German term for the concept of "adjustment." Rather Brill's frequent use of the term "adjustment" and "maladjustment" in his translations of Freud, and his own writing on psychoanalysis, made it easier for Freudian thought to be folded into an emerging discourse of "social adjustment."

This broader discourse of adjustment drew together diverse strains of American social thought. The first was progressive ideals about social progress and social welfare. Another was the social hygiene movement, which emerged out of anxieties over physical health amidst urbanization and industrialization. And a third was the mental hygiene movement. From the 1910s on, mental health clinicians and educators frequently blurred the distinction between "psychological adjustment" and "social adjustment," aligning psychological health with social conformity. Failures to conform to social convention, or simply achieve social and economic success, were grouped alongside mental illness, all as failures to "adjust" properly to one's environment.[42]

This ambiguous conception of adjustment was put into even wider practice during and immediately after World War II. During the war, military psychiatrists sought to normalize reactions like fear, while providing training and strategies to improve soldiers' mental preparedness. Combat was treated as a stable variable, to which the individual needed to adapt. A similar stance was taken to civilian life following the war. The 1944 GI Bill was formally called the Servicemen's Readjustment Act and aimed to ease the transition back to "normal" life.[43] At the same time, the incentives the GI Bill provided—for education, mortgages, and businesses—scripted what readjustment should look like, reasserting the primacy of the bread-winning and home-owning male.

The federal government's endorsement of the male-dominated, breadwinner-homemaker household resonated with advice literature, marriage counseling services, popular print media, and film.[44] But it was especially echoed and supported by psychologists. Psychoanalyst Therese Benedek, for example, explained in her 1946 book, *Insight and Personality Adjustment: A Study of the Psychological Effects of War*, "The woman at home is the measure of the masculinity and emotional maturation of the man." Benedek conceded that men and women's economic roles were changing as women moved into the workforce, but she insisted that their basic psychosexual and emotional needs remained the same: "The ability to love—mature, heterosexual love—is an expression of strength; the desire to be loved is the emotion of the weaker one. The man conquers to love; the woman surrenders to be loved."[45] Psychoanalysts like Benedek would gain increasing influence in the 1950s within US psychiatry, social work, and American popular culture, particularly through the model of American ego psychology, with its emphasis on psychological defenses and adaptation. Yet many psychoanalysts and psychoanalytically-informed therapists and writers essentially deployed Freudian developmental concepts to reaffirm middle-class gender, sexual, and marital conventions. Adapting to marriage became not only socially desirable—it was widely understood as developmentally normal.[46]

As heterosexual marriage was made a mark of maturity, homosexuality was increasingly understood as a neurosis: a symptom of maladjustment.[47] One of the most outspoken supporters of this view was psychoanalyst Edmund Bergler. Putting aside "passive-feminine" men and "masculine" women, Bergler characterized homosexuality as a defense mechanism and viewed long-term homosexual relationships as inherently pathological, if not impossible. As Bergler wrote on gay male couples: "Their quarrels—especially in jealousy—surpass everything that occurs, even in the worst heterosexual relationship: They simply act out the mechanism of 'injustice collecting.'"[48] Bergler and other psychoanalysts spent far less time analyzing long-term lesbian relationships, in part because they assumed lesbians were more likely than gay men to be heterosexually married. Lesbian desire, Bergler surmised, manifested itself primarily as frigidity, and frigidity, he argued, was easier to hide from a spouse than male impotence. When Bergler did discuss lesbian relationships, it was primarily as an extension of his theories of male homosexuality, focusing again on masochistic "injustice collecting."[49]

At the same time, the underlying ambiguity of the term "adjustment" presented opportunities for social scientists to question psychological diagnoses. Alfred Kinsey argued in a passage of *Sexual Behavior in the Human Male* that measures of social and psychological adjustment ultimately relied on arbitrary conceptions of "normal" behavior. Extending the term "abnormal" from bodily health to social or sexual activities, Kinsey argued, "involves subjective determinations of what is good personal living, or good social adjustment; and these things are not as readily determined as physiologic well-being in an organic body." Kinsey was, ironically, quite vague about his own definition of good adjustment but seemed to equate it largely with self-acceptance. Sexual variations were problematic only if they disturbed the individual.[50]

Evelyn Hooker wielded similar language and logic in her 1957 study, "The Adjustment of the Male Overt Homosexual." Hooker demonstrated that trained clinicians could not distinguish homosexual and heterosexual subjects when presented with results from three tests—the Rorschach ink-blot test, an attitude scale, and a life history interview—suggesting that homosexuals were no different from heterosexuals beyond their sexual object, and just as likely to be well- or maladjusted. The test analyzer's comments, moreover, reveal again how arbitrary judgments of "good" adjustment could be: "He takes essentials and doesn't get lost in details. A solid citizen, neatly and solidly integrated with no specific defenses." "He has intense involvement with people. . . . He practically acts like a husband and father." Like Kinsey, Hooker did not do away with the discourse of adjustment. She utilized it to argue for greater acceptance of homosexuals and to encourage homosexuals to be more accepting of themselves.[51] Adjustment was not, in the end, a stable measure but an open and malleable discourse, one that could be put to various uses by various actors, whether to normalize particular behaviors and people or to pathologize them.

Homophile activists, too, reframed the language of adjustment to argue for the acceptance of homosexuality, though not without some adaptation. The articles of incorporation of the Mattachine Society of San Francisco listed fourth among its methods of advocacy, "To aid in the adjustment to society of such persons as may vary from the normal, moral and social standards of society and to aid in the development of a highly ethical, social and moral responsibility in all such persons."[52] Every issue of *The Ladder* similarly included a statement of purpose, emphasizing the "integration of the homosexual into society," beginning with "education of the variant, with particular emphasis on the psychological, physiological and sociological aspects, to enable her to understand herself and make her adjustment to society in all its social, civic and economic implications."[53] Kinsey's and Hooker's emphasis on self-acceptance had offered an important model for developing an alternative conception of mental health—one in which homosexual desire was no obstacle in and of itself.

The homophile movement's use of the language of adjustment stemmed from a broader engagement with psychology and social science. From the 1950s into the early 1960s, leaders of organizations including the Mattachine Society and the Daughters of Bilitis developed a diverse social and political agenda that included advocating for legal reform, countering negative depictions of homosexuals in popular media, and supporting gay men and lesbians in need of personal support or legal counsel. They saw social scientists as critical allies in all these battles: they hosted talks by psychologists and counselors, published original essays and assessments of research in homophile journals, and assisted researchers in recruiting subjects.[54] The ONE Institute also developed its own social services division, while *ONE* magazine featured an advice column by psychiatrist Blanche Baker.

The emphasis on mental health was strategic. From the 1930s into the Cold War, the presumption that homosexuality was a sign of mental illness underpinned a wide range of discriminatory legal, military, and police practices. At the same time, psychology also provided an influential and presumably objective language for advocacy and education—both to encourage outsiders to see homosexuals as more "normal" and to encourage homosexuals themselves to behave differently, all in the name of integration.

ROMANTIC ADJUSTMENT

Homosexual marriage emerged in this context not merely as a path to romantic bliss but as a step toward social and psychological maturity. In *The Homosexual in America*, a landmark work of nonfiction published in 1951, Edward Sagarin, under the pseudonym Donald Webster Cory, argued that successful homosexual relationships were rare and difficult to establish. Still, when they were possible, they seemed an ideal form of homosexual life. "Whatever the pattern, the ages, the races, the nature of the adjustment to the outside world, the degree of sexual fidelity involved, it can be said without equivocation that those who have found a stable relationship or a true love have gone a long way toward solving the problem of the adjustment of the homosexual in a hostile society, although not to a hostile society."[55] Cory's distinction between "adjustment in" and "adjustment to" society captures again some of the ambiguity of the term and its usefulness: through the stability of a long-term relationship, Cory argued, gay men would grow more accepting of themselves, even if they could not change how they were viewed and treated by others.

Beginning in the mid-1950s, the homophile journals the *Mattachine Review* and *The Ladder*, both published out of San Francisco, also highlighted the question of homosexual marriage. The *Mattachine Review*, published by members of the Mattachine Society, for example, featured a first-person account of "twilight marriage," written by a pair of men who had both left their wives and moved in together.[56] *The Ladder*, meanwhile, published by the Daughters of Bilitis, featured a short article titled simply "Lesbian Marriage," written by Barbara Grier (under the pseudonym Gene Damon), discussing her six-year-long relationship with Helen Bennett. Grier acknowledged that living together long-term was not always easy, but insisted the problems "are almost always overcome if the people involved really are in love." She reflected, "We are lucky enough to have a lovely apartment, and our own furniture and car, free and clear. We love our work, each other and life in general."[57]

Both the Mattachine Society and Daughters of Bilitis also hosted speaking events on the topic of marriage. In 1956, for example, the Mattachine Society of San Francisco hosted a public discussion, "The Need for a Permanent Relationship," led by Basil Vaerlen, a psychotherapist and Mattachine research director. The group's newsletter described it as "perhaps one of the finest meetings yet held." Vaerlen defined marriage as a "cooperative adventure in growth" that included "constant compromise and a continual willingness and awareness of seeing and understanding the other person's viewpoint." The major message was that long-term relationships took constant effort and reflection to last.[58] Readers of *The Ladder* were evidently less enthusiastic: a listing for a second talk by Vaerlen promised, "Those of you who didn't get a chance to take Mr. Vaerlen to task after his lecture in December will have a second whack at him"—perhaps because of Vaerlen's assumptions about male and female differences (the feminine approach to marriage, he argued, was "basically emotional," the male approach "primarily intellectual").[59]

The link between homosexual marriage and psychological adjustment was made most explicit in January 1959, when the ONE Institute hosted its annual conference in Los Angeles on the topic of "Mental Health and Homosexuality," including the presentation, "Adjustment Through Partnership." The forty-five-minute-long session stressed the need for "courtship" before a homosexual marriage and the importance of "basic friendship, companionship, common interests and community property" to a long-term relationship.[60] Homophile writers and activists did not emphasize love and fulfillment in their endorsement of marriage. Rather, they followed the lead of psychologists and marital experts in rationalizing romance.

One key area of tension was monogamy. In practice, many gay male couples accepted some degree of sexual contact outside the relationship. At a discussion on "permanent relationships" held in 1957 by the Los Angeles Mattachine Society, participants warned against "possessiveness" and agreed, "A great tolerance must be developed by both parties in the inevitable side-affairs." Still, "extra-partnership adventures" were discouraged for the anxiety they could cause.[61] Another discussion group, hosted by the New York Mattachine Society that same year, stressed the point more strongly. As the group's newsletter described, "The problem of infidelity was admitted to be a crucial one, possibly more so for the homosexual couple than for the heterosexual because of the lesser emotional stability of the first." Participants specifically discouraged going to gay bars and called for "self-discipline": "Emotional maturity is thus the key to a lasting relationship, for it renders a person capable of withstanding temptations to promiscuity in order to achieve a superior joy, the blessings of a shared life and true love."[62] Echoing popular discourses of heterosexual marriage, homophile activists reread the sentimental appeals of partnership in psychological terms and looked to marriage to "contain" unruly sexual desires.

This tendency to promote homosexual marriage in psychological terms was perhaps greatest among the writers and editors of the homophile magazine ONE, published out of Los Angeles and led primarily by gay, white, middle-class men. Throughout the 1950s and 1960s, ONE's writers again and again positioned homosexual marriage as the highest form of homosexual relationship and a sign of maturity. As Canadian writer and activist Jim Egan put it, "The successful homosexual relationship is composed of many elements: love, trust, mutual respect, co-operation, and above all the determination on the part of both partners to remain together in spite of what family, friends or anyone else thinks, says or does."[63] In "Reflexions on Love and Marriage," the author Didgeon advocated for careful consideration in choosing a partner: "Just as a man decided whether a given woman had the qualities he wanted in a wife (is she beautiful, rich, intelligent, a good housekeeper?), and just as a woman knew what she wanted in a man (is he handsome, gallant, ambitious, a good provider?), so we should fix our standards according to what we want in our mate."[64]

ONE's discussions of long-term relationships particularly reflected the expanding influence of marital counseling, which framed marriage as work. As historian Kristin Celello has shown, marital counselors and advice literature in the 1940s and 1950s frequently emphasized that marriages succeeded when husbands and especially wives approached marriage as an ongoing challenge. Healthy couples took responsibility for their problems to understand themselves and stay together.[65] In the pages of ONE, this discourse of marital work often led writers and activists to take a dim view of gay men who chose not to pursue long-term relationships or failed to sustain them. As Didgeon explained, "Many of us are too egotistical—or too spoiled—to make allowance for another's peculiarities, while remaining too tolerant of our own; . . . let's face it—many of us lack the emotional stability which we would require in order to make a success of marriage or of anything else." In a long essay published in 1963, "Let's Push Homophile Marriage," Randy Lloyd bemoaned "these homosexuals who want to get married, but instead of doing anything intelligent about it and working at it, have just plain given up the fight in a great big tizzy of petulance and despair and flown off into either a fit of cynical celibacy with frequent hot flashes, or into a fit of cynical promiscuity." He went on to warn prospective husband-hunters, "Don't expect to be continually amused and unbored every hour of the day you spend with a prospective marriage partner. If you're the gay type that tries to be continually amused, you're not only unsuited for marriage, you just haven't grown up."[66]

The magazine further presented couples in long-term relationships as role models. In 1964, Dorr Legg (under the pseudonym Valentine Richardson) penned a long profile of Don Plagmann and Jon Lawson, a pair of midwestern transplants who had moderated the 1959 ONE Institute session on "Adjustment Through Partnership." They were known among their friends as the "Heavenly Twins" for their remarkable resemblance, despite a twenty-five-year age difference. Plagmann and Lawson had met in the 1950s cruising in a park in Kansas City, Missouri: Plagmann was married, with three children; Lawson, in his twenties, lived at home with his parents. After Plagmann's wife discovered the relationship, Plagmann and Lawson moved in together and faced a range of harassment: Plagmann was fired from his longtime job, their car tires were slashed, and their lease was canceled, yet they continued to live together, despite the advice of Plagmann's divorce lawyer. Plagmann left the marriage with nothing, and the two men moved from Missouri to Monterey Park, Los Angeles. They quickly became known, both among neighbors and friends, for their lavishly decorated home, with a collection of antique music boxes, Wedgwood china, Chinese gongs, and physique portraits by artist George Quaintance, plus fountains and Greek statues on the lawn. They were also active in the local community, winning awards for their Christmas decorations and giving gifts to children in the neighborhood. They credited the strength of their relationship to their religious beliefs—both in Kansas City and Los Angeles, they attended church together; they abstained from cigarettes and alcohol; and, as Legg wrote in *ONE*, they "thoroughly frown upon promiscuity, partner-switchings, bar-hopping and separate dates." They saw and presented themselves as an "ordinary" couple. As Legg reported, "They're just too normal even for their heterosexual friends, they say."[67]

Over and over, writers interpreted homosexual commitment through the language of adjustment—of maturity, capacity, stability, normalcy, and self-control—adding psychological ramifications to romantic pursuits. In one sense, this reading was deeply subversive of postwar discourses of family, home, and mental health: by upholding marriage as an ideal and presenting it as a real possibility, *ONE*'s writers essentially wielded psychological appraisals of married men as "well adjusted" to complicate, even short-circuit, the appraisal of homosexual men as "maladjusted." The capacity to form a lasting partnership—romantic adjustment—had emerged not merely as a source of emotional fulfillment but a means of contradicting psychological discourses that described homosexual men as sick—of managing, if not entirely countering, the stigma of homosexuality.[68] At the same time, positioning homosexual marriage as the pinnacle of emotional maturity reinforced stigma against more open models of sexual expression—derided simply as "promiscuity."

The lesbian writers of *The Ladder* appear to have been, on the whole, far less focused on marriage as a social form to emulate and, when they did discuss marriage, far less prescriptive. There were significantly fewer articles and letters that presented long-term lesbian relationships as desirable, and never with the same imperative as the gay male writers of *ONE*. Many writers of *The Ladder* were more concerned with helping readers cope with, or leave, existing heterosexual marriages. Into the 1960s, writers of *The Ladder* repeatedly reported on the experiences of lesbians isolated in marriages to men, often blaming themselves for failing to satisfy their husbands.[69] As one woman explained, her husband was "not selfish and demanding as many husbands are. . . . But, right from the beginning of my marriage, I have never been able to fulfill my wifely duties without imagining that it was the other way around, i.e., that I was the husband."[70] This sense of the heterosexual home as oppressive looked forward to later feminist critiques of postwar marriage: in March 1963, *The Ladder* ran a laudatory review of

Betty Friedan's *The Feminine Mystique*, for exposing "the myth that marriage and motherhood in themselves constitute fulfillment for women."[71]

Gay male activists may also have had more to gain in homosexual marriage than lesbians. While marriage was often depicted in popular culture as a "trap" for men, postwar readjustment literature also depicted men as more vulnerable than women and more in need of the stability that marriage and fatherhood allowed.[72] And while marital roles grew more complementary in the 1950s, the breadwinner-homemaker model still ultimately empowered husbands over wives. Gay men, more than lesbians, were also defined by psychoanalysts and in popular culture by their promiscuity. For gay male activists especially, marriage seemed a clear way of asserting their respectability, their normalness, and their social stability through sexual constraint. Much as the heterosexual, reproductive household was expected to "contain" straight men's sexual desires, homosexual marriage was portrayed as a way of channeling and ennobling same-sex sexuality.[73]

In their emphasis on adjustment to white middle-class norms, homophile activists also typically failed to consider how queer people of color were multiply marginalized. Indeed, most homophile organizations tended to avoid, if not outright resist, discussing the intersections of oppressed identities. While homophile activists of the 1950s frequently compared the plight of gay people to African Americans, for example, they rarely explored the experiences of African American gay men and lesbians. Instead the homophile movement consolidated and naturalized an emerging white gay and lesbian middle class—their homosexuality the only obstacle to full citizenship. This vision of the homophile citizen as white and middle class particularly shaped homophile activists' faith in home as a private domain, secure from police or state surveillance, in ways people of color would be less likely to assume.[74]

This is not to say there were no queer people of color who participated in the homophile movement or held key leadership positions. Mexican American artist and performer Tony Reyes, for example, was an original founder of ONE, Inc., alongside his long-term partner, Don Slater. For more than a decade, Reyes served as a board member for the organization and staff artist for the magazine. He also worked professionally as a flamenco dancer at El Paseo Inn, a Mexican restaurant in downtown Los Angeles, and organized instructional sessions on dance at ONE conferences.[75] Across the country, Tony Segura, a Cuban American chemist, led the formation of the New York chapter of the Mattachine Society in the mid-1950s. He was soon named Mattachine's national public relations director, as well as "Member of the Year" at the organization's national convention in 1957.[76] African American activist Ernestine Eckstein was elected vice president of the New

York Daughters of Bilitis in 1965, and she appeared on the cover of *The Ladder* the following year.[77] Yet despite the contributions of people of color, homophile organizations remained predominantly white and largely failed to consider race and racism in their strategies of integration.

Some gay men and lesbians actively pushed back on the language of adjustment and the prioritization of marriage as new forms of repression. In 1961, a *ONE* reader from Brooklyn responded to an editorial that criticized men who collected physique photos as deeply maladjusted: "WELL NOW ADJUSTMENT AND BEING WELL-ADJUSTED SOUNDS TERRIBLY INTELLIGENT IN THE TALK, BUT I FIND IT VERY DIFFICULT TO FIND WHAT IT *MEANS*. . . . IT SOUNDS TO ME THAT THEY MEAN 'WELL, *YOU* KNOW, LIKE ME.'"[78] Another *ONE* reader, Miss D in Pasadena, similarly dismissed "adjustment" as mere conformity: "To achieve a personal and social identity does not require life-long subservience to society-conceived, unproven theories of what constitutes a normal, well-adjusted human being."[79] In 1960, a young man from Seattle, who had recently been arrested and suspended from his college, responded to a question in the members-only newsletter *ONE Confidential* about whether homophiles should seek to legalize marriage. He wrote, "If the time comes that we are faced with a compromise proposition like legalizing and consequently institutionalizing marriage in order to get 'acceptance' for ourselves, we must resist. . . . 'Acceptance' means recognizing our right to be different." In fact, the writer contended, the homosexual's freedom from marriage made for "his noticeabl[y] greater emotional maturity."[80]

Resistance to mental health discourses and marriage grew only more common among lesbian and gay activists in the late 1960s. In 1965, a thirty-six-year-old man from Los Angeles wrote to the Philadelphia gay magazine *Drum* explaining he had "had many affairs" but "none has lasted long. Does this mean I am neurotic?" *Drum* replied, "Some persons are happiest with lasting mates; others are happiest without them. Neither state, itself, suggests neurosis."[81] In 1968, Martha Shelley—who a year later helped to found New York's Gay Liberation Front—offered a pointed critique of the New York chapter of the Daughters of Bilitis. As Shelley wrote, "I have encountered a great many people who seem to think that the only proper alternatives are a straight marriage or a gay one, and who regard me as 'queer' for desiring a different way of life. But I, too, have the right to choose, and I believe that DOB should defend the rights of those of us who prefer not to marry." This "minority," Shelley argued, "are not necessarily 'immature,' a term the psychiatrists apply to anyone who does not fit into their notions of what is right and proper."[82] Shelley's critique revealed a widening generational divide within the gay and lesbian rights movement, one that grew only more pronounced after the Stonewall riots. But it also suggested the limits of homosexual marriage, romantic adjustment, and privacy as modes of social integration: they primarily devolved into forms of self-policing.

PRIVACY AND THE DILEMMA
OF DOMESTIC CITIZENSHIP

In his 1963 book, *Stigma*, sociologist Erving Goffman explored the ways various marginalized subjects "managed" their difference through social performance. Goffman was primarily concerned with "good adjustment" as a performance intended to elicit tolerance from the dominant group, and he pointed to representative speakers who could "provide a living model of fully-normal achievement." These "heroes of adjustment," as Goffman put it, provided proof both to insiders and outsiders "that an individual of this kind can be a good person."[83]

Within the homophile movement, gay and lesbian couples were often held up as similar role models. In 1967, the Kansas City-based homophile journal *The Phoenix* published an essay advocating for gay wedding ceremonies, as a means of making homosexual marriage less secret. The author explained, "Like people in public office, we must try to live as if the public were watching our every move." He wrote particularly with young people in mind, hoping the model of marriage would offer "a stability they cannot find elsewhere" and "lend dignity, recognition and meaning to the hopes of two young women or men, determined to live together in love and companionship."[84] In the mid-1960s, *The Ladder*, meanwhile, ran a regular column, titled "Living Propaganda," aimed at empowering readers to promote positive images of the lesbian as a productive citizen. In one installment, author Marilyn Barrow explained how she intentionally avoided any "subterfuge" about her sexuality and dropped "we" and "our" in conversation until people came to think of her and her "friend" "as a couple—a married couple."[85]

Still there remained an underlying tension whether the primary audience for homosexual marriage was other gay men and lesbians or straight society. Homophiles valued homosexual marriage for producing ethical, sexually contained, and emotionally mature subjects, yet they acknowledged that most gay and lesbian couples also felt a need for discretion. In a 1959 *ONE* column titled "The Successful Homosexual," for example, an elementary school teacher under the pseudonym "Don Winters" explained that he shared an apartment with another man he'd been with for three years. Winters was proud of the relationship he and his partner had built: "You see, with a homosexual, it's something of a merit badge. Partners have no legal ties, no family, and no financial obligations to bind them. So when a couple can make a go of it together, it means something."[86] Still Winters and his partner lived far from the school where he worked, so as not to run into other teachers or school parents. Winters also emphasized the importance of being a "model citizen" in public, avoiding open displays of affection with other men, or discussing improper topics, like sex. To be a respectable citizen meant being in a stable relationship, but being part of a community also meant being careful not to impose yourself on that community either.

The trouble for many gay men and lesbians of the 1950s and 1960s was in balancing a variety of affiliations—both those among gay men and lesbians and within a largely straight world around them. In the 1964 government report *Homosexuality and Citizenship in Florida*, the researchers shared the letter of a twenty-four-year-old Tampa woman who wrote to the committee:

> First of all, let me say that I do not feel shame for what I am. I have made a good adjustment to my way of life. I am happy as I am. I do not want to change. Many well adjusted homosexuals feel as I do. . . . Like many others, I lead a quiet, and apparently normal life. I have a well paying, responsible job, I own my own home, I am active in church and community affairs and I command the respect of those who know me. I love the woman I live with and . . . I regard my personal relationship as having all the sanctity of marriage.[87]

She admitted that she thought homosexuality a "dread disease," but still resented the ways homosexuals were all treated as criminals. "Must I be stripped of my privacy and all the pride and dignity that I enjoy as an American, simply because some element in my environment, some incident in my childhood, or some faulty parental relationship has produced an individual who chooses to love one of the same sex?" For this woman, as for many others, her "adjustment"—including her relationship with her lover—entitled her to the same respect and privacy accorded all good citizens.[88]

A woman from Saint Paul wrote to the editors of *The Ladder* in 1958 that she and her "friend of the heart" had lived together for ten years and considered themselves "well adjusted, happy, and contented—to a point." "We have a house, reputable standing in the local suburban community, in the church of our choice and the professional positions we hold. . . . Our private life matters only to us and we make every effort to conceal it from the world with which we are forced to compromise." They looked down on women who frequented the "local 'gay spot'" and longed for friends "like ourselves with a home and position, who are discreet, careful and NOT OBVIOUS."[89] Like the woman from Tampa, the author strived to fulfill and perform the demands of domestic citizenship—owning a house, contributing to her community and church—at the cost of concealing the private life she maintained at home.

Such discretion could itself take a toll on a relationship. Carol Bradford, writing in *ONE*, explained that homosexual marriages were "constantly harassed" by anxiety: "'Be careful how you look at me in public,' 'Uncle John's coming to visit, push the beds apart so he won't suspect,' 'We can't buy a house together, how will I explain it to my folks,' . . . 'Don't wear your matching little-finger ring when you drop by the office today, someone might notice,' and on and on." Bradford concluded, "It's a miracle we all aren't on constant sedation for a nervous condition."[90] One *Ladder* reader similarly observed, "The act of behaving furtively breeds of itself a furtiveness of spirit which can quickly corrode into guilt." This behavior, she continued, was not only "psychologically harmful to the partnership," it did nothing "to encourage acceptance by others of the close relationship."[91] The desire to achieve and demonstrate healthy adjustment through homosexual marriage was seen as being directly in tension with the discretion such relationships required.

The homophile movement's support for homosexual marriage ultimately pitted the need for "positive" representation against the prioritization of privacy, and the need for privacy won out. Homophile discussions of homosexual marriage rarely, for example, raised the question about whether such relationships should be legally recognized. In 1954, *ONE* put homosexual marriage on the cover, with an essay titled, "Marriage License, or Just License?" Author E. B. Saunders reflected, with some surprise, that there was little discussion of seeking to legalize same-sex marriage, whether among homophile activists or gay people in general. To do so, Saunders concluded, would take a massive shift in homosexual culture, choosing the monogamous norms of marriage over the relative sexual freedom gay men and lesbians currently enjoyed.[92] Nine years later, *ONE* put marriage on the cover again, with Randy Lloyd's essay, "Let's Push Homophile Marriage." Yet in five and half pages of text, Lloyd made no mention of the possibility of legal same-sex marriage, even as he argued that "married" homosexuals would be the first to be accepted by straight society.[93]

The cover illustration for Lloyd's essay also raised larger questions about whether marriage would be enough to normalize gay men. The playful drawing by Mark Haldane, printed as a single image back cover to front (fig. 1.8), drew on popular visual tropes to picture three potential couples standing in a row: a pair of effeminate men on the left (their wrists limp, their shirts

FIGURE 1.8. Mark Haldane's illustration for *ONE* magazine's June 1963 cover story depicted a range of gay people in pairs, suggesting that homosexual marriage could work for everyone, however fey or butch. Courtesy of ONE Archives at the USC Libraries.

loose); a pair of clean-cut men in collared shirts, suits, and sweaters on the right; and in the middle, a more ambiguously gendered pair, one figure tall and muscular, the other short and round. At least two figures are also racially ambiguous, their skin dotted, perhaps to identify them as people of color. The mirroring of the two couples on the end (and the apparent mismatch of the middle couple, split by the fold of the cover) may suggest the importance of finding a like-minded (or at least like-dressed) partner. But several readers objected to the apparent effeminacy of the figures depicted. One reader criticized the cover for depicting "prancing, nelly faggots" when the magazine was sold at newsstands all over the country. Another asked how he could possibly share the issue with a "non-homophile friend," wondering whether "such drawings on the cover page contribute to giving the public a notion of homosexuals as normal healthy people?"[94]

This tension between public presentation and discretion was hardly unique to gay men and lesbians but rather reflected a broader paradox inherent to postwar models of domestic citizenship: it promised the comfort and containment of privacy, at the same time it demanded private, domestic life be performed publicly. In 1961, Daniel Boorstin pointed to the picture window—a large window opening out of and into a suburban living room—as a primary symbol of postwar domestic life, displacing the front porch of an earlier small-town era. "The picture window is as much to look into as to look out of. It is where we display ourselves to ourselves."[95] The postwar domestic citizen was both the performer and the audience member, the home both a retreat and a stage.

This paradox posed a particular challenge to homophile activists, who elevated romantic adjustment as a path toward integration without fully acknowledging its limitations: pitting the need for privacy against the desire for public affirmation. Since the 1980s and 1990s, arguments for gay marriage have tended to center on rights and the recognition of the state. But debates around homosexual marriages in the 1950s and 1960s centered on privacy as a right to be left alone.[96] Homosexual marriage allowed gay men and lesbians a sense of connection and meaning, but it was also difficult to separate from the dominant norms of marriage as a mode of communal and national belonging. It was, to put it another way, a double-bind: it allowed gay men and lesbians a sense of maturity, but one that could rarely be put on display.

CHAPTER TWO

"Oh Hell, May, Why Don't You People Have a Cookbook?": Camp Humor and Gay Domesticity

On Wednesday, December 1, 1965, the *New York Times* ran an advertisement for *The Gay Cookbook* by Chef Lou Rand Hogan, whether "for that very special man in your life or for the jaded hostess whose soufflés no longer stand on their own." The ad, sponsored by Doubleday Book Shops, filled a quarter of the page and featured an image of a slender man wearing a flowery apron, his hand limply holding a steak over a grill. It did not go unnoticed. A month later, in January 1966, *Time* magazine printed a twenty-five-hundred-word essay, "The Homosexual in America," its longest article yet on the lives of gay men and lesbians. In the introduction, the author named several signs that homosexuality was "more in evidence" than ever before: the addition of "beefcake" magazines to newsstands, explicit jokes in the most recent Rock Hudson movie, and Doubleday's "smirking ads" for *The Gay Cookbook*.[1]

The publication of a "gay cookbook" (fig. 2.1) four years before the Stonewall riots, typically acknowledged as the start of gay liberation, undoubtedly surprises many readers who stumble on a surviving copy today.[2] But Lou Rand Hogan's book was not entirely unprecedented. As courts struck down obscenity laws in the early 1960s, books and magazines about and targeted to gay men proliferated as never before—and could be produced and purchased with far less fear of legal sanction. The gay mail-order catalog Guild Book Service, for example, included more than 100 books in its 1964–65 catalog, from paperback editions of William Burroughs's *Naked Lunch* and James Baldwin's *Another Country* to *The Gay Coloring Book* and *The Beginner's Guide to Cruising*.[3] Mainstream magazines like *Life* and *Time* and newspapers like the *New York Times* and the *Washington Post* discussed homosexuality regularly, both as a topic of serious fiction and theater, and as a social problem in need of solving. What might have surprised

FIGURE 2.1. The dust jacket of *The Gay Cookbook*, published in 1965, tied the book directly to the camp craze inspired by Susan Sontag.

Times readers was not the subject of the ad but its blithe and quirky tone. When the *Times* ran an ad for Jess Stearn's best-selling exposé *The Sixth Man* in 1961, it promised a "shocking revelation" of homosexual life.[4] The ad for *The Gay Cookbook* promised "the answer to your holiday gift shopping problem."

That carefully humorous tone, or "smirk" as *Time* put it, was hardly accidental. *The Gay Cookbook* was published amid a wave of interest in gay culture set off by Susan Sontag's essay "Notes on 'Camp,'" published in 1964 in the *Partisan Review*. Rather than provide a stable definition of this "camp" sensibility, Sontag offered numerous, sometimes contradictory, aphorisms, including "Camp sees everything in quotation marks" and "It is the love of the exaggerated, the 'off,' of things-being-what-they-are-not." Still, Sontag made one thing clear enough: there was an undeniable connection between camp and gay men. As she wrote, "While it's not true that Camp taste *is* homosexual taste, there is no doubt a peculiar affinity and overlap."[5] *The Gay Cookbook* capitalized on this sudden fascination with gay male taste, down to the tagline on its cover, the "complete compendium of campy cuisine."

Yet Hogan's version of camp did not align easily with Sontag's assessment. Sontag presented "Camp," in its highest form, as a way of *seeing* the world—of exposing, and treasuring, artifice and excess in popular culture.

Hogan's style of "camping" was a way of *being in* the world, a strategy of everyday performance derived from the working-class gay subcultures he first encountered in his teens and twenties. For Hogan, as for many other gay men of his generation, camping was a way to negotiate cultural constructions of gender and sexuality and, at the same time, make community.

Hogan's style also contrasted sharply with early gay rights activists' emphasis on "respectable" self-presentation.[6] Since the 1950s, homophile groups had largely concentrated on integrating homosexuals into American society, stressing the need for gender-normative behavior. Many self-identified homosexual men also criticized, and sought to distance themselves, from so-called swishes, whose visible effeminacy was seen as affirming dominant conceptions of homosexual deviance.[7] Hogan embraced camp humor, and its play on gender, as central to gay culture.

The Gay Cookbook was most innovative in using camp humor to reimagine gay domestic space. In the 1950s and 1960s, when mainstream journalism, movies, and popular sociology portrayed the lives of homosexuals, they typically conveyed an image of a dangerous, immoral, and unhappy "gay world"—seedy bars and street corners where men covertly ventured to find a companion for the night. At the same time, popular representations of the effeminate gay decorator persistently linked male homosexuality with an excessive interest and investment in other people's domestic consumption, while still denying gay men home lives of their own. *The Gay Cookbook* challenged these representations, for both gay and straight audiences. Hogan depicted the home as a central stage for shaping gay life and relationships, a site of humor, community, and pleasure. At a time when many homophile activists and their followers still prioritized privacy, Hogan's cookbook made the gay home public, embracing the culture of Cold War domestic consumption only to challenge its gender and sexual norms.

My reading of Hogan's cookbook builds on Lizabeth Cohen's conception of the consumers' republic, to consider how and why LGBTQ people turned to the consumer market to assert their right to social and political inclusion.[8] I also build on the expanding field of food studies, which has troubled conventional views of domestic space as simply apolitical or private. Feminist scholars in particular have revealed the complex and unexpected ways that food acquisition, preparation, consumption, and representation both reflect and shape understandings of gender, class, and ethnic and racial identities—connecting individuals to the market, structuring social performance, and inspiring political activism.[9] Foodways should be conceived in Michel Foucault's terms, alongside sexuality, as a "dense transfer point for relations of power," serving multiple actors, strategies, and ends.[10] In combining the form of the cookbook with the aesthetics of camp, Hogan exposed the underlying potential of food and foodways as sites of social and political creativity, even within the constraints of the consumer market.

CAMPING QUEENS AND CAMP MAVENS

Louis Randall—the future Lou Rand Hogan—was born in May 1910, near Bakersfield, California (fig. 2.2). He was the only son of George D. Randall, a Pennsylvania-born oil driller, and his Canadian wife, Lucille Hogan.[11] Their marriage was not destined to last. In 1920, when Hogan was ten, his father left California for Borneo, where he was sent to work for Royal Dutch Oil.[12] By 1931, George was still working overseas, and Lucille filed for divorce, blaming the "Borneo cuties" her husband mentioned in his infrequent letters.[13] At the time Lucille was living in Los Angeles with Louis and her widowed mother, Jane Hogan; Lucille was employed as a copyist for the county clerk, Louis as a municipal clerk.[14]

Even in his teens, however, Hogan had gained a foothold in two worlds where conventional gender and sexual norms were suspended: the burgeoning theater scene of Los Angeles and San Francisco, and the tourist industry. As Hogan recalled in "The Golden Age of Queens," a serialized memoir published in 1974 under the pseudonym Toto le Grand, he got his first part in a production at Gilmor Brown's Pasadena Playhouse and went on to perform in the chorus lines of two popular touring musicals—*Desert Song* and *Good News*—listed in the program only as "Sonia Pavlijev." As Hogan reflected, "What could be wrong with a polish (?) name for a young Irish (!) faggot . . . ?"[15]

FIGURE 2.2. Photograph of Lou Rand Hogan, c. 1969. Originally published in *Avanti*. Photographer unknown. Reproduction courtesy of the Human Sexuality Collection, Rare and Manuscript Collections, Cornell University Library.

Hogan's stage career nonetheless floundered, and in 1936 he began working as a steward and cook on the newly launched Matson luxury cruise line, on trips to Hawaii, Australia, Japan, and the Pacific Islands.[16] The job itself was hardly glamorous: while passengers swam, dined, and lounged, many crew members remained below deck and slept in crowded quarters. Still, Hogan was in good company. Of the 500 men in the steward's department, Hogan wrote, "Probably 486 were actively gay!"[17] Indeed, as Allan Bérubé revealed in his unfinished work on the Marine Cooks and Stewards Union, the steward's department of the Matson line largely consisted of gay white men, all with camp nicknames like Miss Cook, Miss McCormick, Miss Leprosy, and the African Queen. The ships themselves earned nicknames as well: the *Lurline* was known as the "Queerline," the *Matsonia* the "Fruit-sonia," and the *Mariposa* the "Mary-" or "Fairy-posa." Camping provided a private language for the crew members to make light of their living and working conditions, and to parody conventional views of housekeeping and personal service as work limited to women and people of color.[18]

The campy "sisterhood" of the Matson line more broadly reflected an expanding "camp" subculture that had emerged in the 1910s and 1920s in a number of American cities, including New York, Newport, and Chicago. This camp culture was epitomized by the "fairy"—people assigned male at birth who challenged, intentionally and unintentionally, conventional male gender performances, embodying mannerisms and linguistic styles coded as "feminine." Fairies, like the stewards on the Matson line, might also refer to each other by female nicknames and joke about their sexual exploits and desires. Such camping gained further circulation in the 1920s and 1930s through popular fiction, vaudeville, and pre-Code Hollywood films.[19] Hogan himself fondly recalled Robert Scully's widely circulated 1932 book, *A Scarlet Pansy*: it followed a heroine named "Fay Etrange" (French for "strange fairy") on the prowl for "rough trade"—and provided Hogan a model of "gay talk."[20]

After World War II, Hogan landed back in San Francisco, but his history from there is harder to document. In one byline, from the late 1960s, he claimed to have cooked for restaurants, clubs, and luxury hotels in Los Angeles and San Francisco; served as the personal chef for the industrialist Henry J. Kaiser and the Sultan of Johor; and written for *Gourmet* and *Sunset* magazines (though there is no concrete evidence that he ever did).[21] He occasionally peppered later bylines with the titles of books he never wrote.[22] Yet whatever the full truth of Hogan's biography, the story he presented matters just as much. Hogan saw his own history as deeply intertwined with that of California: its expanding cities, burgeoning entertainment industries, and growing gay communities.

Hogan capitalized on his intimate knowledge of San Francisco in his first publishing endeavor, a parody of classic noir, *The Gay Detective*. Released in 1961 under the slight pseudonym "Lou Rand," the novel followed Francis Morley, a private investigator trying to solve the murder of a young gay man.[23] The novel's humor depended on the characters' complicated play with the conventional gender norms popularized in hard-boiled crime fiction. In one scene, Morley proves his masculinity by challenging his new assistant, Tiger, a former football star, to a boxing match—easily defeating him. But Morley also refers to other gay men affectionately as "girls" and seems initially more interested in redecorating his office than getting down to work. He adopts his "gayest manner, even to a slightly mincing step" at the homosexual hangout "The Bait Room." The clientele, the headwaiter informs him, often "just sit and camp" into the early morning.[24] More than a mere reflection of gay life, the book provided a guided tour of postwar San Francisco places and personalities, loosely fictionalized but still recognizable.[25]

The Gay Cookbook, published four years later, offered readers guidance of a different sort—not to bars and bathhouses but to their own apartments. The cookbook most closely resembled the irreverent, anecdotal style of Peg Bracken's best-selling 1960 cookbook, *The I Hate to Cook Book*. But while Bracken's book conjured images of a beleaguered housewife, Hogan depicted a new kind of cook. As Hogan explained in his introduction, there now seemed to be cookbooks for every demographic, so an editor suggested, "Oh hell, May, why don't you people have a cookbook? After all, you're supposed to be 'one-in-six,' and that's a lot of cooking!"[26] The popular claim that "one-in-six" men were homosexual was typically treated as reason for alarm. Hogan cited it as reason for publication—a kind of culinary identity politics, where every "type" of individual deserved a guide to the kitchen.

The publisher's motives were likely more profit driven. Sherbourne Press was an up-and-coming press founded in the early 1960s as part of a larger West Coast publishing boom. Its primary goal was targeting previously "invisible" markets—whether sci-fi fans, movie fanatics, or biography junkies. Its ads in the mainstream press were virtual testaments to 1960s market segmentation, placing books for film buffs side by side with those for jazz connoisseurs.[27] It also published a fair number of books on sexual subcultures—*The Swap Club*, *The Erotic Revolution*, *Sex-Driven People*, among others—in addition to a still-wider range of pulp and erotica titles through its paperback imprint Argyle (including a reissue of *The Gay Detective*). Publishing *The Gay Cookbook* was daring, but it was also an obvious extension of its business model—identifying a new readership.

The gay press confirmed Sherbourne's instincts that a gay audience was just waiting for mainstream publishers to notice it. The San Francisco–based newspaper *Citizens News* estimated in 1964 that each gay man and woman would spend, on average, $123 a year on reading and education, compared with $110 a year on alcohol: "In short," the editor concluded, "the gay dollar has not yet really been tapped."[28] A year later, when *The Gay Cookbook* was published, no full reviews appeared in the mainstream or gay press, but several gay mail-order services picked up the book. A flyer circulated by the Dorian Book Service went so far as to boast that the book was hardcover, with a "Washable Binding for Kitchen Use!" The catalog's writers, like Hogan, did not imagine the book merely as a novelty item to sit on someone's coffee table—it was designed to be used (fig. 2.3).[29]

The book eventually sold an estimated 10,000 to 12,000 copies—but gay readers were only one segment of the book's intended audience. Sherbourne advertised the book in mainstream venues as well, including the *New York Times*, the *San Francisco Examiner*, and *Publishers' Weekly*.[30] That same fall the book was also reprinted in smaller hardcover format by the Bell Publishing Company, an imprint of Crown Publishers in New York. The Los Angeles radio station KPFK even featured a thirty-five-minute interview with Hogan, rebroadcast the following week on WBAI radio in New York.[31] The potential gay audience does not seem enough to explain why *The Gay Cookbook* was so readily picked up by two mainstream publishers and why it received such unprecedented publicity. How did the publishers and promoters expect straight audiences would understand the book?

It was only a year earlier that Sontag had popularized the concept of camp as a distinct "sensibility" defined by "its love of the unnatural: of artifice and exaggeration."[32] She acknowledged the most traditional or "vulgar" use of the verb "to camp" as enacting "flamboyant mannerisms," but she was more interested in camp as it applied to movies, clothing, furniture, architecture, music, and literature. These cultural products were not campy in themselves, but could be transformed by "Camp taste," a way of looking that honors theatricality and style over sincerity or content. "Camp taste" has the power to look at art a "serious" critic might consider "bad" and revalue its failures as "good," be it a Tiffany lamp, *The Maltese Falcon*, a Busby Berkeley musical, or Flash Gordon comics. Gay men, Sontag argued, epitomized this taste for the artificial. Elevating gay men to cultural mavens and trendsetters, she called them "the vanguard—and the most articulate audience—of Camp."[33] Not that she did so without hesitation. She did not address the connection of camp to gay men directly until note 50 of 58, and derided the very form of camp humor most central to gay culture since the

The **Gay Cookbook**

$5.95   by Chef Lou Rand Hogan

Hard-Cover Edition

Big 7x10 size!

Washable Binding for Kitchen Use!   **280 pages!**

Read the Introduction to this Wild Wacky Book

In these sensuous sixties, when we're all waiting for someone to drop that big one, and hoping — for goodness sake — that there isn't a cake in the oven at the moment, one pauses to note those perennial offerings of the literary entrepreneurs - cookbooks.

Of course, there's nothing really new about cookbooks — some of the earliest known volumes remain from the time of those gay Caesars. Were they ever the ones! They'd eat it laying down; then, when they'd had all they could take, they'd swish into a handy room and spit it all out!

Of course, there've been some changes. Even fifty years ago many things weren't as good as they are now, including cookbooks. We had (yes, Myrtle, I do remember) some rather rough French translations in

this line (no pictures!) and the NEW BOSTON, or was it OLD FANNY FARMER?

Later, as the 20th century rolled on - and on - and on, cookbooks developed character, and characters developed cookbooks. Brawny wrestlers found that a well-publicized sponge cake tossed off while waiting for their wave to set was good business. Tired old burley queens offered cookbooks. Maine guides came out with 'em as did ministers, masons, and morticians.

In consequence, there are books on How to Cook a Wolf, and presumably vice-versa, a Book of One-Arm Cookery (it must be assumed that the other arm was cooked the week before) and so on. And there are the specialty cookbooks. Mad, girl, mad! Wine cookbooks, vegetable cookbooks, all-meat cookbooks, no-meat cookbooks (that's a life, dearie-some has it, some don't!)

In any case, there seem to be new jazzy cookbooks for everyone, for every type, every temperament. A mad, mad editor coyly suggested: "Oh, hell, May, why don't you people have a cookbook? After all, you're supposed to be 'one-in-six', and that's a lot of cooking!"

Well, why not? As a popular writer and columnist put it, "You used to guess whether one 'was' or 'wasn't'! Now it's damned hard to tell who isn't'!" To repeat, why not? Many sad souls come home from a rough day over the ribbon counter, or from working over a hot comptometer, or even from 'down on Madison' (it's rough down on Madison, competition-wise) and face the prospect of wading into that grim little kitchenette to whip up something cheap and filling.

Yes, in that magic hour 'tween day and dark, after effacing the ravages of the day's toil and before the night's serious cruising, ya gotta take on some food. Man, woman, or child, a girl has got to eat!

So we'll offer here a sort of non-sensical cookbook for the androgynous (don't bother to look it up, Maude - it means "limp-wristed"). And while we can't guarantee the quality of the guests these dishes may be set before, we assure the reader that all preparations and recipe details are honest.

Here then is THE GAY COOKBOOK, which some queen will promptly call FAGGOT'S FARE!

Order your copy today — A433

CHAPTERS INCLUDE:
— SALADS AND DRESSINGS, INCLUDING LE FRENCH — THAT TIRED OLD FISH — IN YOUR OVEN — SWISH STEAK — OYSTERS, LOBSTERS, SHRIMPS, AND WHAT TO DO ABOUT CRABS — WHAT TO DO WITH A TOUGH PIECE OF MEAT — and others just as succulent! Every recipe entirely useful!
Over 30 riotous drawings add spice to every chapter

FIGURE 2.3. This flyer for the Dorian Book Service, a gay mail-order catalog, presented *The Gay Cookbook* not as a novelty item but a useful addition to any home, "Big 7 x 10 size!" with "Washable Binding for Kitchen Use!" Reproduction courtesy of Beinecke Rare Book and Manuscript Library, Yale University.

1920s. "Pure Camp is always naïve," Sontag argued. "Camp which knows itself to be Camp ('camping') is usually less satisfying."[34]

In the weeks and months after "Notes on 'Camp'" appeared, major newspapers and magazines began promoting camp as a hip new trend. *Time* magazine printed an enthusiastic summary, noting that "it is to homosexuals' self-interest to neutralize moral indignation, and this Camp does by promoting playful estheticism." Soon after, the *New York Times Magazine* ran a four-page spread by Thomas Meehan proclaiming that growing ranks of New Yorkers were now using camp as "a catch-all term to describe a previously unnamed sensibility, a third stream of taste, entirely apart from good taste or bad taste," with photographs of Barbra Streisand (intentional camp), Batman comics (low camp), and many other examples to guide the camp novice. Gloria Steinem, in *Life*, also weighed in, and Sontag quickly became known as the "Camp girl."[35] Following Sontag's lead, however, nearly all these popular commentaries overlooked the older style of outrageous, effeminate camping.[36] Sontag made camp widely appealing by downplaying its potential for gender and sexual parody—precisely the qualities Hogan most prized.

If anything, *The Gay Cookbook* fell on the lowest rung of Sontag's camp ladder, not pure, unintentional camp, but rather intentional camping. Amid long and detailed recipes, Hogan frequently included an aside directed toward the "ladies," a community of gay readers whom he referred to by camp names like Sue Ellen or Gussie (fig. 2.4). In the middle of gazpacho instructions, for example, Hogan imagined a complaining reader and responded, "I know, Maude. You're all impatient, with your 'what the hell is it?'" Even the copyright page warned, "All rights reserved, Mary." Hogan also alluded to his, and his readers', effeminate affectations. In a recipe for carrot salad he warned that grating "can be very rough on the manicure, so watch it!" He told readers not to "swish" into the butcher's and "get all impatient at having to wait. Smile at the S.O.B., as you gayly ask, 'How's ya meat today, Butch?'"[37] (The cookbook was also the first time he used the name "Lou Rand Hogan," appending his mother's maiden name to the pseudonym he invented for his novel.) The book at once seized on the mainstream fascination with camp and reclaimed it for gay men.

THE CULTURAL POLITICS OF GAY DOMESTICITY

What was more unique still was where Hogan located camp culture—not in public but at home. Imagining a homosexual, let alone a happy one, in the home was a radical innovation in 1965. Social scientists, journalists, and filmmakers of the 1950s typically depicted gay men as outsiders, if not threats, to the ideal heterosexual household—lonely figures who lurked in city streets, bathrooms, and bars in search of a one-night stand. Representations of gay culture multiplied in the early 1960s, yet the idea of a happy homosexual seemed to many observers unfathomable. Mental health experts, for one, largely regarded homosexuality as a symptom of neurotic beets. Canned, sliced salad beets are best to use; these are drained, saving most of the liquid. Onions and garlic are prepared as for cucumbers. To about 2 cups of the juice, add one cup of cider vinegar. A couple of tablespoons of salt, and one of sugar (may be brown) are tossed into this juice. A little pickling spice may be added; at least a dozen or so whole cloves. The liquid is poured over the beets, and they are put away for a day or so. These too, are simply drained and served on crisp, cool lettuce, with possibly a minor sprinkle of green chopped parsley. Very pretty; very tasty.

FAVORITE SALAD

A great many men prefer — as a salad — just plain sliced tomatoes. Some like 'em with dressing, almost any kind; others want to sprinkle a little sugar and vinegar on them. The tomatoes must be firm, ripe, cold, and in nice thick slices.

FRUIT SALAD

As a fitting finale to this chapter, let us spare a few kind words for the Fruit Salad. (Oh! Behave, Gussie!)

At Happy House we use both fresh and canned fruits; first dumping the canned — with all the can juice — into a large bowl; then the cut-up apples, orange, banana, melon, or whatever. We add a good cup of heavy sherry (wine!) and put it all in the icebox to chill for an hour or so. With a slotted spoon (so we get no juice, see), we spoon it out onto lettuce cups, and pour a little honey mayonnaise over it. Then, if we feel really gay, we garnish with a few mint leaves, a large fresh strawberry, or even a cherry! It's swell!

HONEY MAYONNAISE

1 cup mayonnaise (or 'type')
2/3 cup honey
Good squeeze of lemon juice

Mad on a fruit salad. What do we do with the leftover juice and sherry? Why, we bake a ham in it, silly boy!

This seems to cover the salad bit; with these ideas you can take it from here. Try and remember, the simpler the salad, the better.

❖

32

FIGURE 2.4. This sample page from *The Gay Cookbook* exemplifies Hogan's campy style of humor, replete with double entendres, like "Fruit Salad," and asides to friends ("Oh! Behave, Gussie!"). It also reveals Hogan's earnest dedication to cuisine, with liberal use of canned food common for cookbooks from the period.

maladjustment—whether a "flight from masculinity" or the result of un-resolved parental conflict. Popular sociological and journalistic accounts tended to be more sympathetic, but still regarded gay men as pathologi-cally promiscuous and, very likely, pedophilic.[38] As Jess Stearn put it in *The Sixth Man*, "While he often says he prefers a lasting relationship, the adult homosexual seems quite ready to indulge in sex for sex's sake. And when he ventures forth on the prowl, he generally prefers somebody younger."[39]

This image of gay men as anti-domestic coexisted, paradoxically, with the popular stereotype of gay men as hyper-domestic, embodied by the fig-ure of the effeminate gay decorator. When interior decorating first emerged as a trade in the 1870s, it was dominated by male manufacturers, contrac-tors, and distributors of furniture, wallpaper, carpet, and tiles. By the turn of the century, however, prominent female decorators, most centrally former actress Elsie de Wolfe, moved to redefine the field, emphasizing women's "natural" aesthetic expertise. Male decorators still dominated the profes-sion, yet, over the 1910s and 1920s, they increasingly appeared misplaced, parodied in periodicals and film as effete and hysterical.

One of the earliest comic depictions appeared in 1917 in *Vogue* magazine, in a satirical portrait titled "Interior Desecration," by Dorothy Parker (then Rothschild), focusing on a fictional decorator named Alistair St. Cloud. Touring a mansion St. Cloud has recently decorated, the narrator noted that nearly all the rooms seemed wildly overdone, with bright bold colors. The guest room, the narrator explained, was "painted scarlet" with tas-sels hanging "from every possible place: no matter how anything began, it ended in a tassel."[40] But St. Cloud's decorative style was only an extension of his extravagant, eccentric, and effeminate self-presentation. As Parker described St. Cloud, "He has phenomenally long nervous hands, white and translucent, which are used principally for making languid gestures."[41] The accompanying illustrations depicted St. Cloud with his hand on his hip, his black jacket emphasizing an hourglass-shaped figure (fig. 2.5). Another image depicted him in a "Chinese dreaming robe, gazing upon goldfish"—with one more tassel hanging down from the waist (fig. 2.6).

Similar representations appeared increasingly in the decades to come, in popular literature, cartoons, film, and television, persistently linking male homosexuality to an excessive investment in surface, style, and con-sumption. Typically the stereotype was played for laughs. In the 1950 film *The Jackpot*, starring Jimmy Stewart, British character actor Alan Mowbray plays a decorator named Lesley, who redoes the main character's suburban home as part of a radio show prize. Touring the house, Lesley exclaims, "Divine, absolutely divine—we won't be able to use a thing."[42] Others were more expressly critical, blaming decorators—both gay men and single

"It took me two weeks to arrange that fruit," he said, "and now you have upset it"

That photograph of him clad in a Chinese dreaming-robe, gazing upon goldfish

FIGURES 2.5 AND 2.6. These illustrations of fictional decorator Alistair St. Cloud appeared in *Vogue* magazine in 1917, accompanying "Interior Desecration," an article by Dorothy Parker (then Rothschild) parodying the kind of decorating advice and decorators the magazine regularly celebrated. Courtesy of Condé Nast.

women—for undermining the goals of the heterosexual household, aggravating wives' anxieties and alienating husbands from their home. As psychologist Milton Sapirstein, writing with Alis De Sola, explained in *Harper's*: "With few exceptions, these people are fundamentally hostile to the normal purposes of homemaking: children, family life in general, are outside their range of interest." In either case, the decorator was rarely imagined to have a home or family of his own. He constructed postwar domesticity at the same time he was excluded from it.[43]

When observers did depict gay men at home, they often did so with derision—even when the writers were gay themselves. In *The Homosexual and His Society*, for instance, Donald Webster Cory (a pseudonym for Edward Sagarin) and John P. LeRoy (his young lover, Barry Sheer) presented gay domesticity as a contradiction in terms. "Home: Where is that?" Cory and LeRoy's everyman-homosexual reflected. "A place without people, where the last roommate moved out a week ago, and the guy who stayed over Saturday night—oh, well, what was his name, anyway?" In their eyes, the gay home was not a refuge from a hostile world but a lonely, isolating space, where someone might, at best, stay for a night of anonymous sex. Sagarin and Sheer did not ignore gay men who *were* at ease in the domestic sphere—men who were "handy with the thread and needle" or knew "a thousand ways to make the same kind of spaghetti sauce taste different." Rather, echoing popular psychoanalytic accounts, they depicted these men as sick and effeminate, "fleeing from manhood."[44]

Hogan's representation of gay domesticity deflected such stereotypes, depicting gay men neither as lonely wanderers in search of sex nor as taste-makers obsessed with other people's décor, but rather domestic citizens of a different kind, working to build home lives of their own. His imagined reader may have been single, but he entertained frequently and needed to be prepared: "There always comes a time when someone drops in to call," whether "late afternoon or early morning." For side dishes, he advised, "Most (alleged) he-man types don't want vegetables; but sometimes ya get a guy who digs them." Elsewhere Hogan celebrated a cup of coffee not only for warming you up but for giving you "a chance to get acquainted with that stray pickup." That carrot salad, too, was perfect for parties: Halloween, Thanksgiving, not to mention "bashes, buffets or drag dinners."[45] The book also overflowed with double entendres and sexual innuendos: "seafood" (sailors), "quickie," "frenching," "browning," "chicken queens," "crabs," and "loose ends." He titled one chapter "what to do with a tough piece of meat," and warned against soggy canapés: "As you all know too damn well, a limp delicacy is neither pretty nor tasty."[46]

The line drawings by freelance artist David Costain further contributed to the book's portrayal of the home as a principal stage of queer social and sexual connection (fig. 2.7). In an illustration for French dressing, Costain depicted Hogan dancing with two men in European corsets and skirts. Next to a paragraph about choosing beef grades, Costain drew Hogan as a matador taming a wild bull. In another the chef literally netted a muscular man in a bathing suit. Where Alistair St. Cloud was delicate and uptight, Costain's gay chef was playful and passionate.

This irreverent presentation of everyday queer life, with its frequent allusions to sexuality and gender nonconformity, was emblematic of a broader shift in gay politics and culture. Since the mid-1950s, homophile groups like the Mattachine Society and ONE, Inc., presented the typical gay male as normal, well adjusted, and masculine to the point of invisibility.[47] By 1965, however, a new wave of gay rights organizations had begun to challenge these strategies. Founded in San Francisco in 1964, the Society for Individual Rights (SIR) pledged to represent "*all* expressions of the homosexual community." SIR hosted events to attract a diverse crowd, from dances and bowling nights to drag shows and musical performances.[48] On

FIGURE 2.7. David Costain's playful illustrations for *The Gay Cookbook* depicted the gay home as a space of gay social and sexual connection—images that were virtually unprecedented in postwar gay or mainstream culture.

the East Coast, Clark Polak took over the Philadelphia-based Janus Society in 1963 and made a repeated point of defending the "masculine woman" and the "feminine man" against the conformist stance of older organizations.[49] He also founded *Drum* magazine to put, in his words, "'sex' back into homosexuality," mixing physique photography with political essays, cultural reviews, and campy cartoons. In Polak's hands, camp, gender nonconformity, and sexual expression became modes of militancy, essential ways to reject normative ideals, both inside and outside the gay rights movement.

Hogan's flamboyant writing style fit well with these nonconformist strategies, but he also valued the discretion and control that domesticity allowed. Only a few months after *The Gay Cookbook* was published, in February 1966, Hogan mailed an excerpt from a new book-in-progress called *Kitchens and Tea-Rooms* to Mattachine Society leader Hal Call. Here Hogan bluntly depicted gay life in bars and coffeehouses (as well as sex in parks, movie houses, and bathrooms) as exciting but undeniably dangerous, with the constant threat of arrest. On the flip side, Hogan wrote, "There are more couples of men (as well as more couples of women) living quiet, 'decent' lives together here than you would believe. And—this is in every walk of life; not just the obvious 'arts' people, but many professionals."[50] "Respectability" was, for Hogan as for the Mattachine Society, a pragmatic approach to protecting individuals against discrimination and police entrapment. Yet even as Hogan praised the "quiet," "decent" life, his own cookbook shouted to readers from the pages of the *Times* and *Publishers' Weekly*. In the context of the early gay rights movement, the cookbook was a paradox: making privacy public.

The expansion of a gay consumer market more largely functioned to blur divides between public and private gay life. Some mail-order catalogs, like the Dorian Book Service, operated by Hal Call, primarily distributed fiction and nonfiction—including some produced by another Mattachine-owned company, the Pan-Graphic Press. The book service of Guild Press similarly distributed books from mainstream publishers, as well as magazines and novelty books produced in-house. Yet other services branched out further. The 1965 *Vagabond* catalog, for example (operated by the Minneapolis-based company Directory Services, Inc.), sold not only books and magazines but also wall calendars, greeting cards, erotic photographs, records, sex aids, decorative statues, and "towels with a gay touch" (one pictured a singing rooster with the words "For a Gay Old Cock").[51] Such services transformed the home itself into a site of gay cultural consumption. You no longer needed to go to a bar to "come out" into the gay world. Domestic consumption was now an extension, and expression, of sexual desire and identity.

Hogan's recipes themselves ranged from easy standards to the gourmet—meat loaf to beef bourguignon, Texas chili to Cantonese chicken, codfish cakes to wiener schnitzel—while including such staple ingredients of the 1960s as MSG and canned Campbell's tomato soup. Hogan added a few surprises, too, like gefilte fish: "You could simply call them 'fish balls' (being very gay about it!)," he remarked, in case you are the kind of "ninny who would hesitate to serve an item with the racial connotation of gefilte."[52]

This variety was shaped in part by broader trends in American cuisine in the 1940s and 1950s, chief among these a heightened interest in Continental cuisine. Fascination with European foods would take off even more in the mid-1960s with the ascendance of food writers including Julia Child and Craig Claiborne.[53] Hogan's cosmopolitan cookery, however, was likely inspired as much by his experiences aboard the Matson cruise ships. Matson menus, when Hogan was aboard, routinely included foreign-sounding dishes alongside familiar ones—not just Roast Chicken with American Stuffing but also Leg of New Zealand Lamb Boulangere, Cold Veal Loaf with Russian Vegetable Salad, Consomme with Vermicelli, and Parisienne Potatoes. Hogan's cookbook also bore more specific marks of the routes he served, including Hawaiian barbecue and a Philippine dish for dried cod and potatoes.[54]

The culinary range of Hogan's cookbook, like others of the period, also reflected a longer cultural development that Kristin Hoganson calls "cosmopolitan domesticity"—whereby consumption enabled men and women to bring the foreign and exotic into their homes.[55] By the 1960s, food had arguably come to dominate as a key component in cosmopolitan domesticity. Nora Ephron, in her classic 1968 essay on the gourmet food establishment, for example, pointed to "the curry development" of the 1950s—whereby curry dishes began appearing everywhere from the frozen food aisle to "fashionable homes."[56] But while domestic cosmopolitanism may have allowed Americans to signal their class status and creativity, it also tended to fetishize the foreign as objects to be acquired or literally consumed—reaffirming existing racial, economic, and national hierarchies while giving white, middle-class Americans access to everyone else's culture.

Often Hogan used humor to disrupt any sense of affluence. In his section on soups, for example, he explained the ingredients in *Consomme Madrilène en Gelee* and *Consomme Poivrade*, only to add, "Jeez! Ain't we elegant; French names 'n everything!" Hogan, after all, was himself working class—and he frequently made suggestions for cutting costs. But Hogan's humor could also rely on racial fetishizations. He joked that sushi would give readers "a chance to wear that mad kimono!" In a section on spaghetti sauces, he suggested, "Why not just find a foot-loose Italian for your weekend houseguest and turn him loose in the kitchenette." And he ended his recipe for Hawaiian barbecue by explaining, "Of course this type meal is made much jazzier if someone is plunking at a guitar or a ukulele—with everyone wearing a good coat of all-over tan, and a hibiscus bloom behind each ear, leis all over the place . . . and aloha to you, too."[57] *The Gay Cookbook* may have offered readers a way to resist conventional gender, sexual, and class codes. It could not, however, so easily overcome the racial logic of American domesticity and culinary cosmopolitanism.

GAY DOMESTICITY AFTER LIBERATION

The explosion of the gay liberation movement after the Stonewall riots of June 1969 immediately began to reshape gay politics and gay culture across the United States. In large part, gay liberation leaders succeeded in building a visible base so quickly because they radically redefined "coming out" as a personal political act, or as John D'Emilio put it, an "ends and means for young gay radicals."[58] Before Stonewall, "coming out" had meant entering gay society—revealing your identity to other gay men and lesbians—but after Stonewall, "coming out" came to mean disclosing your identity to heterosexual family and friends. But while the leaders of the gay liberation movement rejected the integrationist principles of earlier activists, they ironically followed their predecessors' lead in rejecting "effeminate" gay men and behavior—particularly when it came to domesticity.

Already in December 1969, *Esquire* printed a long report by Tom Burke hailing the new, hippie-inspired "homosexual of the Seventies." In the first paragraph, Burke declared dead that "semi-neuter" who "lives in a white and silver Jean Harlow apartment, drinks pink gin, cooks *boeuf Bourguignon*, mourns Judy [Garland], makes timid liaisons on Forty-second Street, . . . and masturbates while watching televised swimming meets." Burke later quoted a twenty-four-year-old graduate student who had worked as a waiter in a gay bar, where patrons frequently arrived with their poodles in tow. Once, the student remembered, one of the men invited him home for dinner, but he was appalled by the man's taste for Ethel Merman and Judy Garland records. And his apartment "looked like the Castro showroom on Times Square, only not as masculine. Everything . . . *embellished*. You know: not a straight line in the whole apartment." How much time you spent at home, how you decorated, what you listened to had become critical ways to separate the "old" homosexual culture of camp and effeminacy from the "new" homosexual culture of masculine virility.[59]

This critique of gay domesticity was hardly limited to the mainstream press. In the tenth issue of the radical Berkeley newspaper *Gay Sunshine*,

Craig Alfred Hanson published "The Fairy Princess Exposed," echoing *Esquire* in simultaneously deriding camp, effeminacy, and domesticity. Hanson argued that an aging breed of campy, extravagant fairies was imprisoned by egocentric fantasies and predicted that they would "simply linger on unto death as past relics of a bygone era in their fantasy world of poodle dogs and Wedgewood [*sic*] teacups." To sharpen the blow, Hanson argued that these fairies did not even create the roles they played, whether "bitchy male hairdressers" or "snobbish antique dealers." Rather, straight people imposed the roles and kept the fairies like "pampered pets in gilded cages." The old fairies both lived in a world of camp and had become camp artifacts themselves.[60] Hanson also singled out Mart Crowley's landmark 1968 play, *The Boys in the Band*, for scorn. The play, and its 1970 film adaptation, centered on a Manhattan apartment where eight gay men gather for a birthday party. But while Crowley took pains to represent a range of characters (Jewish, black, Catholic, single, coupled), Hanson focused on the figure of Emory, a lisping, camping, cooking antiques dealer, as a prime example of the "fairy princess," or in the words of a fellow character, "a natural born domestic."[61] For Hanson, gay domesticity simply reaffirmed stereotypes of gay effeminacy, passivity, and weakness, at a moment when gay activists were calling for masculinist militancy.[62]

Not everyone shared this disdain for camp and gender transgression. Carl Wittman's widely circulated "Gay Manifesto," first published at the end of 1969, celebrated "nellies" and "queens" as "our first martyrs," for being visible before many other gay men were.[63] In the third issue of *Gay Sunshine*, Mike Silverstein lauded camp as "a guerilla attack on the whole system of male-female roles."[64] Camp did not simply disappear after the founding of the gay liberation movement, but its political value was suddenly thrown into serious doubt, inspiring passionate and extreme arguments both from its defenders and from its skeptics. Other gay men seemed to reinvent camp, still calling each other by female pronouns, but making their jokes more sexually explicit and thereby more "masculine."[65]

Lou Rand Hogan, too, seems to have realized that he would need to adapt the camp humor he cultivated in the 1960s for a new audience. In March 1970, Hogan began writing a food column for the Los Angeles–based newspaper the *Advocate*. The column was called "Auntie Lou Cooks" and, in many ways, mirrored the style and content of *The Gay Cookbook* (fig. 2.8). Hogan frequently referred to himself as "Mother," evoking a maternal sentiment while returning to older camp modes of gender reversal.

At the same time, Hogan changed the tenor of his jokes. In the 1965 cookbook, Hogan frequently winked at his audience: he might have alluded to an easy double entendre, but he resisted making it outright. When

how 'bout a tall, blond lamb?

by LOU RAND
Author of *The Gay Cookbook*

Well, hello Dolls, Auntie Lou has been whipping her memories and, happily, came up with an old trip to Norway many, many years ago. Fun in the fjords! Long past, of course, but we still have some peculiar recollections. Beautiful tall blond beasts in Bergen—and yards of lace curtains.

More pleasant eating was the national dish, a sort of lamb stew, though I recall it was often made with young venison. And not too expensive; a sort of family dish; suitable, too, for a coven of witches!

THE FJORDS GAVE ME A BETTER IDEA!

LAMB-AND-CABBAGE (Får-i-Kål)—for 6 to 8:
- 2½-3 lbs. lean lamb or mutton, in 1½-in. dice.
- ¼ c. butter PLUS 1 Tbs. oil.
- 1½ tsp. salt PLUS 1 tsp. Accent.
- 2 tsp. whole peppercorns.
- 2 lg. bay leaves.
- 2 c. water.
- 1 sml-to-med cabbage, cored, cut in 8ths.
- 1 c. dairy sour cream (½ pt.).
- 6 med. potatoes, peeled, sliced thick or in quarters.

Now, Tess, how'ya gettin' on with your butcher? You'll need about 3 lbs. of chunky, lean meat. (Yah! Who doesn't?) You can buy about 3 to 4 lbs. of lamb loin, in one piece; take it home, and carefully cut meat away from bone (both sides); trim off excess fat, then cut into 1½-in. or 2-in. cubes.

OR you can buy a small leg of lamb—say 5 lbs.—have Butch cut 3 steaks, nearly an inch thick from the center. Then you take it all home; wax-paper and foil-wrap each steak, put away for another time.

With that little, sharp knife, cut away all the rest of the lamb from the bone; peel away the thin outer skin of the lamb, cut off excess fat. Make your dice or chunks of the lean meat. Save bones.

Take bones, and a tired ol' carrot, a quartered onion, a half stalk of celery, and 3 cups of water. Bring to boil, reduce to simmer for an hour. Strain, discard vegetables, remove fat—and you have about 2 c. of good lamb stock.

Then, or next day, let's make our Får-i-Kål. We'll figure a little over an hour from stove to table. No, Maude, that'll have to wait. . . .

Brown lamb pieces in hot butter-and-oil; toss with the seasonings and spices, cover with the 2 cups of lamb stock, or plain water if you didn't bother, or canned consomme, and simmer 45 to 50 min.

In a second pot of water, put potatoes on to cook, about 20 min.—should only be half-cooked. Add cabbage around on top of meat; drain potatoes and lay in on top of cabbage. Do not stir—try not to break up either cabbage or potatoes. Cover, simmer 15 to 20 min. Pour the sour cream over all, shake down into the pot; heat through, but do not boil.

Carefully spoon out—or use flat skimmer—onto large deep platter, including the whole peppers. These are, carefully—but elegantly, of course—spit out like olive seeds; you'll look surprised when you bite into one, and the whole family will giggle at you (family fun among the Norse!). Anyway, ladle it all out, perhaps potatoes in center, cabbage around, and the lamb over all. Pour all the juice over the meat. This is actually a very tasty dish, and—as Mother says—not too expensive.

Of course, some don't like lamb, a Western heritage, or something. All those stories about the horny sheepherders. Next time, something else; write in for recipes you'd like.

Until then, cook it nice, do it pretty, and don't get busted! . . . says . . . Auntie Lou.

FIGURE 2.8. Building on the success of *The Gay Cookbook*, Hogan wrote the column "Auntie Lou Cooks" for the *Advocate* from March 1970 to April 1974. The column shared the cookbook's camp humor, but it was often more sexually suggestive, now targeted to an exclusively gay audience. Sample column, March 3–16, 1971. © 1971 Pride Media. Reprinted with permission. All rights reserved. Reproduction courtesy of Beinecke Rare Book and Manuscript Library, Yale University.

he referred to California as "the land of fruits and nuts," for instance, he added in parentheses, "(yes, we know, Bessie, a camp. But pull y'self together . . .)."[66] The aside both alerted straight readers to a joke that might have easily gone over their heads and tamed the gay humor to a more "respectable" level for publication. Yet when Hogan began writing for the *Advocate*, he more or less abandoned those winking asides in favor of more aggressive camping. The shift was evident from his first column, which began, "EVERYBODY LOVES HAMBURGERS—if the meat is tasty! Of course, my dears, there are those unsubtle ones we all know, who, when making a new friend (read: pick up a trick) at once rush him into the nearest dark alley."[67] Here, the parenthetical aside did not hint at a euphemism's meaning; it made that meaning explicit.

Hogan's racial assumptions, too, became more explicit. In one column titled "Fabulous Curries," he called on readers to pay more attention to "Eastern dishes," moving swiftly from the culinary to the sexual: "There is a general idea that all Oriental numbers are small 'appetizers.' Well, 'tain't necessarily so." He went on to literally size up various groups of Asian and Southeast Asian men, determining who was and was not "well-equipped, both physically and erotically, to please a busy palate." These newly aggressive fantasies about foreignness and men of color reflected the *Advocate* and urban gay culture's increasing consolidation of the homosexual's presumed racial, class, and gender privilege—white, middle class, and masculine.[68] The column was a success (it regularly featured requests for cooking advice from readers across the country), but in April 1974 Hogan left (or was asked to leave) the *Advocate*—only to turn up three months later in the pages of the tamer San Francisco–based *Bay Area Reporter*.[69] Here, his new cooking column, "The Gourmet Shoppe," showed surprisingly little trace of camp—no double entendres, no asides to Maude and the other "ladies." The camp culture Hogan had known seemed to be disappearing, and his domestic world along with it. As the increasing range of advertisements in the *Advocate* attested, the gay entertainment industry expanded rapidly in the 1970s—bars, clubs, bathhouses, stores, movie theaters, dating services. Making privacy public had ceased to appear politically or socially pragmatic. What came to matter instead was occupying public space, visibly and en masse.

Hogan, in turn, was left feeling nostalgic for what seemed like a lost era. Just two months after he began "The Gourmet Shoppe," the *Bay Area Reporter* began running his six-part memoir, "The Golden Age of Queens." Flamboyantly campy and conversational, the memoir resurrected Hogan's "Mother" persona, only to look back on the California he knew before World War II. "Yes," Hogan wrote, "'twas better back then, when there were

MEN! Men who treated a 'girl' like a lady. . . . A 'trick' was for a whole week-end, or 48 hours, or longer. Many even lasted out the year, possibly the next, too. And, you stayed at home, and cooked and drank a little, and loved, and lived!"[70] To many younger readers, Hogan's vision of gay domesticity must have seemed quaint, but, well into the 1970s, he never stopped defending it. Hogan, and others like him who deployed domestic consumption to imagine and make homes of their own, did not simply embrace and reproduce white middle-class norms but parodied, augmented, and reinvented them.

TWO

REVOLUTIONS

CHAPTER THREE

"The Ultimate Extension of Gay Community": Communal Living, Gay Liberation, and the Reinvention of the Household

In the fall of 1975, the Berkeley-based magazine *Gay Sunshine* ran a classified ad placed by a group of men seeking others to join their urban commune: "Fort Hill Faggots: We are creating a radicalized faggot community in Boston. Interested?" Similar ads appeared frequently in North American gay and counterculture periodicals throughout the 1970s. A 1974 issue of the Canadian magazine *Body Politic* contained four listings for communes, including one that balanced the practical and political: "Gay male commune seeks seventh person. Cooking and gay liberation politics considered assets." An ad in *Kaliflower*, a Bay Area commune newsletter, read, "OUR GAY COMMUNE HAS ROOM FOR TWO MORE. CALL AND RAP." Communal living could even prove a useful real estate pitch: the *Empty Closet*, a gay liberation newsletter published in Rochester, New York, included this ad in 1973: "HOUSE AVAILABLE FOR GAY COMMUNE: 3BR, kitchen, dining room, large living room."[1]

Although largely neglected in most accounts of 1970s gay politics and culture, communal living—sharing a house, an apartment, or land—was widely discussed and practiced as a central strategy of gay male liberation. Following several nights of riots at New York's Stonewall Inn in June 1969, gay liberation groups emerged in cities and on college campuses across the country, encouraging gay men and lesbians to "come out" and come together.[2] Gay communal living was immediately conceived as a vital component of this revolution. In his widely reprinted essay "A Gay Manifesto," Carl Wittman wrote that the creation of gay liberation communes was an important step toward creating what he called a gay "free territory"—free from the economic exploitation that characterized many straight-owned bars and baths in the "gay ghettos" of New York City and San Francisco.[3] In *Homosexual: Oppression and Liberation*, an early synthesis of gay liberation theory, Dennis Altman wrote, matter-of-factly, "The ultimate extension of gay community is the gay commune"—"in essence an attempt to create a new form of extended family."[4] And *Life* magazine's 1971 article, "Homosexuals in Revolt," included a photo of rural "communalists" among gay liberation's many "experiments with different life-styles."[5]

It is impossible to say precisely how many gay male communes—or living collectives, as they were often called—formed in the 1970s. The earliest, and most self-conscious, emerged between 1969 and 1972 out of newly formed gay liberation groups in major cities. But many more, shaped by gay liberation if not always tied to gay liberation groups, would appear in the years that followed, in urban as well as rural areas. These communes varied in their specific goals, their size, their longevity, and their spaces. Many were predominantly populated by white middle-class men, but others were multiracial and cross-class: the homophile movement of the 1950s and 1960s had been predominantly white, and the domestic ideal it upheld was based on white middle-class norms. Gay liberation groups were much more widespread in numbers and location, and attracted relatively more people of color and more people of working-class backgrounds—in large part because of a coalitional approach with the Black Power movement.[6] That diversity was reflected in a few of the communes as well, which espoused a broader ideal of a multiracial gay belonging. What all gay communes shared was a belief in communal living as a vital alternative to the reproductive household and a potential pathway toward personal and collective change.

Gay men were hardly alone in seeking to create communes. Between 1960 and 1975, communes in the United States multiplied exponentially— from a few hundred to many thousand—and became a common topic of conversation, study, and media coverage. Back-to-the-land communes, founded by young "hippies" who sought escape from contemporary technology and consumerism, were the most frequently discussed and depicted in popular magazines and newspapers. In a 1967 story on hippies, *Time* magazine explained the appeal of the commune: "nature-loving hippie tribesmen can escape the commercialization of the city and attempt to build a society outside of society." In July 1969, *Life* magazine put communes on the cover—a photo of five adults and three small girls, in front of a log cabin, with the caption: "The Youth Communes: A New Way of Living Confronts the U.S." Their credo: "Getting out of the cities isn't hard, only concrete is." By the end of the decade, the hippie commune had made its film debut as well, in the comedy *I Love You, Alice B. Toklas* (1968), where a square lawyer becomes a hippie pot smoker, and in the motorcycle odyssey *Easy Rider* (1969). Within the span of five years, communes had become a central expression and emblem of the burgeoning national counterculture.[7]

But while anticapitalist, antiurban youth communes were the most visible to middle-class readers, they were only one manifestation of a more diverse communal movement. Many communes were founded as religious or spiritual communities—from so-called Jesus freaks like the Oregon Family, to Eastern-inspired collectives like the Ananda Cooperative in California. Some, like Harrad West in Berkeley, were based in ideals of "group marriage," inspired by Robert Rimmer's novel *The Harrad Experiment*. Still others emerged out of the antiwar and student movements. Even hippie communes were significantly more diverse in their motives and practices than mainstream accounts often suggested: at Millbrook, founded in upstate New York in 1963, members and visitors led by Timothy Leary experimented with psychedelic drugs; at Drop City, founded in 1965 in Colorado, members built geodesic domes out of car roofs and created conceptual artwork from paintings to film; in 1966, the Diggers in the Haight-Ashbury district of San Francisco began living communally, gathering discarded meat, vegetables, and bread to cook and distribute, and setting up "stores" where customers could take any item for free. What all these communes shared was an eagerness to flee convention, whether in art, spirituality, labor, or family relations. Their members were predominantly white, educated, and middle class—"refugees from affluence," as *Life* put it.[8]

More broadly, communes consolidated, and came to stand in for, a larger critique of middle-class domesticity and, with it, the nuclear family household.[9] One 1971 essay published in the *New York Times Magazine*, titled "The Family is Out of Fashion," featured a drawing of a nuclear family literally surrounded by men and women on horseback, representing, the caption explained, "intellectuals, Women's Lib, population controllers, advocates of the commune." The author, novelist Anne Roiphe, particularly weighed the benefits and drawbacks of collective living, the "much-discussed alternative to the nuclear-family problem"—an opportunity to transform the natal family into "a chosen one, of friends who share cultural, social, political outlook."[10] By the late 1970s, the term "alternative lifestyles" had come to encompass a wide variety of "nontraditional" domestic relations including communes, cohabitation, group marriage, heterosexual singles, single-parent households, "swingers," and same-sex relationships.[11]

The creation of gay male communes most closely paralleled the development of feminist and lesbian communes. As early as 1969, women began forming working and living collectives in cities across the United States as a means of building women's culture and politics. In Iowa City, for example, most of the editorial board of the feminist newsletter *Ain't I a Woman?* lived together and frequently reflected in print on the opportunities and challenges of collectivity. Part of the motivation, one member reflected, was to combine resources: by living as a group, rather than individually or in pairs, they could reduce the burden of everyday tasks like cooking and allow some house members to devote less time to work and more time to political action.[12]

Living collectives like this one quickly took on heightened meaning with evolving ideas about lesbian feminism and women's separatism. More and more, feminist activists argued that social and sexual separatism from men was essential to combatting patriarchal norms and developing a new women's culture. For many women, that also meant redefining lesbian identity, desire, and intimacy as key forms of political resistance. In 1971, for example, a group of twelve activists in Washington, DC, broke away from the mainstream women's movement to form the Furies, a lesbian feminist collective. From 1971 to 1972, the collective lived and worked together producing their own newsletter, centering lesbian desire and relationships as a political strategy. Lesbian feminist communities across the United States also gave rise to living collectives where lesbian mothers shared childcare responsibilities and sought to raise and educate children outside of patriarchal gender norms.[13]

By the mid-1970s, many lesbians also advocated for the creation of "womyn's lands"—separatist intentional communities in the country. Womyn's lands were typically larger and more open than earlier urban communes: some women lived on the land long-term, but many welcomed others to visit for shorter periods; some urban communities also had ongoing connections with rural communities. They primarily attracted white, educated, middle-class women, but women of color also moved to womyn's lands and sometimes worked to create their own. Puerto Rican lesbian activist Juana Maria Paz, for example, moved to a womyn's land in Arizona in 1977, looking for a place outside of the city to raise her daughter. The middle-class white women who lived there, however, largely avoided and rejected her. Within a few months, she moved to Northern California to join an emerging womyn's land for lesbians of color called La Luz de la Lucha (Light of the Struggle).[14]

Gay male activists, too, pressed on the boundaries of private and public life—reinventing domestic practices, spaces, and relationships not as a retreat from politics or community but a form of everyday political and social rebellion. Yet while they drew inspiration and momentum from other political, social, and sexual radicals around them, gay male activists also invested communal living with unique meaning, as a primary strategy for reinventing gay social and sexual culture. The gay liberation movement was diverse in its tactics and theories, yet one common theme was that male heterosexual power held oppressed people apart. This analysis drew particular inspiration from radical and lesbian feminists, who sought to expose and resist culturally inscribed gender and sexual norms—or "sex roles" as they were commonly termed at the time—and, with them, male-dominated power structures, most centrally the patriarchal family. Gay liberation activists, in turn, blamed male sex roles for one of the primary problems facing gay men: loneliness—a sense of isolation and alienation from each other. In centering loneliness as a psychological challenge, gay male activists echoed pathologizing accounts of male homosexuality from the decades before, which depicted gay men as isolated, alienated figures. But where psychiatrists and other social scientists called for gay men to change their social and sexual patterns, gay liberation activists advocated for new forms of queer community—new modes of belonging.

"Belonging" and "belongingness" were keywords of postwar social science and popular thought. As conceptualized by influential psychologist Abraham Maslow, the term "belongingness" framed the search for love, friendship, and community as a primary human need and source of motivation. By the early 1960s, however, many intellectuals, artists, and writers were questioning normative models of homemaking, community, and citizenship as modes of conformity. As Paul Goodman put in his 1960 book, *Growing Up Absurd*, "Our social scientists have become so accustomed to the highly organized and by-and-large smoothly running society that they have begun to think that 'social animal' means 'harmoniously belonging.'" Others redirected discourses of belonging, emphasizing authenticity in seeking connection, and an end to alienation. As "A Gay Manifesto" put it, "We're all looking for security, a flow of love, and a feeling of belonging and being needed."[15]

Gay male activists across the United States built on these psychological discourses, centering communal living as a means of combatting psychological oppression, encouraging new forms of connection rooted in emotional authenticity, sexual openness, and shared practices of homemaking. In 1976, a man named Jack Childers expressed his desire to form a communal household this way: "I want a gay commune. I want to surround myself with gay people who care for me as a person and not just a sex object. I want to know the joy of sitting quietly amid my gay friends and enjoying their company for just that, their company. I want to grow old in their company and know that when I die they will mourn me as a friend."[16] Gay liberation activist Ron Dayman, who had lived in two communes in Toronto and Ottawa, similarly reflected, "Living together with other gays helps one to come to grips with one's gayness. It is not only a sharing of space and necessities but a sharing of lives and experiences. This can be especially valuable in raising the consciousness of those just coming into the movement. But it is an opportunity for all to learn to relate to other gays and to be ourselves on a daily basis, something which few can do in the straight world."[17]

In her work on the New Left, Wini Breines usefully distinguishes strategic politics—largely characterized by "organization building"—from prefigurative politics—efforts to "create and prefigure in lived action and behavior the desired society."[18] Gay communalism partook of a similar prefigurative logic: the commune was a microcosm of the new society gay liberation activists envisioned. Gay commune members saw themselves, and were seen by others, as modeling a new kind of family, elevating social and sexual relationships among gay men as a source of intimate and communal belonging. It was a glimpse of an alternative future, where the home would be unbound to monogamy, to capitalism, to patriarchy, and to the state, molded only to the needs, desires, and ideals of its makers.

GAY COMMUNAL LIVING IN THEORY

Gay communes emerged at a moment of dramatic change for gay male communities and politics. Gay male social life of the 1950s and 1960s had been shaped fundamentally by fear of persecution by the police and exposure to friends, family members, and employers. Vice squads staked out gay men in known gathering spots, including public bathrooms, and conducted routine raids on bars. People who were arrested might also find their names published in local newspapers, only to be fired by their employers.[19] Gay activists, in turn, had largely advocated for the integration of gay men and lesbians into American society as "normal" middle-class citizens, through legal reform and education—though some had already begun to move toward more radical sexual and social inclusivity by the mid-1960s.[20]

A younger generation of activists, beginning in the late 1960s, took a more publicly antiauthoritarian stance under the banner of gay liberation, positioning homosexuality as a revolutionary assault on the American socioeconomic system. Inspired and emboldened by the New Left, Black Power and Third World Liberation, second-wave feminism, and the counterculture, gay liberation brought together three major threads of 1960s social activism and social thought. The first was a revolutionary stance against capitalism and the state; the second was a belief in personal "authenticity"; and the third was a rejection of the nuclear family.[21] Radical feminism incorporated all three, rejecting consumer culture and heterosexual, reproductive domesticity as obstacles to women's self-discovery. Building on Karl Marx and Friedrich Engels, feminist writers framed the nuclear family household as both the foundational unit of modern capitalism and a major force of patriarchal power, conscripting women to limited gender and sexual roles.[22]

Gay liberation activists built on these analyses, adding heterosexuality to the list of the family's oppressions. As Wittman put it, "Right from the beginning we have been subjected to a barrage of straight propaganda. Since our parents don't know any homosexuals, we grow up thinking that we're alone and different and perverted." Heterosexual marriage, too, was largely understood as a repressive institution. Wittman, who had been married briefly himself, warned gay men against mimicking marriage in their own romantic relationships: "To accept that happiness comes through finding a groovy spouse and settling down, showing the world that 'we're just the same as you,' is avoiding the real issues, and is an expression of self-hatred."[23]

Such ideas circulated well beyond Wittman's manifesto. Third World Gay Revolution, a subgroup of black and Latinx activists within the New York Gay Liberation Front (GLF), put the point sharply in their manifesto, "What We Want, What We Believe": "We want the abolition of the institution of the bourgeois nuclear family," which "perpetuates the false categories of homosexuality and heterosexuality by creating sex roles, sex definitions and sexual exploitation."[24] Japanese American activist Kiyoshi Kuromiya similarly claimed in the Philadelphia Free Press: "Homosexuals have burst their chains and abandoned their closets. . . . We came to challenge the incredible hypocrisy of your serial monogamy, your oppressive sexual role-playing, your nuclear family, your Protestant ethic, apple pie and Mother."[25]

Gay liberation activists also looked down on past modes of gay domesticity—particularly a mode of flamboyant "camp" domesticity, which they aligned with effeminacy, inauthenticity, and bourgeois capitalism. This assessment of gay homes of the past was not without reality—some gay men of the 1950s and 1960s, like Gay Cookbook author Lou Rand Hogan, did embrace a self-consciously over-the-top domestic aesthetic. But gay activists pathologized such homes as hopeless role-playing, parroting cultural stereotypes of gay effeminacy.[26]

Gay communes promised an alternative to both modes of domesticity—both the heterosexual nuclear family and the "bourgeois" gay home. One of the earliest calls for gay male communes, Steven Dansky's essay "Hey Man," published in the gay liberation newspaper Come Out in summer 1970, promoted communal living as an essential means of remaking gay sexuality and sociality. As Dansky explained, "In order that we fight our oppressor we must band together" in what he called "Revolutionary Male Homosexual collectives." Collective living would allow gay men to challenge the romantic norm of monogamy and "begin to remould our homosexuality by developing a communistic sexuality of sharing, cooperation, selflessness and total community." Dansky went further to suggest gay male living collectives might adopt and raise homeless gay teenagers so "that they do not acquire the male supremacist ideation of manhood."[27]

Dansky's discussion of sex roles was informed, in great part, by feminist critiques of male supremacy—including that of gay men. Dansky specifically cited recent articles by Robin Morgan and Rita Mae Brown from *Rat*—a two-year-old newspaper recently taken over by radical feminists. In "Goodbye to All That," Morgan wrote, "No getting away, no matter how else you are oppressed, from the primary oppression of being female in a patriarchal world. It hurts to hear that the Sisters in the Gay Liberation Front, too, have to struggle continually against the male chauvinism of their gay brothers." Brown wrote more pointedly, "Most male homosexuals I know are desperately clinging to the externals of cock privilege while secretly fearing they aren't really men. One of the ironies that clearly demonstrates this exists within some of the political homosexual groups—they are often male supremacist." Morgan's and Brown's critiques were just two markers of the growing rift between gay and lesbian activists, and increasing advocacy for women's separatism from men, straight and gay.[28] Dansky redirected such critiques to call for gay men to examine their own sexism through intentional separatism of their own.

Dansky also presented communes as a corrective to existing gay social and sexual outlets, which he viewed as perpetuating gay male oppression and alienation. As Dansky wrote, "G.L.F. must demand the complete negation of the use of gay bars, tea rooms, trucks, baths, streets, and other traditional cruising institutions. These are exploitative institutions designed to keep gay men in the roles given to them by a male heterosexual system."[29] Dansky's view of commercial gay spaces, cruising, and public sex tapped into a broader critique of capitalism as a source of alienation—a stance shared by many gay liberation activists. It also discounted the role of commercial gay spaces in shaping gay identities, communities, and politics—spaces that would become only more important in the years to come, not only through the proliferation of gay bars but also the rise of disco and dance clubs.[30]

Nevertheless, the broader message of Dansky's article and others like it clearly resonated for many young gay men. San Francisco activist Gary Alinder echoed Dansky's critique in his essay "My Gay Soul": "I need to be together with other Gay men. We have not been together—we've not had enough self-respect for that. Isolated sex and then look for another partner.

Enough of that, that's where we've been. Let's go somewhere else." What gay men needed, Alinder argued, were new spaces that would allow for new patterns of social and sexual interaction—communes among them.[31] Many gay liberation writers of the 1970s questioned a sharp homosexual/hetero-sexual binary, calling upon activists to "free the homosexual in everyone."[32] But calls for gay communes, like Alinder's, tended to affirm same-sex desire by essentializing and naturalizing "gayness"—and with it maleness.

The emphasis on interpersonal connection was undoubtedly appealing to many gay men because it challenged dominant stereotypes that most would have encountered if they picked up almost any mainstream account of gay life in the 1960s—images popularized by accounts like *The Sixth Man* or those in *Life* magazine and *Time*, of lonely, depressed men, capable of furtive encounters and one-night stands but not long-term relationships. Even the covers of pulp novels aimed at gay audiences tended to represent gay men as tortured, alienated figures—"sad young men" lost in the dark-ness of the city, their gaze averted, their eyes downcast.[33] Gay liberation activists reinterpreted this affective script: the feelings of failure and isola-tion many gay men experienced were not caused by any psychological dys-function, nor were they essential in some way to homosexuality; rather the instability and "sadness" of gay life was caused by society itself, which had programmed gay men to value unreasonable and unhealthy norms.

The gay liberation critique of gay male culture found its clearest repre-sentation in German filmmaker Rosa von Praunheim's film *Nicht der Homo-sexuelle ist pervers, sondern die Situation, in der er lebt* (*It is Not the Homosex-ual Who Is Perverse but the Society in Which He Lives*). The film was released in Germany in 1971, and von Praunheim brought the film to New York City in spring 1972 for a series of screenings—two at the Museum of Modern Art and another at the Gay Activists Alliance Firehouse, spearheaded by activist and film critic Vito Russo. Self-consciously pedagogical (with "theoretical assistance" from German sociologist Martin Dannecker), the film follows Daniel, a young gay man, on a picaresque of gay spaces: at the beginning of the film, he meets another man and goes back with him to his ornate Berlin apartment. They soon become a couple, but Daniel quickly grows dissatisfied, moving on to glamorous parties and, later, leather bars. He is finally rescued by a radical gay collective who bring him back to their urban commune, where Daniel confesses the errors of his past ways: he is glad he has not become a member of the bourgeoisie, with a wife and kids, but he also regrets his failure to connect with other gay men despite sleep-ing with so many of them. As one of the men explains, "You've become a career queer. All you're interested in is sex and how to get it. You've become a whore who's not getting paid. You've become incapable of a human relationship. You live like a million other gays."[34] Gay communal living promised to provide a new route out of this psychological trap.

GAY COMMUNAL LIVING IN PRACTICE

The exaltation of the commune was more than mere rhetoric or representation. In the early 1970s, gay liberation groups formed communes in major cities across the United States, including New York, Los Angeles, San Francisco, Louisville, Boston, Philadelphia, and Chicago—though there were many more without direct ties to gay liberation groups.[35]

Within Manhattan and Brooklyn alone, GLF formed five gay male living collectives, known by their street: 95th, 23rd, 17th, 12th, and Baltic. The spaces and membership varied. The ten members of the 17th Street Collective lived in a large loft of a commercial building, between the offices of the raunchy and radical *Screw* magazine and the Communist Party. In his book *The Gay Militants*, published in June 1971, Donn Teal wrote that the apartment "breathed variety," with "nine or ten rugs; work tables; a sewing machine and spotless kitchen; a huge planter suspended from the roof light; a World War I helmet; a bulletin board; and posters of Che and Picasso's *Don Quixote* that did not seem incompatible." Many of the members had already been heavily involved in New Left and civil rights politics: Allen Young had worked for Liberation News Service; Guy Nassberg (later known as Jason Victor Serinus) had worked for the Southern Christian Leadership Conference; and Jim Fouratt had been a key member of the Yippie movement. Several members had also visited and worked in Cuba with the Venceremos Brigades, to show solidarity with the Cuban Revolution.[36] Young later recalled, "More than mere living space, our loft served as a meeting space for hundreds of gay men from all over the city as well as from across the U.S., Canada and beyond. Dances, parties, consciousness-raising groups, political meetings, orgies, acid trips, hot affairs, fast friendships—all these and more constituted the life of the collective."[37] A few blocks away, Argentine activists Néstor Latrónico and Juan Carlos Vidal formed the 23rd Street Collective along with four other men and a tuxedo cat named Gato. They too saw their personal lives and political goals as intertwined: as Latrónico later recalled, they regularly hosted meetings of Third World Gay Revolution and shared all their money and belongings, "even if one of us didn't have any."[38]

One of the most detailed and widely read accounts of gay collective living came from John Knoebel, who published a personal essay on the 95th Street Collective in an early gay liberation reader, *Out of the Closets*. GLF had been a transformative experience for Knoebel, as it had been for many others. Knoebel had grown up in Wisconsin and spent five years in a Catholic seminary before going to college at University of Wisconsin in Madison. In the summer of 1969, he moved to New York to attend NYU's graduate program in comparative literature; by November, he began attending GLF meetings. "Everything seemed to come alive for me then, like it had never been before," Knoebel later wrote. "I was gay! Gay! With ribbons streaming and bells ringing." By July 1970, at another GLF meeting, three members of the 95th Street Collective, who had organized a month earlier, invited him to join them. Knoebel had gotten the attention of the collective after speaking at a GLF meeting about his experience getting beaten up in the Village two nights before the first parade commemorating the Stonewall riots (he had to get fourteen stitches). He quickly agreed to move in, surmising that the living collective would be an opportunity to extend his involvement in GLF and join others experimenting with alternative modes of living. Their apartment, located on the second floor of a twelve-floor apartment building on the Upper West Side, was small and sparsely decorated—two bedrooms, an eat-in-kitchen, and a living room. The walls were painted bright red, and the only items of furniture in the living room were five mattresses, covered in sheets and strewn around the room—an ideal arrangement for hosting larger GLF meetings and out-of-town activists.[39]

The collective soon expanded on the theory behind their communal living in a jointly authored article titled "Five Notes on Collective Living." The accompanying photograph encapsulated both the spirit of gay liberation and gay communalism. The five members were naked, suggesting the importance of authenticity and self-revelation. Each one had a flower in his hand or hair, suggesting his rejection of masculine gender performance; and each one lightly touched the arm of the man in front of him, suggesting both an emotional connection and the potential for erotic contact. The article itself carefully balanced individualism and collectivity—each of the five members wrote one section but did not sign his name. The first note began, "Any group which calls itself radical and revolutionary must concern itself with providing an alternative way for people to live and work together than the competitive, role-oriented model which heterosexual, capitalist society offers." The revolution, they insisted, needed to account for the psychological patterns of daily domestic and work life if it were to make a lasting impact.[40]

The collective worked hard to put such ideals into practice: they held two group meetings every week—one to discuss the practical details of living together, the other to discuss their feelings and relationships. They strove to spend as much of their spare time together, too, turning every apparently personal experience into a subject for group discussion. "If I was reading a good book," Knoebel wrote, "it was my responsibility to share it with the group, as well as my mother's letters. If I had to make a decision about something that affected me alone, like an argument with a friend, I still brought it to the group."[41] Any disagreement between members was also brought out before the entire group for resolution. Everyone was expected to function as "equals" within the house—sharing all ideas and making all decisions together, however long it took.

Such ideals of sharing extended to romantic and sexual practices as well—though not quite as successfully. At its most idyllic, the collective functioned as a kind of plural marriage: "In the evenings," Knoebel wrote, "we often took walks in Riverside Park, all of us holding hands. It was romantic, in a very different way than any of us had experienced before." Living together led them to question the boundaries of love. But their collectivity faltered when they tried to extend their principles to sexual contact. Knoebel explained, "We tried to be physical together, holding one another, kissing each other in greeting. We learned to be naked together, around the apartment and sitting at meetings. . . . Several times we moved mattresses into the living room and all slept together." Despite their efforts, though, most of the sexual relationships members had during their time in the commune were with outsiders. "Theory," Knoebel wrote regretfully, "was not supported by our feelings."[42] What little sex there was within the household, far from uniting them, often led to jealousy.

Members of other GLF communes similarly hoped that collective living would enable new forms of connection and cooperation: Nikos Diaman, a member of the Baltic Street Collective, recalled the day the seven members (five of them white, two black) first moved into their three-story house in Brooklyn: "Once we got everything inside, we took a break. . . . One man undressed and lay down on a mattress. Another followed suit. . . . One by one we each undressed and joined the pile of warm bodies. All of us laughed as we playfully rolled around on the mattress. It was difficult to tell where one body began and another ended." They shared cooking responsibilities (even though two were far better chefs than the others); shared clothes (even though some members were bigger than others); and walked around the apartment naked or half-naked, despite the objections of passersby who saw them through the windows. "Openness," Diaman recalled, "was equated with freedom, the elimination of shame. Whatever we did with our bodies was natural and need not be hidden. Someone even suggested removing the bathroom door, but that never happened." The collective found house meetings more tiresome: "Decisions were made as quickly as possible just to shorten the agony." As a result, they ended up vetoing most of each other's artworks as objectionable (a portrait of the Madonna and child, for example, was considered antifeminist). Some members also made decisions without consulting others: one member bought a waterbed, adopted a dog, and used food stamps to purchase a kitchen clock, all without discussion.[43]

Other gay liberation groups formed similar communes in cities across the United States. In fall 1970, in Washington, DC, a multiracial group of gay liberation activists moved into a three-story rowhouse at 1620 S Street NW near Dupont Circle—then an area known as the city's countercultural, activist, and gay center. The house formed directly out of the local GLF chapter and quickly came to serve as a de facto community center. The residents hosted a wide range of functions, including GLF meetings, a coming-out group, a mixed gay and lesbian discussion group, religious rituals, Halloween parties, fundraisers, and dances. They also maintained a phone line for help and information, offered counseling, and provided or arranged shelter for homeless gay teenagers, many of them getting by on sex work.[44]

From the beginning, the house was particularly attuned to issues impacting gay people of color. Many of its members were people of color themselves, including African American activists Theodore Kirkland, Reggie Haynes, siblings Kashi and Shima Rahman, and Puerto Rican activist José Ramos (figs. 3.1 and 3.2). Other members included a pair of white

FIGURE 3.1. The Washington, DC, living collective Gay Liberation House was formed in 1970 by members of the local Gay Liberation Front. House members and visitors pictured here include, in the front row (from left), Reggie Haynes, David Aiken, Bruce Pennington, and Bobby (last name unknown), and, in the back row (from left), Bill Taylor, Howard Grayson, Joseph Covert, Paul Bartels, and Bobby Ulhorn. Photographer unknown. Reproduction courtesy of the Rainbow History Project.

FIGURE 3.2. The DC Gay Liberation House marched together in the second Christopher Street Gay Liberation Day March in New York on June 25, 1971. Here, house founder Reggie Haynes holds a banner with text parodying a popular 1970 song by Crosby, Stills, Nash & Young—"Our house is a very very very gay house"—bringing the queer home to the streets. Photographer unknown. Reproduction courtesy of the Rainbow History Project.

journalists, David Aiken and Bruce Pennington. More largely, multiracial organizing was a clear priority of all house members. In November 1970, the house served as the information center for all gay groups who had traveled to DC for the Black Panther Party's second Revolutionary People's Constitutional Convention. The house was also active in campaigns protesting racial discrimination at gay bars in DC, particularly "double-carding"—demanding two forms of identification exclusively from black patrons. A number of house members later went on to become organizers and members of the DC chapter of the social and activist group Black and White Men Together.[45]

By the mid-1970s, some gay men had also formed communes in rural areas, inspired as much by gay liberation as a desire to get "back to the land." In 1970, for example, unbeknownst to most readers of his manifesto, Carl Wittman left California for Wolf Creek, Oregon, where he soon set up a rural commune with his lover, Allan Troxler. By 1974, Allen Young, who had been in the 17th Street Collective, had left New York and headed to northern Massachusetts, where he established a new commune called Butterworth Farm. And in Washington State, GLF leader John Singer (later known as Faygele ben Miriam), left the commune he helped found in Seattle and moved to the Olympic peninsula to start a farm near the Elwha River. Many of these communes eventually came together to launch *RFD*, a "country journal by gay men," which frequently included reports from rural commune members.[46]

Many of these communes, both urban and rural, saw it as a primary responsibility to advance the broader goals of gay liberation through education and outreach. The 95th Street Collective, for example, hosted a gay night every Sunday night at a nearby coffeehouse. "Upwards of 50 gay people, many of whom had never heard about the gay movement before, came to talk and drink coffee in an atmosphere far more pleasant than any bar," Knoebel wrote. The contrast to gay bars was key: the space of the coffeehouse linked gay liberation once more to the counterculture (the Beats, folk music) and radical politics. The apartment itself also became a base for numerous GLF functions: they housed gay out-of-towners, hosted GLF meetings, and installed a phone listed under "GLF men." Calls flooded in from prospective GLF members wondering how they could get involved; schools, churches, and media venues looking for speakers; and high schoolers looking for support.[47]

Other collectives made similar efforts. The Gay Lib House in Louisville, Kentucky, set up phone lines to connect callers to gay liberation groups and provide counseling. The 17th Street Collective in New York printed a series of pamphlets under the title *Gay Flames*, circulating key texts to an even broader audience. In Los Angeles, GLF members moved to a house on Hoover Street and began planning the creation of a gay community service center.[48] Rural communes hosted conferences, like the "Faggots and Class Struggle" conference held at Wolf Creek in the summer of 1976.[49] And the Elwha commune, founded by Faygele ben Miriam, served as a rehabilitation center. As another Elwha member told a local newspaper in 1976, "We get people sent out here from counseling centers in Seattle, people who for whatever reason need to escape the city and get the good things from country living."[50] The ideal of service also extended to communes that were not formally connected to gay liberation groups: one commune in San Francisco operated a gay bar while another operated a bathhouse.[51]

At the same time, commune members focused their energies inward, toward members' own psychological transformation—a goal epitomized by consciousness-raising (CR), a practice again borrowed from the women's movement. CR was first named and pioneered by New York Radical Women, founded in 1967, and caught on quickly among many other radical feminist organizations. The goal was for members of a group to talk about the ways they felt oppressed as women, as a means of reconceiving personal experiences in political terms.[52] Gay CR groups, frequently formed out of

GLF meetings, similarly sought to help members connect their individual experiences as part of a broader system of antihomosexual oppression— raising awareness of the problem and, at the same time, encouraging a sense of identification both with the immediate group and gay people more generally. An early guide, "Notes on Gay Male Consciousness-Raising," explained that individual sessions would typically move from the individual relating his personal experiences ("of anti-homosexuality," "relationships with family, women, men") to testimony relating to a predetermined topic. The session would then move from the individual toward collective experience, encouraging members to make "connections between people's testimony" and seek "the common root when there are different experiences and feelings." Last, the group would consider relationships between members of the group, and then what projects they planned to work on— including "helping to start new consciousness-raising groups."[53]

Gay male collectives frequently built from, and incorporated, the model of CR. One of the members of the 95th Street Collective explained in "Five Notes" that his entry into the living collective was, in fact, a "direct result of five months of consciousness raising." Through CR, he wrote, "I learned to identify with and trust other gay men. This eased the pain I had felt as an isolated, lonely, 'sick' man." Members of other collectives similarly sought to adapt CR techniques for their group: in the 17th Street Collective, Jim Fouratt brought in a professional gestalt therapist to lead group sessions, and the various gay households at Wolf Creek held regular discussion "circles."[54]

Many gay activists also took communal living as an opportunity to experiment with, and challenge, gender normativity. The members of the 95th Street Collective, for example, identified as "femme males" and aimed to embrace their sensitivity. This "effeminism," as it came to be called, was quite different from the classic form of gay camping. Rather than playing at effeminacy as a mode of humor and performance—for example, calling each other "she" and "Mary"—the femme men of the 95th Street Collective presented their gender expression as "natural," an authentic expression of self that was threatened by the "straight" masculinity of both heterosexual and gay men. Perhaps most tellingly, they still referred to each other as "gay brothers"—not "sisters" as an earlier generation of gay men might have.[55] Other gay men experimented with modes of gender performance that came to be known as gender-fucking. One gay liberation activist, who had lived in communes in both New York City and Boston, wrote, "For the first time in our lives we no longer felt coerced to act as masculine as possible. . . . I experimented with all of them, went in bearded drag from time to time, wearing a bright red dress with a Che Guevara beret with a red star."[56] Bruce Pennington of the DC Gay Liberation House developed his own drag persona named Aurora Borealis.[57]

Such practices overlapped with a broader interrogation of masculine privilege among some gay activists, though this critique of gay masculinity could prove divisive as well. 17th Street Collective member Jason Victor Serinus recalled he had initially joined a "femme" CR group, only to be thrown out and given the nickname "Venceremos Butch."[58] At the same time, transgender identity was largely excluded from the framework, as it was from the larger conversation around gay male togetherness. Femme activists, like those of the 95th Street Collective, may have questioned expressions of masculinity by gay men, but they largely took their own maleness for granted, much as some feminist activists essentialized womanhood. While gay male practices of communal living and consciousness-raising were initially intended to help gay men think about their own masculine privilege, they could also promote gender essentialism.

The trend toward gender essentialism and separatism nevertheless obscured the ways gay men and lesbians actually interacted, and when and why they didn't. The Gay Liberation House in Washington, DC, for example, initially included one woman: Joan Carmody was an early member of GLF-DC and spoke at a large rally for Women's Equality Day about the role of lesbians in women's liberation. Carmody nevertheless moved out of the house after only a few months.[59] Carmody's decision to move out likely reflected larger gender divides within gay liberation. As Genny Beemyn has shown, lesbian feminist activism was initially slow to start in DC, in part because there were few out lesbians in the women's movement. That changed following the second Revolutionary People's Constitutional Convention, when gay and lesbian activists from New York traveled to the city. The Radicalesbians' manifesto, "The Woman-Identified Woman," with its call for lesbian separatism, proved especially influential. By mid-1971, a group of twelve white women formed the lesbian separatist collective that came to be known as the Furies. This growing split between gay men and lesbians was seen as necessary but productive: in 1972, members of the Furies Collective worked with the Skyline Faggots Collective, an offshoot of the Gay Liberation House, to curate a two-part final issue of the radical Methodist magazine *Motive*—one part focusing on lesbian feminism, the other on gay male liberation.[60]

In rural areas, gay male communes and womyn's lands often neighbored and supported one another. Jean and Ruth Mountaingrove, founders of the magazine *WomanSpirit*, moved to Wolf Creek in the 1970s and lived for many years in a cabin on land owned by Carl Wittman. They eventually established a womyn's land but remained friends with Wittman and

Troxler.[61] Similarly, when Trella Laughlin arrived in Fayetteville, Arkansas, in the mid-1970s, she and her partner lived out of a Volkswagen in the parking lot of a radical gay male collective called Mulberry House. As Laughlin recalled, the collective largely identified as "sissies" and "fairies": "They respected us and we respected them." At one point, when some local men threatened the collective, Laughlin recalled, "We said well we're not having that. We're not having it. We, the women, we had brooms and a rake and an old .22 rifle that couldn't shoot straight. . . . And they never came back."[62]

Some gay men and lesbians also formed communes together: in the mid-1970s, a group of young gay men and lesbians created a commune known as Lavender Hill. The collective grew out of an earlier commune of men and women, but it essentially became gay when all the straight men departed and all the women came out. After moving between Staten Island and the Catskills, the members eventually purchased a plot of land further west, just south of Ithaca, New York, and built their own house off the grid. What held the group together was less any overriding ideology of gay liberation than a sense that they had become more than friends—they were in their own words a new kind of family, "a family of choice."[63]

At the same time, gay communes—individually and as a movement—often struggled to create the inclusive communities they imagined. Fort Hill Faggots, founded in Boston in 1975, actively sought to recruit black men but attracted only a handful among the twenty residents who joined the collective over the next two years (fig. 3.3). The challenge to create racial diversity in the collective reflected, in many ways, broader tensions within the city: much of the neighborhood in which Fort Hill Faggots was located had been razed to make way for a controversial, and then canceled, highway extension—allowing the founders to purchase several houses cheaply. Yet for the black and Latinx residents who had long lived there, the commune members appeared as interlopers. One member, John Kyper, recalled that one of the African American residents left the collective after he was held up at knifepoint by two men who lived down the street. As Kyper put it, "It seemed pretty clear that he had been singled out as a . . . 'traitor.'"[64]

Class differences also proved a source of rupture. In Los Angeles, a member of the Highland Park Collective wrote a letter describing the deteriorating atmosphere of the house. He came home from a trip to San Francisco only to find a note berating him for failing to wash the frying pan before he left. Meanwhile another member sat at the kitchen table explaining that he felt unhappy and bored, only to have another member turn to him and say, "We working class people don't have time be bored."[65] Mulberry House in Fayetteville sent an announcement to *RFD* in 1976: "We are white and from working- and middle-class backgrounds. We live and work together

FIGURE 3.3. In April 1976, the Boston gay newspaper *Gay Community News* dedicated a full-page article to the newly formed collective Fort Hill Faggots, under the headline, "Fort Hill Faggots for Freedom: An Experiment in Communal City Living." Photograph by Jane Picard, used with permission. Reproduction courtesy of Northeastern University Archives and Special Collections.

collectively not only for economic reasons, but in order to overcome our heterosexual conditioning as men."[66] Yet in multiple subsequent letters, members of Mulberry House wrote to criticize *RFD*'s "privileged-class perspectives." Looking back on one recent issue they complained, "Every one was white in the photos" and "Sexism is depicted in a subtle way in the photos of faggots in dresses with what appeared to be stuffing to imitate breasts." And finally, "Why wasn't anything written about the privilege around photography? How many people have the free time, money and energy to take pictures especially so-called 'artistic portraits'?"[67]

Yet it was often more mundane problems of daily living that could discourage commune members and disrupt their idealism. In "Five Notes," one member of the 95th Street Collective wrote, "We are all encumbered with all kinds of irrational habits and petty hang-ups. Some of us are shy about sex or nudity or expressing our emotions. Some of us smoke too much, or have developed little rituals about sleeping or eating or going to the bathroom." The authors urged patience and commitment to overcome these small differences.[68] Members of a Boston gay collective, who sought to run their home as both a commune and community center, lamented the collective's collapse in the pages of the Boston newspaper *Fag Rag*, "Our bourgeois training makes us uncooperative individualists." An unpublished draft elaborated some of the material problems: "they failed to apportion 'menial tasks' properly; dirty dishes were in the sinks, garbage in the hall. Many men failed to become their own servants."[69] Gay communes established a new set of domestic norms and a new model of personal politics—only to find that these were all difficult to maintain.

Some gay communes also encountered resistance from outside. In 1976, shortly after the Elwha commune was featured in the *Port Angeles Daily News*, someone drove by the house at three in the morning and threw a Molotov cocktail into a woodpile, starting a fire.[70] A similar firebombing incident occurred three years later at the Creekland commune in Oregon, one of several gay and lesbian communes in the area: on January 12, 1979, an unknown arsonist threw two Molotov cocktails into the main farmhouse of the commune and burned it down (fig. 3.4). The incident drew attention to underlying hostility between the area's gay and straight residents. As the *Oregonian* put it, "Creekland residents consider the wearing of female clothing on occasion a political act, a defiance of sexual roles arbitrarily assigned by society. But some old-timers in Wolf Creek—and even some recently arrived longhairs—may not have been prepared for the sight of a hairy, bearded man in a skirt or an ex-priest dressed as a nun." Local residents had also expressed concern that the commune was raising two boys—most likely children from neighboring lesbian separatist communities, which

FIGURE 3.4. This photograph of residents and visitors of Creekland accompanied a pair of articles in the *Oregonian* about the growth of communes near Wolf Creek and responses from the community. Photograph by Foster Church, originally published in the *Oregonian*, July 22, 1979. © 1979 Oregonian Publishing Co. All rights reserved. Used with permission of the *Oregonian*.

frequently excluded boys or imposed an age limit. After six months, the state police and the local sheriff's office had done little to investigate the attack, with one county official referring to the collective as "that bunch of fruits living up there in Wolf Creek."[71]

In the end, many of the gay communes that formed in the 1970s lasted only a short time—typically six months to two years, though some, rural communes in particular, lasted longer. In some cases, personal and political conflicts led collectives to split. As John Knoebel recalled, the 95th Street Collective dissolved soon after it was discovered a founding member had been sleeping every night with a member Knoebel had recently brought in.[72] This led to feelings of jealousy and resentment, as well as accusations that a monogamous sexual relationship between two members was disruptive to the functioning of the collective. Other collectives split more amicably, after individual members decided to move away or when a lease ran up.[73]

By the early 1980s, the widescale impulse to create gay living collectives and communes had largely ended—though not entirely. The Radical Faeries, a spiritual movement of gay men led by homophile pioneer Harry Hay, emerged out of the rural communes in the late 1970s and continues to this day, operating sanctuaries across the United States for individual visitors and larger gatherings. These sanctuaries, including Short Mountain in Tennessee and Nomenus in Wolf Creek, Oregon, were frequently founded on or near land previously occupied by gay communes, and they continue to be occupied and run by small living and farming collectives. These sanctuaries diverge in important ways, as well: anthropologist Scott Morgensen has critiqued the Radical Faerie movement for its appropriation of indigenous spiritual traditions by mostly white urban gay men—a trope largely absent from the organizing of earlier gay living collectives.[74] In the last ten years, new queer communes have also emerged in places like Northern California and Tennessee—although not with the same visibility as gay communes of the 1970s.[75]

DOMESTIC LIBERATION

The impact of gay communes in the 1970s ultimately rested not in their numbers or longevity but in their broader reframing of domestic life. Although many gay communes lasted only a short time, the idea and image of the gay commune circulated widely, in newspapers, magazines, film, and books—emerging as a central discourse of gay liberation, even if not everyone practiced it. A journalist named John Murphy explained in his memoir how the members of his CR group came to understand their place in the movement: "Most of us were not completely into the gay lib life style of constant meetings, constant confrontations with every aspect of the straight world and communal living. We subscribed to a lot of the movement's aims without subscribing to them all personally."[76] For others, the language of communalism lent new emotional and political weight to domestic practices they might have pursued anyway—even just sharing an apartment. In many ways, living in a collective was not qualitatively different from living with roommates, but the discourse of gay communalism gave the practice new meaning. One man in Boston described his decision to seek a roommate this way: "What first needed to be done, I felt, was to change the isolation of my living situation and get into some sort of communal living arrangement with other gay people." He invited a friend to move in, and they agreed that a larger collective might be the next step: "No more way station on the road to liberation, we were looking for a liberated way to live."[77]

Gay men throughout the second half of the twentieth century imagined and constructed domestic spaces, lives, and relationships that diverged, to varying degrees, from heterosexual, reproductive norms, but rarely would they do so with as much self-consciousness, and as great a sense of possibility, as gay liberation activists did in the early 1970s. Homophile activists of the 1950s and 1960s had frequently looked to legal reform to protect their privacy, while later gay activists of the 1980s and 1990s turned increasingly to the state to recognize and protect their relationships, in the form of domestic partnership, civil union, and marriage legislation.[78] Gay liberation activists, in contrast to both, largely rejected the state and a model of national belonging and domestic citizenship predicated on normative forms of domesticity, prioritizing instead a sense of intimate and communal belonging—though still one rooted in the home. Some gay commune members struggled to balance those commitments, finding it difficult to attend equally to relationships with men in and outside the home. Nor were relations within communes ever as utopic as many members hoped—some experienced alienation and disenchantment. Nevertheless, gay communes, for their members and observers, exposed the norms of home, gender, and family with new clarity, and opened up possibilities for collective creativity and revision.

There was, after all, something always unfinished about all the gay communes as they were represented in personal testimonies like those of the 95th Street Collective, and in outsider's accounts, as in Altman's *Homosexual: Oppression and Liberation*. The communes, it seemed, were always on the brink of falling apart, changing members, or moving—and in some cases, they had already collapsed. And yet this very instability, impossibility, might also account, in part, for the commune's attractiveness—it was always waiting to be tried again, modified, perfected.

Much early gay liberation thinking can be characterized by what José Esteban Muñoz calls a "logic of futurity." Muñoz gives the example of Third World Gay Revolution's manifesto: "We want a new society—a revolutionary socialist society. . . . We believe that all people should share the labor and products of society, according to each one's needs and abilities, regardless of race, sex, age or sexual preferences." The "we" here, Muñoz writes, is not the simple "we" of gay identity politics but a "future society that is being invoked and addressed at the same moment"—a "we" that has not yet arrived, where all might belong in their difference.[79] The gay commune, as experience and representation, partook of a similar hopefulness. It became an emblem of the social utopia many gay men desired, a space for experimentation—new forms of self-awareness and self-expression, new forms of sexual and social connection—even when reality failed to match. For many gay men, both those who joined communes and those who read about them, the commune remained a utopian ideal—of what gay community and gay lives could look like—precisely because it could never be completed.

CHAPTER FOUR

"Fantasy Is the Beginning of Creation": Imagining Lesbian Feminist Architecture

In November 1971, thirty-eight-year-old architect Phyllis Birkby was surprised to find herself pictured in the pages of the radical magazine *Ramparts*, accompanying an article on gay liberation.[1] The photograph had been taken at the gay pride march in Manhattan that June and captured Birkby embracing another woman (fig. 4.1). Birkby had pursued romantic and sexual relationships with other women from the time she was in college in the 1950s, but, by her own account, the rise of gay liberation and lesbian feminism in the late 1960s and early 1970s represented, for her, a reawakening. Nevertheless, Birkby struggled to define herself at a moment when the world of architecture and design was almost entirely dominated by men and the women's movement was still led largely by straight women. In 1972, she attended an event on "Women in Architecture." In a letter to her lover of the time, novelist Bertha Harris, she described the event as "a bizarre gathering of architectural females of varying levels of consciousness." "CHRIST IT WAS PAINFUL," Birkby wrote, "Coming out is not always the breeze one wishes it to be." When the time came for her to speak, Birkby wrote, she "looked down and found such unfriendly territory, I rocked back into my spare closet and felt a failure, why the hell can't I fly?" Birkby thought the *Ramparts* article would have done the coming out for her, but apparently, Birkby reasoned, "architects don't read *Ramparts*." Birkby's most radical suggestion was that women first needed to figure out "what we all mean by the absurd term Women in Architecture," and do so away from "'Them'— that is, away from men. The experience provoked Birkby to make a promise to Harris: "I am going to make a gay architecture, a lesbian architecture, and I am going to give it to you."[2]

For Birkby the tasks of understanding what it meant to be a woman in architecture and what a lesbian architecture might look like were intimately intertwined and would guide much of her work over the next decade. At the

FIGURE 4.1. Phyllis Birkby (left) and Frances Doughty at the second Christopher Street Gay Liberation Day March, June 25, 1971. The photograph, by Michael Abramson, originally appeared in an article on the gay liberation movement in the magazine *Ramparts* in November 1971. © Michael Abramson, from the Black Star Collection at Ryerson University. Courtesy of the Ryerson Image Centre.

core of both questions was home itself. Since the late eighteenth century, American understandings of gender, sexuality, and the built environment were tightly bound: private domestic space was frequently understood to define, confine, and protect the feminine body and female sexuality. Yet home was also a site of principal contradiction—it was defined as "female space," yet still determined, controlled, and largely designed by men. Birkby argued that reimagining private space was an important step in remaking women's lives and identities. Birkby's work and life provide a critical lens into the ways lesbian feminists of the 1970s sought to expose the gendered power of architecture, to renegotiate the public-private divide, and imagine a new built environment oriented around what she framed as women's sensibilities and needs.

Birkby's call for a lesbian architecture stemmed from a longer thread of second-wave feminist thought and activism that targeted postwar domestic norms as sites of social and psychological oppression. Betty Friedan's *The Feminine Mystique*, published in 1963, diagnosed a "strange stirring" among suburban housewives, finding many women dissatisfied with the vision of middle-class married motherhood promised by psychiatric experts and American magazines. Friedan was not alone in the critique: as Eva Moskowitz argues, postwar women's magazines, in fact, were just as likely to praise domesticity as they were to voice a "discourse of discontent." Friedan's book amplified and reframed this postwar dissent in psychological terms, adapting for women the terms and conclusions of 1950s social criticism focused on men. Like William H. Whyte's *The Organization Man* (1956) and Sloan Wilson's *The Man in the Gray Flannel Suit* (1955), Friedan assumed that the problem facing American women was not poverty but affluence.[3] Later feminist critiques continued to frame normative models of home and family as a trap. Pat Mainardi's widely reprinted essay "The Politics of Housework" (1970) argued that even sexually and professionally "liberated women" were still conditioned and expected to do the "dirty chores" of everyday life—groceries, dishes, and laundry—and called on women to enact more egalitarian politics at home.[4] The international movement Wages for Housework pushed this analysis further, identifying the family, in Marxist terms, as a site of capitalist oppression and demanding compensation for women's unwaged household and reproductive labor.[5]

Yet while many feminist thinkers critiqued the conventional American household, Birkby was among the first to locate women's oppression in the built environment itself. In 1973, Birkby began running a series of workshops in which she asked women to imagine and draw their ideal living spaces, free of any pragmatic constraints. Birkby believed only through fantasy could women shake off their psychological conditioning and begin to imagine new spaces. Birkby followed the project, in the late 1970s, with an investigation of women's "vernacular architecture"—living spaces independently built by women across the United States in the countryside and the desert. Through both projects, Birkby hoped to empower women to realize what she called a woman-identified architecture and environment, an environment rooted in women's shared aesthetic and emotional values.

Since the 1980s, feminist historians and queer theorists have tended to take a critical view of projects like Birkby's that rely on discourses of gender essentialism. In *Daring to be Bad*, published in 1989, Alice Echols outlined what has since become a standard historical narrative of second-wave feminism: while radical feminists of the early 1970s had called for a complete overthrow of the gender system, later activists—lesbian feminists chief among them—largely "retreated" to "cultural feminism." In advocating for women's separatism, women's culture, and women's spaces, Echols argued, cultural feminists revalued traditional female values and gender roles only to recapitulate the gender binary as a "natural" distinction.[6] Queer theories of gender, most centrally work by Judith Butler, have also challenged essentialist constructions of femininity, pointing instead to gender's social construction through embodied performance: gender gains its reality through its repetition.[7]

More recent work, however, has begun to complicate historical assessments of lesbian feminist activism and thought. In *Feeling Women's Liberation*, Victoria Hesford argues that historians have tended to approach the archive of women's liberation and lesbian feminism as "evidence of specific and coherent theoretical and ideological standpoints" rather than "an array of rhetorical materials that sought to persuade and enact a new political constituency and world into being."[8] That is, historians have tended to treat reconceptualizations of "woman," "lesbian," and "lesbian feminist" during the 1970s as unified and stable from the start and look past the messiness of their emergence and evolution. Joan Wallach Scott, too, has argued that historians have tended to treat the category of "women" as a given rather than track its changing and contingent meanings. Scott instead frames identity itself as a "fantasy," though a productive one: as Scott writes, "Fantasy can help account for the ways subjects are formed, internalizing and resisting social norms, taking on the terms of identity that endow them with agency."[9] As Agatha Beins writes in her study of 1970s feminist periodicals, feminism itself should be understood as "an accumulation of repeated discursive tropes that are performative, semiotic, and affective": concepts like "sisterhood" gain the appearance of intrinsic meaning through their repetition, even as their repetition introduces the potential for difference and disruption.[10] A case in point is the treatment of transgender women within feminist activism: while a few prominent feminist thinkers, such as Janice Raymond and Sheila Jeffreys, have long relied on essentialist framings of womanhood to represent transgender experience as a symptom of patriarchal power, many other feminist groups and thinkers have been inclusive of transgender people as far back as the 1970s.[11] Hesford, Scott, and Beins all push scholars to attend to the unstable and evolving deployments of women's identity to better understand their social meaning and strategic uses.

In this sense, I read Birkby's conceptualization of a woman-identified environment for its emergence and evolution, not as a stable theory but an ongoing process—a performative intervention that builds on lesbian feminist theory without necessarily "arriving" at a final answer. In his essay "Performing Essentialism," Greg Youmans analyzes the early work of lesbian filmmaker Barbara Hammer—a close friend, lover, and collaborator of Birkby's. Youmans argues that works like Hammer's *Dyketactics* and *Superdyke* are easy to decry as essentialist, yet to do so misses Hammer's filmmaking as performance and process—how Hammer's films, in their humor and their rituals, seek to construct new ways of being. Hammer's essentialism is ultimately contradictory: as Youmans explains, "During the 1970s, both feminists and gay activists saw the 'truth' of themselves as something radically, historically new and in the fragile process of invention, and also, at the same time, as something buried deep within themselves, long suppressed and obscured by heteropatriarchy, that needed to be excavated and set free."[12] Birkby, in a similar mode, presented her environmental fantasy and vernacular architecture projects as uncovering hidden or repressed female needs, desires, and ways of relating, yet also worked to constitute them—imagining new modes of social and political identification alongside new forms of home and belonging.

In this chapter, I trace the origins and impact of Birkby's feminist pedagogy and practice as a means of unpacking lesbian feminism's engagement with the built environment and its ties to broader feminist conceptualizations of oppression and solidarity. Birkby elaborated and materialized lesbian feminist theory to reveal American domesticity as a prescriptive fantasy, endowed with force by men's prolonged prominence in architecture and planning. The only way to combat that script, Birkby argued, was to produce new fantasies, with the hope of building new environments and realizing new modes of self-expression. My reading of Birkby's work and life also demonstrates the ambiguities and dualities of early lesbian feminist theory: Birkby's rhetoric in print was often essentialist in its framing of womanhood, but her archive—her diaries, letters, recordings, and architecture, as well as the fantasy and vernacular designs she collected—reveals a more capacious critique of architecture and power, one that began with a focus on women but ultimately encompassed people who were poor, elderly, and disabled. At the same time, Birkby questioned the heteronormative, reproductive household, calling for home design and urban planning that could meet the needs of alternative family forms. Scholars and architects working alongside and after Birkby, including Leslie Kanes Weisman, Dolores Hayden, Susana Torre, and Jos Boys, would echo and expand many of her key concerns about gender and power, but Birkby was herself a pathbreaker.[13] By addressing the ways the built environment constrained women, Birkby moved toward a more fundamental re-visioning of home as a queer and inclusive site of liberation.

Birkby also built on emerging activism within architecture, aimed at diversifying the profession. In 1970, there were roughly 56,000 architects in the United States. The vast majority—51,400—were white and male. Of the remainder, 2,600 were men of color, 1,900 were white women, and 200 were women of color.[14] The rise of the women's movement encouraged many women in architecture to form new professional organizations, including the Alliance of Women in Architecture in New York, which Birkby helped to found. Those efforts paralleled activism by African American architects, urban planners, and community organizers both to diversify the field and respond to the needs of their communities. In 1968, Whitney M. Young Jr., director of the National Urban League, gave a stinging speech to the largely male, and nearly all white, membership of the American Institute of Architects (AIA), calling on them to take responsibility for the poor living conditions in many American cities, advocate for better housing, and work to bring more people of color into the field. The AIA responded two years later by creating its first minority scholarship, and in 1971, twelve African American AIA members—all of them men—formed the National Organization of Minority Architects.[15] Nevertheless, Birkby argued, diversifying the field would not necessarily lead to new designs: as she later quipped, "Traditional schools of architecture don't discriminate. Most tend to graduate white, middle-class male designers regardless of whether you were Third World and/or a woman when you entered!"[16] Birkby's intervention was to move beyond demographics to consider how psychological conditioning shaped both perceptions of and designs for the built environment. In his 1993 essay, "A Note on Race and Architecture," Cornel West called on architecture critics to attend to the "political legitimacy" of architecture—to analyze "how authority warrants or does not warrant the way in which buildings are made" and better understand architectural practices as "power-laden cultural practices," shaped both by institutional and historical forces.[17] Birkby centered fantasy as the best means for both design professionals and laypeople to unpack those power dynamics embedded in architecture and begin to resist and reinvent them.

ALIENATION AND LIBERATION

Birkby discovered architecture at a young age but quickly encountered its barriers, too. Born in 1932, Birkby grew up in an upper-middle-class family in the predominantly white suburb of Nutley, New Jersey, the youngest of three children. Her father, Harold, worked in sales and advertising in the textile industry; her mother, Alice, stayed at home.[18] Birkby was frequently sick as a child and spent hours confined to bed, drawing detailed plans for cities and towns, "down to the food on the tables," she later recalled. She drew inspiration from a visit to the 1939 World's Fair in Queens: she was entranced by the General Motors "Futurama" display, a model city of a world to come, designed by Norman Bel Geddes. By high school, however, career counselors discouraged Birkby, despite her aptitude tests: "Well Miss Birkby," she was advised, "it appears that IF YOU WERE A MAN you should be studying architecture." By Birkby's account, she immediately "formed a math block" and "swallowed the implication that there just weren't any women architects." The implication was largely right: in 1950 women represented less than 2 percent of architects nationwide—400 women total.[19] Her ambitions dashed, Birkby decided to pursue a more "womanly career" as a painter and enrolled at the Woman's College of the University of North Carolina in Greensboro, at the time the largest women's college in the nation. Still, she secretly explored her interest in architecture: as Birkby recalled, she and a friend frequently made "furtive trips" to the library "to read the latest architecture journals," but "still neither of us dared to think too seriously about it."[20]

The Woman's College, known to students as the WC, also gave Birkby a space to explore her desires for other women. Crushes and intimate friendships among students were relatively common at the WC: Key Barkley, a professor of psychology at the school in the 1940s, later recounted, "There grew up a practice on that campus, as well as many other places, on allowing women a great deal of leeway with respect to homosexual expression with respect to each other—hug each other, kiss each other, caress each other, and so on."[21] Birkby shared her own first glimpses of lesbian life with a student from Charlotte, North Carolina, nicknamed Mac. Birkby recalled, "Mac was the woman I shared so many 'first views' with, views of anything—Hesse, Stein, *Nightwood*—and oh god the *Well of Loneliness* (everybody's introduction to lesbians 101)."[22] The WC also gave Birkby her first exposure to a long-term lesbian relationship—and domesticity: one of the school's health teachers lived with her lover and regularly invited gay students over to their home on weekends. They acted, Birkby recalled, as mentors and role models: "they taught us about the word 'dyke' and 'gay' and what the bar scene was like in New York, if we ever got up there where to go."[23]

Despite this support, Birkby's early relationships were stifled by shame. Birkby had her first sexual relationship in 1951 with a student named Kay. "Not the first 'love,'" Birkby later wrote, "but the first to discover what that meant. Both innocent, it took us several months to dare. Ended by guilt and madness (hers)." Two years later Birkby fell deeply in love with a young Jewish woman named Ebba, a student two years below her, who entranced her in a production of Chekhov's *Three Sisters*. Yet Ebba, Birkby recalled, felt ashamed too. Birkby was unwilling to hide her desires. As she later recalled, "I wasn't hiding my love for another woman, didn't think there was anything 'wrong' with it—I was even then defending it in discussions with my dormitory mates who seemed only more confused than hostile." Her openness ultimately drew the ire of the school administration. In early spring 1953, Birkby was suspended, officially for drinking a beer, though her sexuality was clearly the cause. She returned the following year but was ultimately expelled just before graduating. Birkby had cherished the WC as a space of women's connection and culture; now she felt a deep sense of failure and betrayal. The worst part, she recalled, was feeling abandoned by her friends. "Still can't accept my sisters' silence, those silent backs—we don't know you anymore, you let us down and got caught at being stupidly human."[24]

Birkby soon followed her health teacher's advice and moved to New York, landing in an apartment at the edge of Greenwich Village. By the 1950s, the Village was home to an emerging lesbian subculture anchored by a circuit of bars Audre Lorde referred to as the "gay-girl scene." Bars like the Bagatelle and the Sea Colony were mostly Mafia-run and especially popular among working-class lesbians, though they attracted bohemian artists and writers as well.[25] But even Greenwich Village guaranteed no escape from guilt. Birkby's first serious relationship after college was with Esther, in Birkby's words, "an elegant dyke from Wellesley," studying to be a psychologist.[26] Esther's letters give a sense of the tensions of the time: she spent evenings traveling between the gay bars in Greenwich Village and had a group of lesbian friends. Still she saw the option of choosing a "gay life"—a term she did not like—as isolation. "The problem," Esther wrote, "is not so much how this will effect one while you're young but how much alienation can you tolerate for a life time especially if this may mean rejection in other areas of activity when there might have been accomplishment later in life."[27] For Esther, embracing a lesbian life ultimately meant a life of estrangement. Over the next fifteen years, Birkby fell in and out of love with a host of artists and writers: painter Yvonne Jacquette; sculptor Lorinda Roland; Chinese art historian Alberta Ming-Chi Wang; painter Louise Fishman; and artist Frederica Leser, who built dioramas for the American Museum of Natural History and threw 1920s theme parties in her Village townhouse. At the time, Birkby identified as bisexual and dated a few men, too, but she found her most meaningful relationships were still with women. Nevertheless, Birkby struggled to attain a sense of belonging and self-worth, and by the late 1960s, fell into depression.[28]

It was during this same period that Birkby went back to school to pursue a career in architecture. As she later wrote, "I began to feel the need to be involved in an art that encompassed more of life. Painting was too remote, too ivory tower, and architecture presented itself to me as a real and hopefully honest involvement with the world around me ... it held ... the promise of engagement with life in all its facets." In 1959, she enrolled in free night courses in the school of architecture at Cooper Union. She also began working for a series of small architecture firms. It was good training but revealed the gender discrimination in the field. As she later wrote, "I was not only the draftswoman but also the model maker, the receptionist, the secretary, the file clerk, the bookkeeper, the building department liaison, the phone hustler and just as often as not the catering service." Graduate schools of architecture and design were still dominated by men as well. When Birkby enrolled in 1962 in the master's program at the Yale School of Architecture, she was one of six women in a class of 200 and faced considerable harassment from male students. She recalled being told "women shouldn't/couldn't be architects, or you're only here to find a rich husband, or your critic would flirt instead of crit and on and on." Still, she wrote, "we set our jaws and forged ahead."[29]

A career in architecture nevertheless meant working for men. In 1965, during her last year at Yale, Birkby took a position as a project designer at the firm Davis, Brody & Associates, an emerging star of the New York architecture world—named for its two male founders, Lewis Davis and Samuel Brody. Birkby worked on a range of projects that were widely discussed in the media, including Waterside Plaza, a mixed-income housing development on Manhattan's East River. She was also the lead project designer for the Library Learning Center at Long Island University in Brooklyn, an integral part of the campus's redesign. Still, Birkby's name rarely appeared in press discussing the work.[30]

It was lesbian feminism that radically reshaped Birkby's life. During the late 1960s, the women's movement grew exponentially. An older generation of professional women spearheaded the creation of the National Organization for Women (NOW) in 1966, to push for equal treatment of women through legislative reform. At the same time, a younger generation of women began to push for more expansive "liberation" and "revolution," drawing inspiration from the antiwar movement, student radicalism, and Black Power. The movement spread rapidly, not only through protests and periodicals but through autonomous consciousness-raising (CR) groups: across the country, small clusters of women began coming together to discuss and think through their experiences of oppression. The place of lesbians in this movement was deeply contested: although lesbians had been involved in the women's movement throughout the 1960s, many felt compelled to hide their sexuality in order to be included. The rise of gay liberation in 1969 and 1970, however, encouraged many women in the movement to speak out, spurring the rise of radical lesbian groups across the United States.[31]

Birkby suddenly found herself at the center of a new lesbian feminism. Birkby's first encounter with the feminist movement had been in graduate school, when one of the other female students shared a copy of *The Feminine Mystique*, but Birkby did not identify with its discussion of housewives and the suburbs.[32] Lesbian feminism made Birkby feel like she could be part of the movement. In 1971, she joined one of the first lesbian feminist CR groups in New York, organized by activists Sidney Abbott and Barbara Love—a "supergroup" intended to bring together lesbian leaders from various New York organizations, including NOW, Gay Liberation Front, and the Daughters of Bilitis.[33] Other group members included Kate Millett, author of *Sexual Politics*, and Alma Routsong, author of *Patience and Sarah*, an early and popular work of lesbian historical fiction. Each meeting the group chose a topic—bisexuality, butch-femme, straight. They would then spin a bottle and whoever it landed on shared their story for discussion, before spinning the bottle again.[34] The process was, for Birkby, a revelation: "newly defining and yet recapturing my old gay pride, my sisters giving it back to me after all those years . . . a new adolescence, a passion rose in me, turned on to myself, to all women, and eventually a few came into focus."[35] The group did not come to answers but provided a space for reflection and validation of each member's experience, looking backward to move forward. As Birkby reflected, "Through a political analysis of my experience things started to make some sense—and lo, the depression lifted, connections were made, and a new way of dealing with the world began to take hold."[36] The next step would be bringing her new consciousness to her career.

FROM LESBIAN NATION TO WOMAN-IDENTIFIED ARCHITECTURE

Patriarchy, it turned out, was paralyzing: during graduate school, Birkby failed a project for the first time, and her drawing arm literally went numb.

Encountering the sexism of the Yale School of Architecture was, Birkby wrote, "like hitting a concrete wall—not one but an entire enclosure." To survive, she needed to camouflage: "Like so many other women students in this situation I learned to tiptoe through this male-defined garden of delights, kept pace with their rhythm, and conformed as much as one could."[37] Feminism disrupted Birkby's cover. She reflected, "After about two years of feminist involvement in general, I began to think more specifically in terms of my own work and the sphere I dwelt in as a creative and professional person."[38] The most immediate impact was leaving her job at Davis, Brody & Associates to open her own practice and begin a career in teaching. It was at this point that Birkby began running workshops to encourage women to imagine their "fantasy" environments—the spaces they would like to inhabit. Birkby wrote, "All we had around us was originally fantasized by men since they were the ones, I too acutely felt, that dominated the very processes that controlled and led to physical form that shaped our very existence."[39]

Birkby began gathering small groups of women to talk and then draw. Always a visual thinker, she believed that drawing would enable women to tap into hidden or repressed beliefs and needs that were diminished by male culture. Birkby's interest in unconscious beliefs was shaped, in part, by her experience in psychotherapy with a male analyst, but CR was her ultimate model. Birkby reflected: "I had become aware that in order to break though conditioning one had to dig deep under the roots. . . . In consciousness raising, we talked, externalized verbally but in the fantasy workshops we externalized visually. People tend to 'say' things in drawings and three dimensional expressions what often eludes us when we confine ourselves to words."[40] She specifically sought out women who had no professional training because she believed women who had attended architecture programs had already been "conditioned to male-defined processes in a male-dominated atmosphere and are apt to become male-identified in their approach to design problems."[41] She called instead for a "woman-identified environment" and a "lesbian architecture," but she had more questions than answers. In 1974, Birkby recorded a list of queries in her notebook: "Is there a woman's aesthetic? Do women design differently than men? If so is it a biological fact or rather a culturally induced phenomena? . . . How much does 'myth' play a part in woman's own conditioning? In a man's conditioning? . . . Does the term 'man-made environment' do anything to you? Would you ever say 'woman-made environment'?"[42]

Birkby later cited multiple sources of inspiration for the project. One source was her participation in a groundbreaking feminist action: in 1971, Birkby's CR group joined with 100 women to take over a vacant building in the East Village and create a new women's center, with programs designed to meet the needs the city refused to fund, including a day-care program, health clinic, women's shelter, food co-op, and continuing education. For twelve days, women worked to make the building into a functional women's center—fixing the boiler, replacing windows, providing food and day-care services. Although the original organizers were white, several Latina women also rose to leadership roles as the takeover stretched on. The city sent officials to negotiate with the activists but ultimately arrested twenty-one participants and shut down the building. For Birkby, the takeover was nevertheless an important model of activism in and around the built environment. Birkby created a silent film documenting the activities at the building and the many signs and graffiti posted along the walls: "Adelante las hermanas en la lucha" ("Go Forward Sisters in the Fight"), "Lesbians and Straights Together"; "Sisters Unite!"; "This Building Is *Ours.* The Price? Our Commitment."; "Gay Pride!"; "Lesbians Unite! Love Each Other Love Ourselves Love Each Other."[43]

Birkby also credited her relationship with novelist Bertha Harris for inspiring a renewed interest in fantasy. Birkby met Harris through Kate Millett in January 1972, and they quickly hit it off. Born and raised in North Carolina, Harris had attended the WC shortly after Birkby. She married and had a child but soon separated from her husband and, by the start of 1972, was teaching at University of North Carolina in Charlotte. Over the next six months, Birkby and Harris developed a long-distance relationship, largely by letter and phone. Fantasy and symbolism were major themes of Harris's fiction—and her romantic relationships too: Harris pondered the meaning of Birkby's names and addressed Birkby in one letter as "Myth." It was Harris, Birkby thought, "who at one point said something about fantasy being the basis of creativity, and my mind, still searching for doorways, lit up with the idea of what if? What if women fantasized about environment? What would we find?"[44]

More broadly, Birkby's fantasy environment project tapped into wider currents of feminist thought of the 1970s. Birkby's language of being "woman-identified" or "male-identified" stemmed directly from broader lesbian feminist discourse on gender, social conditioning, and women's separatism, originating with the widely read and discussed essay "The Woman-Identified Woman." The essay, published in 1970 by the New York-based group Radicalesbians, was one of the earliest conceptualizations of lesbian desire not as a biological given but a political choice: "What is a lesbian? The lesbian is the rage of all women condensed to the point of explosion."[45] The authors specifically rejected the label of "lesbian" as it was defined within a male-dominated system of sexual and gender roles—a term used to discount a woman who strives to be man's equal and discourage women from forming bonds with one another. Women needed instead to break away from men, male culture, and male definitions of "femininity" and "see in each other the possibility of a primal commitment which includes sexual love." They needed to cut the psychic and sexual cords to patriarchy. "Irrespective of where our love and sexual energies flow," the essay put it, "if we are male-identified in our heads, we cannot realize our autonomy as human beings."[46] Alice Echols argues that the essay aimed to disarm straight women's homophobia, disrupting associations between lesbianism and maleness, and centering lesbian sensuality over sexuality.[47] But it also effectively repositioned lesbianism as revolutionary strategy. The ultimate answer was separatism: to leave men behind and devote oneself socially, politically, and sexually to other women.

Many prominent feminist thinkers built on the idea of the "political lesbian," but the writer who may be most responsible for popularizing its ideals was Birkby's close friend and early interlocutor, writer Jill Johnston.[48] A longtime dance critic for the *Village Voice*, Johnston emerged as a kind of lesbian celebrity in the early 1970s after she came out and shared increasingly personal reflections in her *Village Voice* column. Those reflections became the basis for her 1973 book, *Lesbian Nation: The Feminist Solution*.[49] The book, published by a mainstream press, was a largely personal, freewheeling account of Johnston's own exploration of lesbian identity and desire, written in a Dadaist style, with the free-associative narratives and run-on sentences that had become typical of her *Village Voice* columns. It was also steeped in emerging gay liberation and lesbian feminist thought, citing "The Woman-Identified Woman" alongside Kate Millett's *Sexual Politics*, Valerie Solanas's "SCUM Manifesto," and Carl Wittman's "Gay Manifesto." Johnston specifically echoed and amplified calls for lesbian separatism, identifying heterosexuality as a key obstacle to women's liberation: "A personal solution or exceptional adjustment to a political problem is a collusion with the enemy. The solution is getting it together with women. Or separatism. . . . Tribal groupings of such women, the fugitive Lesbian Nation, have begun and will continue to serve as sustaining support and psychic power bases within the movement."[50] The language of "Lesbian Nation" specifically echoed calls for black nationalism, but "tribal groupings" reflected a broader nostalgia within lesbian feminism for an imagined, premodern women's culture, centered on the mythical image of the Amazon warrior.

Many women had already begun to develop separatist communities—both urban communes, like the Furies Collective in Washington, DC, and rural communities, known among lesbian feminists as "womyn's lands."

Many other activists had begun to develop women's restaurants, bookstores, publishing houses, and health centers.[51] While they intended to be radically inclusive for all women, many black feminists specifically rejected separatism because, they argued, it essentialized women's gender experience and ignored the compounding impacts of racial oppression. Many women's spaces—though not all—also excluded transgender women, an area of ongoing contestation.[52]

For Johnston herself, Lesbian Nation was as much a sensibility as a space—as performance studies scholar Sara Warner puts it, "more an endeavor than an actual entity." Johnston, Warner argues, was vague about her plans for a lesbian nation, aiming to inspire not "an actual geopolitical entity" but "emotional states of rapture and joy." Warner characterizes Johnston's intervention as an act of "joker citizenship": "the joker pushes the boundaries of acceptable behavior and makes a mockery of the arbitrary institutions and authorities, precepts and protocols that govern our worlds."[53] Johnston embraced joy and fun as modes of political action that Warner calls "national gaiety." Johnston's Lesbian Nation was, in this sense, a gay fantasy, an imagined community that inspired not because of its pragmatism but because of its playfulness—an open and utopian vision of a future that provoked, seduced, amused, and enchanted.

Birkby was one of its earliest acolytes. Birkby and Johnston met while they were both at the WC in the 1950s, but they did not cross paths again until the early 1970s. Johnston regularly hosted what she called "lesbian camp weekends" at her country home in upstate New York, and Birkby was a frequent visitor.[54] They also worked together on *Amazon Expedition*, one of the earliest anthologies of lesbian feminist writing, edited with Bertha Harris, anthropologist Esther Newton, and Johnston's lover, Jane O'Wyatt. The sense of sisterhood was intoxicating for Birkby: she joked to Johnston that they should take "the Trojan mare down through north carolina and go around snatching all those women we knew out of their closets and take them to lesbian nation, so watch out, th' mo'oment gonna getcha."[55] In spring 1973, Birkby, Johnston, and O'Wyatt looked into purchasing some land together in the Berkshires of Massachusetts. As Birkby relayed to Harris, they met with three banks about a loan, and after playing it "coolish" all morning, Birkby burst out, "Now we can have the lesbian architecture!"[56]

Birkby captured the excitement of that moment in her Super 8 films documenting Johnston's weekend retreats. Birkby's finished short silent film *Amazon Weekend*—first screened at a women-only film festival in 1974—cut together footage from one retreat, recasting lesbian love and desire as continuous with nature. It begins with a woman on a raft in the middle of a pond; in another scene two women lie together, one naked,

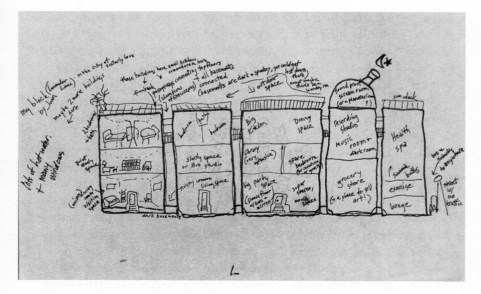

FIGURE 4.2. "My Block by Joan (Lavender Lane) in the City of Sisterly Love," was one of the earliest fantasy environment drawings collected by Birkby, c. 1974, reimagining a row of apartment buildings as a lesbian collective and community center, with a recording studio, grocery store, health spa, and "big party space." Noel Phyllis Birkby Papers, Sophia Smith Collection, Smith College, Northampton, MA.

caressing each other, kissing long and deep; a group of women play volleyball, sit in the grass, and drink wine. All of the women are white, except for one African American woman who dances for the camera.[57] The images of women loving women were virtually unprecedented. In her autobiographical novel *Flying*, Kate Millett recalled her reaction seeing Birkby's films for the first time: "I see a whole world of women, they are all Lesbians and they are beautiful. . . . Always I have been ashamed of us that we were ugly. Now we are transformed into a whole world that is us."[58] The films reconstructed the everyday as a utopic fantasy, a world of women held in suspension.

Birkby's environmental fantasy project similarly sought to give women space to explore a utopic future, to make space for unspoken and unspeakable desires and imagine new ways of organizing self, space, and community, free of the conventional constraints of the "man-made" environment. Birkby ran her earliest workshops in 1973, among small groups of women she knew through feminist, art, and literary circles in New York—nearly all of them identifying as lesbians. It's unclear exactly how Birkby prompted the conversation, but most participants imagined women-only environments, where women could connect with each other socially and sexually.

During a workshop at their apartment, sculptor Ann Pollon and her part-ner, Gail, imagined a communal women's home with one large bed where everyone could sleep together. It would be ideal, they agreed, "if you were the right kind of woman."[59] Another early participant named Joan reenvi-sioned a city block with rowhouses connected by bridges and basement passageways—she called it "Lavender Lane" (fig. 4.2). It included a large shared kitchen; a "big party space" with a "dance floor with bars and mir-rors," a "superstereo," and movie screen"; a recording studio, dark room, and art studio; plus a "soundproof scream room."[60]

Birkby published her first article about the project in the lesbian femi-nist magazine Cowrie in April 1974, under the title "Amazon Architecture." The article was based on a workshop with the magazine's editor, artist Liza Cowan, and two of her friends, Mary and Cheryl—both of them carpen-ters. Birkby's article largely quoted from the conversations, stringing lines together like a poem: "Turn off the power and the World Trade Center will crumble in 20 years. . . . ," "Relearn how to live from the ground up. . . . We are faced with the problem of how the changes in our internal lives can have effect on our work, our loving, our living arrangements, our shelter, spaces, environment." The article, and the issue cover, featured a drawing by Birkby, trying to visualize this new community: an Amazonian network, circular, organic bubbles streaming between the decaying urban centers, represented by dense, linear grids.[61]

A recording from the visit gives a deeper sense of the conversation. With Carole King playing in the background, Liza, Mary, and Cheryl discussed the challenges of adapting internal spaces and feeling limited by existing walls: "You're already given a geometry." What if the residents of a co-op all agreed to tear down the walls and create more communal spaces? Chil-dren's space on the tenth floor, a shared kitchen on the ninth? Birkby asked how they might form an "Amazon Community." Another participant asked, "We mean that there are no male children?" It was agreed that by "Ama-zon" they were thinking of a future in which women had evolved to have only female children, so they wouldn't have to kill off the men. And they could create a "lesbian ark" ("three giraffes, but they're all girls!"), abandon the cities, go out to sea, and wait thirty years for the cities to decay—then start over. Following the conversation, Birkby asked everyone to draw their fantasy environments. Cowan imagined an adobe-like hut, with a woman inside preparing a communal meal.[62] Birkby's project allowed participants to name a feeling of constraint and alienation and begin to imagine an alternative.

Birkby's work resonated with a larger conversation about women and architecture that was just beginning to take off. In September 1972, the magazine *Architectural Forum* ran a long report by senior editor Ellen Perry Berkeley, titled "Women in Architecture," investigating the lack of opportunities for women in the field and the ongoing gender gap in architecture graduate programs and professional organizations.[63] In May 1974, *New York Times* architecture critic Ada Louise Huxtable wrote her own groundbreaking essay on women in architecture, titled "The Letterhead is Solidly Male," reporting on the low number of women in the profession as well as discrimination those women faced. Huxtable also asked whether women design differently from men: "Is there, or isn't there, then, a difference in sensibility between the male and the female designer? Do women perceive the environment differently from men?" The answer, Huxtable answered, was yes, but this was less innate than cultural—shaped by women's traditional role in the home. Women, Huxtable wrote, "often (but not always) design better houses and apartments than men, because in their housewife hats they are more intimately concerned with this particular kind of environmental success or failure. A woman who has had to spend a lot of time in a windowless kitchen will break her neck to give the kitchen a view. . . . She understands the relationships between space and privacy and pleasure, operational efficiency, and the potential human violations of a bad plan."[64]

Spring 1974 was a major moment of crossover for Birkby's work. The journal *Design & Environment* published a special issue on "Women in Design," featuring Birkby's environmental fantasy project. Birkby's description of the project was reduced to a paragraph, but a full page was devoted to drawings from the project, including those by Cowan.[65] That March, Birkby also presented the environmental fantasy project at one of the first conferences on architecture and gender, "The Women in Architecture Symposium," organized by a group of graduate and undergraduate students at Washington University in St. Louis. The goal, the program explained, was "to explore the many concerns of professional women in architecture— role conflicts, professional attitudes and design capabilities." The program indicated that Birkby would present a video depicting how the built environment was "disabling for a woman in NYC with three small children," but she focused instead on the fantasy environment project.[66]

Birkby's earlier workshops had been primarily with feminists without professional training; this was the first time she was presenting the project to an audience of design professionals. She was terrified of rejection, she later reflected, but the response was overwhelmingly positive: "To my surprise and delight there were those who expressed joy and gratitude, feelings that spoke of repressed processes, of not having been 'allowed.'"[67] In a journal entry, she wrote, more emphatically, "Beautiful images today— showing the drawings of charleen, mandy, julia, frances, liza, ann, etc. where are the women who were my projections of love passion fantasy? fantasy is the beginning of creation I roared in my heart and spoke so softly and they responded with orgasmic output . . . orgasm is output not input after all. . . . I made love and they did it."[68] For Birkby, women's environmental fantasy provided a deep sense of connection—it was erotic, bodily, and manifested the feeling of a utopian feminist space.

The conference also gave Birkby an opportunity to connect with other architects, scholars, and writers who shared her concerns and passions. Among the other presenters was Leslie Kanes Weisman, a professor at the University of Detroit and the only woman in the school's architecture department. Like Birkby, Weisman was deeply interested in the impact of male-dominated architecture programs on women. Birkby and Weisman quickly developed a professional and romantic relationship. The relationship was at first long distance, with Weisman in Detroit and Birkby still in New York, but after a year, Weisman left her husband, got a job at the New Jersey Institute of Technology, and moved in with Birkby in Lower Manhattan.[69]

Over the next two years, Birkby and Weisman took the fantasy workshops to a broader public across the United States. They presented together at the second annual conference of the Gay Academic Union (GAU) on the theme "Toward Community" in fall 1974 and a conference on "Women in Design: The Next Decade" at the Women's Building in Los Angeles in 1975. They also gave a guest lecture for the Environmental Design Program at University of Wisconsin-Green Bay, as well as presentations for community groups, including the Woodstock Women's Center in the Catskills and a local NOW chapter in Westport, Connecticut.[70] In each session, Birkby and Weisman would begin by explaining the project and sharing slides of sample environmental fantasies. They would then ask women to get on the floor around large sheets of brown craft paper, take a magic marker, and draw "their ideal living environment." After twenty or thirty minutes, they would come back together to discuss their drawings—as Weisman later summarized, "What does it look like? What size and shape? What is it made of? Where is it located? What do you do there? Is there anyone else there?"[71] Each woman, Birkby and Weisman wrote, needed to "become her own architect, that is she must become aware of her ability to exercise environmental judgement and make decisions about the nature of the spaces in which she lives and works."[72]

Birkby and Weisman elaborated many of the key concepts underlying the project in published writings on environmental fantasies. In the feminist magazine *Quest*, Birkby and Weisman used the term "environmental oppression" to reframe architecture and the built environment as instruments of patriarchal power.[73] In the magazine *Liberation*, they coined the term "patritecture" to think about the patriarchal structure of the built environment, writing, "Architectural machismo confronts and affronts us continuously. The 20th century urban skyscraper, the pinnacle of patriarchal symbology, is rooted in the masculine mystique of the big, erect, and forceful. . . . Each building competes for individual recognition and domination in this schema, while the value of human identity is impoverished." And they defended the use of fantasy itself: "Fantasies are psychically free spaces in which to construct the vision of an environment in our own self-image, free from the narrow constraints of linear thinking. They are a serious and powerful means for developing an environmental consciousness, the first step in the actualization of change."[74]

The environmental fantasy workshop also became one of the core programs in another of Birkby's key collaborations: the Women's School of Planning and Architecture (WSPA). Beginning in March 1974, at the St. Louis conference, Birkby, Weisman, and five other women—Ellen Perry Berkeley, Katrin Adam, Bobbie Sue Hood, Marie Kennedy, and Joan Forrester Sprague—began making plans for an annual summer program, a two-week educational retreat where women in the design professions could meet and learn together. The first was held over two weeks in August 1975, in Biddeford, Maine, with roughly fifty women attending. Among the goals, as Weisman and Birkby wrote, was to provide "a separatist experience that is supportive and analytical of our unique experiences, perceptions, and common concerns as women within male-dominated fields."[75] Housed on a college campus, the school became a kind of temporary women's commune, allowing women to live and work together. Birkby and Weisman led a session on "Women and the Built Environment"—first asking women to talk about their memories of their childhood homes and neighborhoods, to consider where their "environmental perceptions and values" come from, before drawing and discussing their fantasy environments (fig. 4.3). The program was transformative for many women, both professionally and personally. One participant wrote to Birkby and Weisman shortly after the first retreat to share that she was planning to go back to school to pursue a master's degree. She also noted that the retreat was where she had her first lesbian experience. "I am certainly more in touch with my more active bi-sexuality, and not too fearful of it anymore."[76]

Birkby and Weisman ultimately collected hundreds of drawings from a broad array of participants—"older women, housewives, female kids, nuns, career women, lesbians, straights, writers, painters, doctors, secretaries, factory workers, mothers, daughters, sisters, grandmas."[77] The participants ranged in age from their teens to their seventies, though most were white and well educated, either working or looking for work.[78] Most of the

FIGURE 4.3. Birkby and Leslie Kanes Weisman included the fantasy environment exercise in their core course, "Women and the Built Environment: Personal, Social, and Professional Perceptions," at the first session of the Women's School of Planning and Architecture in Biddeford, Maine, August 1975. Women's School of Planning and Architecture Records, Sophia Smith Collection, Smith College, Northampton, MA.

drawings, archived now with Birkby's papers at Smith College, depicted women-only spaces—retreats from men—suggesting that if not all participants were ready to commit to living in a women-only, women-identified community, they were ready to fantasize about it.

One common theme across the drawings was flexibility—an ability to control and adapt space to changing needs. As Birkby and Weisman put it, the environments in the drawings were "not static and monolithic, but manipulable, expanding and contracting, organically evolving—stretchable nets, systems of attachment and separation, multiple purposes, recyclable forms" (fig. 4.4).[79] One woman created a home with walls that could, she explained, "move in and out according to your psychic needs and the number of visitors."[80] Another participant imagined an "edible house" that could be altered by consuming it.[81] Still another envisioned a house made from gelatin—the houses would be made with Jell-O molds, only to melt and be made again. One participant drew a home protected by a dome, visible or invisible, opened or closed on demand, shielding the dweller, she annotated, from "demands" and "noise" with a path to a private beach, "invitation only."[82]

Many participants also expressed a frustration with the isolation of single-family houses or apartments and sought through their fantasies to renegotiate the balance between privacy and community. One woman

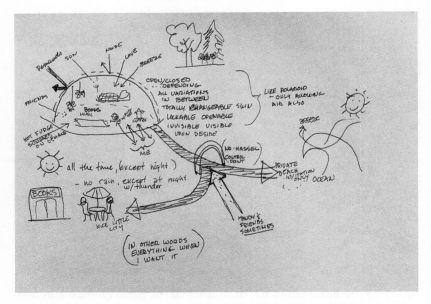

FIGURE 4.4. This fantasy environment drawing, c. 1974, included a dome that could be variably opened and closed, allowing friends in but keeping demands out. Noel Phyllis Birkby Papers, Sophia Smith Collection, Smith College, Northampton, MA.

from the Connecticut suburbs, for example, drew a closed-circuit TV with a push button to summon the "nurturer of your choice" after "you get over wanting to be alone."[83] Many other participants divided homes into communal spaces and more private rooms, to give options to be together or alone. One drawing featured an "introvert" room, a room for "multiple experiences," and, on the roof, an "ultra-extrovert space" (fig. 4.5). Some were also distinctly erotic: one drawing presented a "community for 10 women" including a "community room for lovemaking" and a "pool for group swims," but also a "private retreat" and a "pool for me."[84]

Much of the space depicted in the drawings were simply given to pleasure, play, and creativity. Charleen Whisnant, a North Carolina–based writer, drew a tower-like home, with a tall glass elevator moving up to an all-glass dome, with a dance floor and bedroom, and down to an underground waterfall that served as a shower.[85] Another participant drew a tower with a large room at the top labeled "my space," with glass all around. It contained 100 pillows, giant closets, 5,000 books, a grand piano, a "cozy corner," and lots of room for friends. Children were given their own wing of the house, with no one under twenty-one admitted. She also included a garage with vehicles for each mood—a van, a motorcycle, a camper (fig. 4.6). In many drawings, women simply imagined more time and space for learning and

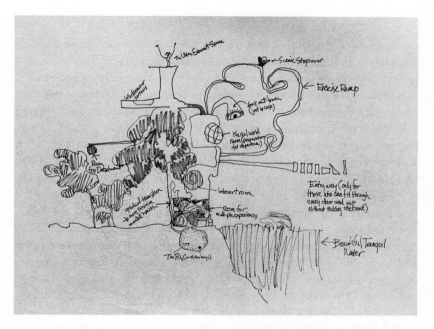

FIGURE 4.5. This fantasy environment drawing, c. 1974, featured both an "introvert" room and a rooftop platform for "ultra-extroverts." Noel Phyllis Birkby Papers, Sophia Smith Collection, Smith College, Northampton, MA.

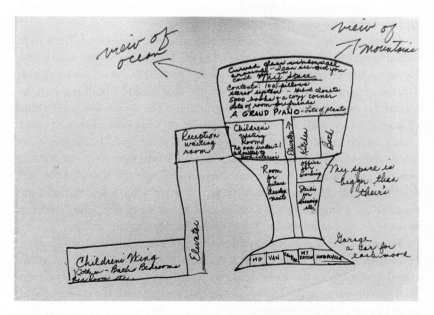

FIGURE 4.6. One participant in the fantasy environment workshops, c. 1974, designed a house with a separate "children's wing," leaving greater space for creativity and self-expression. Noel Phyllis Birkby Papers, Sophia Smith Collection, Smith College, Northampton, MA.

creating—vast libraries, rooms for art, media, and music. One drawing even anticipated the internet, envisioning a TV screen with "instant access to encyclopedic information (no heavy books, just up there on a screen)."[86] Participants did not necessarily object to cooking and kitchens, but they often made the kitchens communal or open. Many women also expressed a desire for greater connections to the natural world. Most of the drawings featured views of forests, mountains, meadows, or oceans—though often with the city still accessible. The problem that women in the workshops repeatedly returned to was not home itself but the isolation of hetero-normative domesticity.

Architecturally, the most common design in the drawings was the dome. The form of the geodesic dome was originally conceived by architect Buck-minster Fuller and grew popular in the communal architecture of the 1960s and 1970s. The appearance of the dome in the workshop drawings suggests how deeply feminist critique of the family was shaped by a larger counter-culture critique of the nuclear family household and, with it, the suburban built environment. The dome was an emblem of a more enlightened future. As Bill Voyd, a resident of the influential commune Drop City, explained, "To live in a dome is—psychologically—to be in closer harmony with nat-ural structure. Macrocosm and microcosm are recreated, both the celestial sphere and molecular and crystalline forms. . . . Corners constrict the mind. Domes break into new dimensions."[87]

Other drawings located new feminist spaces underground, from indi-vidual homes to whole communities. In 1974, Weisman worked with fellow Detroit activists Valerie Angers and Joanne Parrent to draw a prototype for a "fetus of matriarchy" or "feminist womb," that could be built beneath the "pinnacles of patriarchy"—that is, skyscrapers. The womb was itself a kind of women's city, with a feminist commune, printing press, feminist credit union, health center, library, and health food store, with the largest space manipulable for dancing, "soft conversing," or something else. The drawing was not pure fantasy: Angers and Parrent had recently founded the first feminist credit union in the country, at a moment when it was virtually im-possible for a woman to get a credit card of her own. Imagining women's space was a way of imagining women's autonomy and connection.[88]

For many women, that new autonomy and connection was also deeply connected to their sexuality. One of the participants at the GAU conference noted that many of the early drawings featured womblike imagery: "I see these small spaces in the fantasy drawings, this coziness, the underground, as an opportunity for women to say 'I too miss the womb,' openly express-ing through sisterhood these feelings we were never permitted to express. I feel very sure that my lesbianism is a part of this."[89] Weisman, Angers, and

Parrent also envisioned new modes of transportation, including the "Great Goddess Percolation System." Women could take elevators and "percolate" to a platform in the sky, only to come back down to any spot in the country within fifteen minutes. The drawing imagined material connections across a feminist network, across geographic regions, at a time before email and when long-distance phone calls were expensive. They also drew plans for an "Amazon Airways" plane—part of a fleet of alliterative lesbian feminist transportation options including "Hera's Helicopter Service," "Lavender Limousine," and "Sappho Sea Travel."[90]

Participants in Birkby and Weisman's workshops, however, did not need to wait for Amazon Airways to connect with other women: the workshops served, in themselves, as a way of breaking down isolation. Listening to recordings of the feminist fantasy workshops, what is most striking is the sense of playfulness. At the GAU conference, Birkby's slideshow of images from the project was punctuated with waves of laughter—at the playfulness, pleasure, and creative vulnerability of the drawings. Birkby shared one of her own drawings: a complex constellation of domes for a range of sexual relationships, inspired by her own travels in lesbian feminist circles. There was a monogamy dome, a cluster of "multiple relationship domes," a line of "serial monogamy domes," and a round of "rotating relationship domes" (fig. 4.7). The audience roared with recognition. Birkby said when she was creating the drawing, she was "just having fun, but it was also serious."[91]

That balance of seriousness and fun bore traces of Johnston's influence: Birkby brought Johnston's joker citizenship to architecture and freed women to express unspoken desires. Birkby saw that conventional domesticity and housing—whether in the suburbs or the city—atomized women, isolated them from one another. CR groups, the women's building, weekends on Johnston's farm fired her heart and imagination. She sought to imagine a feminist environment that would both counter the sharp phallocentric, patriarchal forms of conventional, male-dominated architecture and challenge their spatiality—clustering women together.

ACTUALIZING WOMEN'S ARCHITECTURE

Birkby always imagined the environmental fantasy project was a beginning, not an end in itself. To realize new architectural forms, women needed to explore their fantasies first. But the revolution in women's design and architecture had already begun. In late February 1977, Birkby received a letter from a woman named Caroling, an artist living in Monte Rio, California. Caroling had read Birkby and Weisman's 1975 article on the environmental fantasy project in *Quest* and found the piece resonated with her own

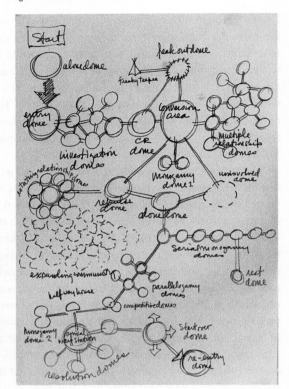

FIGURE 4.7. Birkby presented her own fantasy environment drawing at the Gay Academic Union conference in Fall 1974, featuring a monogamy dome, serial monogamy domes, and "multiple relationship domes." Noel Phyllis Birkby Papers, Sophia Smith Collection, Smith College, Northampton, MA.

work. She had recently built a dome entirely out of stained glass, fourteen feet in diameter, which she called Wholeo. "It is my main fantasy," Caroling wrote, "which, Goddess willing, became a dream come true." Caroling also shared an article she published about the dome in the magazine *Glass Art*. Since childhood, she explained, her consciousness had been dominated by a "'male' vision of reality"; the stained glass dome was the result of liberating her "'female' intuition." (She placed male and female in quotes, she noted, because she was "not sure of these assumptions and sorting bins labeled male and female.") Birkby wrote back delighted, noting that the dome was "amazingly similar to a fantasy drawing done by a friend of ours who will love seeing it."[92]

The friend was Frances Doughty, who had appeared with Birkby in the *Ramparts* photograph in 1971 and participated in an early environmental fantasy workshop. Frances described her fantasy environment this way: "The place I am in is in a high rounded space: big, airy... like the inside of a patchwork zeppelin built of stained glass. . . . It's like being in a warm sea of colors or living in a kaleidoscope ... to swim, to move slowly exploring the play of color and motion."[93] The similarities between Caroling's dome and Frances's description were, indeed, striking, and they set Birkby out on the next phase of her environmental fantasy project—documenting what she called "women's vernacular architecture," the spaces women had actually built.[94]

By the mid-1970s, more and more women had, in fact, sought to construct new environments from scratch, typically without any formal training. Much as Birkby had proposed, many women found that taking control of their home spaces—apart from men—was an important step in taking control of their lives. One of the primary venues for exploring those efforts was the magazine *Country Women*. As Scott Herring has chronicled, *Country Women* was founded in 1973 by a collective of working- and lower-middle-class women in Albion, California, shaped as much by a back-to-the-land ideology as lesbian separatism. The collective was led by Jeanne Tetrault, who had fled Berkeley, California, for the country in 1968, along with her lover, Carmen Goodyear, their five dogs, seven cats, and a baby goat. Not all women who wrote for, or read, the magazine identified as lesbians, but as journalist Kate Coleman wrote in *Mother Jones*, "It was lesbianism . . . that provided the protective, sisterly umbrella under which these women were far freer to break out of conventional roles as helpmates, mothers and lovers."[95]

Country Women was both reflective and instructive—authors routinely shared their experiences moving to the country to help other women follow in their footsteps. In January 1974, they dedicated an issue to "Structures," investigating the meanings, and methods, of home and shelter. It began with a meditation, in the form of a poem:

> Clear yourself a clean space in your head.
> Forget what you think you know about "houses," what they look like and what they are.
> Forget about corners and windows and heating and toilets.
> Forget about shelves, closets, and rooms.
> Throw away all the pictures in your mind, all the things you've been taught to think you and a house should have.
> And think about yourself, about who you really are.
> And think about the land you wish to live on. . . .
> Your shelter will reflect and provide a frame for you and your life.[96]

Articles and photographs in the issue went on to document women building homes out of adobe bricks, putting up yurts, constructing octagonal barns. Like Birkby's fantasy project, the issue redefined homemaking—not as a rigid process ruled by convention but a creative process that responded to women's needs and desires.

Birkby's growing interest in women's vernacular architecture coincided with another period of change in her life. After two years, she broke up with Weisman, shortly after the second WSPA conference in 1976. They continued to work together over the next few years, both on an article about the history of the WSPA and a book they never completed on the fantasy drawings, but the relationship deteriorated as they struggled over ownership and rights to the project. At the same time, Birkby moved to Venice, California, to live with a new lover, architect Ena Dubnoff. When that relationship too ended, Birkby decided to stay in Los Angeles, teaching adjunct at the Southern California Institute of Architecture and later University of Southern California.[97]

The time in California was challenging for Birkby personally and professionally, but it also gave her an opportunity to explore a wide range of new women's spaces and communities coming together in California and the Southwest. She started in February 1978 with a visit to Caroling in Monte Rio to see the Wholeo Dome (fig. 4.8). She was accompanied on the trip by

FIGURE 4.8. Birkby visited artist Caroling's stained glass Wholeo Dome in Monte Rio, California, in February 1978, at the start of a new project on women's vernacular architecture. She also created a film featuring her friend and lover, filmmaker Barbara Hammer. Noel Phyllis Birkby Papers, Sophia Smith Collection, Smith College, Northampton, MA.

a new friend and lover, Barbara Hammer. They were a good match: Hammer was slowly becoming known as a leading lesbian filmmaker, with playful, experimental films centering on lesbian culture and desire. In Monte Rio, Birkby filmed Hammer in the Wholeo Dome, the colored light striking her nude body, linking sexuality and spirituality.[98] She wrote in her notes, "Entering this space is an act of transformation—light itself unifies all who enter here with a sense of wonder, immediate connection with each other, an instant sense of being of the same universe."[99]

Birkby went on to visit many other women's spaces and conducted interviews with their makers. In Albion, California, she visited Tye Farm— home of the *Country Women* collective—where residents had erected yurts and an octagonal barn for the goats.[100] Many women she met were also working in and adapting indigenous architecture. In Española, New Mexico, she visited with Rain Parrish, a Navajo artist, who constructed a traditional hogan—a hut made from clay and branches. The house recalled for Birkby a long tradition of women's construction—"the women of the ages taking the clay, surrounding inner space, creating inner space, the vessels of life to hold the human and all her/his needs."[101] In Santa Fe, she interviewed Anita Rodriguez, a woman of Pueblo descent and a professional *enjarradora*—a builder of traditional adobe fireplaces.[102] The influence of adobe architecture was visible among many white artists as well: in Taos, Birkby interviewed painter and printmaker Marcia Oliver, who built an oval house out of clay: "I wanted something round, not square and boxy, I wanted it to be soft, to have contours and curves. . . . I wanted it to look as if it just grows out of the earth."[103] The fascination with indigenous architecture followed recent historical accounts, like Doris Cole's 1973 book, *From Tipi to Skyscraper*, which sought to reclaim architecture as a traditional women's art—though typically for white women.[104]

For Birkby, women's vernacular architecture hinted at the possibility of an underlying and essential women's sensibility. In a special architecture issue of the feminist journal *Heresies*, she published an essay on her research titled "Herspace," putting photographs and plans for actual women's homes alongside drawings from the environmental fantasy project. She described how Santa Fe artist Virginia Gray built a round adobe addition to an existing rectangular house, trying to break away from square designs and right angles. Images of Gray's home were paired with a drawing of a "sea shell snail house"—a home designed as a spiral, moving inward with each circle from public to more and more private space. She also described Caroling's dome and reproduced Frances's description of her fantasy home. The parallels provoked Birkby to ask whether there was indeed a common feminine architecture, across time and culture: "Aren't these signs of a common foundation for the expression of a uniquely female imagery of built form? Doesn't this show a creative process that emphasizes those qualities our culture associates with the female principle, with a greater reliance on feeling and intuition, on things not too carefully planned by choice?"[105] Birkby remained undecided about whether the differences she observed between male and female architecture were ultimately innate or cultural. What mattered was that men and women alike had been conditioned to accept and value modes of architecture and design that were associated with male patterns of behavior.

By the late 1970s, Birkby had come to a new language to describe this mode of patriarchal architecture: pornographic. In a 1981 essay for *Ms.*, she explained, "A continued refusal to accommodate women's needs with physical spaces constitutes an abuse of power as severe as the violence in pornography, battering, and rape."[106] Birkby's new framing drew on an emerging antipornography, antiviolence movement of the late 1970s: in November 1978, Birkby attended the first national conference of antipornography feminists, held in in San Francisco. The conference had a major impact on Birkby's thought, particularly a talk by lesbian poet Terry Wolverton (Birkby recorded and transcribed the talk herself). As Wolverton explained, "Pornography is the sensibility of severance, the ultimate alienation of the life force, a non-identification with women, nature, life." For Wolverton, this meant specifically the "annihilation of female bonding" and "eradication of lesbian vision"—separating women from their own source of creativity, specifically "lesbian creativity."[107] Wolverton's views resonated with Birkby's own ideas about male- and female-identified architecture. In *Ms.*, she quoted Wolverton and condemned the modern American city with distinctly bodily language: "Freeways slash through the cities, slicing the urban body into disconnected real estate plots for exploitation; the phallic symbol of the skyscraper advertises male dominance of public life and space; vast areas of pavement and hard-line geometries scar natural topographies, clumsily force the earth into unnatural acts."[108]

Birkby heralded instead a more feminine force—an erotic architecture. The erotic sensibility was, Birkby wrote, a "sensibility of connection," one "based on shared power and open-ended modes of thinking and action."[109] Birkby's conceptualization of the erotic drew especially on Audre Lorde's essay, "The Uses of the Erotic," which Lorde presented at the same 1978 conference. Lorde identified the erotic as "a resource within each of us that lies in a deeply female and spiritual plane, firmly rooted in the power of our unexpressed or unrecognized feeling." The erotic was not limited to sexual expression but enabled a broader sharing of joy—feeling the world deeply, connecting with oneself and others. Birkby quoted the last lines of Lorde's essay in her draft of the *Ms.* essay, "Recognizing the power of the erotic within our lives can give us energy to pursue genuine change within our world, rather than merely settling for a shift of characters in the same weary drama. For not only do we touch our most profoundly creative source, but we do that which is female and self-affirming in the face of a racist, patriarchal, and anti-erotic society." In her draft, Birkby also created a list of pornographic and erotic qualities: pornographic included restriction, isolation, manipulation, competition, goal orientation; erotic included mobility, contact, inclusion, cooperation, and process orientation.[110]

Birkby's increasingly essentialist split between male and female, pornographic and erotic, modes of expression placed her in line with other activists of the late 1970s and early 1980s who historians have come to identify as "cultural feminists." Where early forms of radical feminism sought to undo gender and embrace androgyny, cultural feminism largely upheld a male-female binary—albeit, to revalue what they defined as female perspectives and sensibilities.[111] Many cultural feminists also came to rigidly monitor and police expressions of sexuality: as Jane Gerhard summarizes, "For sex to be consistent with feminism, it had to reflect women's values by prioritizing intimacy, nongenital touching, and emotional nurturing."[112] Birkby herself was far from doctrinaire—her letters to Hammer, for one, detail their passionate sexual connection. Yet she also found essentialist, and antipornographic, discourses productive to break free of restrictive models of architecture and home, not only for women but for many oppressed minoritized groups. A woman-identified environment, she argued in *Ms.*, would mean "designs that recognize the 'messiness' of life." That included "environments that accept children as an integral part of society" as well as "spaces that admit that not all women will be mothers." She took inspiration from "the revival of midwifery and creation of birthing centers; the growing militance of the disabled providing a greater mobility for pregnant women and young children," as well as new designs for cooperative housing aimed at meeting "the needs of low-income women living outside of male-headed households." And she called for new "inclusionary zoning"—zoning, as she elaborated in her notes, that encouraged "overlaps, not divisions . . . the integration of culture, the aged, the disabled, children, life work play . . . respect for different lifestyles, collective/communal arrangements."[113] For Birkby, patriarchal and pornographic modes of architecture demanded people conform to existing models of home and family life; a more women-identified, erotic, and emotional architecture would mean adapting environments to fit human needs and encourage human connection.

Birkby herself had relatively limited opportunities to realize her own architectural fantasies. Although she opened a private practice in 1972, she had a relatively small number of commissions for her own constructions. There were a few exceptions. In 1973, sculptor David Jacobs commissioned her to build a sculpture studio for him at his family's home in Sea Cliff, Long Island (figs. 4.9 and 4.10). The design was relatively simple: a double-gabled roof, wooden siding with sliding doors, and ceilings of skylights to provide natural light. Birkby's modernist designs also resonated with Jacobs's sculptures, which played with simple forms, raw materials, and negative space.[114]

Birkby also designed a few houses, including one for a lesbian couple: in 1977, Debra Lobel and her partner, Beverly Dash, commissioned Birkby to design a house for them in East Hampton, New York. The project could

FIGURE 4.9. One of Birkby's first commissions as an independent architect was a sculpture studio for artist David Jacobs at his family home in Sea Cliff, Long Island, New York. Photograph by Phyllis Birkby, 1973. Noel Phyllis Birkby Papers, Sophia Smith Collection, Smith College, Northampton, MA, with permission of Joan Jacobs.

FIGURE 4.10. Painted steel sculptures by David Jacobs outside studio designed by Phyllis Birkby, Sea Cliff, Long Island, New York, 1973. Photograph by Phyllis Birkby. Noel Phyllis Birkby Papers, Sophia Smith Collection, Smith College, Northampton, MA, with permission of Joan Jacobs.

have been a good testing ground for Birkby's environmental theories: she had initially planned sloping ceilings and walls, on multiple levels, but the contractors' bids came in too high; Birkby redesigned it as a cube, though still with a deck for the pool. The project ultimately had little of the playfulness of the environmental fantasy drawings, but the living room and dining room were open, to allow more communal space, and the building was set on an angle so that residents could see over the cliffs down to the water, echoing some of the common features in the fantasy project (fig. 4.11).[115] Birkby also oversaw the creative redesign of a warehouse into twenty-four loft-like condominiums in Little Ferry, New Jersey.[116] She strived in all these projects to evoke a sense of continuity between the building and the natural environment, with large windows, skylights, and sharp lines.

Birkby was nevertheless held back, undoubtedly, by being a woman. During the same period Birkby was working, architect Horace Gifford made a name for himself designing modern beach houses for gay men in the Pines on Fire Island. Gifford, who never completed his architectural degree, shared many of the same ideals as Birkby. As architect and historian Christopher Rawlins shows, Gifford had a distaste for suburbia and wanted

FIGURE 4.11. This house, built for Debra Lobel and Beverly Dash in East Hampton, Long Island, was one of the few houses Birkby completed, from design to construction, as an independent architect. Photograph by Phyllis Birkby, c. 1977. Noel Phyllis Birkby Papers, Sophia Smith Collection, Smith College, Northampton, MA.

his houses to flow naturally from the beach. They included great walls of windows and pool decks steps from the boardwalk, and he prioritized communal spaces and conversation pits.[117] But money was rarely an obstacle for the wealthy, white gay men who sought Gifford out. Few women had the resources to match: Birkby worked for a number of women over the 1970s and 1980s, but most often doing small kitchen and bathroom renovations. Birkby's most fanciful design was in the mid-1970s for lesbian poet Anne Witten—a circular three-story house that closely resembled many of the fantasy drawings. But the house appears never to have been built. She also spent months designing a hotel in the Bay Islands of Honduras, to be called Watering Place Resort, but the plans were eventually abandoned because of escalating conflict between Honduras and the Sandinistas.[118]

After Birkby moved back to New York in the 1980s, much of her income came instead from designing affordable housing and supportive care facilities for larger firms. From 1980 to 1982, she designed eldercare residences for Gruzen & Partners, and from 1984 to 1985, multifamily affordable housing for Lloyd Goldfarb & Associates. She also worked on multiple public projects for the New York State Facilities Development Corporation, including a halfway house for women on Staten Island. In many cases, Birkby was tasked with converting existing buildings to new use: on Long Island, she turned suburban homes into transitional housing for a local psychiatric center; she turned a school in the Bronx into an adult day treatment center; and she helped develop SROs (single-room occupancy housing) for people with low incomes in Brooklyn. The jobs were not glamorous but they fit with another of Birkby's ongoing research projects on supportive housing for people marginalized by mainstream designs. Her interest in housing for the elderly seems to have been particularly long lasting: Birkby began working on housing for the elderly while still at Yale and, in 1981, received a Marshall grant to visit and research communal homes for the elderly in Scandinavia.[119]

One unexpected site where Birkby's work in eldercare, accessible housing, and lesbian architecture converged was in her work in the 1980s for another lesbian couple: Thea Spyer and Edie Windsor. Spyer was born in Amsterdam, and her family fled to the United States as the Nazis took power in Europe. She went to Sarah Lawrence College in the 1950s but was thrown out after a security guard saw her kissing another woman. She went on to gain a PhD in clinical psychology. In the early 1960s, she met Windsor, a mathematician for IBM, at a restaurant in Greenwich Village. They soon moved in together and married in Canada in 2007. When Spyer died in 2009, however, Windsor lost $350,000 in estate taxes because their marriage was not recognized by the federal government. Windsor sued, eventually leading the US Supreme Court to strike down the Defense of Marriage Act.[120]

Spyer and Windsor are best known today for their place in the history of same-sex marriage, but their story also has important intersections with histories of disability, eldercare, and domestic design. In 1977, Spyer was diagnosed with multiple sclerosis, and in 1986 she and Windsor approached Birkby to redesign their bathroom in the summer house they owned in Southampton. The work was relatively simple: they replaced the vanity with one that was wheelchair accessible, tore out and reconstructed the shower, and added support bars throughout the room. Five years later, Birkby made similar renovations to Spyer and Windsor's bathroom at their apartment in New York City.[121] Birkby's renovation of Spyer and Windsor's bathrooms is likely not what she had in mind when she first dreamed of lesbian architecture in the early 1970s, yet it resonates with her fundamental critique. The environment as it had been constructed was, for many people, simply disabling: architecture and design were manifestations of the normative assumptions and ideals of their makers—the majority of them white, heterosexual, middle-upper-class, able-bodied men.[122] Birkby wanted to change that, to allow women to dream of new spaces for themselves and others, not as an end in itself but a beginning. Birkby believed in the power of fantasy, but she also knew the importance of adaptation and renovation—design, as she put it, for "the messiness of life."

Viewed today, Birkby's commitment to a lesbian feminist architecture can seem sharply out of line with understandings of gender and sexuality as performative and socially contingent. Birkby was deeply committed to women's and lesbian culture, and frequently relied on essentialist framings of "woman" as a discrete and natural category, often with little attention to class and race and no attention at all to trans women. She rooted that work in the evidence of her own experience—decades of oppression in her education and career, as well as the frequent disappointments and alienation of her romantic and sexual life—that only occasionally resembled the lesbian feminist spaces she imagined. But Birkby also found in lesbian feminist theory a resource for challenging and expanding the built environment: her fantasy of lesbian architecture was founded on a more fundamental critique of male power and the script of the heterosexual household. Ultimately, Birkby's work should not be read as a restrictive or exclusive vision of women's territory, but a broader rejection of male-centered and controlled space and the model of domestic citizenship it upheld. In the fantasy project, she aligned women's architecture with emotion, love, and care, yet in her practice, she hoped those values might transform the built environment, and the everyday world of home, for everyone.

By the early 1990s, Birkby had moved nearly full time to Great Barrington, Massachusetts, in the Berkshires. She had been diagnosed with cancer, and her friends created a schedule so that someone could come every weekend to visit her. One friend explained in a note that she primarily needed help around the house with "jobs that require bending, such as changing the sheets, cleaning, etc." She continued, "I urged her not to think, 'Oh my god, I've got to get this garbage out of here, the Sisters are coming.' We'll do the garbage." They called themselves the Sisters of Birkby—SOBs for short. The Sisters included many of the women from Birkby's CR group in the 1970s: Kate Millett, Alma Routsong, Barbara Love, Sidney Abbott, as well as Jane O'Wyatt, a coeditor of *Amazon Expedition*, and Artemis March, one of the original authors of "The Woman-Identified Woman."[123] In the early 1970s, Birkby joked to Jill Johnston that they should get in the car and head south to bring their old friends to the Lesbian Nation. "Watch out," she said, "th' mo'oment gonna getcha." At the end of her life, the Lesbian Nation had come back to enfold her. It was a fantasy, but it was a dream that would sustain her. Lesbian Nation was not only found on rural communes, in bookstores or restaurants, but in the quotidian acts of home care, too.

THREE

REFORMS

CHAPTER FIVE

"Some Hearts Go Hungering": Homelessness and the First Wave of LGBTQ Shelter Activism

F. E. Mitchell arrived in San Francisco in June 1971 with dreams of liberation. As Mitchell recalled a few years later, "This meant being free, black
and in hope of being able to learn how to live in a gay world happily."
Mitchell first lived in the Tenderloin and within eight months moved to
the Haight-Ashbury district. Both areas had long been known as magnets
for youth who had run away or been pushed out of their family homes, and
in the Haight, Mitchell began "taking in crashers, trying to help them obtain employment or welfare." He also observed many young men engaged
in sex work simply to "survive from day to day." While Mitchell came to
San Francisco to enjoy its queer nightlife, his encounter with the poverty
of the Tenderloin and the Haight led him to begin volunteering for Emmaus House, a gay drop-in center opened in 1971. The center operated a
regular coffeehouse, discussion sessions, and a phone switchboard, aiming
to help LGBTQ people in the city find jobs and places to stay, and more
broadly to promote self-acceptance. Mitchell remarked that he felt a sense
of "amazement" finding "people who really spent their time and energies
in the interest of social improvement within the gay community." By 1973,
Mitchell had become director of Emmaus; soon after, he built a new model
of gay social services in the city, "Survival House"—a longer-term home for
LGBTQ people facing a range of social and economic challenges.[1] Mitchell's work on behalf of homeless people was groundbreaking, but it was not
without precedent: Survival House represented a larger, and now largely
forgotten, movement by LGBTQ activists throughout the 1970s and early
1980s to address homelessness among LGBTQ people—what I am calling
the first wave of LGBTQ shelter activism.

  LGBTQ homeless people were a visible presence within urban gay
communities and active leaders in LGBTQ politics throughout the 1960s
and 1970s. Joey Plaster, Jennifer Worley, and Christina Hanhardt, for example, have documented how homeless queer and transgender youth in San

Francisco's Tenderloin came together in the mid-1960s to form the early gay liberation collective Vanguard, publishing their own magazine and taking brooms to the street to stage a protest of police sweeps.[2] Susan Stryker, David Carter, and Martin Duberman have documented the central role of homeless queer and transgender youth—especially young people of color—in resisting police harassment, both at Compton's Cafeteria in San Francisco and the Stonewall Inn in New York City. Soon after Stonewall, Sylvia Rivera and Marsha P. Johnson formed the collective Street Transvestite Action Revolutionaries to support and advocate for transgender people within and beyond Gay Liberation Front (GLF).[3]

At the time, the most common terms for LGBTQ homeless people, often used by homeless youth and adults themselves, were "street people," "street kids," and "street queens." As Donn Teal footnoted in *The Gay Militants*, his 1971 narrative of the gay liberation movement, "'Street people' is a term homosexuals use to describe gays who have no apartment or at best a poor one and who may spend some of their time hustling."[4] This diverse group included transgender women and men, drag queens, "hair fairies," sex workers, military veterans, people with drug and alcohol dependencies, and teenagers who had run away from home or been thrown out by their families—though these categories all could and did overlap. I use the acronym "LGBTQ" here, although not used at the time, to recognize the breadth of individuals in this group, including gay, lesbian, and bisexual youth as well as transgender and gender-nonconforming youth (most commonly referred to at the time as transvestite or transsexual), although I do not mean to suggest that those identities were necessarily uncontested.

Bread Box, an early gay liberation collective formed in Washington, DC, sought to capture the range of LGBTQ homeless people and the challenges they faced in their own words in a series of newsletters published in 1970. They described themselves on page one of the first issue:

> We are gay people and we are poor. We are refugees from straight America—women and men of many nationalities and races. We live in the gay community which surrounds Dupont Circle. We are here because the dying American empire has no place for us. We are constantly unemployed or made to work at shitty jobs for shitty wages. We are often forced into living off the streets—begging, stealing, selling our bodies and dealing dope in order to survive. We are all outlaws.... We have no careers and no security. The system is our biggest enemy. Our only hope for the future lies in revolution.

The writers understood their homelessness as a symptom of oppression, in line with the larger revolutionary ideologies of GLF and the Black Panthers.

One contributor called for organizing and protests, as well as "crash pads, cheap healthy food, free clothing and entertainment" that would make organizing possible. They used the term "street person" but put it in quotes, recognizing its common usage while simultaneously calling into question how it othered people without stable housing.[5]

Despite their central role in gay liberation, however, LGBTQ homeless people met with indifference, discomfort, or rejection by many other gay men and lesbians, activists and nonactivists alike. Gay liberation activist Bob Kohler, for example, recalled raising concern for LGBTQ homeless people at a Mattachine meeting in New York—the first meeting to follow the Stonewall riots. As Kohler told Donn Teal, he "got a quarter from one person" and "somebody else got up and told me to shut up and sit down and that the queens were irrelevant."[6] For some, LGBTQ homeless people seemed to represent all the stereotypes of deviance that many homophiles, gay liberation activists, gay rights activists, and lesbian feminists sought to displace—gender variance, mental illness, and promiscuity, among others. The Bread Box collective noted that they had been kicked out of their home when the "bourgie hip types who control the house we live in decided our room (there's four of us) would serve them better as a living room. No kidding."[7]

These dynamics of indifference and disavowal slowly began to shift in the 1970s, with the emergence of social service programs aimed at helping LGBTQ homeless youth and adults. This cluster of programs emerged out of the convergence of two larger grassroots movements of the 1960s and 1970s—activism on behalf of runaway and homeless youth, and LGBTQ health and social service activism.[8] By the mid-1970s, activism on behalf of LGBTQ homeless youth was widespread enough to constitute a movement in its own right. It encompassed a constellation of disparate and diverse organizations and strategies—referral services, crash pads, emergency shelters, group homes, and foster care advocacy. What they all shared was a belief that housing was fundamental and that the needs of homeless youth and adults should be central to LGBTQ activism. These programs came during a decade of expanding and increasingly positive public visibility for gay men and lesbians, as well as a growing commercial world of bars, bathhouses, bookstores, and dance clubs.[9] The LGBTQ shelter movement, by contrast, represented a focused effort to secure private space for those most marginalized within urban LGBTQ communities. Many of these initiatives collapsed by the mid-1980s, yet they nevertheless laid a foundation for ongoing advocacy and activism around LGBTQ homelessness that continues today.

At the same time, LGBTQ shelter activism of the 1970s was emblematic of an emerging strategy in LGBTQ politics that saw local, state, and federal governments as potential allies. Early homophile activism—as well as some strains of early transgender activism—typically centered on rights to privacy: asking the state essentially to stay out of "personal" matters of sexuality and gender expression. Gay liberationists often made more radical demands, calling for revolution and making personal visibility a new ideal, yet they too largely wanted police and the government to leave LGBTQ people alone. By the mid-1970s, the tenor of lesbian and gay activism had shifted toward more conventional rights-based rhetoric and more focused efforts to change the system from within, through the courts and the ballot.[10] LGBTQ shelter activists were among the first to see government agencies not as the enemy but as partners in working to help marginalized LGBTQ people. The partnership went in both directions: LGBTQ shelter services needed government funding to survive, but by the mid-1970s, government welfare agencies also increasingly reached out to gay and lesbian social service activists for guidance in working with LGBTQ clients. This collaboration reflected rapidly changing, though not uncontroversial, beliefs about the nature of LGBTQ identities as stable rather than situational, even among young people. It also reflected a growing respect for LGBTQ social service providers and advocacy groups, which were quickly evolving from radical grassroots initiatives to more established and professionalized organizations.[11]

The partnership ultimately succeeded because government agencies and LGBTQ shelter activists shared core assumptions about the importance of a stable home and family for supporting social development and integration. As LGBTQ shelter programs became more bureaucratized, with recognition and funding from government agencies, gay and lesbian social service activists increasingly sought to reform LGBTQ homeless people into their vision of "well adjusted" and respectable citizens. Internal documents and published brochures from these various programs, in particular, reflect organizers' efforts to socialize residents into the values and performances of productive middle-class citizenship—moving swiftly from self-acceptance to self-improvement. In framing LGBTQ homelessness in terms of self-determination and self-sufficiency, shelter activists failed to consider whether an economic and social system predicated on productive, independent citizenship might have been a root cause of youth homelessness to begin with. Shelter activists mobilized discourses of home and family to reframe LGBTQ homeless youth as young people in need of support but also the social reform only a stable home could provide.

This chapter focuses on two major forms of shelter activism: first, efforts to establish homeless shelters and transitional housing in two centers of LGBTQ activism, Los Angeles and San Francisco; and second, the emergence of LGBTQ foster care advocacy and group homes, focusing on the Eromin Center, a center for sexual minorities in Philadelphia. I use the term "youth" here to refer to people roughly between the ages of thirteen and twenty-six, although the groups I examine use "youth" and "kids" variously depending on the specific context. The age of eighteen is often significant legally—the age when young people reach majority and age out of foster care systems—but some housing programs defined "youth" more broadly. Some programs also served both young people and adults, but young people were typically the focus of LGBTQ social service efforts as well as gay and mainstream media attention. These examples, and the first wave of LGBTQ shelter activism more broadly, reveal how domesticity itself was mobilized simultaneously as a space for social control and social change.[12] Although the LGBTQ shelter movement began by creating alternative domestic spaces, in the end it largely reaffirmed values of middle-class individualism and family life.

LOCATING THE QUEER RUNAWAY

Throughout the 1960s and 1970s, journalists, social scientists, and activists centered increasing attention on the problem of the runaway teenager. Before the 1960s, social researchers tended to regard running away as a sign of individual pathology and potential criminality, identifying runaway boys and girls as coming from lower-class and "broken" families, marked by parental separation or divorce.[13] An apparent rise in rates of adolescents running away from their family homes in the 1960s, however, challenged these assumptions and the juvenile justice system they upheld. These "new" runaways came largely from relatively affluent, white, middle-class homes. Explanations varied, but most news articles tended to understand runaways as part of a broader counterculture rebellion against the family and authority. Psychologist David Cole Gordon wrote in the progressive magazine the *Humanist*, "Our children are running away in increasing numbers. They are leaving apparently 'good' homes and 'loving' parents to join the hippies and flower children in a poorly articulated and vague search for the good the true and beautiful. . . . They prefer to live in squalor, in increasing danger, in vermin infested pads, to panhandle, to wear filthy clothes, to go hungry and suffer illness rather than return."[14] In November 1967, *Life* magazine devoted a cover story to "runaway kids" flooding "hippie slum areas" of various cities. They named three major areas—the East Village in New York, the Haight-Ashbury neighborhood in San Francisco, and Sunset Strip in Los Angeles—where young people could be found panhandling, getting high on methamphetamines, and sleeping in communal "crash pads."[15]

While it is difficult to give exact numbers, it was commonly estimated that between 500,000 and one million young people ran away every year in the late 1960s and 1970s.[16]

Growing concern for young runaways led activists in cities across the United States to pioneer new forms of social services—the runaway house and the drop-in center. For decades, young people who ran away from home were at constant risk of being picked up by police and placed in the juvenile justice system. Runaway houses sought to provide an alternative— addressing the immediate material needs of young people while providing social support. Their major intervention was to take seriously the young person's reasons for leaving home, and either help to reunify young people with their families or, when not possible, place them in suitable group or foster homes.[17]

Huckleberry's for Runaways, one of the earliest runaway houses, was representative. The house was founded in San Francisco in June 1967, at the start of the "Summer of Love," to provide counseling and short-term shelter to runaway youth in the Haight. The program was supported by the progressive Glide Methodist Church and named by the house's director, Reverend Larry Beggs, after Mark Twain's classic runaway figure, Huckleberry Finn. Its major goal was to support young people in reconnecting with their families of origin, allowing for a greater sense of shared understanding between parents and children. (Legally, Huckleberry's could not house young people under the age of eighteen without notifying police or parents.) Within six years, Huckleberry's was incorporated and moved to develop longer-term counseling and housing programs, including Greenhouse, a group home where young people could stay up to six months either to transition back to living with their guardians, move into foster care placement, or develop skills to live independently. With increasing numbers of city and federal government contracts, programs like Huckleberry's soon became the national model for interventions with runaway youth: in 1974, Congress passed the landmark Runaway Youth Act, providing long-term funding for runaway houses across the United States.[18]

LGBTQ youth undoubtedly sought help at runaway houses, but they were rarely a major programming focus. Huckleberry's, for example, developed services to address the needs of young people of color in the early 1970s but did not develop a specific set of programs around sexual identity until 1977.[19] In contrast, LGBTQ-focused interventions tended to be smaller in scale and received little attention in the mainstream or gay press. In January 1967, six months before Huckleberry's was formed, a collective of youth workers and ministers in San Francisco formed Central City Hospitality House, a drop-in center for runaway youth in the Tenderloin.

Located downtown, the Tenderloin was known as one of the city's major vice districts. As the report *The Tenderloin Ghetto: The Young Reject in Our Society* put it, the neighborhood was "notorious for prostitution, drunkenness, newsstands selling trashy pulp magazines, pimping, pill pushing, robbing and rolling, shoplifting, and other misbehavior." It was also the neighborhood where many young people who had fled their families wound up. *The Tenderloin Ghetto* reported, "The young person in the Tenderloin invariably comes from a deprived family background. A poor relationship with father or mother, a broken home, or no home at all is the rule rather than the exception." There was a need, the report argued, for programming to help "the outcasts of society, these young people who are unloved and unwanted because they don't seem to fit into society's general idea of productive citizenship."[20] Hospitality House grew out of this report, to provide counseling, medical advice, and referrals, and to help young people find jobs, finish their education, and obtain housing and food assistance.

Sister Betsy Hague, a member of the Medical Mission Sisters and a nursing student, volunteered at Hospitality House beginning in the summer of 1968. She provided a vivid portrait of the center and the young people who came there in the *American Journal of Nursing*. Their visitors ranged in age from twelve to twenty-eight and included, in Hague's terms, male and female homosexuals, bisexuals, transsexuals, and drag queens. Most of them lived in the cheap hotels of the Tenderloin, for an average of $66 a month. Accompanying photographs showed a large couch and chairs, set up around a shag carpet, and a jukebox, the walls covered in posters, including one of Ringo Starr holding a dove (fig. 5.1). As Hague explained, "The house was planned as a recreation center where they could feel welcome and accepted as they were. These were all youngsters who had left home and wandered to the Tenderloin, for one reason or another. Indeed, there was a community spirit among them, a feeling of group unity which gave them the only security they seemed to have. . . . They were trapped in a vicious circle: they could not go home and they could not go on." One of the young people explained to Hague how many street kids ended up dependent on drugs: "You're somebody society doesn't like—a homosexual, ex-convict, or a member of a minority group. You attempt to escape harsh reality through the use of drugs. The 'trip' or 'high' period of drugs distorts reality almost to the point of nonexistence. But when the effects wear off, you've got to adjust to the reality you tried to escape."[21] Yet even though Hospitality House had the support of homophile activists, same-sex sexuality and gender variance might still be understood as situational rather than authentic self-expressions, in keeping with broader contemporary understandings of homosexuality as a psychological condition. Hague and

FIGURE 5.1. Hospitality House, founded in San Francisco in 1967, was one of the first drop-in centers in the country for LGBTQ young people without stable housing. This photograph accompanied an article by Sister Betsy Hague in the *American Journal of Nursing*, October 1969, with the caption, "Shunned by society, Tenderloin youth find refuge in Central City Hospitality House." © *AJN: American Journal of Nursing*/Wolters Kluwer Health, Inc.

the center organizers, for example, assumed that some—though not all—visitors were merely experimenting sexually and might change their behavior, and their identification with homosexuality, with effective counseling.

Later LGBTQ-focused housing efforts continued to follow the mold of programs like Huckleberry's and Hospitality House in seeking to develop a model that affirmed young people's autonomy. And like many runaway houses, LGBTQ housing programs also sought to win government funding and ally with government agencies, in ways that inevitably led activists to reassert dominant paradigms of home and citizenship. But critically, they also saw how the experiences and needs of LGBTQ youth might differ from straight youth. First and foremost, they assumed that sexuality (and sometimes gender variance) was a stable part of a young person's identity, rather than a site of confusion. And second, they did not assume that reuniting young people with their families of origin should or could be the goal.

LIBERATION HOUSING AND THE QUEER FAMILY

In the two years after the Stonewall riots, with the spread of gay liberation groups across cities and college campuses around the country, housing slowly emerged as a focus of LGBTQ organizing. LGBTQ phone lines or switchboards were established with the goal of offering referrals for a variety of health, mental health, and social needs—including emergency and temporary housing or "crashing," as it was more commonly listed [22] Gay community centers and gay liberation communes frequently provided overnight or short-term housing.[23]

Transgender activists in New York were among the first to provide long-term shelter for homeless youth. In 1969, Street Transvestite Action Revolutionaries (STAR), led by Sylvia Rivera and Marsha P. Johnson, created an informal group home known as STAR House. At first, they set up a home in the back of a tractor trailer on the West Side, until the truck drove away with one person still sleeping inside. Soon after, the group began renting an apartment in the East Village at 213 East 2nd Street, just off Avenue B.[24] As Rivera later recalled, "It was only four rooms, and the landlord had turned the electricity off. So we lived there by candle light, a floating bunch of 15 to 25 queens, cramped in those rooms with all our wardrobe. But it worked. We'd cook up these big spaghetti dinners and sometimes we'd have sausage for breakfast, if we were feeling rich."[25] The older members of the household paid the $200 a month rent through sex work and panhandling and "liberated" food from the local A&P. They were finally kicked out of the house after eight months when one of the house founders, Bubbles, left for Florida without passing on the rent money to the landlord. *Village Voice* writer and gay activist Arthur Bell chronicled their eviction in July 1971 in a front-page article titled "STAR Trek." He quoted house resident Bambi, "I'd have liked to stay here—save our money—get something nice for the fall and move from the East Village. We can't do that now. We'll have to spend our money on eating out and sometimes on hotels, and if the cops come, it's too bad. At least in this hole you could always come home."

A major factor in the house's demise was the lack of support STAR received from gay and lesbian activists in the city. As Bell noted, STAR did not fit easily with the politics of the Gay Activists Alliance (GAA)—the gay rights organization that had come to displace GLF New York. Where GLF had explicitly sought to ally with the Black Panthers and other revolutionary groups, GAA treated gay rights as a single issue and aimed for government reform. STAR's philosophy, Bell wrote, was "to destroy the system. . . . Sylvia and Marsha and Bambi and Andorra with their third world looks and their larger-than-life presences and their cut-the-crap tongues do not 'fit' at a GAA meeting."[26]

At roughly the same time STAR House's residents were evicted, activists in Los Angeles developed their own model for helping homeless LGBTQ youth. In the summer of 1971, the *Advocate* ran a three-page article on a new venture in Los Angeles: Liberation House, a one-story bungalow on North Edgemont, half a block from Santa Monica Boulevard. The house opened in June and provided a home for ten men who had previously been sleeping on the floor of the coffeehouse run by the local GLF. But when the coffeehouse was shut down in June, several GLF leaders sought to establish a residence for "street kids." Liberation House aimed to address the needs of poor young men in an immediate, and lasting, way, combining material and emotional support.[27]

Runaway houses like Huckleberry's prioritized family reunification, but the organizers of Liberation House assumed that the parents of gay runaways would not affirm their sexual and gender variance. Instead, Liberation House specifically hoped the structure of the house would provide homeless youth with a new kind of kinship. The "family," as the *Advocate* put it, in many ways encapsulated the larger ethos of gay liberation communalism. An accompanying photograph pictured six of the ten members sitting on a couch, one with a kitten in his lap (fig. 5.2). Another pictured two of the men "pulling KP"—"kitchen patrol" (fig. 5.3). As activist, social worker, and head of the house John Platania explained, "If this group becomes fully cohesive, it may become a self-supporting collective—a real social alternative for gay people. Or it may break up. You can't tell. But we got them off the streets and kept them together so far. These guys literally have nobody but each other now." All ten house members were expected

FIGURE 5.2. Liberation House at 1168 N. Edgemont Street, Los Angeles, was one of several residences created by the Gay Community Services Center to provide a new home and family for LGBTQ young people. This photograph of residents with activist and social worker John Platania (on couch, second from left) was featured in the *Advocate*, August 4–17, 1971. Photograph by Lee Mason, courtesy of ONE Archives at the USC Libraries.

to contribute $1.50 per day toward the monthly rent of $175—whether through work or welfare. Platania reasoned, "Anybody who really wants to get his life together can pay that."[28]

The Liberation House model emerged from and became a critical component in a broader movement to develop social service and health support programs for LGBTQ people in Los Angeles. Beginning in 1970, the Gay Survival Committee of GLF Los Angeles, including Platania, Don Kilhefner, and Morris Kight, began discussing how GLF might address the psychological and medical challenges facing gay men and lesbians in Los Angeles. Within a year they formulated plans to launch the Gay Community Services Center (GCSC), one of the earliest social service and health centers in the United States dedicated to LGBTQ people. Housed in a dilapidated mansion, the center quickly developed counseling programs, discussion groups, employment services, and VD testing. Key to their work

FIGURE 5.3. Liberation House
residents Joe Scopp and Jay Richardson
"pulling KP" (kitchen patrol), as featured in the *Advocate*, August 4–17, 1971.
Photograph by Lee Mason, courtesy of
ONE Archives at the USC Libraries.

was a theory of what they termed "oppression sickness"—a belief that
lesbians and gay men were oppressed psychologically with much larger
ramifications. As historian Katie Batza summarizes, "Oppression sickness
encompassed physical, mental, financial, and political issues and ailments
common in the gay community." This concept "pushed beyond the rigid
boundaries of a medical understanding of health and illness . . . , blurring
the lines between medical issues and political ones."[29] Under the model of
oppression sickness, poverty and homelessness could be understood not
simply as a personal economic problem but as a symptom of larger social
injustice and alienation.

The Liberation House on Edgemont opened a few months ahead of
the GCSC, but quickly became the model for the GCSC's larger housing intervention.[30] To meet demand, the GCSC founders leased a second,
larger house a mile and a half away on North Van Ness Avenue only a few
months later. Its fourteen rooms could house up to twenty-five people.[31] In
December 1971, the GCSC also joined with several feminist groups includ-

ing the Daughters of Bilitis, the Gay Women's Service Center, and Lesbian Feminists to open Sisters Liberation House, with beds for twenty women of any sexual orientation. June Herrle, a clinical social worker and another founder of the GCSC, told the feminist newspaper *Proud Woman*, "We get women who are facing a lot of negative situations, to the point of being almost mentally ill. . . . To these women, morale and warmth is tremendously important. . . . We don't call this a crash-pad and we don't call the women crashers. They're temporary guests. This is all part of self-respect and of our respect for them."[32] The three houses together were the beginning of a full-scale housing program. Over the next four years, the GCSC supported the creation of several more houses to provide short-term and long-term housing, some specifically for men, others for men and women.

The GCSC estimated that the housing program served 400 men and women in its first year and more than 4,300 men and women over four years.[33] There are no specific statistics for racial and gender breakdown within the housing program, but it likely mirrored that of the center overall: in June 1974, the GCSC's programs served roughly 5,000 people—62 percent were identified as men, 38 percent as women; 70 percent of clients were white, 10 percent black, 9 percent Mexican American/Latinx. In terms of age, 40 percent of clients were between twenty-one and thirty years old. They did not report on any clients under the age of twenty-one, which was still controversial, but other records show that they did see teenagers as clients. The inclusion of transgender clients is more difficult to discern: the GCSC developed a transgender counseling program in the first three years, but transgender clients were rarely mentioned in programming materials, grant applications, or media coverage. Surviving records—a sample of intake forms and index cards issued for residents—give a better, if incomplete, sense of the people who came to the houses. They came from all over California and the United States—Hawaii, Indiana, Mississippi, Ohio, Oregon, to name the few places that are recorded—and ranged in age from their teens to their early forties. Some stayed for one week, some for a month, some longer. Others stayed for two weeks, only to return months later for another short stay.[34]

Other housing programs were available for homeless youth in Los Angeles, but few were affirmative of LGBTQ identification. In 1972, the GCSC did a survey of housing services in the county, only to find that there were no other housing programs directed at gay people. "More importantly," a later report summarized, "out of the 27 agencies surveyed in Los Angeles County, only 4 indicated a willingness to accept referrals from the Gay Community Services Center." The report reiterated, "It is not uncommon for gay people to be excluded from housing facilities simply because they are gay; or to feel uncomfortable and unwelcomed." What the Liberation Houses could provide that other services—and many clients' own families—could not was a "positive, accepting home environment."[35]

The program ultimately aimed not only to provide shelter but to encourage a positive self-image. As one brochure from 1972 described, "The Center's pioneering Liberation House projects provide a warm, supportive and loving environment where the individual is encouraged to express a positive view of his or her gayness with openness and pride."[36] Diane Trzcinski was a literature graduate student at University of Arkansas who came out to Los Angeles for spring break and stayed at Sisters Liberation House. She was expecting a more open, feminist environment, but "because of my three years of conditioning (oppression?) I was hardly prepared for the relative strength and incredible health of the LA lesbian/feminist movement. My bewilderment wore off as my admiration grew."[37] Residents were also encouraged to volunteer a few hours at the GCSC—a reflection of the center's larger model of cyclical service, where those seeking help came to help others.[38]

The program lasted as long as it did—several years longer than STAR House—largely because it was backed by a broader, and better funded, contingent of gay and lesbian activists, many of them with college and professional degrees. The increased scale and organization of the program also meant, however, that some of its early goals faded to the background over time. The first Liberation Houses were framed as alternative families, akin to gay communes, but the program became, by necessity, increasingly bureaucratized as it grew. The records indicate a range of challenges house staff encountered. Some residents left owing money to the house. A handful of residents had also evidently caused enough trouble to be listed as "persona non grata" on their index cards. One man, who stayed at one of the houses for only a few days, was listed as "psychotic—do not admit to lib house, but do try to help." For one house, the agreement form that residents signed stipulated a series of rules, which likely reflected problems staff had previously encountered: residents were not allowed weapons or drugs; they were allowed to bring guests into the house but not beyond the living area without permission of the house manager; and anyone "disrupting the house with bum alcohol or drug trips" or failing to pay rent would be asked to leave.[39] The extent of homelessness in Los Angeles also meant that the Liberation Houses increasingly emphasized temporary, short-term crisis housing rather than ongoing collective living.

This tension between the program's initial emphasis on creating new families and their later, more targeted and monitored approach comes through most clearly in a conflict that erupted in 1973, concerning the second Liberation House on Van Ness Street. In March 1973, Don Kilhefner wrote to the members of the Van Ness Liberation House to inform them that they would need to vacate the house within thirty days, as the GCSC planned to develop the house into a housing program for people recovering from alcohol or drug use. Since the formation of the house that past December, Kilhefner wrote, "it has become apparent that the Van Ness residence is not self-sustaining; nor has there been much indication that the experiment in collective living is working there." Residents responded with a six-page later, rebuking Kilhefner and the board as "slum lords." They argued that the letter showed the board's underlying sexism for failing to include two of the women living in the house among those addressed. More largely, they rejected the very term "Liberation House," arguing that the name had come to be synonymous with "crashing" rather than true collective living. The board, the residents argued, had become their oppressors. Residents further suspected that the plan to shift the function of the house was fundamentally financial: the GCSC had received federal funds to support a drug and alcohol recovery program, at the cost of gay people "whose needs don't serve to get you that establishment funding." Despite their protests, the residents were soon evicted, and GCSC redeveloped Van Ness as a recovery program, in partnership with Alcoholics Together, a gay counseling program.[40]

The Van Ness collective's argument, that the GCSC board was privileging programs and needs that could more easily be funded, reflected a larger question about the professionalization of the GCSC and the influence government support might have. From the beginning, the Liberation Houses had relied on state funding and support in various forms. Rent for the first house, on Edgemont Street, was paid for, in part, through individual government assistance: two of the house members qualified for assistance under the Los Angeles County Juvenile Welfare Program, another under the General Assistance Program. Another house member, a veteran of the ongoing war in Vietnam, qualified for disability. The Los Angeles court system additionally released several young people on probation to the house, with Platania named legal guardian for several minors.[41] By the mid-1970s, GCSC staff also pursued grants specifically for the housing program: in 1975, the Los Angeles County Department of Urban Affairs granted the center nearly $50,000 for the housing program.[42] That increasing collaboration with government agencies mirrored shifts in the GCSC on the whole. As Batza has shown, the GCSC increasingly relied on local, state, and federal grants to grow in its first decade: in 1978, the center was serving over 13,000 people a year with government grants totaling $750,000, including from the US Department of Health.[43]

Nevertheless, the housing program struggled financially almost from the start: many of the Liberation Houses lasted only a short time before they had to be shuttered, only for another to open soon after. By 1977, Fountain House was the only remaining home operated by the GCSC but was barely paying the rent after the 1975 county grant expired. The GCSC applied for a new grant but, in January 1978, closed the program. Only the Van Ness Recovery House remained in operation.[44]

It was not the end of the homeless youth services in Los Angeles, however: a month later, a similar residential program called Hudson House opened at the corner of Hudson and Yucca, spearheaded by longtime Los Angeles resident and erotic filmmaker Pat Rocco with the help of GCSC cofounder Morris Kight and radical pastor Reverend Bob Humphries. The program was supported by Humphries' religious nonprofit, the United States Mission, but, unlike the GCSC, it depended largely on donations and private fundraising—initially through a "Greasy Guy Contest," where male contestants dressed in the style of the 1950s, with their hair slicked back. As Ian Baldwin has argued, the reliance on private funds was a response, in part, to rising social conservativism as well as California's 1978 "tax revolt," which dramatically curtailed funding for social welfare programs.[45]

Shelter activists in San Francisco similarly struggled to reconcile their radical liberation politics with the need to appeal to the state for funding. That tension played out most vividly in the case of Survival House, the shelter for LGBTQ homeless youth and adults founded by F. E. Mitchell in 1973.

Little is known about Mitchell (fig. 5.4) before he arrived in San Francisco. Born in Pennsylvania in 1945, Mitchell's given name was Florzell, but he mostly went by "Mitch." He attended Porterville College, about 250 miles southeast of San Francisco, performing in a school production of *The Fantasticks* and working on the school yearbook.[46] But by his own account, he did not begin coming out until moving to San Francisco, buoyed by living and working at Emmaus House. The drop-in center/switchboard was run and staffed by volunteers and offered aid in finding food, housing, and jobs, as well as weekly "raps" and "social nights." As Mitchell put it, "These people sacrificed the luxury of privacy in the home and the many weekends that could have meant 'far-out' parties, etc., etc., etc. These people were also working at jobs part time in the interest of keeping the switchboard going. They spent their money on all the costs involved in keeping in existence their switchboard."[47]

Housing was a critical part of Emmaus's work: it provided housing for up to three nights, helping almost 1,100 people in one year. But it did not have the resources to provide long-term shelter and was left referring people to other agencies, which were often not affirming of gay and transgender

FIGURE 5.4. Survival House founder, F. E. Mitchell, at the organization's office, 944 Market Street, Suite 512, San Francisco, 1977. Photograph by Bruce Pavlow. Courtesy of the artist.

identities. To address this need, Emmaus House announced in March 1972 its plans to open a "combination drop-in-center and residence house similar to Los Angeles' Liberation Houses."[48] It would take another year and a half to raise the funds, but in October 1973, it opened "Golden Gate Gay Liberation House" in a previously condemned, three-story house on Page Street in the Lower Haight (fig. 5.5). The house, managed by Mitchell, soon moved around the corner to 758 Haight Street—renamed "Survival House"—and continued to operate there until 1978 (fig. 5.6).[49]

Like the Liberation Houses in Los Angeles, Survival House served a

FIGURE 5.5. Golden Gate Gay Liberation House (also known as Survival House) was founded in 1973 in San Francisco, modeled on the Liberation Houses in Los Angeles. This illustration from an early report (c. 1974) listed the range of services available at the house, including counseling, food, and employment support. Courtesy of the Gay, Lesbian, Bisexual, Transgender Historical Society.

FIGURE 5.6. Survival House moved from 934 Page Street to this Victorian at 758 Haight Street by 1976. It can be seen here in 1977, as photographed by Bruce Pavlow. Courtesy of the artist.

wide range of people, including young runaways, sex workers, veterans, and people on parole or probation. Grant applications from 1977 and 1978 give some further sense of the people served. Nearly half were under the age of twenty-one, with another 30 percent between the ages of twenty-two and forty-four. About 45 percent were white, 33 percent African American, 9 percent Latinx, and 2 percent Asian. Staff also estimated that 40 percent of their clients had drug-related issues, and many were estranged from their families.[50] The majority were cisgender men, but there were also significant numbers of cisgender and transgender women.[51]

Clients could stay for a short time without paying, but after that, they were expected to pay a small amount, either from work or government assistance, toward food and housing. They were also encouraged to participate in house programming, including educational and vocational training, counseling for drug addiction and alcohol dependency, employment and financial assistance, as well as other counseling programs specifically targeted to transgender clients. The average stay was two months, but some stayed six. Mitchell explained,

> What happens is that these are people who run away and they come to San Francisco because this is the place where they're supposed to be able to live free and expressing who they are. . . . But they don't have any money. . . . What we want to do is to . . . offer them the alternative to hustling, shoplifting, dealing dope; you know, whatever the street crimes are that could just wipe them out the rest of the way.[52]

A documentary filmed in 1977, but never widely released, offers remarkable evidence of daily life in Survival House. Bruce Pavlow was a young architecture student at the University of California, Berkeley, taking a new course on gay spaces. For the final project, he visited the house on Haight Street over several months, interviewing, photographing, and videotaping its residents (figs. 5.7 and 5.8).[53] Pavlow captured the residents sitting down for dinner around several communal tables, putting on makeup and doing each other's hair for a night out, watching television, and dancing together.

Some of the residents explained to Pavlow how they came to stay at the house. A young man from Kansas named Tom, for example, had been committed to a mental institution at age fourteen, after setting fire to the home he shared with his sister (his legal guardian). When he was released at age eighteen, he briefly worked at a bookstore in Kansas City, Missouri; he then decided to move to California, where he had previously lived with his uncle. But after two years, working and trying to go back to school, he was evicted from his apartment and wound up, literally, on the street. "I know what it's like to eat out of garbage cans and to bum money from people, and

FIGURE 5.7. Architecture student Bruce Pavlow photographed and filmed residents of Survival House in 1977, as part of a course on gay spaces at University of California, Berkeley. Residents at Survival House, 1977. Photograph by Bruce Pavlow. Courtesy of the artist.

to sleep out in the cold," Tom told Pavlow. The house was not perfect—the food wasn't very good, and disagreements came up among residents—but it was, Tom thought, "basically a good place." A young man named Jonathan, meanwhile, explained how he began sneaking out of his family home to go down to the boardwalk or beach, only to be offered money for sex. He later found an apartment of his own and began doing sex work in a local bathhouse. But many other residents did not offer a clear narrative of how they wound up homeless—they simply needed a place to stay.[54]

Living communally could be difficult, of course. A few of the residents complained about the chaos of the house. Fanny, the one cisgender woman who appears in Pavlow's film, commented that "Survival House" was an appropriate name: the term referred to "survival services," but Fanny explained that the house itself required you to "deal with so many things and people. When you can survive here you can survive anywhere."[55] Another of Pavlow's interviews was interrupted when three of the trans residents of the house began expressing concern about an apparent stranger on their floor—actually a new resident—who they worried might try to steal from them. A few also complained about the logistical difficulties of receiving welfare.

But more residents expressed a sense of connection to the house and a feeling of family. A young man named Attila (fig. 5.9) recalled being referred to the house when he first arrived in San Francisco: "I didn't have

FIGURE 5.8. Resident at Survival House, 1977. Photograph by Bruce Pavlow. Courtesy of the artist.

FIGURE 5.9. Attila (left) had been at Survival House about two weeks at the time of Pavlow's interview. He recalled that he had dropped out of high school after being harassed by other students. Attila with friend at Survival House, 1977. Photograph by Bruce Pavlow. Courtesy of the artist.

any place to stay, I didn't have any money. And I was very lonely too at the time and I needed someone to talk to. And I think it's sort of like this is my family now in a way." A transgender African American resident named Janis (fig. 5.10) explained, "I like helping people, and here at the house there's a lot of things that you wouldn't normally experience, you know, at home or living by yourself. You learn about various peoples' lives, their lifestyle. It helps you understand people better." And another transgender woman named Chesty told Pavlow she didn't mind living with thirty other people. "It's sort of really nice. I like being around a lot of people. It's not like being at home by yourself in your own room. You're out in the open."

For many residents, in fact, the house provided a profound sense of relief. An older resident named Carl read the opening lines from a poem he had written, exploring the sense of isolation he had felt: "Some hearts go hungering through the world and never find the love they seek. Some hearts breathe softly, sigh, and hope that they will be noticed by someone." Against such feelings of isolation, Survival House provided a space to construct a new kind of family, where residents felt accepted and understood, and together transformed shelter into home.

Yet as in Los Angeles, the desire to build a new kind of queer home rested in tension with the need for residents to leave the house and make

FIGURE 5.10. Janis moved to San Francisco from Chicago and had been at Survival House for nine months at the time of Pavlow's interview. Portrait of Janis at Survival House, 1977. Photograph by Bruce Pavlow. Courtesy of the artist.

room for others. Survival House promised family, but as a residence, it could only ever be temporary: residents needed to move out and live on their own. Internal documents and published brochures, in particular, reflect organizers' efforts to socialize residents into the values and performances of productive middle-class citizenship. Grant applications for Survival House explained that the house aimed to "enable a person who is estranged to become aware of himself as a functional member of society," to "develop skills and insight toward taking control of his life," "to live a more productive life-style," to "recognize his own resourcefulness," and to become "a responsible citizen."[56] Similarly, a 1975 grant application for the housing program of the GCSC explained the importance of helping residents find employment: "This helps the residents, most of whom have no marketable skills and low self-image as far as being employable, to have a source of income and thereby break a negative pattern of dependency. This newfound sense of financial independence and accomplishment results in a new sense of self-esteem and positive behavior by the residents."[57] These were justifications for funding and likely reflect organizers' strategic appeals to the values espoused by government agencies as much as their own. They repeatedly attempted to persuade government officials that LGBTQ people qualified as a minority whose needs could not be met by existing agencies. That meant emphasizing outcomes that would be recognized and approved by the state—not communal living, but economic and social independence. That language may have started as strategic, but organizers' alignment with the state would ultimately have a deeper influence.

The shift to a short-term rehabilitation model was also a result of the overwhelming demand. In a 1978 meeting, the newly formed board of Survival House openly discussed the underlying dilemma of the program. If the rogram was going to continue, it could not, in the words of board member Lois Dolan, be "all things for all people."[58] Dolan's involvement with the house stemmed from her work as director of the Sexual Trauma Center of San Francisco, where she advocated for and worked with young victims of sexual abuse. "I think one of the points we need to look at right away," Dolan said, "is do we want to run a sheltered environment type situation, or are we really dedicated to getting people into a comfortable situation in their own life, in other words, where they are living in the community, where they are having their own income, making their own decisions?" As Dolan put it, did they want to create a "nest"—where people would stay—or a "womb"—from which they would emerge to go elsewhere? By the end of 1978, they could no longer do either: despite multiple attempts and multiple letters of support from various city agencies, Survival House's application for federal funds through the San Francisco Employment and Training Council was denied—not, it seems, because the program was poorly designed but because the council did not recognize gay people as a distinct minority group in need.[59]

The emergence and collapse of the Liberation Houses in Los Angeles and San Francisco reflected one of the broader trends of LGBTQ politics in the years after gay liberation. Organizations like the GCSC and Survival House saw the pressing needs of young people who arrived in their cities without funds or stable housing, and these groups increasingly looked to the state to support new LGBTQ-targeted initiatives. They also understood and articulated the link between psychological and material oppression, hoping to create homes that could address both needs—to address the loneliness and alienation of homeless LGBTQ people as a means to help them achieve a new social and material stability. They saw Liberation Houses as transformative spaces. But their efforts were consistently hampered by a relative lack of support: where mainstream organizations like Huckleberry's benefited from ongoing federal funding lines like the Runaway Youth Act, LGBTQ organizations needed to constantly demonstrate the unique, unmet needs of LGBTQ people. The pragmatics of running a long-term social service program, especially an underfunded one, also meant that the programs inevitably struggled to hold onto the radical spirit of communalism that first motivated them.

REMAKING FOSTER CARE

The model of runaway houses was not the only way activists sought to help LGBTQ homeless youth in the 1970s, nor was it the only way they sought to collaborate with the state. Activists also sought to work directly with the foster care system—through both individual foster care and group homes. Yet where Liberation Houses were started by gay and lesbian activist organizations, many LGBTQ foster care placements were initiated by agency social workers. Liberation Houses demonstrated how LGBTQ social service activists might draw on state support and recognition, but foster care programs demonstrated how the state needed LGBTQ social services, too.

From the start of gay liberation, several newly formed gay rights and social service organizations advocated for placing LGBTQ youth with gay and lesbian foster parents. They reasoned that only gay and lesbian parents would understand the difficulties LGBTQ youth encountered. As early as 1970, New York GLF activist Steven Dansky proposed that gay male living collectives adopt homeless gay youth to raise them outside of conventional forms of masculinity.[60] The following year, the GCSC advocated for placing LGBTQ wards of the state with gay and lesbian foster parents, but the deputy county counsel blocked their effort, arguing that placing a homosexual child with a "confirmed homosexual" would in turn "confirm" their homosexuality as well, placing the child at both an emotional and financial disadvantage. The counsel argued that the child might even, upon turning eighteen, sue the state for "causing him to become a confirmed homosexual to his financial and emotional detriment." The counsel concluded, "We do not believe it is a reasonable rehabilitative goal to make a 'well adjusted' homosexual out of ward." As a result of the judgment, affirmed again in 1975, the GCSC could provide housing for LGBTQ youth under eighteen only unofficially and temporarily in Liberation Houses or in private homes.[61]

One of the most vocal leaders for gay and lesbian foster care was the National Gay Task Force, founded in New York in 1973. In 1974, Tom Smith, the director of community services for the Task Force, explained to the *New York Times* that gay foster parents "want to help the child face the same kind of agonizing problems of discrimination and self-image which they had to face." With the love of accepting parents, the young runaway would ideally grow more self-accepting, as Smith put it, "convinced that he is not a freak of nature, but just an ordinary person." The demand, Smith explained, did not come from gay men and lesbians seeking to be foster parents. It came, instead, from child service agencies across the country, which found themselves unable to adequately help lesbian and gay youth who had been thrown out of their family homes or bullied out of youth shelters. As Smith explained, "They just don't know what to do with these kids."[62] The Task Force saw the need firsthand. In August 1973, the group received a call from Project Contact, a youth crisis center in New York, requesting help finding shelter for a gay fifteen-year-old who had run away from a homophobic foster home. The following year, Smith toured four of the temporary child residences operated by the New York City Bureau of Child Welfare, only to find that they were ill equipped to work with LGBTQ young people. The director of Jennings Hall, a short-term boys' group home in Brooklyn, for example, asked leaders of the Task Force to visit after one of the residents began "cross-dressing" in women's clothes. The teen reported being harassed by other residents as well as staff. The director, however, rejected the idea of a gay foster home placement, and the teenager later ran away. Seven other residents told the Task Force that they were gay, reporting physical, verbal, and sexual abuse by other residents. At a girls' residence, the Task Force found no evidence of abuse but found that lesbians formed "surrogate family groups"—even though the director claimed there were no lesbians who lived there.[63] By the end of 1974, the Task Force had helped to place thirty-two gay male children in foster homes, twelve with gay male couples, the others with single gay men. Underlying these early efforts was an assumption that children needed modeling and support from a parent of the same assigned sex: the Task Force had received calls about girls as well, but reported that they could not help to place them, as they were unable to recruit any openly lesbian foster parents.[64]

Over the next decade, LGBTQ youth were sporadically placed with lesbian and gay foster parents in counties across the United States. In 1973, for example, the magazine *Chicago Today* reported that the Illinois Department of Children and Family Services had placed several children with gay foster parents. A district office staff member explained the placement plan was "full of problems, but so is the plight of the young homosexual who is virtually barred from a normal placement situation and has been the object of scorn all his life." The placements seem to have been made largely without the foreknowledge of the agency director, who was quick to note that he generally opposed such placements. His major objection—one that many other lawmakers would echo in the years to come—was that teenagers who identified as LGBTQ might still grow out of it, and that gay and lesbian foster parents would encourage them to accept their sexuality as already fixed. As the director put it, "I believe that the social pressure exerted on a youngster that we label as a homosexual, by virtue of such a placement, would be too great to risk unless we are quite sure of a lifelong pattern of such behavior."[65] Media reports document that several other state agencies, including in California, Minnesota, New Jersey, Pennsylvania, and Washington, made similar placements, though it is likely that other agencies did so as well, without media attention.[66] In other cases, gay and lesbian foster parents may have hidden their sexual identities from agencies. As legal historian Marie-Amélie George argues, all these cases demonstrate how social workers in government agencies began to pave an alternative path toward gay and lesbian rights, through the administrative state: agency social workers relied on their own judgment to decide the best interests of the child, often without the oversight or knowledge of officials.[67]

Lesbian and gay foster placements nevertheless could cause controversy when they were discovered or made public. David Sindt, a gay social worker and ordained Presbyterian minister, had arranged at least two placements for gay teens in Chicago. When he presented on gay foster care placements in 1974 at the National Conference on Social Welfare, however, he was accused of breaching case confidentiality, although he had not revealed any client names. He did not lose his job but soon learned that the agency was not allowing him to review potential placements with single men.[68] Sometimes courts themselves intervened: in 1975, Randy Shilts reported in the *Advocate* on the case of a sixteen-year-old boy who was removed from the home of a gay couple by a Washington State court. A local children's agency had already attempted to place the teenager—Shilts gave him the pseudonym Bob—in multiple homes, including with his mother, his father, and two group homes, but in each case, he was rejected because of his sexuality. Fear of "confirming" the teenager's sexuality won out: the biological father, who still refused to take his child in, testified to the court, "If Bob is put in a gay foster home, there isn't too much chance for him to come out straight."[69] There were some cases, however, where courts ruled in favor of gay foster parents: in 1976, activist Bruce Pennington became one of the first gay men licensed as a foster parent in Washington, DC. He wound up caring for a gay teenager, but just weeks before the boy turned eighteen, his birth parents sued for custody. The court ruled Pennington the "superior" parent.[70] By the mid-1980s, some states would enact bans on gay and lesbian foster parents, but during the 1970s, most LGBTQ foster placements were made, and judged, on a case-by-case basis.[71]

A more extensive example of how LGBTQ organizations navigated the foster care system are the programs operated by the Eromin Center in Philadelphia. The center, named Eromin for "erotic minorities," opened in 1973 with the goal of providing affirmative psychological counseling to LGBTQ people and later developed one of the first comprehensive LGBTQ youth programs in the country.[72] In September 1980, the center was approved as a licensed children and youth social service agency and began recruiting gay and lesbian individuals and couples as potential foster parents. Applicants were carefully screened regarding their backgrounds, their reasons for seeking to become foster parents, and their comfort with various potential "foster child behavior," including sexual activity, smoking, drug use, gender-nonconforming dress, and other forms of transgender expression.[73] Eromin hoped that gay foster parents would serve as "role models" for LGBTQ youth and prioritized gay people who accepted their own sexuality. The center also worried about the potential for sexual exploitation: it initially sought to license only couples, believing this would reduce the chances of inappropriate sexual activity, but it did begin licensing single people when recruiting couples proved difficult.

Eromin staff noted they had surprising difficulty recruiting lesbians as foster parents. Tacie Vergara, who headed Eromin's youth programs, thought this might be unique to Philadelphia, but the National Gay Task Force had encountered similar challenges only a few years earlier. It is possible that many lesbians who wished to have children preferred to do so through in-vitro fertilization or adoption rather than the foster system. At the same time, Eromin appears to have received fewer referrals for cisgender girls needing foster care, perhaps because they were more commonly overlooked in their family or group homes or because girls' gender presentations were generally less policed.[74]

That same year, the Eromin Center also initiated a more groundbreaking strategy to help LGBTQ youth: the creation of an LGBTQ group home called Eromin House. The house was initially created in response to an unusual request by the federal Immigration and Naturalization Services (INS). In 1980, Fidel Castro announced that all Cubans who wished to leave the country could do so: within a few months, nearly 125,000 Cuban immigrants arrived in the United States, as part of what became known as the Mariel Boatlift. As Susana Peña and Julio Capó have shown, those numbers included many queer refugees. The Cuban government had long stigmatized and persecuted "effeminate" and "passive" homosexuals who "obviously" transgressed gender and sexual norms. Now the government encouraged their exit as a means of eliminating a population long deemed undesirable. As Peña notes, many of those "undesirables" were likely happy for the opportunity, whether to flee persecution or seek new economic opportunities in the States.[75] At the same time, most of the queer Marielitos (some might today identify as transgender) came without immediate family. In October 1980, INS approached Eromin in the hopes the center could help settle and orient a group of LGBTQ-identified Cuban youth.

The residential program Eromin developed for this group of Cuban youth was initially established in Doylestown, Pennsylvania, but it soon moved to Philadelphia, at 6000 Wayne Avenue, in the rectory of St. Peter's

Episcopal Church in Germantown. The rectory had six bedrooms and the potential to house twelve people. The program was developed in partnership with the Nationalities Service Center, a decades-old organization dedicated to working with immigrants and refugees, and the Pennsylvania Council of Voluntary Child Care Agencies. Alternative group homes for youth in the foster care system began to emerge in the 1970s, often directly out of runaway house programs, with the goal of being run more cooperatively and democratically than traditional foster care facilities.[76] But dedicated LGBTQ group homes within the foster care system were virtually unprecedented.[77] The program notes and case records from Eromin House have since been archived at the Urban Archives at Temple University. Many of these materials are restricted; where information is available about individual residents, I have changed all names to preserve confidentiality.[78]

Most of the Cuban youth were referred to Eromin House because they had identified themselves as homosexual at Fort Indiantown Gap, the army base in Pennsylvania where nearly 5,000 Cuban refugees were initially placed to prepare for resettlement. At Eromin House, the teenagers were enrolled in programs to learn English, took part in counseling and recreational programming, and were instructed in basic life skills including cooking and self-care, to get them ready for independent living once they turned eighteen. The house staff also worked with local businesses to help the residents find jobs. An overview of the program, written by Eromin counselor and social worker Sofia Novoa, indicated that most of the Cuban youth had been harassed by police and placed in forced labor camps or prison while in Cuba. Now in the United States, they "felt lost and neglected by the traditional relief organizations." The first step, Novoa wrote, was to establish a relationship of trust. Yet their integration was also complicated because the US government officially excluded homosexuals from attaining citizenship or permanent resident status.[79]

Available progress and discharge reports for six residents between October 1980 and April 1981 give some sense of both the support Eromin staff provided and the challenges residents posed for them. In general, residents of the house seem to have been well supported in learning language skills and adapting to life in a new country. They shared group meals, attended church, and took trips into Center City. Yet the case records also describe occasional incidents of violence: one resident, for example, was discharged early in the program after two attempts to attack staff members, once with a hammer and broken glass, and soon after, with a broken broom handle.[80]

A more consistent challenge for staff was managing the teenagers' sexual expression. A progress note from January 1981 described one resident as "generally cooperative and pleasant" and reported that he appeared to be doing well in his English classes. He had learned to cook while in Cuba, in both a prison and a restaurant. He also, however, had many scars from "stabbings" and self-harm behaviors of cutting. His major hope was to reunite with a lover who was now in Tennessee, but Eromin recommended against this, interpreting their relationship as "sado-masochistic."[81] Another young refugee, Mateo, was described as "intelligent and well-adjusted" with a "decorator's flair for setting the table"; however, he also appeared to be engaging in "sexual favors" for money during trips into Center City, raising staff concern about arrest.[82]

Gender-nonconforming behaviors were also a major concern for staff. Many of the young people at the house had engaged in "cross-dressing" while in Cuba and continued to do so after arriving in the United States. At Fort Indiantown Gap, the military police officially banned gender-nonconforming dress and makeup, though many of the queer Marielitos did so anyway.[83] It is not clear whether Eromin staff regarded this as a sign of psychological maladjustment or merely an obstacle to integration into the United States. They may also have worried about the safety of the residents from police, straight teenagers, and others. Regardless, they sought to teach the refugees to "contain" such behaviors. One discharge report noted, for example, "The most noticeable improvement was the containing of his cross-dressing behavior after initial clothing was purchased; the cross-dressing was assigned an entertainment or stress value and occurred only in those contexts."[84] Several other notes observed approvingly that a resident's gender-nonconforming dress was now restricted to the house itself; the discharge report for Mateo noted that he appeared to have stopped cross-dressing entirely. While the house hoped to help young people adjust to being gay, staff nevertheless had restrictive ideas about what appropriate gender and sexual expression would look like and were not generally affirming of diverse gender identities.

At the same time, Eromin House staff came into conflict with the Pennsylvania Council of Voluntary Child Care Agencies around child placement following Eromin House. In some cases, residents were placed with family members or, when they turned eighteen, were free to live independently with individual sponsors. But Eromin House director Mark Blair raised particular concern about two youth whom the council recommended be placed with foster care families rather than continue living at Eromin House. Foster care, Blair argued, promoted a "greater degree of dependence" than the current group home. But the greater concern was that foster parents, and the agency that would manage the placements over time, were not prepared to facilitate "normal homosexual development." Blair wrote,

The nurturing of the development of gay youth requires special and additional expertises beyond those required for the nurturing and care of heterosexual or straight youth. These expertises include knowledge of resources for the physical health, mental health, religious wellbeing, and social development of youth. . . . Specially trained counselors are needed who can work with these youth to assure that they continue to view their development as normal and worthy of positive self-concept.

Blair also pointed to challenges in mainstream group homes, where LGBTQ youth were sometimes exposed to physical abuse by other residents. Training was necessary for state agencies, as well as private agencies like the council, to properly care for LGBTQ youth—training that Eromin was uniquely positioned to provide.[85] Blair's note revealed a key premise of the program: that a stable and supportive home life was critical for adolescent development, and for lesbian and gay youth, that was possible only if the home affirmed lesbian and gay identities.

That premise was increasingly shared by other youth agencies. Beginning around March 1981, Eromin House began accepting a new set of referrals—this time from Pennsylvania and New Jersey youth service agencies. The majority of those referrals were for African American teens who had run away or been removed from their family homes—most of them gay male identified, in addition to a small number of lesbians. Some of these young people would likely identify today as transgender. For a few months, these local youth overlapped with Cuban youth at the house, but by April 1981, most of the Cuban youth had transitioned to independent living or been placed in other foster care settings. The Cuban placement program had always been intended as a short-term, transitional intervention. The new referrals from the foster system transformed Eromin House into an ongoing group home, with a new goal of building a sense of family.

Yet, as with the Cuban young people, the activities of the new residents were closely monitored, according to an expansive set of rules—meal times, curfews, weekly therapy, house chores. They were forbidden to have sex in the house (either with other residents or with guests)—though other outlets (that is, masturbation) were encouraged.[86] Later rules stipulated that they were forbidden to engage in sex work, that use of drugs and alcohol was not allowed, and that any physical violence would not be tolerated.[87] Staff kept daily logs on all residents, noting when they were "in a good mood," when they spent most of the day in their rooms, and when they broke the rules. The goal, one brochure explained, was to help residents "become more responsible for directing [their] own lives."[88] Yet the teenagers who lived in the house did not necessarily follow those rules: the house records are full of violation reports—residents bringing others back to their rooms, breaking curfew, cutting school, and fighting with other residents. They registered their objections in their disobedience.

That disobedience was undeniably challenging for the staff. Jeff Keith worked at Eromin House from January to May 1981, when the Cuban residents were beginning to move out and African American residents were beginning to move in. Keith was born in 1945 and spent a year in prison as a conscientious objector during the war in Vietnam. He had also married, had a child, and then divorced, coming out into the Boston GLF in the early 1970s. By the time he arrived at Eromin House, he had received a BA in sociology from University of Pennsylvania and was working on a master's degree in Spanish at Temple University. He wanted to like the job but found fighting between residents, and outbursts against the staff, difficult to manage. At one point, he recalled, a group of residents began throwing fruit and other objects at him while he was sitting in the office; he responded less well than he would have hoped. He wrote in his diary, "I wonder what will become of me, if I'll ever come closer to solving this tension: tension between wanting to hold to a radical vision, and yet being confronted a lot by my inability to deal with crazy, violent, or incomprehensible situations." Keith's diary also described a range of other challenges with residents: one took $100 in grocery money and went to New York; others were arrested for shoplifting or staying out past the city's curfew for minors; and some didn't want to go off to school in the morning. Sometimes, Keith wrote, it felt like he was "trying to bail out the ocean." It is clear from the diary that Keith empathized with the residents and felt attached to many of them, but he had little training, and the work ultimately felt too much for him. In mid-May 1981 he quit, after a particularly long, fourteen-hour shift and an unusually bad altercation with a resident, who threw a bucket of water in his face and then a glass of milk.[89] Keith's work was particularly challenging, as he had no formal role in counseling the residents; his role was largely as a disciplinarian.

Counseling itself presented challenges, too, as Eromin staff worked to navigate and instill norms of gender and sexual expression. Much of the rhetoric and strategies deployed by Eromin House to help their residents would have been typical for group foster homes, but Eromin House was also under greater scrutiny because it housed LGBTQ teens. Gender-nonconforming dress was again a particular point of contention—though not a static one. While Eromin counselors had largely discouraged gender-nonconforming dress with Cuban youth, they appear to have developed a more nuanced approach with local African American youth—understanding drag or gender-nonconforming dress as an acceptable form of self-expression. In the house, residents were allowed to wear makeup and dress in clothing coded female—they were even given a $5-a-week cosmetic allowance—but they could not appear in drag outside. One of the major concerns appears to have been the neighbors. The former church rectory that housed Eromin House was located at the corner of a major intersection in a residential neighborhood. One note shows that one of the ministers at the neighboring church (who rented Eromin the rectory) had received complaints about young people on the porch wearing gender-nonconforming clothes (as well as loud music after midnight).[90] The rules specified, "If residents leave the house cross dressed they will be charged fifty (50) cents an article. If they continue to cross dress the clothing they use for this purpose will be confiscated by the staff. If a resident goes on the street with lipstick or nail polish they forfeit their $5.00 cosmetic money for that week." Yet the rules left in one caveat: "Exceptions will be made for individual treatment plans."[91]

The caveat for treatment suggests an evolving understanding of gender-nonconforming behavior as a potential expression of a core identity. Throughout the 1970s and early 1980s, lesbian and gay social service activists often viewed gender-nonconforming dress as a form of self-stereotyping. In the *Los Angeles Times*, for example, social worker Teresa DeCrescenzo advocated for gay and lesbian foster parents, specifically because they were expected to provide gender-normative role models—otherwise boys might become effeminate and girls masculine. As she put it, "They need models to evolve a personal style.... It's important for them to realize there are successful adult human beings who are gay."[92] Eromin, while still restrictive, seems to have been moving toward developing more open ideas.

One example was its treatment of one of the earliest referrals from the Philadelphia Department of Welfare, a black sixteen-year-old from North Philadelphia. Although the initial treatment plan refers to the teenager by a given male name, all subsequent records, including daily logs and incident reports, refer to the teenager by a female name, Denise—although still using he/him pronouns. Denise's mother had asked that she be removed from their family home by the public welfare office because, the report noted, she "consistently truants school, and runs away." Her mother also had trouble accepting her child's "homosexuality and preference to wear female clothing, particularly because of the influence ... on her three younger children." The treatment plan mirrored the general goals of the program—to help prepare Denise to live independently, to discover personal talents and potential career paths, and to develop greater self-worth. But the treatment plan also listed a more specific goal, "To clarify confusion regarding sexual identity and if indicated, begin process for dealing with gender dysphoria" and "participate in weekly group therapy for transsexuals."[93] Eromin

Center had conducted work with transgender people for several years, but the language of gender dysphoria also reflected the broader psychiatric recognition—albeit pathologized—of transgender identities as distinct from homosexuality: in 1980, the third edition of the APA's *Diagnostic and Statistical Manual* was released, including gender identity disorder for the first time.[94]

What may be most striking about the Eromin House records is that gender and sexuality were rarely the explicit focus. Staff worked to help residents stay in school, to develop better relationships with their parents, and gain greater self-confidence. The house logs from November 1982 about Nina, one of the few cisgender girls in the house, for example, noted that she had gotten into a number of fights with some other girls at school and was since having trouble getting out in the morning. But later in the month, she was mostly in a good mood, especially when she convinced the other house members to do a talent show.[95] Even the house violations rarely had to do with sexuality: one case record documented the recurrent difficulties staff had with Michael, a resident who had particular trouble with school—sometimes getting "out of hand" with his teacher, saying he was too sick to leave in the morning, or putting on makeup. One day, he locked himself in his bedroom and didn't give the key to the house counselors until the following day. Three months later, the counselors wrote up a contract in which Michael promised to abide by the rules and expectations of the program, including seeing a therapist, keeping to curfew, attending school on time, and being respectful to other residents and staff.[96]

In working to provide a supportive space for youth development, Eromin staff drew inevitably upon prevailing conceptions of psychological and social maturity: like Survival House, the goal in all these rules was to help prepare residents for independent living—they could not stay at Eromin House indefinitely. They needed to "mature." Eromin did not see being gay or transgender as a barrier to becoming a productive citizen. In that sense, Eromin created openings to make the child welfare system more humane and accepting for LGBTQ youth. At the same time, the largely middle-class professionals who ran Eromin—and sought the cooperation of the child welfare system—were not prepared to question more basic assumptions about what it meant to be a productive adult. The radical family of Eromin House was intended only as preparation for a less radical, more privatized home—but one where queerness would no longer be a personal obstacle or a challenge to others. The vision was imperfect, and yet it was also an improvement.

The evolution of LGBTQ shelter activism represents a key pivot in LGBTQ mobilizations of home. In the 1950s and 1960s, homophile activists identified the home as a site of adaptation to mainstream ideals, as well as protection from surveillance and violence. By the 1970s, gay liberation groups and lesbian feminists heralded more radical forms of domesticity—most centrally collective living. They specifically rejected the reproductive, heterosexual household and worked to imagine alternatives that would open up new social and sexual possibilities. The first wave of LGBTQ shelter activism derived from a similar, utopian idealism but also pointed to the new directions that LGBTQ activism would take in the late 1970s and 1980s—away from revolution and separatism and toward rights and recognition from the state. Those strategies recalled the early homophile movement's emphasis on integration, yet with a new emphasis on authenticity and self-acceptance. The challenge for spaces like Survival House and Eromin House was to bridge those new ideals of authenticity and self-acceptance with expectations of maturity and adjustment. Those expectations, too, resonated with early homophile rhetoric, only now those ideals were imposed on those most marginalized—queer and trans youth—at the same time that a growing gay and lesbian commercial culture espoused ideals of sexual liberation. Echoing earlier social reform movements aimed at immigrants and "juvenile delinquents," LGBTQ activists took up the mission of helping LGBTQ youth—and in many cases did—but, in allying with the state, they also risked reimposing the normative gender and sexual values of citizenship that home and family were conventionally understood to instill.

The tensions between supporting LGBTQ youth to be themselves and helping them to become independent adults, between creating a new family and preparing young people to live on their own, persist today in social services for LGBTQ homeless youth. One challenge is that until the 2000s, few organizations lasted much longer than a decade, limiting institutional and activist memory. As was often the case, Eromin House shut down in 1983 due to a lack of funding: the city ended a $200,000 contract with Eromin to run the house after administrators for the larger agency were accused of mismanaging the funds and hiding shortfalls. Eromin Center closed in 1984.[97] Many of the best programs today similarly foster a sense of acceptance and belonging for homeless LGBTQ youth, but it is temporary and conditional—the priority remains to help LGBTQ homeless youth attain independent and stable housing. These programs, like their predecessors, have little funding or support to create alternatives—to challenge the fundamental terms of domestic citizenship that failed young people in the first place.[98]

CHAPTER SIX

"Picture a Coalition": Community Caregiving and the Politics of HIV/AIDS at Home

In 1995, Liliana Fasanella was a film student at City College in New York when she learned about a caregiving program for people with HIV/AIDS—the buddy program. Fasanella's friend Mark led a team of volunteer caregivers in Queens. Inspired by their work, she got permission to follow and film the team for her class project. The program was run by GMHC, or Gay Men's Health Crisis, founded in 1982, one of the first organizations in the city to provide social services for people living with HIV. Fasanella thought the film could be used as a potential recruitment tool.[1]

The resulting documentary, *Buddies for Life*, focuses on one buddy pair, Juan, a Latino man living with AIDS, and Alexandra, a young Latina woman (fig. 6.1). At the start of the film, both relayed their initial shock at meeting one another: Juan expected "someone old" and Alex expected someone who looked "really sick." Juan explained to Fasanella, in Spanish, "Yo conocí a Alexandra en el momento más difícil de mi vida. Te digo el momento más difícil porque el no tener casa es un momento muy difícil de hecho." ("I met Alexandra during the most difficult moment of my life. I say 'the most difficult moment' because, really, not having a home is a very difficult situation.") At the time, Juan was living in a downtrodden and roach-infested single-room occupancy building called the Carver Hotel in the South Bronx. Alex helped him to move into a new apartment, with furniture donated to GMHC by a client who had recently died. In one shot, Fasanella depicted Juan looking out the window of his new home, as he reflected in the voice-over, "Yo nunca pensé de que ser voluntario, una persona es ser voluntaria, podría darle tanto amor a una persona que esté infestada. Porque yo de ella . . . yo tengo una familia muy grande y yo creo que ella se interesa más en mí que mi propia familia." ("I never thought that a volunteer, a person being a volunteer, could give so much love to an infected person. Because from her . . . I have a very large family, but I think

FIGURE 6.1. Alexandra was paired with Juan through GMHC's pioneering buddy program, which provided support for people living with HIV/AIDS in New York. Video still from *Buddies for Life: GMHC Volunteers* (1996), directed by Liliana Fasanella. Courtesy of Liliana Fasanella and the New York Public Library.

she cares more about me than my own family.") In another scene, Alex reflected, "I never feel like I'm walking on eggshells or I have to hold something back. Even when I think of Juan, I think of my friend, Juan, I don't think 'Juan who has AIDS.'" The buddy program was intended as a form of social and medical support, but for both Juan and Alex, it also provided a new sense of intimacy and kinship, captured by Fasanella's documentary. In one shot, the camera keeps a tight focus on Alex as Juan opens the door to his apartment, greeting each other with a kiss on the cheek.[2]

Juan and Alex's relationship and Fasanella's film were both emblematic of the ways AIDS activists centered and mobilized domestic space as a key arena in their efforts to combat the virus and the social impact of stigma and isolation. GMHC itself began with a meeting in cofounder Larry Kramer's living room, and many of its earliest initiatives, including a telephone hotline, operated out of volunteers' apartments. The organization began as a fundraising group, to help raise money to support medical research, but within a year it developed into New York City's first major provider of social services for people living with AIDS and a model for other programs throughout the city and nation. Within fifteen years, the organization developed a wide range of programming, including crisis counseling, recreation programs, meal programs, as well as youth education and support, while still creating novel ways to raise funds including the now-annual AIDS Walk.[3] But the programs for which GMHC became best known in the 1980s and early 1990s were not its fundraising, advocacy, or outreach programs but its inreach programs—those programs that reached into people's everyday lives and their homes—spaces and moments less readily visible to a wider public.

The history of the HIV/AIDS epidemic has largely played out in people's homes, yet this domestic history of HIV/AIDS has been overlooked in academic and popular histories. Recent histories of AIDS activism, as well as documentaries, have tended to center the direct action group ACT UP—AIDS Coalition to Unleash Power. Founded in New York in March 1987, ACT UP staged dramatic and deliberately confrontational street protests to demand faster testing and release of potentially life-saving drugs. Divided into semiautonomous groups or "cells," ACT UP New York also drew attention to the need for supportive housing, needle-exchange programs, and safe sex education, as well as the indifference, if not antipathy, of many political and religious leaders. The founding of ACT UP has long been heralded as a major turning point in AIDS organizing, for transforming, in Douglas Crimp's words, mourning into militancy, both in and beyond New York. The group quickly spurred the creation of many more chapters across the United States and internationally, which developed similar tactics and goals. By the early 1990s, ACT UP had reshaped popular discourses, and members were working closely with government agencies and the medical establishment to provide better health care to people living with HIV/AIDS.[4]

The focus on public protest, however, has frequently led scholars to miss the vast array of more private interventions that characterized the everyday lives of people living with HIV/AIDS in the 1980s and 1990s—most centrally, caregiving. Caregiving for people with AIDS has often been regarded in the historical literature on HIV/AIDS as essential but limited in its impact—that is, a site of personalized, individual need and intervention, secondary to more public and communal protest, like that of ACT UP. Sociologist Deborah Gould, for example, in her book *Moving Politics*, argues that activists in organizations like GMHC largely maintained a moderate approach to advocacy that foreclosed anger among lesbian and gay activists and restricted their political power.[5]

In this reading, Gould and other historians have tended to follow the lead of novelist, playwright, and activist Larry Kramer in marking a sharp divide between AIDS service organizations like GMHC and later protest groups like ACT UP—both of which he helped to found. After being ousted from GMHC, Kramer grew increasingly critical of the organization for its emphasis on social services. In his semi-autobiographical play *The Normal Heart*, Kramer's stand-in Ned Weeks derides the GMHC-like group he helped to found: "Now they've decided they only want to take care of patients—crisis counseling, support groups, home attendants . . . I know that's important too. But I thought I was starting with a bunch of Ralph Naders and Green Berets, and the first instant they have to take a stand on a political issue and fight, almost in front of my eyes they turn into a bunch of nurses' aides."[6] Kramer derided caregiving as feminized labor, calling on GMHC to take a more militant approach, but he ignored the impact of GMHC's programs—helping people with AIDS to live longer and better with illnesses related to HIV/AIDS.

The sharp distinction between care and protest also obscures how intertwined these practices actually were: many ACT UP members also acted as caregivers for lovers or friends, and some volunteered or worked for AIDS service organizations like GMHC. Caregiving was not only complementary to protest actions but served as a form of political intervention in its own right, blurring the distinction between the private and public and between home, clinic, and community space. This caregiving had immediate impact on the lives of people affected by HIV/AIDS, but it also had wider impact on the ways LGBTQ activists and HIV/AIDS service providers thought about everyday life and home as arenas of political action.

This chapter reevaluates the politics of care and home during the first two decades of the AIDS epidemic, centering on the inreach programs of GMHC as key examples. I focus here on GMHC because it was both a leader and a lightning rod: many of GMHC's earliest programs were groundbreaking and soon reproduced by other agencies in the city, state, and country. Yet, as the first and largest AIDS service organization in New York, GMHC was also repeatedly criticized, first for its early political and sexual conservatism, later for structural racism within the organization. In 1996, for example, three black board members of GMHC, including Dr. Billy E. Jones, a psychiatrist and former head of the New York City Health and Hospitals Corporation, quit after months of feeling their voices and the needs of their communities were largely unheeded: the organization, for example, had focused its search for new office space in Chelsea, a neighborhood known for its community of gay white men, rather than other boroughs where it would be accessible to more people of color.[7] Yet the structural management of any organization does not always align with its street-level operation. A closer examination of GMHC's inreach programs reveals some of the more complex ways the organization navigated sexual, race, class, and gender diversity.

The buddy program was one of GMHC's first, and longest-run, service programs. Over the life of program, from 1983 to 2005 (and restarted in 2015), the buddy program provided support to hundreds of clients a year. While the responsibilities and tasks of a volunteer buddy varied, home was persistently centered as a critical space of intervention. Many people living with AIDS found themselves unable to handle ordinary domestic tasks like cooking, cleaning, and shopping. More fundamentally, isolation at home was persistently identified as a primary danger for people living with AIDS. The program largely began with gay white male volunteers and clients, but buddy coordinators and volunteers quickly found themselves on the leading edge of GMHC's work with a broader community impacted by HIV/AIDS—people of color, women, and people using intravenous (IV) drugs, some of them LGBTQ-identified but many not. The network of volunteers also grew more diverse, expanding to include more women and more people of color.

Another means by which GMHC reached into people's everyday home lives came later in the 1980s, with the weekly television program *Living With AIDS*. From 1987 to 1995, the program aired regularly on public access networks in the New York City area and worked consistently to highlight the needs of people with AIDS who had been largely ignored in mainstream accounts, women and people of color especially. While GMHC also offered these programs for screening in museums and public health spaces, they understood the potential for television to reach into people's homes as a critical means of supporting people impacted by AIDS as well as educating a broader public. The program team also worked increasingly to bring personal stories of HIV/AIDS to television, documenting everyday home lives and acts of caregiving and self-care. At a time when network television still rarely discussed HIV/AIDS, the show represented diverse caregiving relationships and centered stories of people of color at home, imagining and producing a new queer counterpublic.[8]

The experience, performance, and representation of caring at interpersonal and communal levels helped to counter the feelings of isolation and estrangement that many people living with AIDS experienced and became a vehicle for mobilizing activism across the public-private divide. In her now-classic 1997 essay, "Punks, Bulldaggers, and Welfare Queens," Cathy Cohen called for a redefinition of queer to encompass not only lesbian and gay people but a wider range of sexual and racial minorities who failed to abide by normative models of citizenship.[9] Organizations like GMHC were already working, if imperfectly, to produce this expanded vision of queer community and domestic citizenship that imagined family beyond the white, middle-class, heterosexual norm. GMHC's inreach programs reimagined home not as the private, heterosexual, single-family space that right-wing leaders insisted it was but as a porous constellation of spaces that could link individuals and communities across differences. Moreover, in locating domestic space as a crucial arena of AIDS activism, GMHC enabled activists to cross boundaries in the name of communal responsibility, opening up new forms of coalitional intimacy.

With the term "coalitional intimacy," I mean to capture the particular ways AIDS activism called on participants to embody their politics through a focus on care, kinship, and home. Entering someone's private space physically or through media and art can elicit new affective and emotional forms of relation across conventional identity and community divides. Coalitional intimacy is a feeling of closeness and community across differences, that carries the potential to reorganize how individuals see themselves and each other. I build here on a range of work in queer studies and affect studies, including Deborah Gould's and Ann Cvetkovich's work on the emotion, affect, and trauma in AIDS activism, but I take it in a different direction—out of the streets and into the home.[10] I also build on Lauren Berlant's interrogation of intimacy as forms of attachment that bridge the private and public. As Berlant writes, "intimacy" should be understood as a "public mode of identification and self-development." They ask, "How can we think about the ways attachments make people public, producing transpersonal identities and subjectivities . . . ?"[11] GMHC's semi-institutionalized inreach programs raise similar questions about the significance of both ephemeral and ongoing acts of attachment, situated in the interactions between caregiver and client, videomaker and subject, viewer and viewed.

My thinking about home as a center of AIDS activism has also developed out of my work as curator of the exhibition *AIDS at Home: Art and Everyday Activism*, which appeared at the Museum of the City of New York from May to October 2017. The exhibition brought together art and archival materials documenting the history of HIV/AIDS from the 1980s to the present through the lens of domestic space, centering private acts of care and family making, as well as public activism that prioritized housing. Even as I began speaking with artists and activists to research and identify material for the exhibition, I was struck by the feeling of both loss and invisibility: despite growing efforts by museums and documentary filmmakers to look back at the history of HIV/AIDS, many people felt their more private experiences of the virus, and more private interventions, had largely been forgotten. Photojournalist Lori Grinker's installation *Six Days from Forty* draws on diaries of her conversations with her brother Marc near the end of his life. Artist Frederick Weston's photo collage *Searching and Fearless Moral Inventory* depicts all the boxes of personal belongings he had accumulated over years of unstable housing, finally now able to "spread it out"—each box labeled with an aspect of Weston's life and identity: feisty, faith, flaneur, free-wheeler, SRO, virus. Artist and activist Chloe Dzubilo's drawing *HIV Housing* captures her experiences as a trans woman with HIV living in city-supported housing, facing harassment from neighbors. Photographer and performer Kia LaBeija's *The First Ten Years* pictures her wearing her mother's wedding dress ten years after her mother died.[12]

Once the exhibition was up, I was moved, too, by the ways these stories resonated for people without any direct experience of HIV/AIDS—especially those who had cared for family members or friends who were sick with other illnesses. Caregiving, conventionally understood as the labor of women and people of color, has, in fact, typically been treated in American culture as not "real" work at all, its material and emotional impact rarely recognized. Here, I focus on GMHC's inreach programs as a model of carework—what my friend, artist Eric Rhein, once called a "private practice" of AIDS activism and art.[13]

BUDDY PROGRAMS AND HOME CARE

Although largely forgotten today, buddy programs were among the most widespread and most prominently discussed responses to HIV/AIDS from the earliest years of the epidemic into the early 2000s. The model of the buddy program originated with GMHC in 1983, as a means of providing care for gay men with AIDS who might have limited networks of support. It would ultimately serve thousands of clients and attract hundreds if not thousands of volunteers in New York City. There, and in similar buddy programs across the country, volunteer caregivers were paired with people living with AIDS to visit regularly and help with a range of everyday domestic tasks as well as provide more general emotional support.[14] While AIDS service organizations provided various support programs, buddy programs were unique as a form of support that aimed to enter into and transform individuals' everyday lives and spaces—not as professionals but as peers. Buddy programs remade domestic spaces into spaces of community, and in doing so, challenged the LGBTQ community's conception of its own boundaries.

Home was a critical space of care nearly from the start of the epidemic. Initially, many people with AIDS were kept in hospitals for long-term care, but as understanding, diagnosis, and treatment of HIV/AIDS improved in the 1980s, outpatient care emerged as a preferred mode of treatment, allowing people with AIDS to keep working and living as they had before their diagnoses for as long as possible.[15] Many people with AIDS became homebound as illnesses progressed. At later stages of illness, many people with AIDS and their caregivers preferred hospice care at home, as a way to maintain a sense of dignity, particularly given widespread stigma. For many LGBTQ people, home provided a sense of refuge from the homophobia they might encounter in medical settings. Robert Kilgore, whose lover, Mark Holmes, died from AIDS-related illnesses in 1987, explained that caring for Mark at home "gave us a sense of normalcy, and it gave us a life together." He added, "Being at home gave us a sense of control. Mark was in charge of his own destiny, and I wasn't left feeling helpless on the sidelines."[16] Lovers and friends typically played a central role in providing for everyday care, though parents and siblings sometimes served as care providers as well.[17]

At the same time, home could also become a profound space of isolation for people living with or caring for someone with AIDS. Author and activist Sarah Schulman makes the important point that most gay men living with AIDS were supported by their partners and friends, yet popular depictions have often underrepresented their role and focused instead on cases where lovers and friends abandoned people with AIDS to be cared for by others.[18] At the same time, when this kind of estrangement and abandonment happened, and it sometimes did, it compounded feelings of alienation and invisibility. Joseph Interrante, for example, expressed the sense of isolation that he and his partner, Paul, felt after Paul was diagnosed. "Nothing," he wrote, "made me so angry as what I viewed as rejection by others: the fleeting concern of some friends who visited at first and then disappeared, the empty curiosity of some acquaintances, the frightened turning away by friends from whom I expected acknowledgement and assistance." Interrante understood it was a difficult burden to place on friends, as they navigated their own feelings about illness and death. "For some friends," he reflected, "it was simply too painful to stay through those final weeks."[19]

Even those with a strong support network might still be left at home alone during the day while lovers, friends, and family members were away at work. In 1987, a lesbian police officer who went by the name Hunter posted a series of entries on an early internet bulletin board titled "Survivors." The posts described the challenges faced by her friend and fellow officer Frank and his lover, Serge, who was living with AIDS and largely homebound. Hunter wrote, "Serge is alone at home many nights. Last night, he fell in the bathroom and was unable to get up. He'd had a high fever and went into the bathroom to get sick. He lay on the floor until some strength came to him and he was able to rise. Yet, there are days when Serge doesn't have a fever and will take a long walk and sit and relax and then return home. Then there are the night sweats." Hunter emphasized that Serge was, in many ways, lucky—he still had health insurance, a good doctor, and a lover who cared for him—but everyday life could often be a struggle. For Frank, the emotional challenges of caring for Serge were also made more difficult by the need for opacity at work: after Serge was diagnosed, Frank sought to take a day off work, but he could only say "his roommate was ill." The need for privacy in a culture shaped by stigma against LGBTQ people and people with AIDS only added to the sense of isolation that many people with AIDS and their caregivers felt.[20]

The response of GMHC's buddy program was not to provide professional care but rather flexible, informal, and personal support. The program was initially founded by Rodger McFarlane and Mitchell Cutler, two white gay men with little training as caregivers. McFarlane was a respiratory therapist; Cutler was a rare books dealer who began volunteering for GMHC after one of its early fundraisers. Shortly after GMHC was founded, McFarlane began operating a crisis hotline out of his own apartment. Within a few months, he had received calls from a number of people who wanted to volunteer directly with people with AIDS. McFarlane and Cutler soon arrived at the idea of developing ongoing support relationships. Cutler suggested the term "buddy," emphasizing a less medicalized relationship, a kind of friendship. He began managing the program in 1983, assigning volunteers one or more "buddy clients." By that fall, the number of volunteers had grown large enough that Cutler developed a "team" system—dividing volunteers into groups, scattered throughout New York City. By 1986, there were twelve buddy teams operating in all five boroughs of the city, with more than 100 volunteers.[21]

People sought help from the buddy program for many reasons, but dislocation and disconnection were common themes, as documented in the program's extensive archive at the New York Public Library. One client named Lawrence, for example, was incarcerated at Riker's Island and contacted GMHC for help after his release, so he would not need to depend on his mother.[22] Ron was thirty-three years old, bisexual, and a former user of intravenous drugs: his brother had kicked him out after he was hospitalized, and he moved into supportive housing.[23] Paolo was a middle-aged man who was initially cared for by an ex-lover, but after he was hospitalized for pneumonia, his ex-lover disappeared. Paolo was, by that point, too weak to clean his apartment; he was suffering from wasting syndrome—a common effect of AIDS where people rapidly lose weight.[24] Another client, Joseph, needed help cooking and "getting about." Before being diagnosed, his buddy noted, he was a "very gregarious man," but his friends had "abandoned him and left him pretty much alone basically due to the fact that they are uninformed about AIDS and contagion."[25] A buddy regularly showing up could counter the sense that no one cared and connect the person to a wider community.

A major insight of the program was that providing basic forms of support, such as cooking, cleaning, or grocery shopping, could create openings to provide greater emotional support and broader community connection. The GMHC buddy training guide, published in 1983, introduced a buddy volunteer's responsibilities this way: "1. Provides the PWA [person with AIDS] with a support system to solve the problems of daily life. The Buddy should be flexible and adapt to the situation. 2. Assists with housekeeping and performs tasks such as cooking, cleaning, doing laundry, etc." The manual also encouraged buddies to help clients to take part in social and recreational activities and, at the same time, discourage clients from taking on the role of the "professional patient."[26] The role of the buddy was distinguished from another set of volunteers, known as crisis intervention counselors. Crisis counselors were typically the first contact for GMHC clients and operated more as case workers: assessing medical, social, and financial needs, and referring clients to a range of GMHC supportive services. Buddies developed more sustained and informal relationships, with an emphasis on immediate material support. A typical timesheet from Team 1, from May 1985, lists all of the work the buddies did that month, including cleaning, shopping, helping with medications, business assistance, going out to dinner, helping with meals. One GMHC volunteer reflected to his team, after a year of serving as a buddy, "I think all of us in this room have cleaned up more shit and vomit and washed more laundry and floors and toilets and cooked more meals and bought more groceries; spent more time in hospital rooms and in doctors' offices; and on the telephone; rubbed more backs and held more hands; and offered more shoulders to cry on than we could ever summarize in any Buddy Support Report form."[27]

The records begin to reveal the intimacies and nuances of relationships between many buddies, and the emotional, social, and physical regrowth they could sometimes enable. Another GMHC client, Arni, was a forty-six-year-old man who had a history of heart problems and Hodgkin's lymphoma. Following his diagnosis with AIDS, he had become, in the words of a volunteer, "more of a loner than ever before." He had been in a relationship for nine years, but he and his lover broke up shortly before he was diagnosed. His buddy started by cooking for him, to counter the effects of wasting syndrome, and brought him out of the apartment to watch the gay pride parade. Within a few months, with his buddy's help, he connected with other GMHC services, including a photo workshop and a support group. He also started eating healthier foods, gained eight pounds, and began going out for walks on his own.[28] Transformations like these were common. Buddies served as representatives of a larger community, who enabled people with AIDS to connect or reconnect at moments of illness, despair, and alienation.

The program proved tremendously influential, well beyond New York:

within a decade, similar buddy programs were established in cities and suburbs across the United States, including Atlanta; Baltimore; Boston; Houston; Los Angeles; Louisville, Kentucky; Montgomery, Alabama; Philadelphia; San Diego; and Washington, DC, among many others.[29] In 1988, the National AIDS Network, a resource agency formed by GMHC and four other AIDS service organizations, also released a 120-page booklet outlining how groups could create their own buddy programs, with sections on recruitment, screening, training, and guidelines, as well as sample forms.[30] The model's success reflected the vast need for community-based support services throughout the country.

The social service landscape for people with HIV/AIDS in New York City, in fact, mirrored that of other cities in the United States far more than San Francisco, which was more consistently identified as the national leader. In the 1980s, New York City and San Francisco were the two cities with the highest numbers of people with AIDS in the country—accounting for roughly 40 percent of all cases in the United States. Yet almost from the beginning, New York spent far less on patient services and AIDS education than San Francisco, even though New York had the higher caseload. The response of San Francisco health providers was also more integrated: within the first three years of the epidemic, the city established the AIDS Coordinating Committee, the AIDS Mental Health Task Force, and the first AIDS outpatient center in the United States. By the end of the decade, the city was widely recognized for its model of a "continuum of care." Private AIDS service providers, like the Shanti Project, also received much of their funding from the city: one study in 1984 estimated that San Francisco's three leading AIDS service providers received 52 percent of their revenues from the city, whereas GMHC received only 3 percent from New York. Provisions for home care services were particularly disparate. In San Francisco, the nonprofit agencies Hospice and the Visiting Nurse Association developed specialized AIDS home care programs to provide services from nurses, social workers, and home attendants. In New York, home care and hospice services were far scarcer. As a result, one study estimated that the average hospital stay for a person with AIDS in San Francisco was twelve days; in New York, it was fifty, even though it was already clear that people with AIDS fared better at home and that costs for home care were lower.[31]

Yet San Francisco was an outlier: it was widely acknowledged that San Francisco's fast and well-coordinated response depended on the unusual political power of LGBTQ people in the city. It was also known that while most cases of HIV/AIDS in San Francisco were among white gay men, by the mid-1980s a growing number of cases in New York City were among people of color. The relative lack of political power, both of white gay men and LGBTQ and straight people of color in New York, made it far more challenging for people with AIDS to get the health, housing, and general support services they needed. In these ways, government and medical resources for people with AIDS in New York was far more typical of most cities in the United States in the 1980s.

Buddy programs flourished because they required little funding, could be created anywhere, and could provide for a host of needs with relatively little oversight. Ian Lekus and Stephen Inrig, for example, have shown how the North Carolina Lesbian and Gay Health Project founded a buddy program, modeled on GMHC's, to help people with AIDS who found themselves stigmatized by their families or medical providers; the organization had no paid staff and limited grant support.[32]

The dominant framework for understanding the impact of the buddy program, however, was not social services or activism but friendship and alternative family—especially between gay men. A 1984 story by Art Cohen in Boston's *Gay Community News*, "Creating Family Feelings," looked at two men paired through AIDS Action Committee's buddy program. Cohen explained, "Support work is not a part time or extracurricular activity. It means taking on the responsibilities of a family, a family relationship which can be as powerful, as intense and as totally consuming as any family relationship based on blood."[33] A San Diego buddy named Mark described his relationship with his client, Doug, "I've gained a very close friend and someone that supports me and someone I'm able to support."[34]

Devron Kelly Huber, who was diagnosed with AIDS in May 1985, wrote his own reflections about having a buddy in a column he wrote for two years in the *Orange County Register*. His long-term partner asked him to move out of their house soon after he began developing lesions, but his health stabilized after he joined an experimental drug study at UCLA and enlisted local support services. The AIDS Response Program of Orange County suggested he might want a buddy, but Huber expressed reluctance: "I didn't really need anybody to help out around the house. I usually run my own errands. I drive myself to the doctor." Huber finally conceded, "Emotional support was a possibility." He was paired with local volunteer Glenn Dale, who provided a space for Huber to share feelings he couldn't express with other friends or family. The pair spent one afternoon on the beach, talking about the sense of loss and fear they both felt seeing friends suffer from AIDS-related illnesses, and Huber expressed his faith he could "beat" the disease. He reflected, "That afternoon with Glenn I shared more emotional intimacy than I can remember sharing with anybody. . . . I felt a new vigor, a new commitment to life."[35]

Volunteers, too, often expressed a feeling of personal fulfillment and connection in their work. Glenn Dale wrote his own firsthand account for the *Advocate* about his experience working as a buddy, titled "Love, Growth, and Friendship." He reflected how one client, Ken, "taught me so much. Not just factual information, but intimate wisdom—grace under pressure and living as best as one can with one's circumstances. . . . And I asked myself two questions that come up time and again for me as a volunteer: Who is the helper? Who is the helped?" He was even closer with Huber, who Dale wrote "was better at being supportive than 'supported.'"[36]

Indeed, the care work of the buddy program often produced meaningful friendships, but the flexibility of the boundaries between client and volunteer also meant that the relationship produced unique ethical and emotional challenges. Many volunteers, for example, struggled with the quasi-professionalism of the buddy role—whether to understand and treat the buddy relationship as a "real" friendship or not. Many GMHC buddy meeting records emphasize the importance of maintaining some distance when necessary. John Campanella, for example, warned his team to remember that "they are Buddies first and friends (when and if that happens) second. Never compromise your work as an *objective* Buddy by a mutual camaraderie."[37] Another volunteer, Joe Dolce, who joined Buddy Team 7 in 1987, expressed concern about developing "an emotional involvement as a possible friend, and wondered, just how far to get involved. Can you be friends with a PWA?" Another volunteer replied it was easiest "to do your job and keep the lines clear. . . . If however, there *is* a friendship made, if there is a 'payoff' for you, then that's a bonus, and should not necessarily be expected or encouraged." Another volunteer worried that although he and his client had become friends, some tasks might be better fulfilled by other friends and family members. His team concluded that "a balance must be sought between buddies as companions for socialization and being taken for granted as a servant."[38]

Buddies could nevertheless be disappointed when relationships with clients did not develop into friendships. Social work student Michael Williams interviewed fifty-four buddies from Boston's AIDS Action Committee in the mid-1980s, to explore why they chose to volunteer and how volunteering had impacted them. Fourteen participants admitted that they regretted becoming a buddy, typically because of the quality of the relationship. One participant explained, "My first buddy was not someone that I particularly liked and we never became particularly close. My second buddy and I are also quite different and haven't 'bonded' the way I hoped." In a study of buddy relationships in Vancouver, Canada, one participant discussed a client who had died: "I feel funny that I didn't learn to love him to the depth that you hear about with the buddy relationship . . . can't say that you love this guy, he's not your best friend, that you wish that he could be around forever. I don't feel that. . . . I admire things about him. . . . It has to be a real two way thing for a friendship to develop." Another explained about his client, "I don't consider him a close friend that I want to spend a lot of time with for the sake of friendship, but I do enjoy the time we spend together and feel very comfortable within that relationship. . . . It's kind of half way in between [being a volunteer and a friend]."[39]

Burnout was also a major concern of buddy team volunteers and leaders. One month's meeting minutes from GMHC's Team 7, for example, noted, "Buddy Burnout—Beware. Take care of yourself! The commitment GMHC hopes you are making is long term. If you over-exert yourself and burnout with one client, GMHC is potentially losing your much needed help in dealing with future clients."[40] Buddies were advised, essentially, not to overcommit to their clients: at a moment when most people died from illnesses related to AIDS, buddies needed to save their energy with one client so they could be prepared for the next. The extent of need also typically meant that volunteers had little chance to recover after the death of a client. In another set of meeting minutes, for example, a volunteer named Bruce recounts his last visits before the death of his client, David. The team leader suggested he attend an additional volunteer support group before moving on to discuss Bruce's new client.[41] Buddies also had to cope with team members themselves getting diagnosed, growing sick, and dying from illnesses related to AIDS.

A more complex view of the buddy program emerged in the 1985 movie *Buddies*, the first feature film about HIV/AIDS. The film, directed by Arthur Bressan Jr., follows the friendship of two young men: Robert, who is in the hospital with AIDS-related pneumonia, and David, a volunteer buddy who has been assigned to Robert by a local gay center. The film emphasizes the intimacy of the pairing: Robert and David are essentially the only two characters in the film. Other people, including David's mother and lover, are either heard and unseen or seen and unheard. This cinematic sensory deprivation produces an uneasy sense of alienation that mirrors the increasing isolation and closeness of both Robert and David. Most of the action of the film takes place in Robert's hospital room, but a key emotional turn comes when Robert asks David to retrieve his things from his old apartment—his roommate is too afraid to come to the hospital. David enters the empty living room, light streaming in, to find only a suitcase and a few small boxes, as though Robert has already died (fig. 6.2). David sits at the windowsill and begins to look through Robert's photographs and letters. David soon returns to the hospital and watches Robert's silent home movies of himself on a California beach. The hospital room itself soon

FIGURE 6.2. Arthur J. Bressan Jr.'s 1985 film *Buddies* traced the relationship between a volunteer, David, and his buddy, Robert. In this key scene, David visits Robert's apartment to gather photographs and other belongings left behind by Robert's roommate. Courtesy of the Bressan Project and Frameline.

becomes more domestic—David leaves his own VCR for Robert to use and hangs pictures on the wall. David writes in his diary, narrated in voice-over, about the unexpected evolution of his relationship with Robert: "I started out in this buddy thing with reservations. I didn't even like Robert. I almost quit. And now I'm hopelessly lost in his world, that room, and all his dreams and hopes and memories. . . . I've never thought about dying, and now I'm getting attached to a guy who is going to die." The film also included a sexual scene, where David masturbates Robert to orgasm in his hospital bed—an act that most buddy programs would have forbidden. The film represented the program as one essentially defined by boundary crossing—showing how buddy programs created spaces for volunteers and clients to form new kinds of caregiving relationships, not out of preexisting family or friendship ties but a sense of communal responsibility and love.[42]

Volunteers' anxieties about their capacity to connect with and help clients meaningfully took on added urgency as buddy programs began serving a broader population of people impacted by HIV/AIDS—not only white gay men, but also straight and LGBTQ people using IV drugs, women, and people of color. GMHC's buddy programs always served clients who did not fall into their core demographic of white gay men, but client backgrounds began to shift more noticeably in the late 1980s. In 1986, roughly 7 percent of client referrals were people using IV drugs, most of them straight. By 1993, that number had risen to 22 percent.[43] The agency also served increasing numbers of people of color, from 28.5 percent of clients in the year from July 1987 to June 1988, up to 44 percent by 1993. At the same time, the agency served growing numbers of women, who counted for 10 percent of all clients by 1993.[44]

The demographics of the volunteers also slowly shifted, in part through recruitment efforts by GMHC. In 1986, 83 percent of all GMHC staff and volunteers were white gay men, the rest (17 percent) primarily straight women. A later study of volunteers who joined GMHC between December 1988 and February 1990 found that 62 percent were gay men, 28 percent were straight women, 5 percent were straight men, and 4 percent were lesbians. Sixteen percent of volunteers were people of color.[45]

Participation in the buddy program by transgender clients and volunteers is more difficult to determine from the records. GMHC did not list transgender clients in their annual reports until 2000, when they accounted for 0.7 percent of all clients; that number would rise to only 1 percent by 2005, the year the buddy program initially ended. The lack of earlier data likely indicates that GMHC did not begin including transgender identity as an option on intake forms until the late 1990s rather than the absence of transgender clients. It is also possible some clients were not out as trans to staff and volunteers. For the buddy program itself, I was unable to find discussion of transgender clients or volunteers.

GMHC had more extensive involvement with transgender communities in the 1990s through its prevention work with the house ballroom community. The house ballroom community of New York, still thriving today, emerged in the 1970s out of an older tradition of drag balls and competitions: African American and Latinx queer and trans people, beginning with Crystal LaBeija, formed "houses" to provide support to younger queer and trans people of color and to compete together in regular balls. House members do not necessarily live together but function regardless as families, with a designated mother and father. At the balls, each member walks down the runway to compete in a range of fashion categories, ranked by judges on their "realness." In 1990, several GMHC staff members and volunteers formed their own house, the House of Latex, as a form of outreach to the house ballroom community, sharing condoms and information on prevention, and, starting in 1993, hosting their own annual ball.[46]

The expanding demographics of both the clients and volunteers challenged GMHC to redefine the organization, as the population they aimed to serve grew significantly beyond the gay male community they initially sought to help. Buddy volunteers were especially concerned about the increasing number of clients with histories of substance use. Sandi Feinblum, a clinical social worker who became deputy director of client services in the mid-1980s, highlighted the issue in a December 1985 meeting among buddy and crisis counselor team leaders. As the meeting minutes documented, GMHC also had planned trainings for the new year focused on better serving its changing client base. The notes elaborated:

> It was agreed that it is a difficult and terribly complicated issue which goes to the heart of what the organization is about and what its focus is. Concern was expressed that some volunteers would not want to work with straights, or that the priority of the volunteer work should be with gay men and lesbians.... This whole issue of the organization's identity is complicated by a host of social, cultural and political issues, including the fact that the organization receives government monies which means GMHC cannot discriminate in terms of clients.[47]

GMHC essentially could not choose to remain exclusively an LGBTQ organization, but both volunteers and clients were not always prepared to work with others who did not share their identities. Six months later, at another meeting of team leaders, volunteers raised concern about homophobia from straight clients. Feinblum advised, "Without letting the volunteer be psychologically abused by the client, try to identify common interests and issues other than sexuality. Remember that in doing the work we often are effective in changing people's attitudes by example." Feinblum also encouraged empathy and understanding, "Sometimes the hatred and anger may be symbolic; these clients are terrified at their diagnosis and are looking to attribute blame to others."[48] Some gay men were also resistant to working with women, and some women were reluctant to work with men.

Working through these challenges did not take place at the level of GMHC leadership—often volunteers had little contact with the larger organization beyond their team. Rather, volunteers themselves worked through the emotional and material challenges of helping clients who were often quite different from them in their identities and experiences. They sought consultation with other team members and dedicated themselves to connecting with and supporting clients from a wide range of backgrounds. Psychologist J. Brian Cassel argued that two of the strongest motivations for volunteering for GMHC were "helping the gay family" and "joining the AIDS cause."[49] Yet experiences working for the "AIDS cause" also reconfigured conceptions of family and community. Many buddies may have initially volunteered with the goal of helping people like them or like the gay male friends they already had, but the broad impact of AIDS and the expanding client base of GMHC also meant that the buddy program pushed volunteers to form relationships that they did not expect.

This coalitional intimacy can be seen with a closer look at Team 7, in the

East Village—based both on records from the team and documentation by journalist Susan Kuklin, who observed the team for a year.[50] The team was formed in 1986, with about fifteen volunteers by the end of the year. The backgrounds of its members were typical of the larger program. About half of the team members were gay men, the other half straight women. Most were white, though one volunteer, Kachin Fry, had immigrated from Japan, and another, Ernesto Austin, was Puerto Rican. The volunteers were largely employed as artists, actors, writers, stylists, and professionals, and they ranged in age from mid-twenties to fifties. They had been motivated to volunteer with the buddy program for a range of reasons: many had seen friends get sick or die from AIDS-related illnesses; some had been outraged by the prejudice, fear, and homophobia they witnessed. Some gay men in the team also expressed a desire to provide the kind of support they hoped they would receive if they were diagnosed. The team met once a month in one of the co-captain's apartments, and their meetings were loosely organized—team members would review their own clients but also discuss larger issues in working with people with AIDS (figs. 6.3 and 6.4).

The changing buddy client base was an area of ongoing discussion: who

FIGURE 6.3. Photographer Susan Kuklin followed Team 7 in 1987, for a book on the impact of GMHC's buddy program. Here, team members meet for their regular monthly meeting at the home of one of the volunteers to check in about their buddy clients. Susan Kuklin, "Buddy Team 7 Meeting," 1987. Courtesy of the artist.

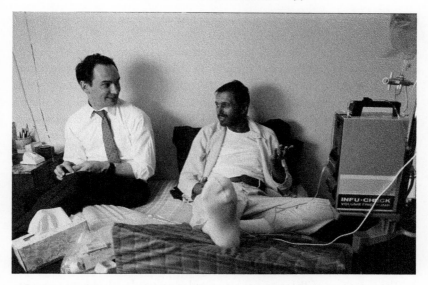

FIGURE 6.4. Ed (left), a member of Buddy Team 7, began working with Steven in May 1986. By fall 1987, he visited every Sunday to have breakfast and help Steven with chores and medication. Susan Kuklin, "Ed and Steven at Steven's Apartment," c. 1987. Courtesy of the artist.

was the program designed to serve, and how could it best help the diverse client population that was emerging? Early on, in August 1986, the group discussed the stereotype of the person with AIDS—"West Village, well-off gay male"—but acknowledged that this did not reflect all gay men or all the people that GMHC served. Six months later, the group discussed rumors that GMHC was planning to change its name, to reduce its emphasis on gay men—rumors that were quickly put to rest.[51]

Gender was a key area of contention. Linda O'Keeffe, a British-born editor, was assigned to help a gay man named Alan, who had lost his vision as a result of AIDS. He was initially resistant to having a woman for a buddy, and then only comfortable allowing her to do housekeeping and shopping. Linda, however, insisted that Alan and his roommate, a former lover named Robert, "deal her in"—at which point, she began to provide more extensive support, including reading to Alan.[52] At one meeting, the group discussed whether women might actually be better care providers for gay men with AIDS, reflecting conventional views of caregiving as women's work. The notes summarized the discussion, "Perhaps, it was offered, women are more nurturing, more 'motherly' in the way in which they handle illnesses. Perhaps gay men are less threatened by women, since they don't represent sexual threats. Or perhaps the daily sights of a healthy 'together' man can cause a PWA lots of resentment." It was agreed, regardless, that more women volunteers were needed.[53]

Volunteers also came to a general consensus that working with people who had contracted the virus through IV drug use was completely different from working with others with HIV/AIDS. One buddy advised, "You have to protect yourself from their stories and abuses, as they are frequently experts at pushing the right 'buttons' to con you."[54] Beverly Gray, for example, was assigned to a client named Joan, whom she and other members found "abusive" and "manipulative"—common words in discussion of people with AIDS who had substance dependencies.[55] But some buddy relationships with people who had used or were using IV drugs proved more impactful. In her account of Buddy Team 7, Kuklin shared the story of Dennis, who had previously struggled with substance use. He was assigned Joe Dolce as a buddy and joined Joe's writing workshop at GMHC. Through his writing, Dennis shared his anguish at both the pain he had caused his family as well as the fear his mother now regarded him with.[56]

The members of Team 7 were also regularly paired with clients across racial difference—and were often surprised by the connections they formed. Stuart Patterson, a white man, worked for several months with a forty-eight-year-old gay Latino man named Edwin who lived on the fourth floor of a walk-up and "seemed to have no one to help him." With GMHC's help, he was able to arrange a home care attendant. A few months later, Edwin passed away without a will, and Stuart consoled Edwin's sister. The buddy meeting report form recounted, "Stuart really grew to admire and respect Edwin towards the end. Although they were two extremely different types of people, Edwin taught Stuart a great deal and it was a valuable learning experience for Stuart to go through."[57] Beverly, a white, British-born hairdresser, worked with Manuel, a Puerto Rican gay man who lived with his lover, a flight attendant who was often away during the day. Manuel was too weak to leave home, and Beverly spent every Sunday with him. One evening, over the phone, Manuel explained that he wanted to have "a really outrageous haircut" before he died. She soon arranged for a friend to come over and dye Manuel's hair bright orange and shave it into a mohawk. Beverly told Kuklin, "He gives me a sense of love. It sounds stupid, but I have a very honest love for Manuel. He taught me that I am able to love someone simply because he's a human being, irrespective of anything else."[58]

For some GMHC volunteers, a sense of injustice based on racism, homophobia, and transphobia could be a major motivation for becoming a buddy. Another Team 7 member, Kachin Fry, a young Japanese fashion stylist who had moved to New York in the early 1980s, joined the buddy program in March 1986 because, as she explained in her first meeting, she wanted to get involved. As she later recalled, "I don't like it when society discriminates. We all look different, and we grow up with different beliefs and ideas." She worked with several clients before she was assigned to Juan, a Spanish-speaking client, who lived with his lover, Michael, in the East Village. The meeting minutes from April 1987 summarized their initial meetings: "Juan, who doesn't speak English very well, is shy, depressed, quiet and non-communicative. Michael is the one with whom Kachin can communicate. . . . Michael has been supporting Juan for about ten years now. Juan doesn't work, has no friends, stays home and has no hobbies. Michael, however, is very active; cooks, cleans, does laundry, does all the talking, likes to go out." Juan and Michael became favorites of the team, and many team members chipped in to provide help: team captain Brooke Alderson regularly picked up their laundry to do in her own home. But within a few months, Juan's health deteriorated, and he was hospitalized. Kachin visited the hospital every day after work, but she also called another buddy, a Franciscan nun named Kathleen O'Farrell, to help. After Juan's death, Kachin and Kathleen continued to work with Michael (fig. 6.5). In October, Kachin and Michael went to Washington, DC, to view the AIDS Quilt

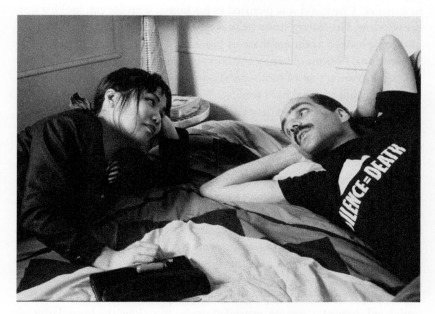

FIGURE 6.5. Kachin, another member of Buddy Team 7, talks with her client, Michael, who is wearing a t-shirt with a pink triangle and the text, "Silence=Death." Susan Kuklin, "Kachin and Michael at Michael's Apartment," 1987. Courtesy of the artist.

the first time it was displayed, including a panel for Juan. Michael, too, died the following year.[59]

By the late 1980s, news coverage of buddy programs in other cities similarly reflected dynamics of cross-identity and cross-cultural intimacy. In December 1987, the *Sunday Boston Herald Magazine* ran a cover story on AIDS Action Committee's buddy program. It began with the story of Maureen McGettigan, a twenty-five-year-old straight white woman who was paired with John Palaza, a thirty-year-old straight white male client who had a history of IV drug use. McGettigan recalled, "I thought I'd be working with a nice gay man or a woman; I never expected to be working with a straight man." The pair nevertheless developed a close relationship: as Palaza told the *Herald*, "A buddy's one thing, but after a while it becomes a friendship. Someone you can call up, that's going to listen to you cry, or listen to you yell, or listen to you talk. Or someone who's going to call you up and ask you how you're doing."[60] Another 1987 article, this one in the *Philadelphia Inquirer*, highlighted buddies for the organization Action AIDS, starting with Anne Greenberg, a forty-four-year-old mother and "one of a growing number of heterosexual women in the city's buddy force." She was paired with David Chickadel, a gay man who had been living with AIDS for four years. Their photo appeared on the cover of the newspaper: Chickadel was pictured in his home, with his cat, looking out the window; Greenberg stood behind him, holding his hand (fig. 6.6). The photograph once again emphasizes home as a space of care but expands conventional notions of family, the cross-gender, cross-generational buddy pairing mirroring that of mother and son. As Chickadel explained, "Anne entered my life at a real hard time. . . . Thomas, my lover, and I would get invited to parties and then disinvited. We lost 99 percent of our friends to AIDS hysteria." Another buddy, a gay white man, described working with a young black man from North Philadelphia: "He asked for a buddy because he wanted a friend. That was my role. I did laundry and cooking, but friendship is beyond that. . . . Most of our time was just sitting together. We met once a week, and it became a friendship in and of itself."[61] Both articles noted that the buddy programs were actively seeking more volunteers from minority backgrounds, to better reach and serve clients of color. At a moment of heightened phobia against people with AIDS, the ability of buddy programs to work across difference was an essential model of caregiving intervention.

The impact of the buddy program ultimately rested on the ways buddies mobilized domestic, private, everyday spaces to redraw the boundaries of care and community. Early media representations of AIDS looked almost exclusively at gay men, and GMHC's buddy program was started with gay

David Chickadel, at home with his buddy Anne Greenberg, says she "got me through some real rough times."

Buddies 'give of their hearts'

FIGURE 6.6. GMHC's buddy program quickly inspired similar support programs across the United States. In July 1987, the *Philadelphia Inquirer* ran a cover story on the Philadelphia AIDS Task Force buddy program, featuring David Chickadel and Anne Greenberg. Photograph by Andy Nelson. © 1987 Philadelphia Inquirer, LLC. All rights reserved. Used under license.

men almost exclusively in mind. But the impact and reach of HIV/AIDS ultimately pushed GMHC—both the organization and its volunteers—to extend their efforts, their empathy, and their identifications as a community. This coalition across difference operated at two scales simultaneously: between clients and volunteers, within an individual buddy relationship, and as a collective community of impacted caregivers, as represented in print and film. Buddies not only provided care; they modeled caregiving as an ordinary and essential act.

HOME VIDEO AND QUEER COUNTERPUBLICS

Video was also a crucial means by which GMHC sought to transform perceptions and experiences of domestic life for people living with AIDS—reframing home not as a site of isolation but one of caretaking and community. *Living With AIDS* was a semi-regular, half-hour-long television news program, produced by GMHC from the late 1980s to the mid-1990s and aired on public access television networks in New York City. The show was one of the first in the country to address directly an AIDS community and featured a wide range of segments, including updates on treatment options; videos on underrepresented communities impacted by AIDS, including women and people using IV drugs; creative public service announcements; and footage from HIV/AIDS conferences and protests. At the time, mainstream news coverage and media representations of people with AIDS were still infrequent and produced implicitly from the perspective of a straight, unaffected majority. *Living With AIDS* altered that media landscape, by not only bringing the voices of an inclusive AIDS community into people's homes, but also frequently representing home life itself. *Living With AIDS* regularly revealed the family bonds mobilized by the AIDS epidemic as well as efforts by people impacted by AIDS to live and help others in spite of illness and loss.

While scholars have previously examined representations of HIV/AIDS in film, documentary, and mainstream news media, little has been written on more localized efforts to represent, discuss, and educate about AIDS through public access television—what by the mid-1980s came to be called alternative television. In the book *AIDS TV*, Alexandra Juhasz documented efforts by activists to mobilize video as a means of educating the general public and health providers about HIV/AIDS, and empowering people with AIDS and caregivers of people with AIDS. Her principal case study was WAVE—Women's AIDS Video Enterprise—a collective of women videomakers that she brought together in New York City. The women in the collective—predominantly women of color, many lesbian or bisexual—learned how to use camcorders and then worked together to create the film *We Care: A Video for Care Providers of People Affected by AIDS*, which was screened at libraries and community centers throughout the country.

At a moment when ACT UP was making headlines for its confrontational protests, *We Care* redefined caregiving as both ordinary—something everyone would do at some point in their lives—and extraordinary, a form of activism in its own right. The video provided guidance and affirmation for people who served as caregivers for people with AIDS and debunked a series of myths about people with AIDS.[62] The core of the film, as Juhasz has recently noted, was her sequence with Marie, an African American mother and grandmother with HIV, whose story I introduced at the start of the book.[63]

But while *We Care* was screened in public or semi-public venues, the videos for *Living With AIDS* were made first and foremost for broadcast into people's homes throughout New York City. In this sense, the show served as an extension of GMHC's work and operated, like the buddy program, to reshape individual experiences and understandings of AIDS in people's everyday lives. At the same time, the show highlighted the importance of home as a space for thinking about illness and activism, both through its broadcast methods and its content.

The lack of scholarly attention to *Living With AIDS* may seem all the more surprising given a rising interest in AIDS video activism in the last twelve years. Roger Hallas's 2009 book, *Reframing Bodies*, for example, includes one chapter on AIDS activist video practice, focusing on two video collectives that emerged in the late 1980s, Testing the Limits and Damned Interfering Video Activists (DIVA) TV. Both collectives may be best known today for documenting demonstrations by ACT UP—videos that have since been used in historical documentaries about ACT UP including *United in Anger* and *How to Survive a Plague*. But while Hallas notes a tendency in writing about HIV/AIDS to take ACT UP as the "'real' beginning of AIDS activism," he acknowledges that his focus on Testing the Limits and DIVA TV largely reiterates this. Hallas also distinguishes these AIDS video activist works from the later "domestic ethnography" of videos like *Silverlake Life: The View from Here*, a 1993 documentary about a gay couple living with HIV in Los Angeles. Hallas, in other words, links activism to public street protest and leaves the domestic aside—and with it other forms of activism and affect.[64] In turning to *Living With AIDS*, I aim to better understand how AIDS videomakers sought to activate domestic space—both as a venue for screening their work and as a site to depict and document the fight against AIDS.

In the 1980s, mainstream news broadcasts periodically featured reports on HIV/AIDS, but *Living With AIDS* was the first television program to provide a regular and dedicated look at the virus. While public access stations originated with cable television in the 1970s, they grew more widely used and watched in the 1980s as cable television became more available. Channel 35 of cable TV provider Manhattan Cable Television, for example, was launched in the 1970s, but it grew both loved and reviled in the 1980s for its late-night programming, much of it pornographic. This included a show featuring "Ugly George," a video maker who went through New York City approaching ordinary young women on the street and asking them to take off their clothes on camera; and *The Robin Byrd Show*, hosted by a former adult movie actress. In 1982, it also became the home of the "Gay Cable Network," founded by Lou Maletta: its programming initially began with *Men & Film*, featuring clips of gay male erotic movies, but quickly expanded into political coverage.[65]

The relative absence of oversight and censorship on public access television also allowed for greater discussion of HIV/AIDS, driven by and directed to the gay community. GMHC identified public access television as a key venue for education and outreach early on. Beginning in 1984, it produced and hosted a regular segment titled "Healthline: Conversations with GMHC" for *Pride and Progress*, the weekly news show of the Gay Cable Network. This was relaunched in 1986 as "Outreach," with slightly better production values. The segments typically paired an interviewer with a GMHC representative or volunteers to talk about a range of GMHC's work and the issues they confronted. Topics included safe sex, volunteering, and the buddy program. The segments were hosted by a progression of GMHC leaders: Federico Gonzalez, GMHC director of education; Diego Lopez, a social worker and director of GMHC's clinical services; and Kevin Mahony, a buddy volunteer who later trained as a social worker. In 1985, GMHC also began producing its own thirty-minute TV talk show, *AIDS Network*, hosted by GMHC's public information director, Lori Behrman. This too largely followed an interview format. In one episode, for example, Behrman interviewed Bill Messina, who led a support group for caregivers of people with AIDS. The close ties to GMHC's clinical, education, and public information programs meant that the programs typically functioned as straightforward educational programming, promotions for GMHC services, or appeals for volunteers.[66]

Living With AIDS was launched two years later and took a different approach, to present original, out-of-the-studio conversations with people living with HIV/AIDS and their advocates. The show was created by Jean Carlomusto, a Queens-born lesbian filmmaker who was completing a master's degree at NYU when she began volunteering for GMHC's educational division. She initially worked part-time on a safe sex video but soon decided to move to GMHC full time as director of its multimedia department. One of her first steps was to convince GMHC to purchase a camcorder, which enabled the group to produce its own content. She also expressly targeted the show to a community of people impacted by AIDS, rather than a "mainstream audience" that imagined people with AIDS as a group of outsiders to be feared or pitied. "So much of the stuff on TV was horrible," Carlomusto explained. "There was a total exclusion of PLWAs [people living with AIDS] in its audience. Instead, everything was reported in terms of a panicked public. I wanted to do a half-hour show devoted to people living with AIDS." For Carlomusto, *Living With AIDS* was a social and political intervention.[67]

The style and segments of *Living With AIDS* often responded directly to mainstream media representations. One early segment, directed by Carlomusto, featured a GMHC Hotline volunteer, Scott Jordan, speaking directly to the camera. The video begins by echoing mainstream media techniques and discourses around AIDS: Jordan is seen in silhouette and says, "When I first found out I had AIDS, my whole world collapsed." But slowly, the lights come up, and Jordan's tone changes from one of defeat to defiance, "Wait a minute, I'm not a bad person. . . . Why should I punish myself, or let others punish me for having an illness? Why should I hide? Why should you hide?"[68] By giving voice to people with AIDS and speaking to a larger AIDS community, *Living With AIDS* aimed to counter phobic media representations.

One of Carlomusto's key collaborators was fellow filmmaker Gregg Bordowitz, who joined her as coproducer in 1988. Bordowitz and Carlomusto first met in March 1987, when they both showed up to the first ACT UP protest at Wall Street with video cameras. Bordowitz had previously been part of the video collective Testing the Limits, which documented various AIDS activist groups in New York; some of that group's footage also appeared on *Living With AIDS*. Like Carlomusto, Bordowitz understood video making as a form of political activism. As Bordowitz wrote in 1988, "We produce a show that can be used as an organizing tool. The cable program is a form of direct action that challenges the ways AIDS has been pictured in the dominant media. On *Living With AIDS*, people with AIDS, ARC [AIDS-related complex], and HIV infection, as well as the people who love and support these people, speak from the point of view of their experience."[69] For Bordowitz and Carlomusto, people impacted by AIDS were the experts.

The approach of the show echoed and drew inspiration from the AIDS self-empowerment movement, spearheaded by the New York-based People With AIDS Coalition. PWAC was formed in 1985 by Michael Callen, a gay musician and activist living with AIDS, along with nine others, to provide a greater sense of community and control to people with AIDS.[70] *Living With AIDS* made its debt to the frameworks of PWAC explicit at the opening of every episode. The title sequence of the show featured a video clip of Max Navarre, another founder of PWAC, speaking at GMHC's 1987 AIDS Walk fundraiser: "I am a person with AIDS. I have a condition which undermines my health, but it doesn't undermine my personhood. I am first and always a person."[71]

Like the buddy program, *Living With AIDS* emphasized ordinary, everyday acts of caretaking and self-care: private acts of support and resilience appeared as personally and politically significant as street protests. In one early video segment, Carlomusto recorded makeup artist Debra Provenzano giving a demonstration on how to use makeup to cover up Kaposi's sarcoma lesions (fig. 6.7).[72] The video was shot at the Living Room, a drop-in center in the basement of PWAC's offices. As the name suggested, the Liv-

FIGURE 6.7. Debra Provenzano and Joey Leonte at the Living Room, a community space operated by the People With AIDS Coalition in Greenwich Village. Video still from "A Kaposi's Sarcoma Makeup Session," directed by Jean Carlomusto for *Living With AIDS*, 1987, produced for GMHC. Courtesy of Jean Carlomusto and GMHC.

ing Room was conspicuously domestic—with a TV, VCR, stereo, fireplace, and a garden—as an early information sheet put it, "a loving, nurturing atmosphere where PWAs and PWArcs can socialize, exchange information, and relax."[73] The makeup session was an important intervention in improving quality of life. As Carlomusto later explained, "The fact that you had these lesions meant that it was going to be hard for you to get a cab. It was going to be hard for you to go into a grocery store. So having a make-up specialist, who was just like any make-up specialist or any good hairdresser— they just put you at ease."[74] Another series of videos highlighted the importance of a healthy diet. In one segment, Frank Abdale, the food services coordinator for GMHC, performed a cooking demonstration in his own kitchen. Another highlighted GMHC's Meals Program, where clients could drop in for lunch or dinner. One volunteer, who had previously been a client, told *Living With AIDS* that the people who ran the program "picked him up" emotionally: "When I first found out, I told my mother I have it, it's like, 'oh, you're not my son.' But here, we're like a big family, we hold each other, we even cry on each other's shoulder every once in a while." By focusing on the everyday, *Living With AIDS* demonstrated continuity between the private and public, and opened conceptions of home and family to connect viewers with a broader supportive community.[75]

From the beginning, Carlomusto and Bordowitz also made it a priority for *Living With AIDS* to represent groups who were underdiscussed in mainstream media, including women, people of color, and people using IV drugs. In 1987, for example, Alexandra Juhasz and Jean Carlomusto directed "Women with AIDS," one of the first documentaries to highlight how women—both straight women and lesbians—were impacted by the virus. Ray Navarro and Catherine Gund directed "Bleach, Teach, and Outreach" to highlight a needle-exchange pilot program. A later episode, "Latino Focus," included video of a performance of Pedro Monge Rafuls's play *Noche de ronda*, about the impact of HIV on a circle of gay Latinx friends.

The show also provided still-rare portrayals of transgender people. In the early 1990s, they filmed a video portrait of Nora Gabriella Molina, a forty-three-year-old Latinx transgender activist and peer counselor at the Gender Identity Project at the city's LGBT Center. Molina, who was HIV positive, called for greater help and understanding for transgender people, "not to be shunned or ridiculed or demeaned." She hoped that appearing in the video would encourage more trans people "to come out, to either get diagnosed or seek out information."[76] In 1990, Carlomusto and Bordowitz also produced a public service announcement featuring transgender African American model Tracey Africa Norman, alongside two dancers from the house ballroom community, Jose Xtravaganza and Aldawna Field. Four year later, African American filmmaker Chas Brack directed another segment focused on the house ballroom community, titled "Having Fun Never Has to End," showcasing the House of Latex's advocacy and outreach.[77]

Most radically, *Living With AIDS* enlisted people with AIDS as experts on their own lives, to talk about their personal experiences: Carlomusto and Bordowitz's early film *PWA Power* featured interviews with a wide range of people with AIDS as a form of self-empowerment.[78] For Bordowitz, it was essential that people living with AIDS, whatever their backgrounds, see and present themselves as united. In a 1987 essay, Bordowitz called on people impacted by AIDS to "proudly identify ourselves as part of a coalition." "Picture a coalition of people," Bordowitz wrote, "refusing to be victims."[79] For Bordowitz, the creation of a social and political coalition could not be separated from its self-representation. "In community television production," Bordowitz reflected, "the ends are the means because new possibilities emerge when the means of production are in the hands of a self-determining group of people representing themselves. A community creates itself as it represents itself."[80] Bordowitz saw coming together across difference as a means to produce new modes of intimacy, and with it, new modes of representation and self-understanding. At the same time, the show resisted defining people with AIDS only in terms of their serostatus: Bordowitz later filmed a series of portraits of people with AIDS at home or work, conspicuously not talking about HIV/AIDS at all.

Surveys from the mid-1990s reflect that the show did indeed draw a broad audience, and many viewers expressly recognized the power of the show to redraw the boundaries of community—to recognize the new cross-cultural, cross-class, and cross-racial coalition that AIDS made necessary. One twenty-four-year-old woman from Queens, who identified as gay and multiracial, wrote that she liked how the series "shows the faces behind the epidemic. It allows people who may not know anyone with AIDS to realize that it can happen to anyone. I also like that it gives visibility to gays/lesbians, by showing that one pain and suffering is no different than anyone else. I think it will help to open some minds." A thirty-year-old straight black woman from Manhattan wrote on her survey, "I just want to thank you for having such a show. It's not easy to ask questions about HIV/AIDS and even harder when you don't know *what* to ask. Your show makes me feel more confident and well informed. Keep it up!" Others specifically emphasized how the show combatted their own sense of isolation. A twenty-two-year-old woman identifying as straight and Latina explained in her survey that her father had been diagnosed with AIDS two years ago. Her favorite thing about watching the show was "not feeling alone, being able to see people experience similar situations that you are going through."[81]

Some gay male viewers objected to the show's broad lens. One fifty-seven-year-old gay white man from Manhattan wrote in his survey, "Although this syndrome knows no bounds—does not discriminate—our society and healthcare agencies DO! Please keep the 'G' in GMHC. Other populations find assistance and care more easily through other venues where help for gay men may still be denied. Please give priority in your agency to those for whom it is named: GAY MEN! Thank you." A sixty-year-old gay white man, also from Manhattan, wrote, "I don't identify with stories of women or former drug addicts but I understand that your program is meant for a wide audience." Another white gay man from Manhattan wrote that he specifically disliked the show's "emphasis on minority community rather than gay community or people with AIDS in general." For some audience members, the show's vision of a diverse AIDS community was a betrayal of what they perceived as GMHC's core mission, to help and speak for gay men. The goals of the producers of *Living With AIDS* were ultimately bigger: *Living With AIDS* mobilized feminist and queer ethics of community, friendship, and family to create a new sense of belonging that embraced gender, sexuality, and racial difference.[82]

Everyday acts of caretaking were, once again, key—nowhere more clearly than in the segments filmed by video artist Juanita Mohammed, now Szczepanski. Szczepanski was raised in Brooklyn and had ambitions from childhood to become a filmmaker. After high school, she enrolled at the School of Visual Arts but found herself isolated—she was one of few students of color in her classes, and one of even fewer working-class students. She eventually dropped out and began working as an inspector for the city's Department of Housing Preservation and Development, which managed affordable housing. During inspections, Szczepanski would often encounter people who were homebound and living with HIV/AIDS. She noted that other inspectors were sometimes disrespectful and insulting. Those experiences motivated her to volunteer with Brooklyn AIDS Task Force, a local service and advocacy group. Through BATF, she also met Alexandra Juhasz, who enlisted her in the WAVE collective. Working with WAVE on *We Care* was a profound turning point in Szczepanski's life, allowing her the opportunity to finally become a filmmaker and the courage to connect with people across the camera.[83]

Szczepanski's position as a black working-class mother from Brooklyn gave her a unique perspective among the staff of *Living With AIDS*. In a recent oral history, Szczepanski remembered seeing many family members in her community in Brooklyn reject children with AIDS. She recalled receiving a call from a friend whose family would not visit him in the hospital. To make matters worse, when she came to visit, she discovered that hospital staff largely avoided contact with him: they posted a sign with the word "AIDS" on the door and would only slide a tray of food into his room. Before her work on AIDS, Szczepanski also had little connection to LGBTQ culture, but while working for GMHC, she entered into her first long-term relationship with a woman: her wife, Evelyn, known as "E," would accompany her on many of her video shoots.[84]

One of Szczepanski's major projects for *Living With AIDS* was a series of videos grouped under the title "Caring," each segment focusing on a different person who was or had acted as a caregiver for someone with AIDS. Szczepanski's commitment to representing a diverse AIDS coalition was clear from the title sequence: as synthesizer music played in the background, a pair of hands, one white, one black, reached toward one another and then clasped (fig. 6.8). By focusing on caregivers rather than people living with AIDS themselves, the series also expanded the reach of the show, to acknowledge the role of caregivers within a larger AIDS community.

Many of the earliest videos were relatively straightforward interviews, but they were shot in the homes of the subjects, contributing to a sense of comfort and intimacy. One early video featured Bruce-Michael Gelbert, a white gay music critic, who was the primary caregiver for his lover, Joe. The video was shot in Gelbert and Joe's backyard, with two flags—a rainbow flag and a Canadian flag—hanging in the background. Gelbert reflected that they needed to slow things down over the last few years, learn to practice safe sex, and manage their anger and despair. He also reflected on the challenges of being a caregiver, "Am I really good for you? Am I really being a good care partner to you? . . . What more can I do? What less can I do? . . . Sometimes Joe feels it very difficult to be in the full glare of my attention."[85]

FIGURE 6.8. The opening graphic for the "Caring" series, directed by Juanita Mohammed Szczepanski for the TV series *Living With AIDS*, featured a pair of hands—one black, one white—reaching out to clasp, an emblem of the show's commitment to building coalitions across difference. Video still from *Living With AIDS*, c. 1992, produced for GMHC. Courtesy of Juanita Szczepanski, GMHC, and the New York Public Library.

Several "Caring" videos focused on mothers who had cared for their sons and daughters. Marilyn Kach had cared for her son, Marcus, at the end of his life. Her video began with an anecdote about her synagogue: "The president of the temple asked me, she said, 'I heard that you have a gay son. What does it feel like to have a gay son?' And I said, what does it feel like to be so stupid as to ask a question like that. And it was then I realized that I didn't need this temple, this was bullshit." She provided a model of an accepting mother: when Marcus came out to her, she told him, "It's what you do in school that's important, not what you do in bed." Her humor and candor were a contrast to popular portrayals of grieving mothers: she proudly recalled how Marcus "lived it up" after he was diagnosed, and how many friends came to his funeral. She also recalled rejecting many of the tenets of the Orthodox Jewish faith she was raised with, including assisting in her son's death by suicide.[86]

Other mothers emphasized the everyday challenges of caregiving, balancing emotional and material support. Florence Rush described becoming a caregiver, both for her son Matthew and his lover, Ron, whose religious family had rejected him. Rush detailed the work of caregiving:

> In addition to the emotional support, in addition to being there . . . letting your child know that you love your child and that you're with your child . . . the caregiving involves that, and it involves hands-on care, which means taking care of

incontinence, cooking, cleaning, laundry, working out a system where you can get, if you're eligible for home health care, for doctors, free medication . . . helping kids work out their income tax, filling out insurance forms when they can hardly hold up their heads.

Szczepanski also interviewed Beverly Rotter, mother of activist Iris De La Cruz. Rotter recalled how Iris came home to live with her and insisted on getting separate plates and towels. "She wouldn't let me touch her, and she wouldn't let me hug her," Rotter told Szczepanski. "She said to me, 'I'm contagious, I'm dirty.'" Soon after, Rotter read more about AIDS and learned it could not be spread through sharing plates or hugging. Still, she recalled, Iris kept her at a distance. "Finally," Rotter recalled, "I put her arm down and I grabbed her and I hugged her and I kissed her. And I said, don't ever do that to me again." Rotter's insistence in the video on holding her daughter was emotionally powerful but it was also educational, refuting popular misconceptions about how AIDS could be transmitted. Both Rush and Rotter also described finding a wider circle of support in groups for mothers of people with AIDS—particularly after the death of their own children. As Rush put it, "I don't have to explain myself. . . . They've become a family to me."[87]

Szczepanski's videos repeatedly represented family as expansive and malleable. One of her best-known segments, "Two Men and a Baby," focuses on a gay African American couple, Ray and Tyrone, who adopted Ray's nephew, Eric, after Ray's sister died from AIDS-related illness (fig. 6.9). Szczepanski first met the couple through her neighbor, Ray's godmother, and proposed putting their story on camera. The film begins by interspersing interview footage with shots of Ray and Tyrone playing with Eric. Szczepanski had seen many families reject children with AIDS, but the film represented a caring community: not only do Ray's and Tyrone's families accept them, but, as Tyrone notes, Eric also has three "gay godfathers" who help to care for him.

The film has the intimacy and candor of a home movie, which masks the art of its construction. The original video files at the New York Public Library include footage that Szczepanski had taken of a social worker with Brooklyn AIDS Task Force who helped Ray and Tyrone to formalize the adoption—though this footage is not included in the final film. If the film skims over the formal, bureaucratic mechanisms by which families are recognized, it does so in service of a larger goal—to make the queer family relatable and ordinary.[88]

Home and family were consistently centered in *Living With AIDS* as a crucial foundation for health. Another of Szczepanski's short films, "Part of Me" (produced with Alisa Lebow), followed Alida "Lilly" Gonzalez, a forty-one-year-old Latina lesbian living with HIV (fig. 6.10). As the video

FIGURE 6.9. One *Living With AIDS* segment, "Two Men and a Baby," followed Ray (left) and Tyrone, who adopted Ray's nephew, Eric, after Ray's sister died from AIDS-related illness. Video still from "Two Men and a Baby," directed by Juanita Mohammed Szczepanski for *Living With AIDS*, 1992, produced for GMHC. Courtesy of Juanita Szczepanski, Jean Carlomusto, and GMHC.

FIGURE 6.10. Alida "Lilly" Gonzalez talks about learning to accept herself and setting up her new apartment, in "Part of Me," directed by Juanita Mohammed Szczepanski for *Living with AIDS*, 1993, produced with Alisa Lebow for GMHC. Courtesy of Juanita Szczepanski, GMHC, and the New York Public Library.

begins, Gonzalez is moving into a new apartment in Queens. As she explains to the camera, "The main thing is I've got a bed, I've got someplace to sleep in. And I've got pots to cook and dishes to eat out of. That's all I needed. The rest will come easy. Oh, and my TV—as long as I've got my TV, that's cool."[89] The film goes on to show Gonzalez with her friends, unpacking and hanging pictures. Home, for Gonzalez, was more than shelter—it provided a sense of stability and the promise of a future. At the same time, Gonzalez's special mention of her television reiterated the potential role of programming like *Living With AIDS*. The television provided a means for GMHC to cross into people's homes and everyday lives, and to bring other people's stories with them.

By the late 1970s, organized gay activism had largely become single-issue, focusing on gay and lesbian rights while recentering experiences and representations of white cisgender men and women. AIDS prompted LGBTQ activists to take on a more coalitional approach—to understand their well-being as bound to the well-being of others. Caregiving programs and videos not only defended the common humanity of people living with AIDS but also expanded the LGBTQ community's conception of its own boundaries—remapping coalitional politics as an everyday, interpersonal process.

In doing so, AIDS activists also remapped the boundaries of domestic citizenship, refusing the conventional norms of the heterosexual, reproductive household and the ways it limited who the state recognized as deserving of care. Instead, they built new modes of kinship and new models of communal belonging, beginning in the spaces of home. Within American culture and politics, domestic citizenship has typically operated as a script, promising recognition for those who followed its rules. But AIDS activists identified domestic citizenship as a practice, too, one whose rules could be rewritten. It was a strategy of domestic remaking, unsettling the restrictions of domestic citizenship to encompass those most marginalized and construct a new public.

EPILOGUE

The Futures of the Queer Home

The undergraduates in my public history course packed into the community room at the John C. Anderson Apartments. The Anderson Apartments are the first apartment development for low-income LGBTQ (and LGBTQ-friendly) elders in Philadelphia. We came that day, on a cloudy morning in April 2019, to conduct informal oral history interviews with a small group of residents. The students sat shyly as residents began to arrive—boisterous, eager to see each other, to welcome us, to talk. I broke the students up into pairs and assigned each pair to a single resident. The room quickly filled with the sounds of their stories. John marched in the 1965 "Annual Reminder," an early gay protest staged on the fourth of July on Philadelphia's Independence Mall; Susan was an early member of Gay Liberation Front and Radicalesbians; Elizabeth came out as transgender in her twenties and appeared in early films by John Waters; Mary and Susan met in a lesbian coming out group. Only a few of the residents knew each other before moving into the apartments, but now, they were a community, spending time together, tending and relaxing in the shared garden and gathering at the nearby William Way LGBT Community Center.[1]

The Anderson Apartments is one of a growing number of affordable housing residences for LGBTQ elders in the United States—a movement that has slowly gained momentum since the 1980s. That effort rests in tension with a more visible form of LGBTQ activism over the last three decades—the movement for same-sex marriage recognition.

Since the 1990s, queer studies scholars have typically been distrustful of domesticity. Building on feminist theory, scholars have critiqued the home as a site of marginalization and constraint, one that singularly reaffirms heterosexist norms. The argument follows that state recognition through normative domesticity, as consolidated in same-sex marriage, may promise LGBTQ inclusion, but only so far as LGBTQ people make themselves legible within dominant cultural frameworks of sexual, romantic, and familial intimacy. The story I have mapped here, however, complicates assessments

of home as necessarily private, unproductive, or apolitical. Rather, looking again at LGBTQ history through the lens of domesticity reveals the
texture of everyday queer lives, and with it the desire for, demands of, and
challenges to cultural belonging. This epilogue reconsiders how and why
LGBTQ activists since the 1980s have come to prioritize the romantic couple as the primary path to cultural inclusion, particularly in the courts; how
that shift was tied to a larger trend of privatization; and how the ongoing
history of LGBTQ homemaking points to the potential for more expansive
models.

INTIMACY AND DOMESTICITY IN THE COURTROOM

Beginning in the 1980s, LGBTQ activists and advocates frequently emphasized the "normal-ness" of LGBTQ people, portraying queer relationships
and the LGBTQ household in increasingly narrow terms: middle class,
conforming to a gender binary, monogamously coupled, and often, if not
always, with children—that is, aligned with conventional American domestic ideals, but for the difference of sexual orientation.[2] The return to
the romantic couple, following the domestic and sexual revolutions of the
1970s, took its most obvious form in the prioritization of same-sex marriage recognition as an LGBTQ rights issue. Domestic partnership legislation has often been upheld as an alternative, but, as Douglas NeJaime has
shown, advocacy for domestic partnership laws in the 1980s and 1990s also
typically reinscribed the primacy of the romantic couple by positioning domestic partnership as "marriage-like."[3]

The prioritization of the romantic couple in LGBTQ legal advocacy is all
the more striking given actual changes to American family life. Since 1970,
the percentage of husband-wife households (with or without children) has
steadily decreased: from 70 percent of all households in 1970, to 55 percent
in 1990, to 48 percent in 2010, while the number of households overall has
increased from 63 million to 96 million. Greater numbers and percentages
of Americans are instead living on their own—including growing numbers
of widows and widowers aging alone. Many others live in single-parent
households or with unmarried domestic partners. Studies also estimate
that roughly 4.5 percent of the population identifies as LGBTQ, with 29
percent of those people raising children. The heterosexual, marital, reproductive household has grown less and less typical of the American home.[4]
Nevertheless, the vision of the romantic couple has continued to hold sway
in popular culture and the law as the surest path to personal happiness and
national belonging.

The return to the romantic couple as the central figure of domestic citizenship was also a strategic move in response to discriminatory legal practices and a broader discourse of "family values" in the 1980s and 1990s, which once again positioned LGBTQ people as outsiders. The value and status of LGBTQ home life has, in fact, been a persistent, if underacknowledged, source of controversy in legal and judicial battles over same-sex sexuality and gender variance since the 1970s. Debates on sodomy laws, rent control and rent stabilization, domestic partnership, child custody, foster care and adoption, and same-sex marriage have all hinged on broader debates not only on the inherent dignity of LGBTQ people but on larger questions about what constitutes a home, a family, and a household.[5] The impact of AIDS in the 1980s and 1990s, in particular, focused attention on the legal ties and barriers facing LGBTQ couples and friends in situations where they were not acknowledged as "family," from hospital visitations to health insurance. Gay men and lesbians also encountered legal obstacles as parents. In the 1970s and 1980s, courts often denied custody or visitation rights to divorced lesbians and gay men, on the grounds that a heterosexual home was better for a child's social and psychological well-being. Transgender parents have faced similar obstacles in child custody cases. Even today, some gay and lesbian couples with children (whether from previous heterosexual relationships, artificial insemination, surrogacy, or adoption) have found they need to pursue "second parent adoption" for both partners to be legally recognized.[6] For LGBTQ activists, appealing to the model of the romantic couple proved the most pragmatic strategy toward securing LGBTQ rights and protections.

That strategy has been most evident in the line of Supreme Court cases taking up sodomy laws and same-sex marriage, beginning with *Bowers v. Hardwick* (1986). Michael Hardwick, an Atlanta bartender, had been arrested in the summer of 1982 for engaging in oral sex with another man in his apartment, a sexual act prohibited by a Georgia state sodomy law. Hardwick's lawyer, Laurence Tribe, working with the American Civil Liberties Union, framed the arrest as an assault on two key values, "the values of intimate association, and of the sanctity of home." Tribe built on two threads of privacy jurisprudence. The first was a line of court decisions that located sexual intimacy within a figurative "zone of privacy," as in the case of birth control, traveling with the person rather than designated to a specific space. The second was a set of decisions recognizing home itself as the most basic and material shield against state intrusion: as Justice Stevens put it in the court's decision in *Payton v. New York* (1980), nowhere was the zone of privacy "more clearly defined than when bounded by the unambiguous physical dimensions of an individual's home." So long as sexual intimacy—gay or straight—was consensual, noncommercial, and confined to the home, Tribe argued, it was beyond the scope of government regulation.[7]

Michael E. Hobbs, the senior assistant attorney general for Georgia, defined the case differently: was there a "fundamental right . . . to engage in consensual private homosexual sodomy"? Hobbs argued that same-sex sexual acts did not fall under culturally legitimated forms of sexual intimacy, nor were homosexual relationships "entitled to heightened sanctuary," as in the case of heterosexual marriage. To find otherwise, Hobbs argued, could lead to a "reordering of our society" and open a "Pandora's box" of challenges against statutes prohibiting polygamy, same-sex marriage, incest, prostitution, and drug use. The court ultimately sided with Hobbs: the home remained a privileged realm, but same-sex sexual intimacy and relationships had no place there.[8]

The *Bowers* case is largely remembered today as a setback in the path toward LGBTQ rights and the legal recognition of same-sex relationships. It would not be until 2003 that the court overturned the *Bowers* decision. But while it failed to convince the court, Tribe's argument was a turning point in the long counterhistory of the queer home. Tribe's argument, that Hardwick should have been protected from arrest based on the "sanctity of the home," recalls the Mattachine Society's early aim, three decades earlier, to "uphold the sanctity of home, church, and state." *Bowers* was the first time such an argument was heard before the Supreme Court. Critically, Tribe did not argue that Georgia's sodomy law was in and of itself unjust, but more narrowly that the home protected Hardwick from its enforcement. Tribe argued for the rights of LGBTQ people under the terms of domestic citizenship. The queer home deserved recognition from the state, if only to stay out of it.

Domestic ideals emerged again in *Lawrence v. Texas*, the 2003 case in which the Supreme Court declared sodomy laws unconstitutional. On the night of September 17, 1998, police entered a two-bedroom apartment on the outskirts of Houston after responding to a phone call claiming there was a black man inside "going crazy" with a gun. No gun was found, but the police arrested the home renter, John Lawrence, a fifty-five-year-old white man, and Tyron Garner, a thirty-one-year-old black man, for allegedly engaging in anal sex. The man who had made the phone call—Garner's forty-year-old white boyfriend Robert Eubanks—was arrested as well, for giving false information to the police. The police report depicted the situation as a "love triangle"—Eubanks had supposedly been jealous of Garner and Lawrence for having sex—but legal scholar Dale Carpenter's investigations into the case cast considerable doubt on this account. Lawrence himself, in a 2011 interview, told Carpenter that he and Garner were not having sex when police arrived, nor had they ever been sexually or romantically involved. Garner and Eubanks, in fact, had a long and troubled relationship—they had met in 1990 and lived together off and on for about eight years. Eubanks was often verbally abusive, and Garner was twice charged with assaulting Eubanks. They were now planning to move into a new apartment together and came over to Lawrence's apartment that night to take some furniture Lawrence was planning to replace.[9]

The team assembled by Lambda Legal to defend Lawrence and Garner nonetheless emphasized what one lawyer called a "mainstream presentation" of the issues, focusing on gay and lesbian couples and families.[10] They emphasized the vital role sexual intimacy—heterosexual or homosexual—can play in committed romantic relationships and within families, specifically within the home. As the team's brief summarized, "For gay men and lesbians, their family life—their intimate associations and the homes in which they nurture those relationships—is every bit as meaningful and important as family life is to heterosexuals," and further, "Gay adults, like their heterosexual counterparts, have vital interests in their intimate relationships, their bodily integrity, and the sanctity of their homes." The legal team defined the stakes broadly, pointing to the increasing number of households headed by same-sex partners (nearly 600,000 according to the 2000 census), and the millions of children with one or more gay or lesbian parent.[11]

That framing was ultimately echoed in the opinion of the court, written by Justice Anthony Kennedy, reversing *Bowers*. As the court put it, anti-sodomy statutes "purport to do no more than prohibit a particular sexual act. Their penalties and purposes, though, have more far-reaching consequences, touching upon the most private human conduct, sexual behavior, and in the most private of places, the home." At the same time, the court understood sexual conduct to be invested with emotional meaning: "When sexuality finds overt expression in intimate conduct with another person, the conduct can be but one element in a personal bond that is more enduring."[12] In their decision, the court sanctified same-sex sexual behavior specifically by tying it to the home. The queer bedroom was no longer the site of deviance but of intimacy and love—deserving of the same treatment as the heterosexual bedroom.

Lesbian and gay rights activists and media outlets like the *Advocate* immediately applauded the decision as a major step forward for gay and lesbian equality.[13] State sodomy laws had their roots in colonial law (and church and English common law before it), covering a range of nonprocreative sexual acts including bestiality and anal sex, regardless of gender. Through the early twentieth century, those laws were rarely enforced, but in the 1950s, sodomy laws were newly mobilized as part of a more sweeping attack on gay men and lesbians. By the 1970s, some states specifically rewrote their sodomy laws to target gay men and lesbians, even as other states removed them. Though still rarely enforced on their own, sodomy laws had what Joseph Landau has called a "ripple effect," providing a rationale for broader forms of discrimination, including denying gay men and lesbians custody of children, refusing employment or promotions, and restricting the discussion of same-sex sexuality and creation of gay student groups in public schools. Striking down sodomy laws, then, both affirmed equal treatment of gay and lesbian relationships in private and dismantled a major mechanism of state oppression.

Still, many queer studies scholars regarded the court's decision in *Lawrence v. Texas* with skepticism. Columbia law professor Katherine Franke read the court's opinion as resuscitating an older form of privacy jurisprudence that privileged private space over personal autonomy. It offered, in Franke's words, a form of "domesticated liberty" that protected and legitimated homebound kinship and romantic ties "while rendering less viable projects that advance nonnormative notions of kinship, intimacy, and sexuality." Franke and other scholars have also pointed to the ways the court's decision overlooked race and class as key factors in determining access to private domestic space and vulnerability to state surveillance and power.[14]

The Lambda Legal team never misrepresented Lawrence and Garner's relationship, but they also chose to shield the men from media inquiry and obscured ambiguities and questions that might have complicated their argument. As Carpenter's research demonstrates, Lawrence and Garner bore little resemblance to the monogamous, middle-class gay couples and families evoked by their legal team, or by the court's opinion. Lawrence had served in the Navy in the 1960s and began renting his two-bedroom apartment in 1978 in a working-class area of Houston. Since the 1980s, he had worked as a hospital lab technician. Two years before the arrest, his partner, Jose Garcia, moved in with him but had recently moved out to care for his ailing brother. Garner, meanwhile, had gotten by on short-term jobs (cook, waiter, dishwasher, housecleaner) and never lived in one place for more than a few months—moving between hotel rooms and the apartments of family members and friends.[15] In masking the details of Lawrence's and Garner's lives, their relationship, and their home lives, the legal team obscured the ways the two men's class status left them more vulnerable to the police than a pair of middle-class white men or women might have been. They also chose not to argue for privacy rights and sexual freedom in broader terms, for all households, and for all individuals, regardless of their romantic and familial status.[16]

Despite its limits, the case provided crucial precedent for future gay and lesbian rights cases: a decade later, the court's decisions in *United States v. Windsor* and *Obergefell v. Hodges* both relied on the *Lawrence* decision to strike down federal and state marriage bans. The decisions, written again by Justice Kennedy, rested on the inherent and equal "dignity" of same-sex relationships in the eyes of the community and the state, with the understanding that legal recognition of those relationships would extend the state's protection. For the court, recognizing the queer home and the sexual acts that took place there became a step toward fully legitimating queer relationships, by folding them into normative constructions of marriage. Failing to recognize those relationships, Kennedy wrote, would "condemn" gay and lesbian people "to live in loneliness."[17]

Critics of the movement for same-sex marriage have long argued that marriage is too normative and too narrow to encompass the range of interpersonal relationships and household forms through which LGBTQ people, and people in general, organize their lives. Legal scholar Melissa Murray, for example, writes that the danger of the *Obergefell* decision is that it legitimates the married couple at the expense of people who are single or in alternative forms of nonmarriage. Indeed, many employers have dropped benefits like health insurance for domestic partners, essentially forcing couples to wed if they want to keep partner benefits. Same-sex marriage could also curtail movement toward more "functional" definitions of family—recognition of households that are "family-like." In the 1980s, for example, New York City courts found that rent stabilization and rent control law should recognize functional family ties—recognizing relationships that operated like families even when individuals were not biologically related or linked by adoption or marriage. Similarly some states have recognized de facto parents in cases of adoption where a couple is unmarried and only one of two parents is legally recognized.[18]

While some queer critics of marriage have argued that romantic relationships and the family should be disentangled from state recognition, most implicitly acknowledge that the state has some place in LGBTQ domestic and family lives, calling instead for the state to recognize still broader forms of kinship.[19] The underlying logic in these claims represents a longer shift in LGBTQ politics, a shift that reformulated the politics of privacy and the home—not as a right to be left alone but a right to be recognized and protected. This shift draws on an underlying principle governing domestic citizenship in the United States—a belief that the state should care about, protect, and regulate its citizens' domestic lives. Yet domestic citizenship has always included by excluding. What is needed is not only a newly expanded model of domestic citizenship but a dynamic and responsive strategy of unsettling, of continual domestic reimagining and remaking.

INCLUSION, EXCLUSION, AND PRIVATIZATION

Since the 1990s, domestic citizenship as a form of cultural membership has gradually expanded to include many LGBTQ people. Yet that recognition has also unfolded against a reprivatization of domestic life and state disinvestment in home and housing. There is a renewed emphasis on performance of normative domesticity, with less promise of support and protection in exchange. The most visible shift in norms and representations of American domesticity has been, on the surface, expanding racial and sexual inclusivity. Studies show that in the last two decades Americans have grown more accepting of interracial marriage and same-gender couples.[20] That has tracked with popular representations, too. The cable network HGTV, for example, regularly features people of color and gay and lesbian couples on their reality shows, all vying to purchase or renovate their homes—an inclusivity that has helped the network to win and maintain a large and diverse viewership. The network scripts a revived model of middle-class single-family homeownership wedded to a post-Clinton multiculturalism where racial and sexual difference are imagined as secondary details rather than obstacles—class status and normative domestic ideals appear to neutralize the racism and homophobia that persist in many neighborhoods and municipalities. HGTV's vision of domestic citizenship reflects the larger ideology of neoliberalism, where citizens and the state look to the market to sort out social prejudice and economic injustice. In reality, portrayals of American home life today, like the programming on HGTV, obscure increasing housing inequality and instability and persistent segregation and discrimination. They also largely leave intact the couple-headed household as the cultural ideal.[21]

This neoliberal faith in the private housing market has gone hand in hand with two other modes of privatization: privatization of care and privatization of security. Melinda Cooper has recently argued that social conservatives and neoliberal policymakers in the 1980s and 1990s found common cause in a return to "family values" and "family responsibility." As cuts were made to welfare and other forms of social insurance, government leaders including Presidents Reagan and Clinton looked to the family and the household to provide care and economic support—essentially reinstating the system of poor laws that predated the New Deal. Clinton's remaking of welfare policy, in particular, sought, as Cooper writes, "to replace public responsibility for the welfare of poor women with a state-enforced system of private family responsibility that actively revived and sometimes created kinship relation *ex nihilo*." That included financing marriage promotion programs and enacting stricter penalties for absent parents who failed to pay child support. Those programs were only expanded under Presidents Bush and Obama.[22] This shift toward a reconsolidation of the heterosexual household, with the father imagined as a major (if no longer the sole) breadwinner, represents not just a return to conventional models of domestic citizenship but a renewed push for policing and enforcement of the familial ideal. Privatization of care, after all, does not necessarily translate into privacy: rather, those receiving government assistance typically face greater surveillance. Since the late 1990s, social welfare programs have, in fact, increased home visits to determine who does and does not deserve government assistance. Privacy, in turn, becomes a reward for performing domesticity correctly.[23]

This increased privatization of home and push for personal and familial "responsibility" have developed in tandem with a heightened security culture. As Elaine Tyler May argues in *Fortress America*, one of the lasting legacies of the Cold War has been "securitization"—a looming fear of danger, coupled with declining faith in the power of the state to provide protection. May points, for example, to the rise of women's self-defense classes, the growth of gated communities, and the development of the private security industry. Joshua Reeves has tracked the rise of neighborhood watch groups since the 1960s, encouraging citizens to be on the lookout for crime in their communities—typically with the cooperation of local police forces. Perhaps the clearest sign of increased securitization of the home is the passage since 2005 of Make My Day and Stand Your Ground laws in at least twenty-five states, giving individuals the right to use lethal force in response to a perceived threat on their own property. As Caroline Light shows, these laws build on the Castle Doctrine tradition in common law, which historically privileged white men—those most likely to own property. Stand Your Ground laws came to national attention in 2013 when George Zimmerman, a neighborhood watch coordinator, shot and killed African American teenager Trayvon Martin, who had been staying in the gated Florida community where Zimmerman lived. Zimmerman was charged with murder but acquitted. This growing securitization of the home and neighborhood has been fed and mirrored by securitization at the national level, with the growth of "homeland security" since 9/11. More recently still, the Trump administration stoked xenophobic fears of "invasion" by immigrants—cast as criminals and rapists—calling for enhanced security at the southern US border and throughout the United States. Undocumented immigrants have lived under heightened threat of deportation since Clinton, but the strategic expansion of home raids by Immigration and Customs Enforcement under the Trump administration mobilized a fascist vision of domestic citizenship, intended to terrorize and destabilize immigrant communities where they live.[24]

The queering of home has in many ways been circumscribed over the last thirty years by this ascendant politics of exclusion, realized through privatization and securitization. The repeal of sodomy laws and recognition of same-sex marriages have brought with them new and widescale recognition of the emotional and social significance of LGBTQ lives, relationships, and homes. At the same time, the dismantling of the welfare state, alongside the empowering of nativist and reactionary political factions, has undermined further efforts to unsettle and expand domestic citizenship in ways so many queer activists have worked for since World War II. Lisa Duggan may be right in her assessment that same-sex marriage has hastened the demobilization and atomization of queer communities.[25] But it is a mistake to conflate marriage, bound to the state, with domesticity. Homemaking, though long devalued, has been and may still be a vital arena for reconceiving queer politics and challenging the boundaries of belonging.

EXPANSIVE MODELS OF DOMESTIC CITIZENSHIP

It has become too easy for historians, queer studies scholars, and activists to assume a teleological narrative, where the arrival of same-sex marriage becomes the sole and inevitable outcome of a decades-long LGBTQ rights movement, necessarily foreclosing alternative domestic forms and other modes of communal and cultural recognition. In fact, one outcome of same-sex marriage recognition appears to be a renewed attention among LGBTQ activists to those whom normative, privatized models of domestic citizenship have necessarily left out—LGBTQ young people without stable housing and LGBTQ elders without family support.

Housing and homelessness had already begun to reemerge as central concerns for queer activists in the late 1980s and 1990s, as awareness grew that many people living with HIV/AIDS in cities like San Francisco and New York were losing their homes. Some people were too sick to go to work, or were fired by employers, and could no longer pay their rent. Some were kicked or pushed out of their apartments after neighbors or a landlord learned they were living with HIV/AIDS. Some were evicted after a partner died because their names were not on the lease and they were not recognized as family. Some were already homeless and living in crowded shelters or neglected SROs.[26] As Sarah Schulman has argued, displacement and deaths in turn sped up gentrification.[27] ACT UP New York's Housing Committee responded by staging a protest in front of Trump Tower on Halloween 1989 (fig. E.1). For ACT UP, Trump Tower was a symbol of injustice: Trump had received $6.2 million in tax abatements to construct his fifty-eight-story skyscraper, while the city provided little funding for dedicated housing for the nearly 10,000 people living with AIDS who were homeless.[28] By 1990, members of the Housing Committee would form Housing Works, to advocate for and provide housing assistance for

FIGURE E.1. Ronny Viggiani borrowed a friend's costume of Dorothy from *The Wizard of Oz* to join a protest by the ACT UP Housing Committee, staged at Trump Tower on Halloween 1989. The protest criticized the city government for its failure to provide housing for people who were homeless and living with HIV/AIDS, even as Donald Trump received generous tax abatements for the construction of Trump Tower. Photograph by Lee Snider, New York, NY, October 31, 1989. Estate of Lee Snider.

people living with HIV/AIDS. In 1997, they opened their first residence, a new model of supportive housing for people living with HIV/AIDS. As of 2021, they operate twelve.[29]

By the late 1980s, there were also renewed efforts to support homeless LGBTQ youth. In 1984, social worker Teresa DeCrescenzo formed Gay and Lesbian Adolescent Social Services (GLASS) in Los Angeles—a group home for homeless LGBTQ teenagers. In 1987, Green Chimneys, a New York City children's service agency founded in 1947, developed housing programs targeted to LGBTQ youth. Other activists formed drop-in centers and shelters for homeless LGBTQ youth—Lambert House in Seattle, founded in 1991; Attic Youth Center in Philadelphia, founded in 1993; the Ruth Ellis Center in Detroit, founded in 1999; and the Ali Forney Center in New York, founded in 2002.[30]

Advocacy and dedicated funding for helping LGBTQ homeless youth have gained new momentum since 2010—in part through an LGBTQ initiative advanced by the federal Department of Housing and Urban Development in 2015 under the Obama administration. Existing drop-in and transitional housing programs for LGBTQ homeless youth in cities like San Francisco, Los Angeles, and New York have expanded, while new dedicated programs have been created in cities including Portland, Oregon; Chicago; Little Rock; Sacramento; and Washington, DC—often with a focus on queer and trans youth of color. Casa Ruby, for example, was founded in 2012 by Latinx trans activist Ruby Corado; the program has since created two transitional living residences for youth between the ages of eighteen and twenty-four, as well as a range of other support services. Their operating funds have come from a mix of private donations and grants, as well as the DC Department of Human Services. Activists in cities including Minneapolis and Philadelphia have also worked to create innovative LGBTQ host home programs, to help young people transition to independent living. Those programs, too, depend on a mix of private donations and grants along with government funding and contracts. These programs recall the early homeless youth services operated by organizations like Survival House in San Francisco but operate today on a much larger scale, with a wider range of services and a greater level of private and government support. Then, as now, however, funding remains precarious and services still only begin to address the actual need.[31]

Affordable housing for LGBTQ elders, while newer, has followed a similar path: grassroots activists and social workers aiming to create new models of care and community by securing a mix of private and government support. Advocacy for LGBTQ seniors first emerged in the late 1970s, with the founding of SAGE—Senior Action in a Gay Environment (now

Services and Advocacy for LGBT Elders). The group launched in 1977 in New York, initially focusing on social services for LGBTQ people who were homebound.[32] Affordable housing for LGBTQ elders, however, has emerged only in the last decade.

The earliest LGBTQ retirement communities were geared to people with the economic resources to purchase homes of their own. One of the earliest efforts came in 1984, when a group in San Francisco created a fund to establish a gay retirement center, using the acronym GALAXY for "Gay and Lesbian Accommodations for the eXperienced in Years." The group lost momentum amid the early HIV/AIDS crisis but identified a demand.[33] By the 1990s, private developers stepped in to build a small number of LGBTQ retirement communities in warm climates. The first was Palms of Manasota in Palmetto, Florida, near Tampa: it opened in the late 1990s and is still in operation today. That was followed by Birds of a Feather and RainbowVision near Santa Fe, New Mexico, and more recently, Stonewall Gardens, an LGBTQ-inclusive assisted living community in Palm Springs, California.

The creation of these communities recognized the desire and need of LGBTQ people to retire and age in accepting communities, pointing to studies showing that LGBTQ people often face discrimination in mainstream retirement communities and nursing homes.[34] They did not, however, aim to take up the economic challenges facing LGBTQ elders: many have not had the job security of straight people of their generation; they may not have family or children to provide support; and many saw their networks of friends, lovers, and partners die in the 1980s and 1990s as a result of HIV/AIDS.

The Anderson Apartments in Philadelphia is part of a new wave of residences specifically built for LGBTQ seniors with limited incomes—with the support of federal, state, and local governments. The project was spearheaded by Mark Segal, an entrepreneurial Philadelphia activist with roots in gay liberation. Raised in a housing project in South Philadelphia, Segal made his way to New York City just before the Stonewall riots and was a founding member of Gay Liberation Front. Segal moved back to Philadelphia a few years later and helped to form a local chapter of the Gay Activists Alliance; in 1975, he created *Philadelphia Gay News*, the city's first LGBTQ newspaper. Segal began seeking funding to open an affordable housing unit for LGBTQ seniors in 2005, recognizing that housing was a growing challenge facing LGBTQ seniors. Over the next nine years, Segal worked to raise funds and support for the project, eventually securing $11 million from Pennsylvania, $6 million from the federal government, and $2 million in low-income federal tax credits. The Anderson Apartments opened in 2014 and was quickly recognized as a national model.[35] The following year,

SAGE started its own elder housing initiative to develop new LGBTQ-friendly affordable housing programs in New York City—one opened in spring 2018 in the Bronx, another opened in Brooklyn in fall 2019. Those developments, too, were government funded, through a mix of city and state support, as well as low-income housing tax credits. Similar projects have also been developed in Boston, Chicago, Houston, Los Angeles, Minneapolis, and San Francisco.[36] All these projects emphasize home as a site of community and belonging—shared space, shared resources, and mutual responsibility.

Home is not only about shelter and stability but also a sense of personal, cultural, and political connection and recognition, from our communities and a larger public. In critiquing domesticity, queer studies scholars risk reifying home's presumed normativity and missing the many ends that home may serve—the normative and the queer, constraint and liberation, isolation and community. The right to the makings and remakings of home—of space, of self, of kinship and community—should be understood as a fundamental component of housing justice.

Early LGBTQ activists of the 1950s looked to the home as a safeguard against state intrusion: they upheld the couple form and the "sanctity of home" as a performance of citizenship. By the 1970s, however, LGBTQ activists increasingly questioned the norms of domestic citizenship—not only the heterosexual, reproductive (and increasingly suburban) home, but also the romantic couple. They worked instead to make space for a wide range of queer domestic forms and increasingly sought government funding to support those forms, even as they wrestled with the constraints. These creative mobilizations of domesticity, like liberation houses and buddy programs, relied on and realized new expressions of care and coalitional intimacy, unsettling social conventions, challenging stigma, and locating new horizons for social and political change.

LGBTQ activists moving forward are unlikely to deemphasize the role of home life in cultural belonging, but they can continue to expand its norms and challenge the boundaries of citizenship itself. A new vision of home and housing can build on the braided legacy of LGBTQ homemaking, recognizing home's normative gravity as well as its potential as a space of radical self-expression and community formation. Domestic citizenship has changed specifically out of the creative tensions produced when outsiders to the home have pressed on its conventions. Making a queerer home means recognizing the material, psychological, and cultural meanings embedded in the everyday practice of homemaking—neither to deny nor reify its power and primacy, but to question and expand its limits.

ACKNOWLEDGMENTS

This is a book about the ways we build a sense of belonging for each other. It should come as no surprise, then, that it has been possible only because of the mentorship, friendship, and family in my own life. I began this project as a graduate student in history of American civilization at Harvard, and my first thanks goes to my dissertation chair, Nancy F. Cott. From the very start, in a first-semester graduate seminar on gender history, Nancy was encouraging of me and my questions about gender, sexuality, and domesticity, even when I was unsure where those questions would take me. She taught me to think as a historian, pushing me to sharpen my analysis, dig deeper into the archive, and complicate my conclusions. In the eight years since I completed my PhD, she has continued to be a trusted mentor, reader, and friend. My two other committee members at Harvard, Robin Bernstein and Glenda Carpio, made me a far better reader of culture and performance and helped me to hold onto my love of theory; the inspiration of their work and their teaching continues to guide me. Margot Canaday joined the committee as an outside reader and has been a constant source of encouragement and feedback in the years since; the model of her scholarship continues to inspire and shape my own efforts to rethink and complicate the stakes of queer histories. I wrote the first draft of what became my chapter on *The Gay Cookbook* in a graduate seminar with Lizabeth Cohen, and I am deeply thankful to her, too, for her careful reading and her enthusiasm for this project from the beginning.

I am very grateful for the funders who supported this project over the last decade. My research and writing were funded by the Charles Warren Center for Studies in American History at Harvard University as well as two postdoctoral fellowships: the Cassius Marcellus Clay Postdoctoral Fellowship in the History of Sexuality at Yale University and the Andrew W. Mellon Postdoctoral Fellowship at the Museum of the City of New York. Extensive travel for research in San Francisco, Los Angeles, Philadelphia, and Ithaca, NY, was supported by a Phil Zwickler Memorial Research

Grant, the Open Gate Foundation of the Harvard Gender and Sexuality Caucus, and the Fund for Lesbian and Gay Studies at Yale University. I thank the Hull Memorial Publication Fund of Cornell University for supporting the publication of the book.

I was honored that this project received early recognition while it was in progress. An article version of chapter 2 was awarded the Crompton-Noll Award by the GL/Q Caucus of the Modern Language Association; a chapter from the dissertation on the interior decorator was awarded the Gregory Sprague Prize by the Committee on LGBT History of the American Historical Association; and an early version of chapter 3 was named best paper or dissertation chapter by a graduate student by the Center for Communal Studies at University of Southern Indiana. The support of these prize committees all came at crucial moments.

This book has also been enriched by conversations with many scholars across disciplines. At Harvard, I was inordinately lucky to share early versions of this work with my friends and fellow travelers, Maggie Gates, Katharine Gerbner, Caitlin Rosenthal, and Tom Wickman, all of whom helped me to hone the project as a graduate student and have continued to support me and this work. I benefited, too, from the friendship, encouragement, and insights of Eitan Kensky, Anna Lvovsky, Sarah Carter, Caitlin DeAngelis, Edward-Michael Dussom, Erin Dwyer, David Francis, Maryam Monalisa Gharavi, Brian Goldstein, Ricky Gonzales, Brian Goodman, Maggie Gram, Jack Hamilton, Jay and Cheryl Harris, Brian Hochman, Rakesh and Stephanie Khurana, Richard Johnston, Ian Lekus, Nancy Lin, Pete L'Official, Brian McCammack, Theresa McCulla, Adam McGee, Tim McGrath, Betsy More, Camille Owens, Eva Payne, Sandy Plácido, Scott Poulson-Bryant, Josie Rodberg, Katherine Stevens, Phyllis Thompson, and Clinton Williams. Joyce Chaplin, Afsaneh Najmabadi, Carol Oja, Werner Sollors, Caroline Light, Steven Biel, and Michael Bronski provided crucial advice and support. I thank, too, Christine McFadden, Arthur Patton-Hock, and Amy Parker.

As a postdoc at Yale, I was given the opportunity to revise and sharpen the manuscript under the guidance of George Chauncey and Joanne Meyerowitz, whose critiques and questions made this a much richer book. This book would not be what it is without George's persistence in pushing for fuller evidence and bolder arguments. A workshop on the full manuscript, with George Chauncey, Joanne Meyerowitz, Regina Kunzel, and Elaine Tyler May, was critical in reshaping the dissertation into a book, encouraging me to broaden the scope of the project. Regina Kunzel has been an ongoing mentor and essential interlocutor since that workshop, encouraging and helping me to articulate what domesticity tells us that is different about queer history and what queer history shows us about the home. I was also deeply fortunate for many long conversations, drinks, and coffee with my fellow fellows—Genevieve Carpio, Dael Norwood, and Rachel Purvis—and a wider community of scholars in the History Department, Women's, Gender, and Sexuality Studies, and the Yale Research Initiative on the History of Sexualities, especially Greta LaFleur, Inderpal Grewal, Kathryn Lofton, Joseph Fischel, Devin McGeehan Muchmore, David Minto, Marie-Amélie George, Joey Plaster, Claudia Calhoun, Lena Eckert-Erdheim, Kate Redburn, Bench Ansfield, Anne Lessy, and David Gary.

My fellowship at the Museum of the City of New York took me in new directions, helping me to hone my voice as a public history scholar. Donald Albrecht was a kind, patient, and passionate teacher as we worked together to curate Gay Gotham, a two-gallery exhibition on New York City's queer creative communities. That experience was fundamental in preparing me to curate an exhibition of my own, AIDS at Home: Art and Everyday Activism, based on an earlier version of the final chapter of this book. My conversations with artists, activists, and other curators helped me to understand the political and emotional stakes of my larger research in new ways and guided me in revising the chapter. I thank deputy director and chief curator Sarah Henry for her faith in the project and in me, and Sarah Seidman, Marissa Martonyi, Nate Lavey, Lilly Tuttle, Becky Laughner, Autumn Nyiri, and Fran Rosenfeld for their friendship, commitment, and collaborations. I also thank MCNY director Whitney Donhauser for her ongoing support, as well as the Mellon Foundation and the Calamus Foundation of New York, along with many others, for funding AIDS at Home. I remain inspired by conversations and collaborations with Ted Kerr, Hugh Ryan, Kia LaBeija, Wanda Hernandez-Parks, LJ Roberts, Susan Kuklin, Lori Grinker, Eric Rhein, Gail Thacker, Rafael Sánchez, Frederick Weston, T De Long, Luna Luis Ortiz, Jean Carlomusto, Maxine Wolfe, Eva Weiss, and, at Visual AIDS, Nelson Santos, Esther McGowan, and Alex Fialho, among many others who contributed to both Gay Gotham and AIDS at Home.

After the MCNY, I spent two years at Bryn Mawr College as a visiting assistant professor, time that was crucial in helping me to integrate and build on my public history work. I thank in particular Sharon Ullman, Janet Shapiro, Madhavi Kale, Carolina Hausmann-Stabile, Monique Scott, Leslie Alexander, Darlyne Bailey, Cindy Sousa, Rosi Song, Anita Kurimay, Colby Gordon, Tamarah Moss, Camilla MacKay, Alex Pfundt, Assef Ashraf, Mary Osirim, and David S. Byers for making Bryn Mawr a home for me and for their encouragement of this work.

I cannot imagine a better place to have completed this project than in the History Department at Cornell University, where I have been an assistant professor since fall 2019. I am deeply grateful for the intellectual generosity and camaraderie of my colleagues. I want to especially thank Tamara Loos, Durba Ghosh, Aaron Sachs, Larry Glickman, Eric Taglia-cozzo, Maria Cristina Garcia, Ed Baptist, Robert Travers, Ray Craib, Derek Chang, TJ Hinrichs, Mostafa Minawi, and Margaret Washington for their mentorship. Durba Ghosh, along with Eric Tagliacozzo, Larry Glickman, and Tamara Loos, helped me to find my footing at Cornell as I worked to complete this book. During a final workshop on the full manuscript, Mar-got Canaday, Robert Self, Durba Ghosh, and Tamara Loos shared gener-ous and generative suggestions that led me to make one last round of revi-sions in summer 2020. Aaron Sachs also read the full manuscript, and his incisive feedback about the book's style and structure reminded me of the careful art in historical writing. I am extremely grateful for ongoing guid-ance and support from Ernesto Bassi Arevalo, Judith Byfield, Peter Dear, Mara Yue Du, Oren Falk, Cristina Florea, Paul Friedland, Sandra Greene, Julilly Kohler-Hausmann, Olga Litvak, Nicholas Mulder, Jon Parmenter, Russell Rickford, Kristin Roebuck, Casey Schmitt, Barry Strauss, Claudia Verhoeven, and Rachel Weil. I also thank Michael Williamson, Georgiana Saroka, Judy Yonkin, Claire Perez, and Barb Donnell.

Beyond the History Department, many other colleagues have made Cornell an inspiring and creative place for my work, especially Brenda Mar-ston, Sara Warner, Lucinda Ramberg, Denise Green, Joan Lubin, Karen Jaime, Austin Bunn, Begüm Adalet, Andrew Campana, Tao Leigh Goffe, Katherine Reagan, Noah Tamarkin, Juno Parreñas, and Derrick Spires.

I have been fortunate to share this work at many conferences, work-shops, and institutions, and to be in conversation with so many scholars whose own work has inspired me and sharpened my thinking. I work-shopped versions of chapters 1 and 3 at two conferences hosted by *Gen-der & History*. I thank participants in those workshops, especially Laurel Thatcher Ulrich, and special issue editors Raffaella Sarti for "Men at Home" and Sarah McDougall and Sarah Pearsall for "Marriage's Global Past." At Cornell, I shared a version of chapter 6 as part of an HIV/AIDS history writing workshop, sponsored by the Central New York Humanities Cor-ridor; I thank Ted Kerr, Tamar Carroll, Benita Roth, Joan Lubin, Daniel Elam, Andrew Campana, and Kwelina Thompson for their questions and suggestions. I shared portions of chapter 6 at the University of Minnesota, and I thank Tracey Deutsch, Martin Manalansan, Elaine Tyler May, and Kevin Murphy. Joanne Meyerowitz invited me back to Yale to present my work on *AIDS at Home*, and I thank her and her students for their clarifying questions and comments. I presented chapter 5 at the University of Bergen in Norway, with many thanks to Tone Hellesund, and at the Wolfe Institute for the Humanities at Brooklyn College, with thanks to Swapna Banerjee. I was grateful to share the earliest version of chapter 4 at a conference in honor of Nancy F. Cott, organized by Ann Braude, George Chauncey, Regina Kunzel, Lori Ginzberg, and Molly Ladd-Taylor. I presented parts of three chapters at the American Studies Association and two at the American Historical Association. I also thank the organizers and participants of the "Queer Places, Practices, and Lives" symposium at Ohio State University and the "Radically Gay" conference at the Center for LGBTQ Studies at the Graduate Center, CUNY.

I spent several summers working on the book at Smith College School for Social Work, where my partner studied and taught. I am grateful to faculty and students there for the opportunity to share this work and for their feedback on an early version of chapter 5. At Bryn Mawr, Sharon Ullman and Janet Shapiro organized a panel where I discussed chapter 5 in conversation with Carrie Jacobs, founder of the Attic Youth Center in Philadelphia. Her comments, along with the discussion of faculty and students, were critical in revising the chapter.

The leaders and members of the Committee on LGBT History of the AHA have been especially important for me as a source of intellectual exchange and solidarity. I thank the committee's past cochairs Emily Hobson, Julio Capó, Nicholas Syrett, Amanda Littauer, Don Romesburg, and Jennifer Brier, as well as AJ Abrams, Rachel Hope Cleves, John D'Emilio, Gill Frank, Alix Genter, Lauren Gutterman, Christina Hanhardt, Kwame Holmes, David Johnson, Will Kuby, Aaron Lecklider, Alison Lefkovitz, Víctor Macías-González, Jen Manion, Kevin Mumford, Anthony Petro, Gabriel Rosenberg, Samantha Rosenthal, Marc Stein, Tim Stewart-Winter, Susan Stryker, and Cookie Woolner.

Many other scholars have also shared feedback, ideas, and encouragement, including Joyce Antler, Marlon Bailey, Morgan Bassichis, Agatha Beins, Joan Berzoff, David Brody, Elspeth Brown, Deborah Cohen, Nicholas de Villiers, Jane Gerhard, Jack Gieseking, Roy Grinker, Tone Hellesund, John Ibson, Holly Jackson, Alexandra Juhasz, Wendy Lee, Serena Mayeri, Patrick McKelvey, Sarah Pearsall, Christopher Rawlins, Hugh Ryan, Kyla Wazana Tompkins, Jeanne Vaccaro, and Jessie Wilkerson. Thank you to Matthew Lasner for sharing sources on an early gay divorce, discussed in chapter 1. My students at Harvard, Yale, New York University, Bryn Mawr, and Cornell have also inspired me with their work and engagement, helping me to stay always attentive to the ongoing resonances of the past.

The research for this book depended on the amazing work of many archives across the United States, and the kindness and patience of many archivists and librarians. I thank Rare and Manuscript Collections at Cornell University, especially Brenda Marston, curator of the Human Sexuality Collection, who I am lucky enough to count now as a colleague and friend; Michael C. Oliveira and Loni Shibuyama at the ONE National Gay and Lesbian Archives at the USC Libraries; Marvin Taylor at Fales Library and Special Collections at New York University; Kate Long and Nichole Calero at the Sophia Smith Collection of Women's History at Smith College; Jason Baumann and the many archivists at Manuscripts and Archives at the New York Public Library; Timothy Young at the Beinecke Library; Brian Meacham at the Yale Film Study Center; Philip Clark and Rob Berger at the Rainbow History Project in Washington, DC; and John Anderies at the John J. Wilcox Jr. Archives at the William Way Center in Philadelphia. In addition, I thank the archivists and librarians at the GLBT Historical Society in San Francisco, the James C. Hormel LGBTQIA Center at the San Francisco Public Library, Archives and Special Collections at Northeastern University, the Special Collections Research Center and Urban Archives at Temple University, the Schlesinger Library at the Radcliffe Institute, the Lesbian Herstory Archives, Archives and Special Collections at University of Connecticut–Storrs, Manuscripts and Archives at the Yale University Library, the Department of Special Collections of Washington University Libraries, and Archives and Special Collections at Amherst College. I am also indebted to Bruce Pavlow and Susan Kuklin for sharing their work and personal collections with me.

Abe Herzog-Arbeitman provided extensive and absolutely essential assistance in conducting research in the Noel Phyllis Birkby Papers in the Sophia Smith Collection. Grace Gallogly generously shared materials from her own research on the Gay Community Services Center in Los Angeles from the ONE Archives. And Carolyn Zola provided important help in obtaining court records from California. Amelia Smith, Dexter Rose, José Hernández, Sarah Jenkins, and Danielle Frank all contributed to a related oral history project I am codirecting with David S. Byers on affirmative LGBTQ psychotherapy, which provided vital context for my research on chapters 5 and 6.

Over the course of writing this book, I have felt impossibly fortunate to speak at length with many people whose stories appear here, many in the context of formal oral history interviews, though some more informally. I thank especially John Knoebel, Steven Dansky, Allen Young, Juanita Mohammed Szczepanski, Bruce Pavlow, Susan Kuklin, Joan Jacobs, Chas Brack, Tommi Avicolli Mecca, Liliana Fasanella, David Hirsch, Allan Warshawsky, Yvonne Fisher, Ron Punit Auerbacher, Chaya Spector, Ned Asta, Zelik Mintz, and Larry Mitchell for entrusting me with their stories. I also thank Ed Miller, senior programs coordinator at the William Way

LGBT Community Center, for coordinating multiple visits and conversations with residents of the John C. Anderson Apartments with the students in my public history courses at Bryn Mawr.

An earlier version of chapter 1 appeared in *Gender & History*, volume 29, no. 3 (2017): 693–715. An earlier version of chapter 2 appeared in *American Quarterly*, volume 65, no. 4 (2013): 877–904. And an earlier version of chapter 3 appeared in *Gender & History*, volume 27, no. 3 (2015): 865–81. I thank the journals for the permission to publish revised versions of those works here, as well as the editors and anonymous readers for their feedback.

At University of Chicago Press, my deep thanks go to the late editor Douglas Mitchell. Douglas emailed me when I was scheduled to present on *The Gay Cookbook* at the American Studies Association as a graduate student and signed the book for the press a year and a half later. His excitement about the project meant a lot to me, and I remain grateful for our conversations and his keen understanding of this project and my hopes for it. Timothy Mennel took over the project when Douglas retired, and I have been grateful, too, for his thoughtful feedback and guidance in taking the book from manuscript to print. The feedback I received from the anonymous readers for the press was enormously insightful and impactful. Thank you also to Susannah Engstrom, Tyler McGaughey, Mark Reschke, and Kyle Wagner at the press, and to copyeditor Lisa Wehrle, proofreaders Natalie Shivers and Dina Theleritis, and indexer June Sawyers.

I will always be indebted to the professors and teachers at Yale who helped me as an undergraduate to begin to see myself as a scholar—Nigel Alderman, Eric Schwab, Jay Winter, Mark Greif, Peter Salovey, Jennifer Baker, and Artemis Christodulou. I thank, too, Blake Eskin, Sara Ivry, and Joanna Rakoff for teaching me so much about writing and editing as a young journalist right out of college. Bryan Lowder and June Thomas of *Slate* were also very encouraging of my publishing popular essays related to this project, and I thank them for their thoughtful edits.

Many other friends have supported me over the years I worked on this project, and I am glad to have a chance to thank them here for both their encouragement and ideas, and sometimes, helping me step away from the book, too. I thank especially Alli Shaloum Brydon, Jonathan Vatner, Morty Rosenbaum, Noah Tamarkin, Juno Parreñas, Jill Constantino, Michael Baran, Noa Wheeler, Nova Cohen-Prohow, Nina Shen Rastogi, Jon Zalben, Peter Terzian, Dan Kitrosser, Danielle Frank, Kris Evans, Christy Tronnier, Kim Webster, Tamarah Moss, and Mary Curry. I regret not having gotten to share this work with Jason Mihalko, who died before the book was completed, but his humor and deep kindness remain with me.

My parents have been my great supporters throughout my life. My father got me my first job as a writer while I was still in high school, as an intern with the *Long Beach Herald*; my mother, without knowing it, instilled in me a love of history, with stories about Long Beach, and the ways it had changed, in the years since she grew up there. I thank them for encouraging me always and giving me space to take risks and go in new directions, too. Karen Byers has been constantly affirming and curious about the project, and especially invested in thinking about the work related to HIV/AIDS. Philip Byers has been encouraging and inspiring in my thinking about the legal histories in this book. My larger family has been a source of joy and much-needed distraction, too. I thank Linda Byers, Jeff and Eileen Vider, Weslie and Craig Surman, Jen and Kevin Hayden, and our nephews and nieces, Sam, Lily, Lilah, Evie, Thomas, and Lydia. As I have gotten older, I have also come to appreciate more how much I gained from my grandmother, Rose Kalish Isenberg, who lived downstairs from us until she died when I was fifteen. In working on this book, I've thought a lot about how the multigenerational, two-family home I grew up in failed to match domestic ideals, and how lucky I was that it did.

My greatest thanks go, without measure, to my partner, David S. Byers. For the last fifteen years, David has been my greatest love and friend. It was David whose encouragement drove me back to graduate school, and David whose support has sustained me since then. This book has lived with us for most of our life together, and it has been shaped in many ways by our relationship and our conversations about history, art, culture, social work, and politics. David has also read every page of writing here multiple times, and his questions, critiques, and suggestions have in every way deepened my thinking and sharpened my prose. David, I am so grateful for the life we have built together and the home in the world you have made for me. This book is undoubtedly for you.

NOTES

INTRODUCTION

1. *We Care: A Video for Care Providers of People Affected by AIDS*, dir. Women's AIDS Video Enterprise, 1990.

2. On production and distribution of *We Care* and history of HIV/AIDS camcorder activism, see Alexandra Juhasz, *AIDS TV: Identity, Community, and Alternative Video* (Durham, NC: Duke University Press, 1995); and Alexandra Juhasz, "A Political Sense of Being at Home with HIV and Video," *Drain Magazine* 13, no. 2 (2016).

3. Alexis Shotwell, "'Women Don't Get AIDS, They Just Die From It': Memory, Classification, and the Campaign to Change the Definition of AIDS," *Hypatia* 29, no. 2 (2014): 509–25.

4. On the history of home and family in the United States after World War II, see especially Elaine Tyler May, *Homeward Bound: American Families in the Cold War Era* (New York: Basic Books, 1988); Joanne Meyerowitz, "Beyond the Feminine Mystique: A Reassessment of Postwar Mass Culture, 1946–1958," *Journal of American History* 79, no. 4 (1993): 1455–82; Barbara Ehrenreich, *The Hearts of Men: American Dreams and the Flight from Commitment* (Garden City, NY: Anchor, 1983); Judith Smith, *Visions of Belonging: Family Stories, Popular Culture, and Postwar Democracy, 1940–1960* (New York: Columbia University Press, 2004); Lynn Spigel, *Make Room for TV: Television and the Family Ideal in Postwar America* (Chicago: University of Chicago Press, 1992); Robert O. Self, *All in the Family: The Realignment of American Democracy Since the 1960s* (New York: Hill and Wang, 2012); Jessica Weiss, *To Have and to Hold: Marriage, the Baby Boom, and Social Change* (Chicago: University of Chicago Press, 2000); and Jane F. Levey, "Imagining the Family in Postwar Popular Culture: The Case of *The Egg and I* and *Cheaper by the Dozen*," *Journal of Women's History* 13, no. 3 (2001): 125–50.

5. Throughout the book, I reference people's sexual and gender identities as much as possible using the language they used at the time—most often gay, lesbian, bisexual, or transgender—though I also use LGBTQ, queer, and trans or transgender as umbrella terms to capture a wide and unstable range of gender and sexual identities and expressions that diverged from cultural norms. People today might draw from a still wider and always changing range of terms to describe their identities and experiences of gender and sexuality.

6. May, *Homeward Bound*.

7. John D'Emilio, *Sexual Politics, Sexual Communities: The Making of a Homosexual Minority in the United States, 1940–1970* (Chicago: University of Chicago Press, 1983).

8. See especially George Chauncey, *Gay New York: Gender, Urban Culture, and the Making of the Gay Male World, 1890–1940* (New York: Basic Books, 1994); Esther Newton, *Cherry Grove, Fire Island: Sixty Years in America's First Gay and Lesbian Town* (Boston: Beacon Press, 1993); Genny Beemyn, ed., *Creating a Place for Ourselves: Lesbian, Gay, and Bisexual Community Histories* (New York: Routledge, 1997); Dangerous Bedfellows, eds., *Policing Public Sex: Queer*

Politics and the Future of AIDS Activism (Boston: South End Press, 1996); Yolanda Retter, Anne-Marie Bouthillette, and Gordon Brent Ingram, eds., *Queers in Space: Communities, Public Places, Sites of Resistance* (Seattle: Bay Press, 1997); William Leap, ed., *Public Sex, Gay Space* (New York: Columbia University Press, 1999).

9. Chauncey, *Gay New York*, 152–63. Similar residential patterns in other cities are revealed by David K. Johnson, "The Kids of Fairytown: Gay Male Culture on Chicago's Near North Side in the 1930s," in Beemyn, *Creating a Place for Ourselves*, 97–118; and Matt Houlbrook, *Queer London: Perils and Pleasures in the Sexual Metropolis, 1918–1957* (Chicago: University of Chicago Press, 2005), 109–34. On residential patterns and sexual expression and sexual identity, see also John D'Emilio, "Capitalism and Gay Identity," in *Powers of Desire: The Politics of Sexuality*, ed. Ann Snitow, Christine Stansell, and Sharon Thompson (New York: Monthly Review Press, 1983), 100–13; and Joanne Meyerowitz, "Sexual Geography and Gender Economy: The Furnished Room Districts of Chicago, 1890–1930," *Gender & History* 2, no. 3 (1990): 274–97.

10. See especially Johnson, "Kids of Fairytown," 105; Eric Garber, "A Spectacle in Color: The Lesbian and Gay Subculture of Jazz Age Harlem," in *Hidden from History: Reclaiming the Gay and Lesbian Past*, ed. Martin Bauml Duberman, Martha Vicinus, and George Chauncey (New York: Meridian, 1989), 318–31; Elizabeth Lapovsky Kennedy and Madeline D. Davis, *Boots of Leather, Slippers of Gold: The History of a Lesbian Community* (New York: Routledge, 1993); and Rochella Thorpe, "'A House Where Queers Go': African-American Lesbian Nightlife in Detroit, 1940–1975," in *Inventing Lesbian Cultures*, ed. Ellen Lewin (Boston: Beacon Press, 1996), 40–61. For an analysis of queer domesticities in the United Kingdom, see Matt Cook, *Queer Domesticities: Homosexuality and Home Life in Twentieth-century London* (New York: Palgrave Macmillan, 2014). See also Christopher Reed, "'A Room of One's Own': The Bloomsbury Group's Creation of a Modernist Domesticity," in *Not at Home: The Suppression of Domesticity in Modern Art and Architecture*, ed. Christopher Reed (New York: Thames and Hudson, 1996); and Sharon Marcus, "At Home with the Other Victorians," *South Atlantic Quarterly* 108, no. 1 (2009): 119–45.

11. D'Emilio, *Sexual Politics, Sexual Communities*, 235–39; Michael Bronski, *The Pleasure Principle: Sex, Backlash, and the Struggle for Gay Freedom* (New York: St. Martin's Press, 1998); Jeffrey Escoffier, "Fabulous Politics: Gay, Lesbian, and Queer Movements, 1969–1999," in *The World the Sixties Made: Politics and Culture in Recent America*, ed. Van Gosse and Richard R. Moser (Philadelphia: Temple University Press, 2003), 191–218; Tourmaline, Eric A. Stanley, and Johanna Burton, eds., *Trap Door: Trans Cultural Production and the Politics of Visibility* (Cambridge, MA: MIT Press, 2017).

12. On history of the "closet," see Chauncey, *Gay New York*, 1–8.

13. Lauren Berlant and Michael Warner, "Sex in Public," *Critical Inquiry* 24, no. 2 (1998): 555, 558; Michael Warner, *The Trouble with Normal: Sex, Politics, and the Ethics of Queer Life* (New York: Free Press, 1999).

14. Lisa Duggan, "The New Homonormativity: The Sexual Politics of Neoliberalism," in *Materializing Democracy: Toward a Revitalized Cultural Politics*, ed. Russ Castronovo and Dana D. Nelson (Durham, NC: Duke University Press, 2002), 179, 189, republished in Lisa Duggan, *The Twilight of Equality? Neoliberalism, Cultural Politics, and the Attack on Democracy* (Boston: Beacon Press, 2003). For a critique of antinormativity in queer studies, see Robyn Wiegman and Elizabeth A. Wilson, "Introduction: Antinormativity's Queer Conventions," *differences* 26, no. 1 (2015): 1–25; and Annamarie Jagose, "The Trouble with Antinormativity," *differences* 26, no. 1 (2015): 26–47. For an alternative genealogy of queer theory, see Michael Hames-García, "Queer Theory Revisited," in *Gay Latino Studies: A Critical Reader*, ed. Michael Hames-García and Ernesto Javier Martínez (Durham, NC: Duke University Press, 2011), 19–45.

15. Heather Murray, *Not in This Family: Gays and the Meaning of Kinship in Postwar North America* (Philadelphia: University of Pennsylvania Press, 2010); Daniel Winunwe Rivers, *Radical Relations: Lesbian Mothers, Gay Fathers, and Their Children in the United States Since World War II* (Chapel Hill: University of North Carolina Press, 2013); Lauren Jae Gutterman, *Her Neighbor's Wife: A History of Lesbian Desire Within Marriage* (Philadelphia: University of Pennsylvania Press, 2020).

16. For discussion of the various meanings of home, house, domesticity, and housing, see introduction to Craig Willse, *The Value of Homelessness: Managing Surplus Life in the United States* (Minneapolis: University of Minnesota Press, 2015), esp. 1–3.

17. Erving Goffman, *The Presentation of Self in Everyday Life* (Garden City, NY: Doubleday, 1959).

18. Judith Butler, "Performative Acts and Gender Constitution: An Essay in Phenomenology and Feminist Theory," *Theatre Journal* 40, no. 4 (1988): 519, 521. See also Judith Butler, *Gender Trouble: Feminism and the Subversion of Identity* (New York: Routledge, 1990); and Judith Butler, *Bodies That Matter: On the Discursive Limits of "Sex"* (New York: Routledge, 1993).

19. Mary Douglas, "The Idea of a Home: A Kind of Space," *Social Research* 58, no. 1 (1991): 290.

20. Robin Bernstein, "Dances with Things: Material Culture and the Performance of Race," *Social Text* 27, no. 4 (2009): 69.

21. Lizabeth A. Cohen, "Embellishing a Life of Labor: An Interpretation of the Material Culture of American Working-Class Homes, 1885–1915," *Journal of American Culture* 3, no. 4 (1980): 752–75.

22. Michel de Certeau, *The Practice of Everyday Life*, trans. Steve Rendall (Berkeley: University of California Press, 1984); and Michel de Certeau, Luce Giard, and Pierre Mayol, *The Practice of Everyday Life*, vol. 2, trans. Timothy J. Tomasik (Minneapolis: University of Minnesota Press, 1998). See also a critique of de Certeau's discussion of strategy and tactics in Ian Buchanan, *Michel de Certeau: Cultural Theorist* (Thousand Oaks, CA: SAGE, 2000), 86–107.

23. Martin F. Manalansan, *Global Divas: Filipino Gay Men in the Diaspora* (Durham, NC: Duke University Press, 2003), 90, 94. See also Svetlana Boym on the everyday and ordinary in *Common Places: Mythologies of Everyday Life in Russia* (Cambridge, MA: Harvard University Press, 1994), esp. 20–23; and Heather Love's discussion of the queer ordinary in "Doing Being Deviant: Deviance Studies, Description, and the Queer Ordinary," *differences* 26, no. 1 (2015): 74–95, and "Playing for Keeps," *GLQ: A Journal of Lesbian and Gay Studies* 25, no. 2 (2019): 257–72. On domesticity, disorder, and deviance, see also Scott Herring, *The Hoarders: Material Deviance in Modern American Culture* (Chicago: University of Chicago Press, 2014).

24. On the emergence of an ideology of domesticity and its connection to privacy, see Michael McKeon, *The Secret History of Domesticity: Public, Private, and the Division of Knowledge* (Baltimore: Johns Hopkins University Press, 2006).

25. Susan Gal, "A Semiotics of the Public/Private Distinction," *differences* 13, no. 1 (2002): 77–95.

26. On home design and privacy in the 1950s, see Clayton Howard, *The Closet and the Cul-De-Sac: The Politics of Sexual Privacy in Northern California* (Philadelphia: University of Pennsylvania Press, 2019), 85–116.

27. Sarah E. Igo, *The Known Citizen: A History of Privacy in Modern America* (Cambridge, MA: Harvard University Press, 2018), 9.

28. Alison Lefkovitz, "Men in the House: Race, Welfare, and the Regulation of Men's Sexuality in the United States, 1961–1972," *Journal of the History of Sexuality* 20, no. 3 (2011): 594–614.

29. For a historiography of domesticity and sexuality, see Stephen Vider, "Domesticity," in

Routledge History of American Sexuality, ed. Kevin P. Murphy, Jason Ruiz, and David Serlin (New York: Routledge, 2020), 166–78. On domesticity as a site of constraint and violence, see Barbara Welter, "The Cult of True Womanhood: 1820–1860," *American Quarterly* 18, no. 2 (1966): 151–74; Ann Douglas, *The Feminization of American Culture* (New York: Alfred A. Knopf, 1977); Nancy Armstrong, *Desire and Domestic Fiction: A Political History of the Novel* (New York: Oxford University Press, 1987); Gillian Brown, *Domestic Individualism: Imagining Self in Nineteenth-century America* (Berkeley: University of California Press, 1990); Lauren Gail Berlant, *The Female Complaint: The Unfinished Business of Sentimentality in American Culture* (Durham, NC: Duke University Press, 2008); Amy Kaplan, "Manifest Domesticity," *American Literature* 70, no. 3 (1998): 581–606; Laura Wexler, *Tender Violence: Domestic Visions in an Age of U.S. Imperialism* (Chapel Hill: University of North Carolina Press, 2000). For alternative takes that give greater emphasis to women's agency, see Carroll Smith-Rosenberg, "The Female World of Love and Ritual: Relations Between Women in Nineteenth-century America," *Signs: Journal of Women in Culture and Society* 1, no. 1 (1975): 1–29; Nancy F. Cott, *The Bonds of Womanhood: "Woman's Sphere" in New England, 1780–1835* (New Haven, CT: Yale University Press, 1977); Mary P. Ryan, *The Empire of the Mother: American Writing about Domesticity, 1830 to 1860* (New York: Haworth Press, 1982); Jane Tompkins, *Sensational Designs: The Cultural Work of American Fiction, 1790–1860* (New York: Oxford University Press, 1986); Joanne J. Meyerowitz, ed., *Not June Cleaver: Women and Gender in Postwar America, 1945–1960* (Philadelphia: Temple University Press, 1994). See also Linda K. Kerber, "Separate Spheres, Female Worlds, Woman's Place: The Rhetoric of Women's History," *Journal of American History* 75, no. 1 (1988): 9–39; and Meyerowitz, "Beyond the Feminine Mystique."

30. bell hooks, "homeplace: a site of resistance," reprinted in *Housing and Dwelling: Perspectives on Modern Domestic Architecture*, ed. Barbara Miller Lane (New York: Routledge, 2006), 69. On domestic ideology and practices under slavery and Jim Crow, see Thavolia Glymph, *Out of the House of Bondage: The Transformation of the Plantation Household* (New York: Cambridge University Press, 2008); and Rebecca Sharpless, *Cooking in Other Women's Kitchens: Domestic Workers in the South, 1865–1960* (Chapel Hill: University of North Carolina Press, 2010).

31. Susan Fraiman, *Extreme Domesticity: A View from the Margins* (New York: Columbia University Press, 2017), 4–5. See also review by Stephen Vider, *Signs: Journal of Women in Culture and Society* 44, no. 1 (2018): 258–61.

32. Douglas, "Idea of a Home," 303.

33. Ann Cvetkovich, *An Archive of Feelings: Trauma, Sexuality, and Lesbian Public Cultures* (Durham, NC: Duke University Press, 2003). For more on the domestic archive, see Stephen Vider, "Public Disclosures of Private Realities: HIV/AIDS and the Domestic Archive," *Public Historian* 41, no. 2 (2019), 163–89.

34. On cultural citizenship, see especially Aihwa Ong, "Cultural Citizenship as Subject-Making: Immigrants Negotiate Racial and Cultural Boundaries in the United States," *Current Anthropology* 37, no. 5 (1996): 737–62. I also build here on Barbara Young Welke's discussion of personhood, citizenship, and belonging in *Law and the Borders of Belonging in the Long Nineteenth Century United States* (New York: Cambridge University Press, 2010); and on discussions of citizenship as practice in Nimisha Barton and Richard S. Hopkins, "Introduction," in *Practiced Citizenship: Women, Gender, and the State in Modern France*, ed. Nimisha Barton and Richard S. Hopkins (Lincoln: University of Nebraska Press, 2019), 1–18; and Derrick R. Spires, *The Practice of Citizenship: Black Politics and Print Culture in the Early United States* (Philadelphia: University of Pennsylvania Press, 2019). See also Margot Canaday, *The Straight State: Sexuality and Citizenship in Twentieth-Century America* (Princeton, NJ: Princeton University Press, 2009); Nancy F. Cott, "Marriage and Women's Citizenship in the United States, 1830–1934," *American Historical*

Review 103, no. 5 (1998): 1440–74; Lauren Berlant, "Citizenship," *Keywords for American Cultural Studies*, 2nd ed., ed. Bruce Burgett and Glenn Hendler (New York: New York University Press, 2014), 41–44; Linda Bosniak, *The Citizen and the Alien: Dilemmas of Contemporary Membership* (Princeton, NJ: Princeton University Press, 2006); and Shane Phelan, *Sexual Strangers: Gays, Lesbians, and Dilemmas of Citizenship* (Philadelphia: Temple University Press, 2001).

35. Teresa Anne Murphy, *Citizenship and the Origins of Women's History in the United States* (Philadelphia: University of Pennsylvania Press, 2013).

36. Cott, *Bonds of Womanhood*. New England domestic ideology would have a dispro-portionate impact on national norms, in large part because of the structure of the American publishing industry: by the 1830s, the vast majority of works were published in Boston, New York, or Philadelphia, with many of its most popular authors based in the North as well. On New England and New York in early book publishing in America, see Robert A. Gross and Mary Kelley, *An Extensive Republic: Print, Culture, and Society in the New Nation, 1790–1840* (Chapel Hill: University of North Carolina Press, 2010), esp. 124–27.

37. Linda Kerber, "The Republican Mother: Women and the Enlightenment: An American Perspective," *American Quarterly* 28, no. 2 (1976): 187–205; Rosemarie Zagarri, "Morals, Man-ners, and the Republican Mother," *American Quarterly* 44, no. 2 (1992): 192–215; Linda Kerber, *Women of the Republic: Intellect and Ideology in Revolutionary America* (Chapel Hill: University of North Carolina Press, 1980); Murphy, *Citizenship and the Origins of Women's History*.

38. Paula Baker, "The Domestication of Politics: Women and American Political Society, 1780–1920," *American Historical Review* 89, no. 3 (1984): 620–47.

39. Nayan Shah, *Contagious Divides: Epidemics and Race in San Francisco's Chinatown* (Berkeley: University of California Press, 2001), 77.

40. Shannon Jackson, *Lines of Activity: Performance, Historiography, Hull-House Domestic-ity* (Ann Arbor: University of Michigan Press, 2000); Nancy B. Sinkoff, "Educating for 'Proper' Jewish Womanhood: A Case Study in Domesticity and Vocational Training, 1897–1926," *Ameri-can Jewish History* 77, no. 4 (1988): 572–99; Victoria W. Wolcott, *Remaking Respectability: African American Women in Interwar Detroit* (Chapel Hill: University of North Carolina Press, 2001). See also Jane E. Simonson, *Making Home Work: Domesticity and Native American Assimilation in the American West, 1860–1919* (Chapel Hill: University of North Carolina Press, 2006).

41. Shah, *Contagious Divides*. Quote from Willard B. Farwell, *The Chinese at Home and Abroad* (San Francisco: A. L. Bancroft, 1885), 9, cited in Shah, *Contagious Divides*, 84. See also George J. Sánchez, *Becoming Mexican American: Ethnicity, Culture, and Identity in Chicano Los Angeles, 1990–1945* (New York: Oxford University Press, 1993); and, for example, Pearl I. Ellis, *Americanization Through Homemaking* (Los Angeles: Wetzel, 1929). For a history of alternative models of domesticity in the nineteenth and early twentieth centuries, see Dolores Hayden's history of material feminism, *The Grand Domestic Revolution: A History of Feminist Designs for American Homes, Neighborhoods, and Cities* (Cambridge, MA: MIT Press, 1981).

42. Advertisement, *Pittsburgh Courier*, April 28, 1923, reproduced in LeeAnn Lands, "Be a Patriot, Buy a Home: Re-Imagining Home Owners and Home Ownership in Early 20th Century Atlanta," *Journal of Social History* 41, no. 4 (2008): 955. See also LeeAnn Lands, "Home-ownership and Park-Neighborhood Ideology, 1910–1933," chap. 4 in *The Culture of Property: Race, Class, and Housing Landscapes in Atlanta, 1880–1950* (Athens: University of Georgia Press, 2009); Brian J. McCabe, *No Place Like Home: Wealth, Community, and the Politics of Homeowner-ship* (New York: Oxford University Press, 2016), esp. chap. 2, "Selling the Citizen Homeowner"; Janet Hutchinson, "The Cure for Domestic Neglect: Better Homes in America, 1922–1935," *Perspectives in Vernacular Architecture* 2 (1986): 168–78; and James L. Greer, "The Better Homes Movement and the Origins of Mortgage Redlining in the United States," in *Statebuild-*

ing from the Margins: Between Reconstruction and the New Deal, ed. Carol Nackenoff and Julie Novkov (Philadelphia: University of Pennsylvania Press, 2014), 203–35.

43. On the foreclosure crisis and the origins of the FHA, see Kenneth T. Jackson, *Crabgrass Frontier: The Suburbanization of the United States* (New York: Oxford University Press, 1987); and Price Fishback, Jonathan Derek Rose, and Kenneth A. Snowden, *Well Worth Saving: How the New Deal Safeguarded Home Ownership* (Chicago: University of Chicago Press, 2013). On the GI Bill, see Suzanne Mettler, *From Soldiers to Citizens: The G.I. Bill and the Making of the Greatest Generation* (New York: Oxford University Press, 2005); and Lizabeth Cohen, "Reconversion: The Emergence of the Consumers' Republic," chap. 3 in *A Consumers' Republic: The Politics of Mass Consumption in Postwar America* (New York: Alfred A. Knopf, 2003).

44. See especially Jackson, *Crabgrass Frontier*; and Richard Rothstein, *The Color of Law: A Forgotten History of How Our Government Segregated America* (New York: Liveright, 2017).

45. Federal Housing Administration, *Underwriting Manual* (Washington, DC: U.S. Government Printing Office, 1936), pt. 2, no. 317; Federal Housing Administration, *Underwriting Manual* (Washington, DC: U.S. Government Printing Office, 1947), no. 1636 (2). Clayton Howard, "Building a 'Family-Friendly' Metropolis: Sexuality, the State, and Postwar Housing Policy," *Journal of Urban History* 39, no. 5 (2013): 933–55; Canaday, *Straight State*.

46. Gail Radford, *Modern Housing for America: Policy Struggles in the New Deal Era* (Chicago: University of Chicago Press, 1996); Rothstein, *Color of Law*; Lisa Levenstein, *A Movement Without Marches: African American Women and the Politics of Poverty in Postwar Philadelphia* (Chapel Hill: University of North Carolina Press, 2009).

47. May, *Homeward Bound*; Nancy F. Cott, "Public Sanctity for a Private Realm," chap. 8 in *Public Vows: A History of Marriage and the Nation* (Cambridge, MA: Harvard University Press, 2000). On marriage in the 1950s, see also Weiss, *To Have and to Hold*.

48. Abraham Maslow, "A Theory of Human Motivation," *Psychological Review* 50, no. 4 (1943): 380–81. On belonging, citizenship, and the family, see Smith, *Visions of Belonging*. The flipside of "belonging" was loneliness and social isolation, another major preoccupation of postwar social scientists. See, for example, David Riesman, *The Lonely Crowd: A Study of the Changing American Character* (New Haven, CT: Yale University Press, 1950); as well as Betty Friedan, *The Feminine Mystique* (New York: W. W. Norton, 1963). See also Daniel Horowitz's discussion of Friedan's feminist revision of popular social science in *Betty Friedan and the Making of* The Feminine Mystique: *The American Left, the Cold War, and Modern Feminism* (Amherst: University of Massachusetts Press, 1998), 205–9.

49. *Boys Beware*, dir. Sid Davis, Sid Davis Productions, 1961. See also Estelle B. Freedman, "'Uncontrolled Desires': The Response to the Sexual Psychopath, 1920–1960," *Journal of American History* 74, no. 1 (1987): 83–106.

50. On the emergence and circulation of the stereotype of the gay decorator, see Stephen Vider, "A Peculiar Talent: Measuring Masculinity, Diagnosing Decorating" (in preparation). On appropriate boundaries of masculinity, see Margaret Marsh, "Suburban Men and Masculine Domesticity, 1870–1915," *American Quarterly* 40, no. 2 (1988): 165–86; and Steven M. Gelber, "Do-it-Yourself: Constructing, Repairing, and Maintaining Domestic Masculinity," *American Quarterly* 49, no. 1 (1997): 66–112.

51. Donna Penn, "The Sexualized Woman: The Lesbian, the Prostitute, and the Containment of Female Sexuality in Postwar America," in Meyerowitz, *Not June Cleaver*, 358–81; Lauren Jae Gutterman, "Another Enemy Within: Lesbian Wives, or the Hidden Threat to the Nuclear Family in Post-war America," *Gender & History* 24, no. 2 (2012): 475–501.

52. Emily Skidmore, "Constructing the 'Good Transsexual': Christine Jorgensen, Whiteness, and Heteronormativity in the Mid-Twentieth-Century Press," *Feminist Studies* 37, no. 2

(2011): 270–300; C. Riley Snorton, "A Nightmarish Silhouette: Racialization and the Long Exposure of Transition," chap. 4 in *Black on Both Sides: A Racial History of Trans Identity* (Minneapolis: University of Minnesota Press, 2017).

53. D'Emilio, *Sexual Politics, Sexual Communities*; Mattachine Society, "Aims and Principles," Homophile Organizations Mattachine Society Coordinating Council Meeting Minutes, August 28, 1953, Donald S. Lucas Papers, 1997–25, Box 1, Folder 21, GLBT Historical Society, retrieved through Gale's *Archives of Sexuality and Gender*.

54. Jim Kepner, Letter to John McKelvey, January 24, 1954, Jim Kepner Papers: Correspondence Series 8, 1936–1997, Box 45, Folder 5, ONE National Gay & Lesbian Archives, USC Libraries, University of Southern California, retrieved through Gale's *Archives of Sexuality and Gender*; Lyn Pedersen, "The Importance of Being Different," *ONE*, March 1954, 4–6.

55. Justin Spring, *Secret Historian: The Life and Times of Samuel Steward, Professor, Tattoo Artist, and Sexual Renegade* (New York: Farrar, Straus and Giroux, 2010). On Steward's Polaroid camera, see particularly 128–35.

56. On sodomy laws, see William N. Eskridge, *Dishonorable Passions: Sodomy Laws in America, 1861–2003* (New York: Viking, 2008). On pornography, see Whitney Strub, "The Clearly Obscene and the Queerly Obscene: Heteronormativity and Obscenity in Cold War Los Angeles," *American Quarterly* 60, no. 2 (2008): 373–98; and David K. Johnson, *Buying Gay: How Physique Entrepreneurs Sparked a Movement* (New York: Columbia University Press, 2019). On vagrancy and public indecency laws, see Risa Goluboff, *Vagrant Nation: Police Power, Constitutional Change, and the Making of the 1960s* (New York: Oxford University Press, 2016); Clare Sears, *Arresting Dress: Cross-Dressing, Law, and Fascination in Nineteenth-Century San Francisco* (Durham, NC: Duke University Press, 2015). On entrapment, see George Chauncey, "The Forgotten History of Gay Entrapment," *Atlantic*, June 25, 2019, https://www.theatlantic.com/ideas/archive/2019/06/before-stonewall-biggest-threat-was-entrapment/590536/.

57. Barry Werth, *The Scarlet Professor: Newton Arvin, a Literary Life Shattered by Scandal* (New York: Nan A. Talese, 2001).

58. Gutterman, *Her Neighbor's Wife*.

59. Robert Hill, "'We Share a Sacred Secret': Gender, Domesticity, and Containment in *Transvestia*'s Histories and Letters from Crossdressers and Their Wives," *Journal of Social History* 44, no. 3 (2011): 729–50.

60. Michel Hurst and Robert Swope, eds., *Casa Susanna* (Brooklyn: powerHouse books, 2005); Susanna [Valenti], "Susanna Says," *Transvestia*, no. 29 (1964): 78; Virginia [Prince], "Wonderful Weekend," *Transvestia*, no. 12 (1961): 16.

61. Jessi Gan, "'Still at the Back of the Bus': Sylvia Rivera's Struggle," *Centro Journal* 19, no. 1 (2007): 124–39.

62. Danny Lyon, *Memories of Myself: Essays by Danny Lyon* (New York: Phaidon Press, 2009), 90–107.

CHAPTER ONE

1. In the Matter of the Estate of Mario M. Firpo, Superior Court of the State of California, No. 138903, transcript of deposition of James Radcliffe Kam, April 4, 1958, in Donald S. Lucas Papers, Box 6, Folder 12, GLBT Historical Society, retrieved from Gale's *Archives of Sexuality and Gender*. Melvyn Mario Firpo, born October 25, 1913, died June 1, 1956, California, Death Index, 1940–1997, Ancestry.com. James Radcliffe Kam, born September 9, 1900, died November 1972, U.S, Social Security Death Index, 1935–2014, Ancestry.com.

2. For histories of long-term same-sex and transgender relationships in the United States

before 1950, see Rachel Hope Cleves, "'What, Another Female Husband?': The Prehistory of Same-Sex Marriage in America," *Journal of American History* 101, no. 4 (2015): 1055–81; Jen Manion, *Female Husbands: A Trans History* (New York: Cambridge University Press, 2020).

3. On the history of the homophile movement, see C. Todd White, *Pre-Gay L.A.: A Social History of the Movement for Homosexual Rights* (Urbana: University of Illinois Press, 2009); Craig M. Loftin, *Masked Voices: Gay Men and Lesbians in Cold War America* (Albany: State University of New York Press, 2012); Martin Meeker, "Behind the Mask of Respectability: Reconsidering the Mattachine Society and Male Homophile Practice, 1950s and 1960s," *Journal of the History of Sexuality* 10, no. 1 (2001): 78–116; Marcia M. Gallo, *Different Daughters: A History of the Daughters of Bilitis and the Rise of the Lesbian Rights Movement* (New York: Carroll and Graf, 2006); and John D'Emilio, *Sexual Politics, Sexual Communities: The Making of a Homosexual Minority in the United States, 1940–1970* (Chicago: University of Chicago Press, 1983).

4. Donald Webster Cory and John P. LeRoy, *The Homosexual and His Society: A View from Within* (New York: Citadel Press, 1963), 11. On Donald Webster Cory (Edward Sagarin) and his coauthor John P. LeRoy (Barry Sheer), see Martin Duberman, "The 'Father' of the Homophile Movement," in *Left Out: The Politics of Exclusion, Essays 1964–2002* (Boston: South End Press, 2002), 59–94.

5. For examples of homophile discussions of privacy, see "New Deal for Deviates," *ONE*, October 1955, 14–15; Del Martin, "Love Is a Private Affair," *The Ladder*, February 1962, 4–5; and Frank C. Wood Jr., "The Right to be Free from Unreasonable Search and Seizure," *ONE*, April 1963, 5–9. See also William N. Eskridge, "Privacy Jurisprudence and the Apartheid of the Closet, 1946–1961," *Florida State University Law Review* 24, no. 4 (1996): 703–839.

6. On privacy in relation to class, race, and sexuality, see Nayan Shah, *Contagious Divides: Epidemics and Race in San Francisco's Chinatown* (Berkeley: University of California Press, 2001); Nayan Shah, *Stranger Intimacy: Contesting Race, Sexuality and the Law in the North American West* (Berkeley: University of California Press, 2011); Peggy Pascoe, *What Comes Naturally: Miscegenation Law and the Making of Race in America* (New York: Oxford University Press, 2009); Stephen Robertson, Shane White, Stephen Garton, and Graham White, "Disorderly Houses: Residences, Privacy, and the Surveillance of Sexuality in 1920s Harlem," *Journal of the History of Sexuality* 21, no. 3 (2012): 443–66; Deborah Nelson, *Pursuing Privacy in Cold War America* (New York: Columbia University Press, 2001); and Sarah E. Igo, *The Known Citizen: A History of Privacy in Modern America* (Cambridge, MA: Harvard University Press, 2018).

7. I adapt here Peter F. Cohen's useful concept of "class dislocation," in "'All They Needed': AIDS, Consumption, and the Politics of Class," *Journal of the History of Sexuality* 8, no. 1 (1997): 86–115.

8. On domestic and sexual containment as a corollary to Cold War political containment, see Elaine Tyler May, *Homeward Bound: American Families in the Cold War Era* (New York: Basic Books, 1988), esp. chapter 5.

9. On the complex ways heterosexual marriage and reproductive ties shaped the lives of lesbians and gay men in the postwar period, see Lauren Jae Gutterman, *Her Neighbor's Wife: A History of Lesbian Desire Within Marriage* (Philadelphia: University of Pennsylvania Press, 2020); Alison Lefkovitz, "'The Peculiar Anomaly': Same-Sex Infidelity in Postwar Divorce Courts," *Law and History Review* 33, no. 3 (2015): 665–701; and Daniel Winunwe Rivers, *Radical Relations: Lesbian Mothers, Gay Fathers, and Their Children in the United States Since World War II* (Chapel Hill: University of North Carolina Press, 2013). Loftin also discusses the social history of heterosexual and homosexual marriage among readers and writers of the homophile magazine *ONE* in "Homosexuals and Marriage under the Shadow of McCarthy," chap. 8 of *Masked Voices*. George Chauncey's 2004 book *Why Marriage?* examines the reasons marriage emerged

as a political goal for the lesbian and gay rights movement but only briefly addresses debates around homosexual marriage in the 1950s and 1960s, see George Chauncey, *Why Marriage? The History Shaping Today's Debate over Gay Equality* (New York: Basic Books, 2004). On gay and lesbian marriage campaigns in the 1970s, see Alison Lefkovitz, *Strange Bedfellows: Marriage in the Age of Women's Liberation* (Philadelphia: University of Pennsylvania Press, 2018), 153–78.

10. Lisa Duggan, *The Twilight of Equality? Neoliberalism, Cultural Politics, and the Attack on Democracy* (Boston: Beacon Press, 2003), 50.

11. The questionnaire was circulated in advance of the 1961 Midwinter Institute conference in Los Angeles, as part of an effort to draft a homosexual "bill of rights." Institute questionnaire discussion, form, and tabulated results reprinted in W. Dorr Legg, *Homophile Studies in Theory and Practice* (San Francisco: ONE Institute Press, 1994), 122–45, 422–36.

12. "Some Facts About Lesbians," *The Ladder*, September 1959, 4–26, and "Some Comparisons Between Male and Female Homosexuals," *The Ladder*, September 1960, 4–25.

13. Jody Shotwell, "Gay Wedding," *The Ladder*, February 1963, 4.

14. Jess Stearn, *The Sixth Man* (New York: Doubleday, 1961), 215–17.

15. On the history of lesbian wedding practices, see Elise Chenier, "Love-Politics: Lesbian Wedding Practices in Canada and the United States from the 1920s to the 1970s," *Journal of the History of Sexuality* 27, no. 2 (2018): 294–321.

16. Will Fellows and Helen P. Branson, *Gay Bar: The Fabulous, True Story of a Daring Woman and Her Boys in the 1950s* (Madison: University of Wisconsin Press, 2010), 79. Reissue of Helen P. Branson, *Gay Bar* (San Francisco: Pan-Graphic Press, 1957).

17. *Homosexuality and Citizenship in Florida* (Tallahassee: Florida Legislative Investigation Committee, 1964), n.p.

18. B. C. letter in Blanche M. Baker, "Toward Understanding," *ONE*, June 1959, 26. See also Loftin on "lonely letters" in *Masked Voices*, 94–96.

19. Buddy Kent oral history, interview by Joan Nestle, January 1983, courtesy of Joan Nestle and Lisa Davis, with thanks to Hugh Ryan. See Hugh Ryan, "The Three Lives of Malvina Schwartz," *Hazlitt*, October 12, 2016, https://hazlitt.net/longreads/three-lives-malvina-schwartz.

20. Suzanne Prosin, "The Concept of the Lesbian: A Minority in Reverse," *The Ladder*, July 1962, 17.

21. For discussion of roles of "husband" and "wife" within gay male couples, see Maurice Leznoff, "The Homosexual in Urban Society" (MA thesis, McGill University, 1954), 184; Marcel Martin (Ross Ingersoll), "A Matter of Language," *ONE*, November 1961, 7–9. James Radcliffe Kam also uses the terms "husband" and "wife" in his deposition, though the terms are introduced by the Firpo family's lawyer, in *In the Matter of the Estate of Mario M. Firpo*. George Chauncey discusses usages of the terms "husbands" and "wives" in working-class and migrant communities before World War II, though these depended more on gender performance and sexual role and were not necessarily linked to shared domestic space. See George Chauncey, *Gay New York: Gender, Urban Culture, and the Making of the Gay Male World, 1890–1940* (New York: Basic Books, 1994), 86–95. Gershon Legman reflected this usage in his 1940 lexicon of gay slang, defining "husband" as "the normal or else more aggressive member of a homosexual liaison, male or female" or a "favorite lover who sees the homosexual regularly." The "wife," in turn, was defined as "the less aggressive member of a homosexual alliance, male or female." See partial reprint of Legman's lexicon in Deborah Cameron and Don Kulick, eds., *The Language and Sexuality Reader* (New York: Routledge 2006), 27, 32, originally published in George W. Henry and the Study of Sex Variants Committee, *Sex Variants; a Study of Homosexual Patterns*, vol. 2 (New York: P. B. Hoeber, 1941).

22. Branson, *Gay Bar*, 79.

23. Craig M. Loftin, "Unacceptable Mannerisms: Gender Anxieties, Homosexual Activism, and Swish in the United States, 1945–1965," *Journal of Social History* 40, no. 3 (2007): 577–96.

24. Philadelphia Gay Wedding Photographs, Coll2012–034, ONE National Gay & Lesbian Archives, USC Libraries, University of Southern California. For more on the photographs, see Nick Fiorellini, "Dear Gentlemen, Your 60-Year-Old Wedding Pics Are Ready," *Philadelphia Citizen*, July 19, 2019, https://thephiladelphiacitizen.org/dear-gentlemen-your-60-year-old-wedding -pics-are-ready/.

25. Photo albums of Philadelphia lesbian couple, Collection 7689, Division of Rare and Manuscript Collections, Cornell University Library. Many thanks to my colleague Denise Green for helping me decipher and describe the two women's clothing.

26. Lee Fuller photograph album, Collection 7667, Division of Rare and Manuscript Collections, Cornell University Library. Fuller is thanked in Francis Marion Pottenger, *The Fight Against Tuberculosis: An Autobiography* (New York: Henry Schuman, 1952), 129. Leach's name is written on the back of a large studio portrait in the album. Phone directories from the late 1940s, digitized on Ancestry.com and the Internet Archive, indicate that H. Lee Fuller lived in residence at Pottenger.

27. On the assault, see "Police Book Youth for Pal's Beating," *Pasadena Independent*, December 5, 1950; "Wins Assault, Robbery Case," *Pasadena Independent*, February 21, 1951; "Martin Found Innocent in Assault Case," *Monrovia Daily News Post*, February 21, 1951. Thank you to John Ibson for linking Leach to this case and the Monrovia nursery, in John Ibson, *Men Without Maps: Some Gay Males of the Generation Before Stonewall* (Chicago: University of Chicago Press, 2019), 25n25. After the closing of the Pottenger Sanatorium, Fuller purchased a new home at 788 Ridgeside Drive, listed for sale on August 30, 1957, in *Monrovia Daily News Post*.

28. Frank W. Leach obituary, *Monrovia Daily News-Post*, April 3, 1973; H. Lee Fuller obituary, *Monrovia Daily News-Post*, April 24, 1973.

29. Gene Damon [Barbara Grier], "Lesbian Marriage," *The Ladder*, August 1958, 12; Joanne Ellen Passet, *Indomitable: The Life of Barbara Grier* (Tallahassee: Bella Books, 2016). On relationships between parents and gay and lesbian children in the 1950s, see Heather Murray, *Not in This Family: Gays and the Meaning of Kinship in Postwar North America* (Philadelphia: University of Pennsylvania Press, 2010).

30. James Radcliffe Kam naturalization petition, #108337 (witnessed by Melvin M. Firpo), National Archives at San Francisco, *Records of District Courts of the United States, 1685–2009, California, Federal Naturalization Records, 1843–1999*, Ancestry.com; Melvin Mario Firpo in 1920 U.S. Federal Census, San Francisco Assembly District 33, San Francisco, California, Ancestry.com.

31. *In the Matter of the Estate of Mario M. Firpo*, Kam deposition transcript; additional trial materials from Civil Records, Superior Court of California, County of San Francisco, case no. 138, 90.

32. "Kam Sentenced in Morals Case," *Californian*, November 9, 1943; Kam naturalization petition.

33. Nancy B. Achilles, "The Homosexual Bar" (MA Thesis, University of Chicago, 1964), 34.

34. Roy Richard Grinker, *In the Arms of Africa: The Life of Colin M. Turnbull* (New York: St. Martin's Press, 2000), 117–53; James A. Ford's letter to James Oliver, March 2, 1964, quoted on p. 151, archived at National Anthropological Archives, Smithsonian Institution, Washington, DC. On Ford, see his obituary, Gordon R. Willey, "James Alfred Ford, 1911–1968," *American Antiquity* 34, no. 1 (1969): 62–71.

35. On enforcement of disorderly conduct, degeneracy, masquerade, and sodomy laws, see William Eskridge, *Gaylaw: Challenging the Apartheid of the Closet* (Cambridge, MA: Harvard University Press, 1999); and William Eskridge, *Dishonorable Passions: Sodomy Laws in America, 1861–2003* (New York: Viking, 2008).

36. See discussion of wedding in Marc Stein, *City of Sisterly and Brotherly Loves: Lesbian and Gay Philadelphia, 1945–1972* (Philadelphia: Temple University Press, 2004), 136. "'Wedding' Entertainment Female 'Groom' Tells Judge," *Philadelphia Tribune*, April 14, 1953; and "'Wedding' Figures Are Held Under $300 Peace Bond," *Philadelphia Tribune*, April 18, 1953. The story and a photograph of the two women appeared again in "Recollection of Interesting Events in the Year," *Philadelphia Tribune*, January 2, 1954.

37. *Hillmer v. Roy Flamm*, 1962–1966, Jack Hillmer Papers, Box 1, Folder 1–2, Bancroft Library, University of California, Berkeley. Many thanks to Matthew Lasner for sharing records from Hillmer and Flamm's legal case with me. On the history of the St. Francis Hotel, see Nan Alamilla Boyd, *Wide Open Town: A History of Queer San Francisco to 1965* (Berkeley: University of California Press, 2003), 58.

38. On marriage in the postwar period, see Barbara Ehrenreich, *The Hearts of Men: American Dreams and the Flight from Commitment* (New York: Anchor, 1983); May, *Homeward Bound*; Joanne Meyerowitz, "Beyond the Feminine Mystique: A Reassessment of Postwar Mass Culture, 1946–1958," *Journal of American History* 79, no. 4 (1993): 1455–82; Jessica Weiss, *To Have and to Hold: Marriage, the Baby Boom, and Social Change* (Chicago: University of Chicago Press, 2000); Robert L. Griswold, *Fatherhood in America: A History* (New York: Basic Books, 1993); and Nancy F. Cott, *Public Vows: A History of Marriage and the Nation* (Cambridge, MA: Harvard University Press, 2000).

39. Albert Ellis, "The Influence of Heterosexual Culture on Homosexual Attitudes," *Mattachine Review*, September 1955, 14.

40. Ellen Herman, *The Romance of American Psychology: Political Culture in the Age of Experts* (Berkeley: University of California Press, 1996), esp. chaps. 4, 5, and 9.

41. Sigmund Freud, *Totem and Taboo: Resemblances Between the Psychic Lives of Savages and Neurotics*, trans. A. A. Brill (New York: Moffat, Yard, 1918), viii.

42. On the emergence of "social adjustment," see especially Edward J. K. Gitre, "Importing Freud: First-Wave Psychoanalysis, Interwar Social Sciences, and the Interdisciplinary Foundations of an American Social Theory," *Journal of the History of the Behavioral Sciences* 46, no. 3 (2010): 239–62. See also John Chynoweth Burnham, "Psychiatry, Psychology and the Progressive Movement," *American Quarterly* 12, no. 4 (1960): 457–65; and Verne Wright, "Summary of Literature on Social Adjustment," *American Sociological Review* 7, no. 3 (1942): 407–22.

43. I build here on Jeffrey Escoffier's discussion of conformism and the "postwar politics of adjustment," in "Homosexuality and the Sociological Imagination: Hegemonic Discourses, the Circulation of Ideas, and the Process of Reading in the 1950s and 1960s," in *American Homo: Community and Perversity* (Berkeley: University of California Press, 1998), 79–98, esp. 82–86. On wartime and postwar psychology, see Herman, *Romance of American Psychology*. On readjustment, see Cott, *Public Vows*, 180–99.

44. Susan M. Hartmann, "Prescriptions for Penelope: Literature on Women's Obligations to Returning World War II Veterans," *Women's Studies: An Interdisciplinary Journal* 5, no. 3 (1978): 223–39; Rebecca L. Davis, *More Perfect Unions: The American Search for Marital Bliss* (Cambridge, MA: Harvard University Press, 2010).

45. Therese Benedek, *Insight and Personality Adjustment: A Study of the Psychological Effects of War* (New York: Ronald Press, 1946), 292, 286.

46. Eli Zaretsky, "Charisma or Rationalization: U.S. Psychoanalysis in the Epoch of the

Cold War," chap. 11 in *Secrets of the Soul: A Social and Cultural History of Psychoanalysis* (New York: Alfred A. Knopf, 2004).

47. Jennifer Terry, "Disease or Way of Life?," chap. 9 in *An American Obsession: Science, Medicine, and Homosexuality in Modern Society* (Chicago: University of Chicago Press, 1999); Kenneth Lewes, *Psychoanalysis and Male Homosexuality* (Lanham, MD: Jason Aronson, 2009); K. A. Cuordileone, "'Politics in an Age of Anxiety': Cold War Political Culture and the Crisis in American Masculinity, 1949–1960," *Journal of American History* 87, no. 2 (2000): 515–45.

48. Edmund Bergler, "The Myth of a New National Disease," *Psychiatric Quarterly* 22 (1948): 82.

49. Edmund Bergler, *Homosexuality: Disease or Way of Life?* (New York: Hill and Wang, 1956), 261–90. See also discussion of psychological and popular accounts of lesbian "pathology" in Lauren Jae Gutterman, "Another Enemy Within: Lesbian Wives, or the Hidden Threat to the Nuclear Family in Post-war America," *Gender & History* 24, no. 2 (2012): 475–501.

50. Alfred Charles Kinsey, Wardell B. Pomeroy, and Clyde E. Martin, *Sexual Behavior in the Human Male* (Bloomington: Indiana University Press, 1998), 201. See also Lionel Trilling's response on this point in *The Liberal Imagination* (New York: New York Review of Books, 2008), 239–41.

51. Hooker defined "adjustment" as "integration of capacities, both intellectual and emotional; ease and comfort in relation to the self and in functioning effectively in relation to the social environment." Evelyn Hooker, "The Adjustment of the Male Overt Homosexual," *Journal of Projective Techniques* 21, no. 1 (1957), 21. On Hooker's study, see Henry L. Minton, *Departing from Deviance: A History of Homosexual Rights and Emancipatory Science in America* (Chicago: University of Chicago Press, 2002), 220–34. Albert Ellis and others pushed back against Hooker's definition of adjustment. See Albert Ellis, "Homosexuality: The Right to Be Wrong," *Journal of Sex Research* 4, no. 2 (1968): 96–107.

52. Homophile Organizations Mattachine Society Articles of Incorporation, 1953–February 19, 1954; Donald S. Lucas Papers, Box 1, Folder 7.

53. Printed on inside front cover of *The Ladder* from 1957 into the 1970s.

54. On homophile cooperation with social scientists, see especially Meeker, "Behind the Mask of Respectability," and Minton, *Departing from Deviance*.

55. Donald Webster Cory, *The Homosexual in America: A Subjective Approach* (New York: Greenberg, 1951), 144.

56. Chris Wetmore and John Arlee, "Twilight Marriage," *Mattachine Review*, June 1956, 6–12.

57. Damon, "Lesbian Marriage," 12–13. For more on *The Ladder's* depiction of lesbian marriage, see Julie R. Enszer, "'Whatever Happens, This Is': Lesbians Engaging Marriage," *WSQ: Women's Studies Quarterly* 41, no. 3/4 (2013): 210–24. On the history of *The Ladder* more generally, see Elyse Vigiletti, "Normalizing the 'Variant' in *The Ladder*, America's Second Lesbian Magazine, 1956–1963," *Frontiers: A Journal of Women Studies* 36, no. 2 (2015): 47–71.

58. "August Speaker," *Mattachine Newsletter*, September 1956, n.p. See also summary of Vaerlen's Daughters of Bilitis discussion, "Is a Homophile Marriage Possible?," *The Ladder*, July 1957, 17–18, 23. Other events on homosexual marriage include a discussion group hosted by the Los Angeles Mattachine Society in January 1957, see "January Discussion Group," *Los Angeles Mattachine Newsletter*, January 1957, seventeen participants; a discussion by the New York Mattachine Society in August 1957, seventeen participants, see "Variations," *New York Mattachine Newsletter*, September 1957; a discussion with psychologist, Leonard B. Olinger, "Keeping the Homosexual Marriage Going," ONE Institute, Los Angeles, fifty-five attendees, November 1961, see *Institute for Homophile Studies Catalog*, 1965–1966; and a pair of "Gab 'n Java" events hosted

by Daughters of Bilitis, New York, "Can a Lesbian Relationship Last?," December 17, 1967, and October 6, 1968, see *Daughters of Bilitis New York Chapter Newsletter*, December 1967 and October 1968.

59. "Calendar of Events," *The Ladder*, May 1957, 16; "August Speaker," n.p.

60. For summaries of conference, see D. S., "Mental Health and Homosexuality," *ONE*, April 1959, 15–16; Sten Russell, "Mental Health and Homosexuality," *The Ladder*, March 1959, 4–6; Del Martin, "Adjustment Through Partnership," *The Ladder*, March 1959, 18.

61. "January Discussion Group."

62. "Variations."

63. Jim Egan, "Homosexual Marriage—FACT OR FANCY?," *ONE*, December 1959, 7. See also Jim Egan, "Blueprint for Partnership," *ONE*, November 1961, 20–23.

64. Didgeon, "Reflexions on Love and Marriage," *ONE*, September 1960, 7.

65. Kristin Celello, *Making Marriage Work: A History of Marriage and Divorce in the Twentieth-century United States* (Chapel Hill: University of North Carolina Press, 2009).

66. Didgeon, "Reflexions on Love and Marriage," 7; Randy Lloyd, "Let's Push Homophile Marriage," *ONE*, June 1963, 7, 8. See also Hermann Stoessel, "The Decline and Fall of Marriage," *ONE*, April 1959, 5–8; and Martin, "A Matter of Language."

67. Valentine Richardson [Dorr Legg], "The Lesson from the Twins: An Interview at Christmas Time," *ONE*, December 1964, 6–11; Jim Kepner, "My First 64 Years of Gay Liberation: 1964–1969" manuscript (c. 1985–97), 31–32, Jim Kepner Papers: Autobiographies Series 2; 1923–1997, Box 6, Folder 3, ONE National Gay & Lesbian Archives, retrieved from Gale's *Archives of Sexuality and Gender*. On their annual holiday party, see "Christmas Party," *Mattachine Newsletter of Los Angeles*, December 1957, 2.

68. On responses to stigmatization, see Erving Goffman, *Stigma: Notes on the Management of Spoiled Identity* (Englewood Cliffs, NJ: Prentice-Hall, 1963).

69. On lesbian wives, see Gutterman, *Her Neighbor's Wife*; and for examples, Marion Zimmer Bradley, "Some Remarks on Marriage," *The Ladder*, July 1957, 14–23; Miriam Gardner, "Behind the Borderline," *The Ladder*, October 1960, 6–11.

70. Georgina Lloyd as told to Joy O. I. Speczynska, "The Experiment that Failed," *The Ladder*, June 1960, 12–13.

71. Nola, Review of *The Feminine Mystique*, *The Ladder*, March 1963, 9. *The Ladder* soon offered the book to readers through its mail-order book service.

72. On male vulnerability after World War II, see Hartmann, "Prescriptions for Penelope."

73. On sexual containment, see May, *Homeward Bound*.

74. For studies of racial politics in the homophile movement, see Emily K. Hobson, "Policing Gay LA: Mapping Racial Divides in the Homophile Era, 1950–1967," in *The Rising Tide of Color: Race, State Violence, and Radical Movements Across the Pacific*, ed. Moon-Ho Jung (University of Washington Press, 2014), 188–212; Christina B. Hanhardt, "'The White Ghetto': Sexual Deviancy, Police Accountability, and the 1960s War on Poverty," chap. 1 in *Safe Space: Gay Neighborhood History and the Politics of Violence* (Durham, NC: Duke University Press, 2013); and Kent W. Peacock, "Race, the Homosexual, and the Mattachine Society of Washington, 1961–1970," *Journal of the History of Sexuality* 25, no. 2 (2016): 267–96.

75. On Tony (Antonio) Reyes, see brief discussion in Lillian Faderman and Stuart Timmons, *Gay L.A.: A History of Sexual Outlaws, Power Politics, and Lipstick Lesbians* (New York: Basic Books, 2006), 116; and schedule for ONE's 1959 Midwinter Institute, Mattachine Society of New York Records, Box 7, Folder 20, New York Public Library, retrieved from Gale's *Archives of Sexuality and Gender*.

76. Whitney Strub, "In Hispanic Heritage Month, Let's Remember Gay Rights Pioneer

Tony Segura," *Slate*, October 10, 2016, https://slate.com/human-interest/2016/10/tony-segura
-may-have-been-the-most-important-early-gay-rights-organizer.html.

77. Kay Tobin and Barbara Gittings, "Interview with Ernestine," *The Ladder*, June
1966, 4–11.

78. Letter from Philip, March 22, 1961, in *Letters to ONE: Gay and Lesbian Voices from
the 1950s and 1960s*, ed. Craig Loftin (Albany: State University of New York Press, 2012), 41,
reprinted from correspondence files, ONE, Inc. Records (ONE National Gay & Lesbian Archives). In response to William Lambert, "Editorial," *ONE*, January 1961, 4–5.

79. Letter from Miss D, *ONE*, July 1955, 19, also reprinted in *Letters to ONE*, 40. In response
to Albert Ellis, "Are Homosexuals Necessarily Neurotic?," *ONE*, April 1955, 8–12.

80. R. S. B. to Don Slater, October 1960, Homophile Organizations, Mattachine Society
Correspondence, Donald S. Lucas Papers, Box 4, Folder 4.

81. "Ask Drum," *Drum*, June 1965, 25.

82. Martha Shelley, "On Marriage," *The Ladder*, October 1968, 47.

83. Goffman, *Stigma*, 121.

84. Evan Mills, "Homosexual Wedding," *The Phoenix: Midwest Homophile Voice*, August
1967, 22.

85. Marilyn Barrow, "Living Propaganda," *The Ladder*, February 1964, 21.

86. Chuck Taylor, "The Successful Homosexual," *ONE*, May 1959, 6.

87. *Homosexuality and Citizenship in Florida*, n.p.

88. *Homosexuality and Citizenship in Florida*, n.p.

89. R. A., letter to *The Ladder*, October 28, 1958, K–L Correspondence—*The Ladder*
Daughters of Bilitis National, 1946–1958, Phyllis Lyon, Del Martin and the Daughters of Bilitis
Collection, Box 11, Folder 3, GLBT Historical Society, retrieved from Gale's *Archives of Sexuality
and Gender*.

90. Carol Bradford, "Invisible Society," *ONE*, May 1962, 11.

91. Jocelyn Hayward, "Readers Respond," *The Ladder*, October–November 1968, 43–44. In
response to Zee Paulsen, "Make It Last, Baby," *The Ladder*, May–June 1968, 2–4.

92. E. B. Saunders, "Reformer's Choice: Marriage License or Just License?" *ONE*, August
1953, 10–12.

93. Lloyd, "Let's Push Homophile Marriage."

94. Letter from Dionysus/Tony Foster, and letter from Marc Daniel (founder of the
French homophile magazine *Arcadie*), *ONE*, September 1963, 29–30.

95. Daniel J. Boorstin, *The Image: A Guide to Pseudo-Events in American Culture*, 50th ann.
ed. (New York: Vintage Books, 2012), 259.

96. On homophile framing of privacy as a "right to be left alone," see Robert Self, *All in
the Family: The Realignment of American Democracy Since the 1960s* (New York: Hill and Wang,
2012), 78–100.

CHAPTER TWO

1. Lou Rand Hogan, *The Gay Cookbook* (New York: Bell, 1965), published earlier that fall
by Sherbourne Press, Los Angeles. The editions are virtually identical except in size. Advertisement, *New York Times*, December 1, 1965; "The Homosexual in America," *Time*, January 21,
1966, 52.

2. As the San Francisco food columnist Michael Procopio remarked on his blog, "A *gay*
cookbook? *Pre*-Stonewall? I never thought any such thing could exist" ("Swish Steak: Camp
Food," *Bay Area Bites*, August 14, 2009, http://blogs.kqed.org/bayareabites/2009/08/14/swish
-steak-camp-food/). Another San Francisco food writer began his blog entry, "What the hell?

The Boys in the Band meets James Beard—a self-consciously campy guide to the kitchen, at a time when gays were still mostly closeted" (John Birdsall, "Is This the Gayest Book Ever Written about Food?," *SF Weekly*, June 26, 2009, https://www.sfweekly.com/dining/is-this-the-gayest -book-ever-written-about-food/).

3. *1964–65 Guild Book Service Catalog* (Washington, DC: Guild, 1964), Vintage Physique Photography, Timinvermont.com. On gay consumer culture, publishing, and censorship in the 1950s and 1960s, see David K. Johnson, "Physique Pioneers: The Politics of 1960s Gay Consumer Culture," *Journal of Social History* 43, no. 4 (2010): 867–92; David K. Johnson, *Buying Gay: How Physique Entrepreneurs Sparked a Movement* (New York: Columbia University Press, 2019); Whitney Strub, "The Clearly Obscene and the Queerly Obscene: Heteronormativity and Obscenity in Cold War Los Angeles," *American Quarterly* 60, no. 2 (2008): 373–98; and Michael Bronski, *Pulp Friction: Uncovering the Golden Age of Gay Male Pulps* (New York: St. Martin's Griffin, 2003).

4. Jess Stearn, *The Sixth Man* (Garden City, NY: Doubleday, 1961); advertisement, *New York Times*, March 21, 1961.

5. Susan Sontag, "Notes on 'Camp,'" in *Against Interpretation, and Other Essays* (New York: Farrar, Straus and Giroux, 1966), 275–92; originally published in *Partisan Review* 31, no. 4 (1964): 515–30. For essential essays and debates on camp, see Fabio Cleto, ed., *Camp: Queer Aesthetics and the Performing Subject: A Reader* (Ann Arbor: University of Michigan Press, 1999); and David Bergman, ed., *Camp Grounds: Style and Homosexuality* (Amherst: University of Massachusetts Press, 1993).

6. Hogan, *Gay Cookbook*, ii, viii.

7. The San Francisco–based Mattachine Society should be distinguished from its predecessor, the Los Angeles–based Mattachine Foundation. On the homophile movement, see especially John D'Emilio, *Sexual Politics, Sexual Communities: The Making of a Homosexual Minority in the United States, 1940–1970* (Chicago: University of Chicago Press, 1983); Martin Meeker, "Behind the Mask of Respectability: Reconsidering the Mattachine Society and Male Homophile Practice, 1950s and 1960s," *Journal of the History of Sexuality* 10, no. 1 (2001): 78–116; and C. Todd White, *Pre-Gay L.A.: A Social History of the Movement for Homosexual Rights* (Urbana: University of Illinois Press, 2009). On effeminacy and gender normativity, see Craig M. Loftin, "Unacceptable Mannerisms: Gender Anxieties, Homosexual Activism, and Swish in the United States, 1945–1965," *Journal of Social History* 40, no. 3 (2007): 577–96; Betty Hillman, "'The Most Profoundly Revolutionary Act a Homosexual Can Engage In': Drag and the Politics of Gender Presentation in the San Francisco Gay Liberation Movement, 1964–1972," *Journal of the History of Sexuality* 20, no. 1 (2011): 153–81; and Barry Reay, *New York Hustlers: Masculinity and Sex in Modern America* (New York: Manchester University Press, 2010), 147–87.

8. Lizabeth Cohen, *A Consumers' Republic: The Politics of Mass Consumption in Postwar America* (New York: Alfred A. Knopf, 2003). For a historiography of consumerism in LGBTQ history, see Stephen Vider, "Consumerism," *Routledge History of Queer America*, ed. Don Romesburg (New York: Routledge, 2018), 344–58.

9. See, for example, Amy Bentley, *Eating for Victory: Food Rationing and the Politics of Domesticity* (Urbana: University of Illinois Press, 1998); Jessamyn Neuhaus, *Manly Meals and Mom's Home Cooking: Cookbooks and Gender in Modern America* (Baltimore: Johns Hopkins University Press, 2003); Hasia R. Diner, *Hungering for America: Italian, Irish, and Jewish Foodways in the Age of Migration* (Cambridge, MA: Harvard University Press, 2001); Tracey Deutsch, *Building a Housewife's Paradise: Gender, Politics, and American Grocery Stores in the Twentieth Century* (Chapel Hill: University of North Carolina Press, 2010); and Kyla Wazana Tompkins, *Racial Indigestion: Eating Bodies in the Nineteenth Century* (New York: New York University Press, 2012).

10. Michel Foucault, *The History of Sexuality*, vol. 1, *An Introduction*, trans. Robert Hurley (New York: Vintage, 1990), 103.

11. California Death Index lists identical information, and Social Security number, for Lou W. Randall, Lou R. Randall, and Lou R. Hogan: born May 4, 1910, California; died August 4, 1976, Los Angeles (*California, Death Index, 1940–1997*, Ancestry.com). George (Ghordis) D. Randall, born November 2, 1883, Smithport, Pennsylvania; Lucille C. Hogan Randall, born February 1, 1881, Montreal, Canada; see George D. Randall passport application, approved April 15, 1920, and Lucille C. Randall passport application, approved October 20, 1920 (*U.S. Passport Applications, 1795–1925*, Ancestry.com); and U.S. Census of 1910, Kern, California (Ancestry.com).

12. George D. Randall passport application.

13. "Island Wrecks Marital Ship," *Los Angeles Times*, February 28, 1931.

14. U.S. Census of 1930, Los Angeles, California, Ancestry.com.

15. Toto le Grand [pseudonym for Lou Rand Hogan], "The Golden Age of Queens," *Bay Area Reporter*, September 4, 1974. Manuscript in Len Evans Papers, Box 1, Manuscript File, GLBT Historical Society, San Francisco, California. Regional productions of the musicals *The Desert Song* and *Good News* played to packed houses in both Los Angeles and San Francisco in 1928 ("Romberg Musical Show Reopens at Majestic Tuesday," *Los Angeles Times*, June 10, 1928; "'Good News' Run Extended for Additional Week Here," *Los Angeles Times*, September 2, 1928).

16. Louis, Lou, or Lou W. Randall appears on at least thirteen passenger and crew lists between 1938 and 1941 on Ancestry.com, including those for the Matson line ships the *Mariposa*, the *Monterey*, and the *Ewa*, as well as three ships from the American President Line, the SS *President Garfield*, the SS *President Harrison*, and the SS *President Coolidge*. For example, Lou Randall, born c. 1910, is listed as a waiter on the SS *Monterey*, arriving in Honolulu from Melbourne, Australia, October 25, 1939; a waiter on the SS *President Garfield*, arriving in New York, from Kobe, Japan, April 18, 1940; and a room steward on the SS *Mariposa*, arriving in Honolulu from Melbourne, July 3, 1940. The records show that his service at sea began around 1936. See *Honolulu, Hawaii, Passenger and Crew Lists, 1900–1959*, Ancestry.com; *New York Passenger Lists, 1820–1957*, Ancestry.com.

17. Toto le Grand, "Golden Age of Queens," *Bay Area Reporter*, September 18, 1974.

18. Allan Bérubé, *My Desire for History: Essays in Gay, Community, and Labor History* (Chapel Hill: University of North Carolina Press, 2011), 294–320.

19. On the fairy and camp culture, see George Chauncey, *Gay New York: Gender, Urban Culture, and the Making of the Gay Male World, 1890–1940* (New York: Basic Books, 1994), 47–63, 286–91; George Chauncey, "Christian Brotherhood or Sexual Perversion? Homosexual Identities and the Construction of Sexual Boundaries in the World War One Era," *Journal of Social History* 19, no. 2 (1985): 189–211; and David K. Johnson, "The Kids of Fairytown: Gay Male Culture on Chicago's Near North Side in the 1930s," in *Creating a Place for Ourselves*, ed. Genny Beemyn (New York: Routledge, 1997), 97–118. The category of the "fairy" also encompassed people who might be better understood today as transgender, see Chauncey's reframing of the fairy in the preface to the 2019 paperback edition of *Gay New York*. On representations and portrayals of the fairy or "pansy," see Chauncey, *Gay New York*, 300–29; Richard Barrios, *Screened Out: Playing Gay in Hollywood from Edison to Stonewall* (New York: Routledge, 2003). For more on links between camp, effeminacy, and language, see Gershon Legman's lexicon, "The Language of Homosexuality," in *Gay/Lesbian Almanac: A New Documentary*, by Jonathan Ned Katz (New York: Harper and Row, 1983), originally published in George W. Henry and the Committee for the Study of Sex Variants, *Sex Variants: A Study of Homosexual Patterns*, vol. 2 (New York: P. B. Hoeber, 1941).

20. Toto le Grand, "Golden Age of Queens," *Bay Area Reporter*, September 4, 1974; and Lou Rand, manuscript, "*The Scarlet Pansy* by Robert Scully: An Introduction," 1965, Len Evans

Papers, Box 1, Manuscript File. See also Robert C. Corber's introduction to Robert Scully, *A Scarlet Pansy* (New York: Fordham University Press, 2016).

21. Introduction to "The Gay Gourmet" by Lou Rand, *Avanti* 1, no. 2 (1969): 20. The *Gourmet* index does not list Hogan as a contributor—though many recipes and articles were published anonymously. The partial index of *Sunset* online (http://sunset-magazine.stanford .edu/html/search.html) also does not list Hogan, but again, many recipes appeared anonymously. The longtime *Sunset* food editor Jerry Anne Di Vecchio says Hogan did not appear as a writer: the magazine was staff-written, though they did publish reader recipes as "reader submitted" (email to author, July 30, 2009).

22. Among books Hogan claimed to write for which there are no records: *It Takes One to Know One* (listed in his first column in the *Los Angeles Advocate*, "Auntie Lou Cooks," March 1970, 34) and *Behind the Green Door* (first column in the "The Gourmet Shoppe," *Bay Area Reporter*, July 25, 1974).

23. Lou Rand, *The Gay Detective* (Fresno, CA: Saber Books, 1961), republished as Lou Rand, *Rough Trade* (Los Angeles: Argyle, 1964; New York: Paperback Library, 1965).

24. Lou Rand, *The Gay Detective* (San Francisco: Cleis, 2003), 74–75.

25. For insightful summary and commentary, see Susan Stryker and Martin Meeker, "Introduction: Mystery as History," in Rand, *Gay Detective*.

26. Peg Bracken, *The I Hate to Cook Book* (New York: Harcourt, 1960); Hogan, *Gay Cookbook*, vii.

27. Sherbourne Press advertisements in *New York Times Book Review*, November 21, 1965, 55; and *Publishers' Weekly*, August 30, 1965, 181. In the years that followed, remaindered copies of the hardcover could frequently be found listed in advertisements for bookstores across the United States; see, for example, advertisement for Pickwick Bookshops, *Los Angeles Times*, July 12, 1968. Sherbourne's history based on interviews by the author with Shelly Lowenkopf, February 3, 2009, and Gil Porter, February 5, 2009. See also Robert Kirsch, "California Opens New Chapter in the Publishing Industry," *Los Angeles Times*, September 12, 1965. On market segmentation, see Cohen, *Consumers' Republic*, 292–344.

28. "A Market Survey," *Citizens News*, August 31, 1964.

29. *The Gay Cookbook* is not listed in *Book Review Digest* (Bronx, NY: H. W. Wilson, 1965–66). My search for reviews in the gay press included *Mattachine Review*, *ONE*, *The Ladder*, *Drum*, and three San Francisco–based publications, *Vector* (published by Society for Individual Rights), *Citizens News* (published by Strait and Associates), and *Town Talk* (published by Pan-Graphic Press). Advertisements appeared in *Drum* (through Trojan Book Service), March 1966 and December 1966; *Town Talk* (through Dorian Book Service), January–February 1966; Dorian Book Service flyer, advertising catalogs and ephemera from Dorian Book Service, Beinecke Rare Book and Manuscript Library, Yale University; and two similar flyers dated January and May 1966 (Directory Services, Timinvermont.com).

30. Advertisements, *New York Times Book Review*, November 21, 1965, 55; *San Francisco Examiner Book Week*, December 5, 1965, 51; and *Publishers' Weekly*, August 30, 1965, 181. Sherbourne's sales figure based on estimates made by Shelly Lowenkopf (interview).

31. Hogan interview on KPFK, Friday, May 13, 1966, listed in *KPFK Program Folio*, April 25–May 22, 1966; rebroadcast on WBAI, May 18, 1966, listed in *WBAI Folio*, May 1966 (Pacifica Radio Archives Digitized Folio Collection, Pacifica Radio Archives, http://archive.org/details/ pacifica). Unfortunately, the recording itself does not appear to have been preserved.

32. Sontag, "Notes on 'Camp,'" 275.

33. Sontag, "Notes on 'Camp,'" 281, 290.

34. Sontag, "Notes on 'Camp,'" 282.

35. "Taste: 'Camp,'" *Time*, December 11, 1964, 75; Thomas Meehan, "Not Good Taste,

Not Bad Taste, It's Camp," *New York Times Magazine*, March 21, 1965, 30; Gloria Steinem, "The Ins and Outs of Pop Culture," *Life*, August 20, 1965, 72. On response to Sontag's essay, see Cleto, *Camp*, 302–7, and bibliography. See also D. A. Miller on Sontag's "phobic de-homosexualization" of camp in "Sontag's Urbanity," *October* 49 (Summer 1989): 93.

36. *Holiday* magazine was one of the few to note the omission. George Frazier, "Call It Camp," *Holiday*, November 1965, 12.

37. Hogan, *Gay Cookbook*, 16, 26, 91.

38. Barbara Ehrenreich, *The Hearts of Men: American Dreams and the Flight from Commit-ment* (New York: Anchor, 1983), 14–28; Jeffrey Escoffier, "Homosexuality and the Sociological Imagination: Hegemonic Discourses, the Circulation of Ideas, and the Process of Reading in the 1950s and 1960s," in *American Homo: Community and Perversity* (Berkeley: University of Califor-nia Press, 1998), 79–98; K. A. Cuordileone, "'Politics in an Age of Anxiety': Cold War Political Culture and the Crisis in American Masculinity, 1949–1960," *Journal of American History* 87, no. 2 (2000): 515–45; Fred Fejes, *Gay Rights and Moral Panic: The Origins of America's Debate on Homosexuality* (New York: Palgrave Macmillan, 2008), 11–52.

39. Stearn, *Sixth Man*, 41.

40. Dorothy Rothschild, "Interior Desecration," *Vogue*, April 15, 1917, 54.

41. Rothschild, "Interior Desecration," 54.

42. *The Jackpot*, dir. Walter Lang, 1950

43. Milton R. Sapirstein and Alis De Sola, "Decorating the Home: A Special Neurosis in Women," *Harper's Magazine*, September 1955, 39.

44. Donald Webster Cory (Edward Sagarin) and John P. LeRoy (Barry Sheer), *The Homo-sexual and His Society: A View from Within* (New York: Citadel, 1963), 136, 71. On Cory/Sagarin, see Martin B. Duberman, "The 'Father' of the Homophile Movement," in *Left Out: The Politics of Exclusion: Essays, 1964–2002* (Cambridge, MA: South End, 2002), 59–94.

45. Hogan, *Gay Cookbook*, 3, 187, 257, 26.

46. Hogan, *Gay Cookbook*, 7.

47. On Mattachine and ONE's strategies of visibility, see especially Meeker, "Behind the Mask"; Martin Meeker, *Contacts Desired: Gay and Lesbian Communications and Community, 1940s–1970s* (Chicago: University of Chicago Press, 2006); and Loftin, "Unacceptable Manner-isms." See also "An Open Letter to Sen. Dirksen," *Mattachine Review*, January–February 1955, 12; and Nan Alamilla Boyd, *Wide Open Town: A History of Queer San Francisco to 1965* (Berkeley: University of California Press, 2003), 184.

48. "SIR Statement of Policy," quoted in D'Emilio, *Sexual Politics, Sexual Communities*, 190. On SIR, see also Boyd, *Wide Open Town*, 227–31.

49. Marc Stein, *City of Sisterly and Brotherly Loves: Lesbian and Gay Philadelphia, 1945–1972* (Philadelphia: Temple University Press, 2004), 200–58.

50. Manuscript of *Kitchens and Tea-Rooms*, with February 10, 1966, letter to Hal Call, Box 4, Folder 29, Harold L. Call papers, Coll2008–010, ONE National Gay & Lesbian Archives, USC Libraries, University of Southern California.

51. *Vagabond*, no. 7 (Minneapolis: Directory Services, 1965), Queer Music Heritage, https://www.queermusicheritage.com/camp14.html; Johnson, "Physique Pioneers."

52. Hogan, *Gay Cookbook*, 84.

53. Harvey A. Levenstein, *Paradox of Plenty: A Social History of Eating in Modern America* (New York: Oxford University Press, 1993), 213–26; David Strauss, *Setting the Table for Julia Child: Gourmet Dining in America, 1934–1961* (Baltimore: Johns Hopkins University Press, 2011); Thomas McNamee, *The Man Who Changed the Way We Eat: Craig Claiborne and the American Food Renaissance* (New York: Free Press, 2012). Claiborne was himself gay but kept his friend-ships and relationships with other gay men secret in the 1950s and 1960s.

54. For representative Matson menus, see John Haskell Kemble Maritime Ephemera, Huntington Digital Library, https://hdl.huntington.org.

55. Kristin L. Hoganson, *Consumers' Imperium: The Global Production of American Domesticity, 1865–1920* (Chapel Hill: University of North Carolina Press, 2007).

56. Nora Ephron, "Critics in the World of the Rising Soufflé (Or Is It the Rising Meringue?)," *New York*, September 3, 1968, 34–39.

57. Hogan, *Gay Cookbook*, 15, 10, 46, 118.

58. D'Emilio, *Sexual Politics, Sexual Communities*, 235.

59. Tom Burke, "The New Homosexuality," *Esquire*, December 1969, 178, 306.

60. Craig Alfred Hanson, "The Fairy Princess Exposed," in *Out of the Closets: Voices of Gay Liberation*, ed. Karla Jay and Allen Young (New York: Douglas, 1972), 266–69; originally published in *Gay Sunshine*, January 1972, 3. See also Allen Young, "Camp Out?" *Gay Sunshine*, August–September 1970, 9.

61. Mart Crowley, *The Boys in the Band* (New York: Farrar, Straus and Giroux, 1968); 1970 film directed by William Friedkin. It was also available as an LP (A&M, 1969). On *The Boys in the Band* and the politics of visibility, see Stephen Vider, "'Nobody's Goddamn Business But My Own': Leonard Frey and the Politics of Jewish and Gay Visibility in the 1970s," in *The Boys in the Band: Flashpoints of Cinema, History, and Queer Politics*, ed. Matt Bell (Detroit: Wayne State University Press, 2016), 190–215.

62. On post-Stonewall gay masculinity and "clone culture," see Martin P. Levine, *Gay Macho: The Life and Death of the Homosexual Clone* (New York: New York University Press, 1998).

63. Carl Wittman, "A Gay Manifesto," in Jay and Young, *Out of the Closets*, 330–41; originally published as "Refugees from Amerika: A Gay Manifesto," *San Francisco Free Press*, December 22, 1969–January 7, 1970.

64. Mike Silverstein, "God Save the Queen," *Gay Sunshine*, November 1970, 2.

65. Levine, *Gay Macho*; and Leila J. Rupp, *A Desired Past: A Short History of Same-Sex Love in America* (Chicago: University of Chicago Press, 1999), 189–94.

66. Hogan, *Gay Cookbook*, 21.

67. Lou Rand, "Auntie Lou Cooks," *Los Angeles Advocate*, March 1970, 34.

68. Lou Rand, "Auntie Lou Cooks: Fabulous Curries," *Los Angeles Advocate*, April 29–May 12, 1970, 9. On race and class in the *Advocate*, see Scott Herring, "Out of the Closets, Into the Woods: *RFD, Country Women*, and the Post-Stonewall Emergence of Queer Anti-urbanism," *American Quarterly* 59, no. 2 (2007): 341–72, particularly 347–52; and David Palmer, "Imagining a Gay New World: Community Identities and the Ethics of Difference in Late-Twentieth Century America" (PhD diss., University of North Carolina, 2011), 20–67. On foreign fantasy and travel in the 1970s, see Lucas Hilderbrand, "A Suitcase Full of Vaseline, or Travels in the 1970s Gay World," *Journal of the History of Sexuality* 22, no. 3 (2013): 373–402.

69. Final installment of "Auntie Lou Cooks" ran in the *Advocate* on April 24, 1974, 32. First column of "The Gourmet Shoppe" appeared in *Bay Area Reporter*, July 25, 1974. This seems to have predated the larger overhaul of the *Advocate* initiated when the publisher Dick Michaels sold it to the investment banker David Goodstein (Stephen J. Sansweet, "Sign of the Times: A Homosexual Paper, The Advocate, Widens Readership," *Wall Street Journal*, November 3, 1975).

70. Toto le Grand, "Golden Age of Queens," *Bay Area Reporter*, September 4, 1974.

CHAPTER THREE

1. *Gay Sunshine*, Winter 1975–76, 35; *Body Politic*, Nov/Dec 1974, 26; *Kaliflower* ad quoted in Herbert A. Otto, "Communes: The Alternative Life-style," *Saturday Review*, April 24, 1971, 20; *The Empty Closet*, November 1973, 4.

2. On the Stonewall riots and their significance, see David Carter, *Stonewall: The Riots That Sparked the Gay Revolution* (New York: St. Martin's Press, 2004); and Elizabeth A. Armstrong and Suzanna M. Crage, "Movements and Memory: The Making of the Stonewall Myth," *American Sociological Review* 71 no. 5 (2006): 724–51. On the gay liberation movement, see Marc Stein's synthesis in *Rethinking the Gay and Lesbian Movement* (New York: Routledge, 2012), 79–114; and Terence Kissack, "Freaking Fag Revolutionaries: New York's Gay Liberation Front, 1961–1971," *Radical History Review*, no. 62 (1995), 104–34.

3. Carl Wittman, "A Gay Manifesto," in *Out of the Closets: Voices of Gay Liberation*, ed. Karla Jay and Allen Young (1972; reprint, New York: Pyramid Books, 1974), 339. Originally appeared as "Refugees from Amerika: A Gay Manifesto," *San Francisco Free Press*, December 22, 1969–January 7, 1970.

4. Dennis Altman, *Homosexual: Oppression and Liberation* (New York: Outerbridge and Dienstfrey, 1971), 124.

5. "Homosexuals in Revolt," *Life*, December 31, 1971, 66.

6. On class and race diversity within gay liberation, see Kevin Mumford, "The Trouble with Gay Rights: Race and the Politics of Sexual Orientation in Philadelphia, 1969–1982," *Journal of American History* 98, no. 1 (2011): 49–72; and Stein, *Rethinking the Gay and Lesbian Movement*, 81–84.

7. "The Hippies," *Time*, July 7, 1967, 22; "The Commune Comes to America," *Life*, July 18, 1969, 21; Timothy Miller, *The 60s Communes: Hippies and Beyond* (Syracuse, NY: Syracuse University Press, 1999).

8. Miller, *60s Communes*; Tim Hodgdon, *Manhood in the Age of Aquarius: Masculinity in Two Countercultural Communities, 1965–83* (New York: Columbia University Press, 2008); Richard Fairfield, *Communes USA; A Personal Tour* (New York: Penguin Books, 1972); Ron E. Roberts, *The New Communes: Coming Together in America* (Englewood Cliffs, NJ: Prentice-Hall, 1971); Rosabeth Moss Kanter, *Communes: Creating and Managing the Collective Life* (New York: Harper and Row, 1973). "Commune Comes to America," *Life*, 16B.

9. Communes and collective living generally, as forms of alternative domesticity, have inspired a rich historiography, particularly on 1960s and 1970s counterculture and the New Left. See especially Miller, *60s Communes*; Blake Slonecker, *A New Dawn for the New Left: Liberation News Service, Montague Farm, and the Long Sixties* (New York: Palgrave Macmillan, 2012); and Hodgdon, *Manhood in the Age of Aquarius*. Miller estimates that the number of communes in the United States went from a few hundred to at least several thousand, if not "tens of thousands" in the 1960s and 1970s, drawing in hundreds of thousands of people, xiii–xx. On communes before 1960, see Donald E. Pitzer, ed., *America's Communal Utopias* (Chapel Hill: University of North Carolina Press, 1997); and Timothy Miller, *The Quest for Utopia in Twentieth-Century America* (Syracuse, NY: Syracuse University Press, 1998).

10. Ann Richardson Roiphe, "The Family is Out of Fashion," *New York Times Magazine*, August 15, 1971, 10, 31.

11. On alternative domesticities in the 1960s and 1970s, see Arlene S. Skolnick, *Embattled Paradise: The American Family in an Age of Uncertainty* (New York: Basic Books, 1991), 75–100; and Elizabeth H. Pleck, *Not Just Roommates: Cohabitation after the Sexual Revolution* (Chicago: University of Chicago Press, 2012).

12. On *Ain't I a Woman?*, see Agatha Beins, *Liberation in Print: Feminist Periodicals and Social Movement Identity* (Athens: University of Georgia Press, 2017). For examples of articles on collective living, see "Living Collective/Collective Living," *Ain't I a Woman?*, April 2, 1971, 3–5; and "Female Culture/Lesbian Nation," *Ain't I a Woman?*, June 4, 1971, 6–10.

13. On women's separatism and lesbian feminism, see Arlene Stein, "Sisters and Queers:

The Decentering of Lesbian Feminism," *Socialist Review* 22, no. 1 (1992): 33–55; Verta Taylor and Leila J. Rupp, "Women's Culture and Lesbian Feminist Activism: A Reconsideration of Cultural Feminism," *Signs: Journal of Women in Culture and Society* 19, no. 1 (1993): 32–61. On the Furies, see Anne M. Valk, "Living a Feminist Lifestyle: The Intersection of Theory and Action in a Lesbian Feminist Collective," *Feminist Studies* 28, no. 2 (2002): 303–32; and Genny Beemyn, *A Queer Capital: A History of Gay Life in Washington* (New York: Routledge, 2015). On lesbian collective households and parenting, see Daniel Winunwe Rivers, *Radical Relations: Lesbian Mothers, Gay Fathers, and Their Children in the United States Since World War II* (Chapel Hill: University of North Carolina Press, 2013), 139–72.

14. On womyn's lands and lesbian separatism, see Dana R. Shugar, *Separatism and Women's Community* (Lincoln: University of Nebraska Press, 1995); Keridwen N. Luis, *Herlands: Exploring the Women's Land Movement in the United States* (Minneapolis: University of Minnesota Press, 2018); Joyce Cheney, *Lesbian Land* (Minneapolis: Word Weavers, 1985). On La Luz de la Lucha, see Juana Maria Paz, "La Luz de la Lucha," in Cheney, *Lesbian Land*, 66–72, excerpted from Juana Maria Paz self-published memoir, *La Luz Journal* (1980). See also discussion of Paz and La Luz in Luis, *Herlands*, 45–72.

15. Wittman, "Gay Manifesto," 334.

16. "More Letters," *RFD*, Summer 1976, 19.

17. Ron Dayman, "The Politics of Gay Communal Living," *Gay Liberator*, Spring 1976, 14.

18. Wini Breines, *Community and Organization in the New Left, 1962–1968: The Great Refusal*, 2nd ed. (New Brunswick, NJ: Rutgers University Press, 1989), xiv.

19. For an overview of regulation of homosexuality in the 1950s and 1960s, see William N. Eskridge, *Gaylaw: Challenging the Apartheid of the Closet* (Cambridge, MA: Harvard University Press, 1999). See also John D'Emilio, "The Homosexual Menace: The Politics of Sexuality in Cold War America," in *Passion and Power: Sexuality in History*, ed. Kathy Peiss and Christina Simmons (Philadelphia: Temple University Press, 1989), 226–40; David K. Johnson, *The Lavender Scare: The Cold War Persecution of Gays and Lesbians in the Federal Government* (Chicago: University of Chicago Press, 2004); Rivers, *Radical Relations*, 11–31; and George Chauncey, "The Forgotten History of Gay Entrapment," *Atlantic*, June 25, 2019, https://www.theatlantic.com/ideas/archive/2019/06/before-stonewall-biggest-threat-was-entrapment/590536/.

20. On 1950s and 1960s gay activism, see John D'Emilio, *Sexual Politics, Sexual Communities: The Making of a Homosexual Minority in the United States, 1940–1970* (Chicago: University of Chicago Press, 1983); Marc Stein, *City of Sisterly and Brotherly Loves: Lesbian and Gay Philadelphia, 1945–1972* (Philadelphia: Temple University Press, 2004); Nan Alamilla Boyd, *Wide Open Town: A History of Queer San Francisco to 1965* (Berkeley: University of California Press, 2003); Craig M. Loftin, *Masked Voices: Gay Men and Lesbians in Cold War America* (Albany: State University of New York Press, 2012); Martin Meeker, "Behind the Mask of Respectability: Reconsidering the Mattachine Society and Male Homophile Practice, 1950s and 1960s," *Journal of the History of Sexuality* 10, no. 1 (2001): 78–116; and Marc Stein, "Canonizing Homophile Sexual Respectability: Archives, History, and Memory," *Radical History Review*, no. 120 (2014): 53–73.

21. For an overview on the 1960s, the New Left, and the counterculture, see Van Gosse, "A Movement of Movements: The Definition and Periodization of the New Left," in *A Companion to Post-1945 America*, ed. Jean-Christophe Agnew and Roy Rosenzweig (Malden, MA: Blackwell, 2002), 277–302. The language of "Third World Liberation" came into common usage following the founding of the Third World Liberation Front at San Francisco State University and University of Berkeley in 1968 and 1969 as a coalition of students of color, calling for decolonization of the curriculum.

22. For examples, see "Redstockings Manifesto," first published in 1969 (https://www

.redstockings.org/index.php/rs-manifesto), and Shulamith Firestone, *The Dialectic of Sex: The Case for Feminist Revolution* (New York: William Morrow, 1970).

23. Wittman, "Gay Manifesto," 335–36, 333.

24. Third World Gay Revolution, "What We Want, What We Believe," in Jay and Young, *Out of the Closets*, 365.

25. Steve [Kiyoshi] Kuromiya, "Come Out, Come Out, Wherever You Are!," *Philadelphia Free Press*, July 27, 1970, 6, quoted in Stein, *City of Sisterly and Brotherly Loves*, 322.

26. Craig Hanson, "Fairy Princess Exposed," in Jay and Young, *Out of the Closets*, 266–69, originally appeared in *Gay Sunshine*, January 1972, 3.

27. Steve Dansky, "Hey Man," *Come Out*, June–July 1970, 6, later republished as *Gay Flames*, Pamphlet No. 8 (New York: Gay Liberation Front, 1970).

28. Robin Morgan, "Goodbye to All That," in *Dear Sisters: Dispatches from the Women's Liberation Movement*, ed. Rosalyn Fraad Baxandall and Linda Gordon (New York: Basic Books, 2000), 56; and Rita Mae Brown, "Coitus Interruptus," in *A Plain Brown Rapper* (Baltimore: Diana Press, 1976), 33. Both essays originally appeared in *Rat*, February 1970.

29. Dansky, "Hey Man," 6.

30. On the role of public space, commercial venues, and consumer culture in gay community and politics, see, for example, George Chauncey, *Gay New York: Gender, Urban Culture, and the Making of the Gay Male World, 1890–1940* (New York: Basic Books, 1994); D'Emilio, *Sexual Politics, Sexual Communities*; Stein, *City of Sisterly and Brotherly Loves*; David K. Johnson, "Physique Pioneers: The Politics of 1960s Gay Consumer Culture," *Journal of Social History* 43, no. 4 (2010): 867–92; David K. Johnson, *Buying Gay: How Physique Entrepreneurs Sparked a Movement* (New York: Columbia University Press, 2019); Stein, "Canonizing Homophile Sexual Respectability"; and Alice Echols, *Hot Stuff: Disco and the Remaking of American Culture* (New York: W. W. Norton, 2010). On emerging forms of masculinized gay social and sexual culture in the 1970s, see Martin P. Levine, *Gay Macho: The Life and Death of the Homosexual Clone* (New York: New York University Press, 1998).

31. Gary Alinder, "My Gay Soul," *Gay Sunshine*, August–September 1970, reprinted in Jay and Young, *Out of the Closets*, 283.

32. Wittman, "Gay Manifesto," 341.

33. Richard Dyer, "Coming Out as Going In: The Image of the Homosexual as a Sad Young Man," in *The Culture of Queers* (New York: Routledge, 2002), 116–36.

34. *Nicht der Homosexuelle ist pervers, sondern die Situation, in der er lebt*, dir. Rosa von Praunheim, 1971. On the history of the film in Germany, see Patrick Henze, "Perversion of Society: Rosa von Praunheim and Martin Dannecker's Film *It Is Not the Homosexual Who Is Perverse, but the Society in Which He Lives* (1971) as the Initiation of the Golden Age of the Radical Left Gay Movement in West Germany," in *Sexual Culture in Germany in the 1970s*, ed. Janin Afken and Benedikt Wolf (Cham, Switzerland: Palgrave Macmillan 2019), 89–118. On the film's screening in the United States, see Michael Schiavi, *Celluloid Activist: The Life and Times of Vito Russo* (Madison: University of Wisconsin Press, 2011), 99; and Vito Russo, "Premiere: Gay Liberation from Germany with Reluctance," *Gay Activist*, April 1972, 9. Thank you to Paul Farber for his help with the German translation.

35. On the Gay Liberation Front in Washington, DC, see Brian Miller, *Here Because We're Queer: Inside the Gay Liberation Front of Washington, D.C., 1970–72* (self-pub., 2020). On the Hoover Street Commune in Los Angeles, see Don Kilhefner, "Creating a Gay Community: The Hoover Street Commune," *Frontiers in L.A.*, Oct 19—Nov 1, 2009, 38. Dennis Altman reported on a GLF commune in a San Francisco warehouse in "One Man's Gay Liberation," *Come Out!*, December 1970–January 1971, 20. The short-lived Gay Lib House in Louisville is discussed in

James T. Sears, *Rebels, Rubyfruit, and Rhinestones: Queering Space in the Stonewall South* (New Brunswick, NJ: Rutgers University Press, 2001), 62–63. On the Boston gay commune formed by Gay Male Liberation, see "WE TRIED/COMMUNITY CENTER," *Fag Rag*, June 1971, 3. Ferd Eggan was a member of a GLF commune in Chicago, see Eggan's essay "Dykes and Fags Want Everything," in *That's Revolting: Queer Strategies for Resisting Assimilation*, ed. Mattilda Bernstein Sycamore (Brooklyn, NY: Soft Skull Press, 2004), 11–18. On communes in Philadelphia, see Stein, *City of Sisterly and Brotherly Loves*, 37–38, 346–47. On gay living collectives in the UK, see Matt Cook's chapter on Brixton squatters in *Queer Domesticities: Homosexuality and Home Life in Twentieth Century London* (London: Palgrave Macmillan, 2014), 199–225.

36. Donn Teal, *The Gay Militants* (New York: Stein and Day, 1971), 162. For more on the 17th Street Collective and its members, see Jason Victor Serinus, "From the Closets of New Haven to the Collectives of New York GLF," in *Smash the Church, Smash the State! The Early Years of Gay Liberation*, ed. Tommi Avicolli Mecca (San Francisco: City Lights Books, 2009), 55–61. See also Ian K. Lekus, "Queer Harvests: Homosexuality, the U.S. New Left, and the Venceremos Brigades to Cuba," *Radical History Review*, no. 89 (2004): 57–91.

37. Allen Young, "Bringing It to the Streets: The 17th Street Collective," *Montrose Voice*, December, 30, 1983, 8.

38. Néstor Latrónico, "My Memories as a Gay Militant in NYC," in Mecca, *Smash the Church*, 52.

39. John Knoebel, "Somewhere in the Right Direction: Testimony of My Experience in a Gay Male Living Collective," in Jay and Young, *Out of the Closets*, 301–14. Interview with John Knoebel by the author, February 23, 2012. See also interview by Christopher de la Torre, July 1, 2009, http://stonewallrebels.wordpress.com/2009/07/02/40-years-after-stonewall-part-3-john-knoebel. Karla Jay also recalls Knoebel's coming out to his roommate (and coming to live with her) in *Tales of the Lavender Menace: A Memoir of Liberation* (New York: Basic Books, 2000), 107–9. For an account of the gay bashing incident, see Angelo d'Arcangelo, "The Limp Arm of the Law," *Gay*, August 24, 1970, 7, though it mistakenly lists the month as January, not June.

40. GLF Men's Collective, "Five Notes on Collective Living," *Come Out!*, December 1970–January 1971, 7.

41. Knoebel, "Somewhere in the Right Direction," 304.

42. Knoebel, "Somewhere in the Right Direction," 305, 306.

43. N. A. Diaman, "The Baltic Street Collective," in Mecca, *Smash the Church*, 234–41.

44. On the history of the Gay Liberation Front of DC and Gay Liberation House, see Miller, *Here Because We're Queer*, and the Rainbow History Project's digital exhibit, https://archives.rainbowhistory.org/exhibits/show/glf. GLF-DC newsletters archived by the Rainbow History Project. See also Bruce Pennington oral history interview by Mark Meinke, January 27, 2001, transcript courtesy of the Rainbow History Project.

45. Pennington oral history; Theodore Kirkland oral history, n.d., Rainbow History Project; David Aiken, "Dethroning the King," *Motive* 32, no. 2 (1972): 46–48. The racial diversity of GLF House, and GLF-DC more largely, contrasts starkly with the earlier Mattachine Society of Washington; see Kent W. Peacock, "Race, the Homosexual, and the Mattachine Society of Washington, 1961–1970," *Journal of the History of Sexuality* 25, no. 2 (2016): 267–96. On alliances between gay liberation groups and the Black Panther Party, and organizing by queer people of color, see Emily K. Hobson, "Beyond the Gay Ghetto: Founding Debates in Gay Liberation," chap. 1 in *Lavender and Red: Liberation and Solidarity in the Gay and Lesbian Left* (Berkeley: University of California Press, 2016).

46. See Charles Shively's biographical entry on Carl Wittman in *Gay Histories and Cultures: An Encyclopedia*, ed. George E. Haggerty (New York: Taylor and Francis, 2000), 1400–1401. On

creation of Butterworth Farm, see Allen Young, "On Human Identity and Gay Identity: A Liberationist Dilemma," in *After You're Out: Personal Experiences of Gay Men and Lesbian Women*, ed. Karla Jay and Allen Young (New York: Pyramid Books, 1975), 297–34. Malden Avenue collective is mentioned in Gary Atkins, *Gay Seattle: Stories of Exile and Belonging* (Seattle: University of Washington Press, 2003). On Elwha commune, see Faygele (ben Miriam), "Elwha," *RFD*, Winter 1974–75, 5–6; and Lyn Watts, "Gay Men Find a Home in a House," *Port Angeles Daily News*, January 14, 1976. On *RFD*, its connection to lesbian separatism, and the Radical Faeries, see Scott Herring, "Critical Rusticity," chap. 2 in *Another Country: Queer Anti-Urbanism* (New York: New York University Press, 2010).

47. Knoebel, "Somewhere in the Right Direction."

48. On the Hoover Street Commune in Los Angeles, see Don Kilhefner, "Creating a Gay Community: The Hoover Street Commune," *Frontiers in L.A.*, October 19—November 1, 2009, 38.

49. *Faggots and Class Struggle: A Conference Report*, published as a special issue of *Morning Due*, November–December 1976.

50. Watts, "Gay Men Find a Home." The commune soon welcomed women as well; see Chris L., "Lesbians Livin' in the Country," *Out and About: Seattle Lesbian Feminist Newspaper*, June 1976, 1–2.

51. On the commune-run gay bar, see Richard Atcheson, *The Bearded Lady: Going on the Commune Trip and Beyond* (New York: John Day, 1971), 73. Atcheson gives a fake name for the bar, but it was likely the Stud, discussed in Konstantin Berlandt, "My Soul Vanished from Sight: A California Saga of Gay Liberation," in Jay and Young, *Out of the Closets*, 54. The commune-operated bathhouse is Fairoaks. See gallery of photographs at http://www.fairoaks-project.com/index.html.

52. On consciousness-raising, see Alice Echols, *Daring to Be Bad: Radical Feminism in America: 1967–75* (Minneapolis: University of Minnesota Press, 1989), 83–84; and Debra Michals, "From 'Consciousness Expansion' to 'Consciousness Raising': Feminism and the Countercultural Politics of the Self," in *Imagine Nation: The American Counterculture of the 1960s and '70s*, ed. Peter Braunstein and Michael William Doyle (New York: Routledge, 2002), 41–68.

53. A Gay Male Group, "Notes on Gay Male Consciousness-Raising," in Jay and Young, *Out of the Closets*, 293–301.

54. Interview with Allen Young and Ron Punit Auerbacher by the author, March 8, 2012. On Wolf Creek, see "Golden Conversations," *RFD*, Summer 1976, 4–12.

55. GLF Men's Collective, "Five Notes on Collective Living." On "effeminism," see Kenneth Pitchford, "Who are the Flaming Faggots?" *Motive*, Winter 1972, 16–19; and "The Effeminist Manifesto," *Double-F: A Magazine of Effeminism*, Winter/Spring 1973, written by Steven Dansky, John Knoebel, and Kenneth Pitchford.

56. "Gay Yoga," *Fag Rag*, Summer 1972, 15.

57. Pennington oral history.

58. Serinus, "From the Closets," 59–60. See also essays on the Cockettes and "genderfuck," Benjamin Shephard, "Play as World Making: From the Cockettes to the Germs, Gay Liberation to DIY Community Building," in *The Hidden 1970s: Histories of Radicalism*, ed. Dan Berger (New Brunswick, NJ: Rutgers University Press, 2010), 177–94; and Julia Bryan-Wilson, "Handmade Genders: Queer Costuming in San Francisco circa 1970," in *West of Center: Art and the Countercultural Experiment in America, 1965–1977*, ed. Elissa Auther and Adam Lerner (Minneapolis: University of Minnesota, 2011), 77–92.

59. "Gay Lib Cruise," *Quicksilver Times*, September 1–10, 1970; Pennington oral history.

60. Beemyn, *Queer Capital*.

61. Heather Burmeister, "Women's Lands in Southern Oregon: Jean Mountaingrove and Bethroot Gwynn Tell Their Stories," *Oregon Historical Quarterly* 115, no. 1 (2014): 60–89; Heather Jo Burmeister, "Rural Revolution: Documenting the Lesbian Land Communities of Southern Oregon" (MA thesis, Portland State University, 2013).

62. Trella Laughlin oral history by Mason Funk, July 7, 2017, *Outwords*, https://theoutwordsarchive.org/subjectdetail/trella-ann-laughlin.

63. 25 to 6 Baking & Trucking Society, *Great Gay in the Morning! One Group's Approach to Communal Living and Sexual Politics* (Washington, NJ: Times Change Press, 1972); Lee Mintz, "City/Country," *RFD*, Spring 1975, 7–11. See also *Lavender Hill: A Love Story*, dir. Austin Bunn, 2013; and Morgan Bassichis, introduction to *The Faggots and Their Friends Between Revolutions*, by Larry Mitchell (Brooklyn, NY: Nightboat Books, 2019).

64. Matthew Perry, "Fort Hill Faggots for Freedom: An Experiment in Communal City Living," *Gay Community News*, April 10, 1976. See also John Kyper, "Fort Hill: Still Crazy After All Those Years?," *Bay Windows*, January 15, 1987; and conclusion in *Bay Windows*, January 29, 1987.

65. Letter, November 22, 1974, from Jeff to M. G. (Christopher Phillips) and Ed (Sanders), Christopher Phillips Papers, Box 29, Folder 52, Yale University Library, Manuscripts and Archives. Thank you to Grace Gallogly for pointing me toward this letter.

66. *RFD*, Fall 1976, 8.

67. *RFD*, Summer 1977, 5, and Spring 1978, 4.

68. GLF Men's Collective, "Five Notes on Collective Living."

69. "WE TRIED/COMMUNITY CENTER," 3. Rough draft of essay, under title "Gay Commune," in William J Canfield Papers, Box 1, Folder 26, Northeastern University Archives and Special Collections.

70. "Elwha Acres Home Firebombed," *Port Angeles Daily News*, February 2, 1976.

71. Foster Church, "Gay Commune Gets Attention of Unwanted Sort," and "'Redneck' Community Home of New Lifestyles," *Oregonian*, July 22, 1979; "Fire Hits Oregon," *Gaysweek*, February 5, 1979. On boy children and lesbian separatist communities, see Elizabeth Alice Clement, "Debating the 'Man Child': Understanding the Politics of Motherhood through Debates in the US Lesbian Community, 1970–1990," *Journal of Women's History* 31, no. 4 (2019): 86–110; and Rebecca Jennings, "The Boy-Child in Australian Lesbian Feminist Discourse and Community," *Cultural and Social History* 13, no. 1 (2016): 63–79.

72. Knoebel, "Somewhere in the Right Direction."

73. The Baltic Street Collective in Brooklyn, for example, ended after six months when several members left, though a few remained until the end of the one-year lease, after which the house was put up for sale. See Diaman, "Baltic Street Collective." In Washington, DC, most of the founders of the Gay Liberation House had moved out by the end of 1971. The collective ultimately shut down in 1973, when the landlord wanted to put the house up for sale. An offshoot, the Skyline Faggots Collective, formed in 1971 and dispersed in 1975. See Miller, *Here Because We're Queer*.

74. On Radical Faeries, see Peter Hennen, *Faeries, Bears, and Leathermen: Men in Community Queering the Masculine* (Chicago: University of Chicago Press, 2008), 59–94; Herring, "Critical Rusticity"; Scott Lauria Morgensen, "Arrival at Home: Radical Faerie Configurations of Sexuality and Place," *GLQ: A Journal of Lesbian and Gay Studies* 15, no. 1 (2009): 67–96; and Jason Ezell; "'Returning Forest Darlings': Gay Liberationist Sanctuary in the Southeastern Network, 1973–80," *Radical History Review*, no. 135 (2019): 71–94. For example, see discussion of Short Mountain in Alex Halberstadt, "Out of the Woods," *New York Times*, August 6, 2015. On the longer history of Short Mountain, see Sears, *Rebels, Rubyfruit, and Rhinestones*, 142–49. For

a discussion of the gay liberation Alpine Project and its connections to settler colonialism, see Hobson, *Lavender and Red*, 34–39.

75. See, for example, Groundswell Community and Retreat Center, https://groundswellretreat.com; and Idyll Dandy Arts (IDA), https://idylldandyarts.tumblr.com/about.

76. John Murphy, *Homosexual Liberation: A Personal View* (New York: Praeger, 1971), 90.

77. Kenneth T. Beck, "Flaming: Autobiographical Explorations into Manhood" (PhD diss., Union Graduate School, 1974), 271, 275.

78. On homophile calls for privacy as a "right to be left alone," see Robert Self, *All in the Family: The Realignment of American Democracy Since the 1960s* (New York: Hill and Wang, 2012), 78–100. On the turn to domestic partnerships, civil unions, and same-sex marriage, see George Chauncey, *Why Marriage? The History Shaping Today's Debate Over Gay Equality* (New York: Basic Books, 2004); and Pleck, *Not Just Roommates*, 209–28. On the relationship between sexuality and the state, see Nancy F. Cott, *Public Vows: A History of Marriage and the Nation* (Cambridge, MA: Harvard University Press, 2000); and Margot Canaday, *The Straight State: Sexuality and Citizenship in Twentieth-Century America* (Princeton, NJ: Princeton University Press, 2009).

79. Third World Gay Revolution, "What We Want, What We Believe"; José Esteban Muñoz, *Cruising Utopia: The Then and There of Queer Futurity* (New York: New York University Press, 2009), 19–20.

CHAPTER FOUR

1. Photograph by Michael Abramson in Allen Young, "Out of the Closet: A Gay Manifesto," *Ramparts*, November 1971, 57.

2. Phyllis Birkby letter to Bertha Harris, 1972, Box 7, Folder 88, Noel Phyllis Birkby Papers, Sophia Smith Collection, Smith College, Northampton, MA. Punctuation added for clarity.

3. Betty Friedan, *The Feminine Mystique* (New York: Dell Books, 1963); Eva Moskowitz, "'It's Good to Blow Your Top': Women's Magazines and a Discourse of Discontent, 1945–1965," *Journal of Women's History* 8, no. 3 (1996): 66–98. On Friedan and popular postwar social science, see Daniel Horowitz, *Betty Friedan and the Making of* The Feminine Mystique: *The American Left, the Cold War, and Modern Feminism* (Amherst: University of Massachusetts Press, 1998). See also Joanne Meyerowitz's important critique, "Beyond the Feminine Mystique: A Reassessment of Postwar Mass Culture, 1946–1958," *Journal of American History* 79, no. 4 (1993), 1455–82.

4. Pat Mainardi, "The Politics of Housework," in New York Radical Women, *Notes from the Second Year: Women's Liberation* (1970), 28–31.

5. Silvia Federici and Arlen Austin, eds., *Wages for Housework: The New York Committee 1972–1977: History, Theory, Documents* (Brooklyn, NY: Autonomedia, 2017).

6. Alice Echols, *Daring to Be Bad: Radical Feminism in America: 1967–75* (Minneapolis: University of Minnesota Press, 1989); and Alice Echols, "Cultural Feminism: Feminist Capitalism and the Anti-Pornography Movement," *Social Text*, no. 7 (1983): 34–53. See also Verta Taylor and Leila J. Rupp, "Women's Culture and Lesbian Feminist Activism: A Reconsideration of Cultural Feminism," *Signs: Journal of Women in Culture and Society* 19, no. 1 (1993): 32–61; Arlene Stein, "Sisters and Queers: The Decentering of Lesbian Feminism," *Socialist Review* 22, no. 1 (1992): 33–55.

7. Judith Butler, *Gender Trouble: Feminism and the Subversion of Identity* (New York: Routledge, 1990); and Judith Butler, "Performative Acts and Gender Constitution: An Essay in Phenomenology and Feminist Theory," *Theatre Journal* 40, no. 4 (1988): 519–31.

8. Victoria Hesford, *Feeling Women's Liberation* (Durham, NC: Duke University Press, 2013), 2.

9. Joan Wallach Scott, *The Fantasy of Feminist History* (Durham, NC: Duke University Press, 2011), 51.

10. Agatha Beins, *Liberation in Print: Feminist Periodicals and Social Movement Identity* (Athens: University of Georgia Press, 2017), 5.

11. See "Trans/Feminisms," special issue of *TSQ: Transgender Studies Quarterly* 3, no. 1–2 (2016), especially Emma Heaney, "Women-Identified Women: Trans Women in 1970s Lesbian Feminist Organizing," 137–45, and Cristan Williams, "Radical Inclusion: Recounting the Trans Inclusive History of Radical Feminism," 254–58; and Jack Halberstam, "Trans* Feminisms," chap. 6 in *Trans*: A Quick and Quirky Account of Gender Variability* (Oakland: University of California Press, 2018).

12. Greg Youmans, "Performing Essentialism: Reassessing Barbara Hammer's Films of the 1970s," *Camera Obscura: Feminism, Culture, and Media Studies* 27, no. 3 (2012): 122.

13. Leslie Kanes Weisman, *Discrimination by Design: A Feminist Critique of Man-Made Environment* (Urbana: University of Illinois Press, 1992); Dolores Hayden, *The Grand Domestic Revolution: A History of Feminist Designs for American Homes, Neighborhoods, and Cities* (Cambridge, MA: MIT Press, 1981); Dolores Hayden, *Redesigning the American Dream: The Future of Housing, Work, and Family Life* (New York: W. W. Norton, 1984); Susana Torre, *Women in American Architecture: A Historic and Contemporary Perspective* (New York: Whitney Library of Design, 1977); Jos Boys, "Is There a Feminist Analysis of Architecture?" *Built Environment* 10, no. 1 (1984): 25–34.

14. *Historical Statistics of the United States*, Millennial Edition Online, Cambridge University Press. For a longer history of women in architecture, and ongoing barriers, see Despina Stratigakos, *Where Are the Women Architects?* (Princeton, NJ: Princeton University Press, 2016).

15. On Young's speech and impact, see Kathryn H. Anthony, *Designing for Diversity: Gender, Race, and Ethnicity in the Architectural Profession* (Urbana: University of Illinois Press, 2001), 99–103.

16. Birkby quoted in Leslie Kanes Weisman and Noel Phyllis Birkby, "The Women's School of Planning and Architecture," in *Learning Our Way: Essays in Feminist Education*, ed. Charlotte Bunch and Sandra Pollack (Trumansburg, NY: Crossing Press, 1983), 234. Birkby's use of the term "Third World" reflected a common usage of the term by feminists and other activists as an umbrella term for people of color, spurred by the formation of Third World Liberation Front at San Francisco State University and University of California, Berkeley, in 1968 and 1969.

17. Cornel West, "A Note on Race and Architecture," in *Keeping Faith: Philosophy and Race in America* (New York: Routledge, 1993), 40, 42.

18. "Birkby Joins Comprehensive Fabrics Soon," *Women's Wear Daily*, March 8, 1944, 16. See also 1940 Census Record for Harold and Alice Birkby and family, Nutley, Essex, New Jersey, Ancestry.com.

19. Biographical information and quotes from Phyllis Birkby, Letter to Margrit Kennedy, 1980, Box 7, Folder 92, Birkby Papers; and Phyllis Birkby, Women in Architecture lecture notes, n.d., Box 21, Folder 312, Birkby Papers. Architecture statistics from *Historical Statistics of the United States*.

20. Background on the Woman's College from Sarah Perry, "A Place of Distinction: Woman's College in Greensboro," *Our State*, December 31, 2013, https://www.ourstate.com/womans-college-greensboro/. Quote from Birkby, Letter to Margrit Kennedy.

21. Transcript of oral history interview with Key L. Barkley, 1991, UNCG Centennial Oral History Project, OH003, Martha Blakeney Hodges Special Collections and University Archives, University of North Carolina at Greensboro, NC.

22. Phyllis Birkby, "Voix du Silence 17 years," October 1971, Box 21, Folder 310, Birkby Papers.

23. Transcript of CR Group One session, "Butch/Femme," 1971, Box 33, Folder 564, Birkby Papers.

24. Phyllis Birkby, Problem solving diary, n.d. ["Fantasies, expectations, desires . . ."], Box 21, Folder 310, Birkby Papers, punctuation added for clarity; Birkby, Letter to Margrit Kennedy; Birkby, "Voix du Silence 17 years."

25. Audre Lorde, *Zami: A New Spelling of My Name: A Biomythography* (Berkeley, CA: Crossing Press, 1982), 177.

26. Birkby, Problem solving diary, n.d. ["Fantasies, expectations, desires . . ."].

27. Anonymous [Esther], Letters to Phyllis Birkby, quote from letter postmarked April 15, 1955, Box 7, Folder 72. Though the folder is marked anonymous, many of the letters discuss psychology classes.

28. Birkby, Problem solving diary, n.d. ["Fantasies, expectations, desires . . ."]. On Leser, see Esther Newton, *My Butch Career: A Memoir* (Durham, NC: Duke University Press, 2018), 145; and Sidney Fields, "She Mimics Nature," *New York Daily News*, March 4, 1964.

29. Birkby, Women in architecture lecture notes. Punctuation added for clarity.

30. Phyllis Birkby lecture, Southern California Institute of Art, c. 1980, https://www.youtube.com/watch?v=7O5d4OD410A; Ada Louise Huxtable, "Breaking the Mold: Architecture," *New York Times*, February 10, 1974; "L.I.U. Library: A Final Campus Link," *Architectural Record*, July 1976, 93–98.

31. On liberal feminism, radical feminism, and inclusion of lesbians, see Ruth Rosen, *The World Split Open: How the Modern Women's Movement Changed America* (New York: Penguin Books, 2000).

32. Birkby, Letter to Margrit Kennedy.

33. Nancy Tucker, "Interview with Barbara Love and Sidney Abbott," *The Ladder*, August/September 1972, 42–49.

34. Transcript of CR Group One session, "Butch/Femme."

35. Birkby, Problem solving diary, n.d. ["Fantasies, expectations, desires . . ."].

36. Phyllis Birkby, Letter to Victoria, Book Proposal, n.d. [c. 1980], Box 24, Folder 374, Birkby Papers.

37. Birkby, Letter to Margrit Kennedy.

38. Birkby, "Some Personal Notes About the Development of This Project," n.d. [c. 1980.], Box 24, Folder 382, Birkby Papers.

39. Birkby, Letter to Victoria.

40. Birkby, "Some Personal Notes."

41. Phyllis Birkby, "Fantasy Environments: An Investigation," n.d. [c. 1974], Box 23, Folder 359, Birkby Papers.

42. Phyllis Birkby, "Symposium Questions" in notebook, c. 1974, Box 3, Folder 39, Birkby Papers.

43. Phyllis Birkby, "Women in the Built Environment" draft, n.d., Box 24, Folder 372, Birkby Papers. Birkby's film of Fifth Street is included in compilation no. 9 created by the Sophia Smith Archives, https://media.smith.edu/departments/ssc/birkby/birkby_playlist.html. For further background, see Liza Cowan, "Side Trip: The Fifth Street Women's Building Takeover: A Feminist Urban Action, January 1971," Dykeaquarterly.com, July 26, 2012, originally written in 1992, https://www.dykeaquarterly.com/2012/07/the-fifth-street-womens-building-a-feminist-urban-action-jan-1-13th-1971-our-hands-our-feet-our-minds-our-bodies.html. Thank you to Carolina Hausmann-Stabile and Rosi Song for consultation on Spanish transcription and translation.

44. Bertha Harris and Phyllis Birkby correspondence, Box 7, Folder 88, Birkby Papers; Birkby, "Some Personal Notes."

45. Radicalesbians, "The Woman-Identified Woman," in *Notes from the Third Year: Women's Liberation* (1971), 81. The essay was first distributed during the Lavender Menace protest at the Second Congress to Unite Women in May 1970. Birkby's partner at the time, painter Louise Fishman, had attended and reported back to Birkby; see Birkby, Letter to Margrit Kennedy.

46. Radicalesbians, "Woman-Identified Woman," 83.

47. Echols, *Daring to be Bad*.

48. On the "political lesbian" and "feminist as lesbian," see Hesford, *Feeling Women's Liberation*; Ti-Grace Atkinson, "Lesbianism and Feminism" in *Amazon Expedition: A Lesbian Feminist Anthology*, ed. Phyllis Birkby, Bertha Harris, Jill Johnston, Esther Newton, and Jane O'Wyatt (New York: Times Change Press, 1973), 11–14; Charlotte Bunch, "Lesbians in Revolt: Male Supremacy Quakes and Quivers," *The Furies: Lesbian/Feminist Monthly* 1 no. 1 (1972): 8–10; Anne Koedt, "Lesbianism and Feminism" in *Notes from the Third Year*, 84–89.

49. On Johnston, see Sara Warner, "Expatriate Acts: Jill Johnston's Joker Citizenship," chap. 3 in *Acts of Gaiety: LGBT Performance and the Politics of Pleasure* (Ann Arbor: University of Michigan Press, 2012); and Jill Johnston, "Lesbian/Feminism Reconsidered," *Salmagundi* no. 58/59 (1982/1983): 76–88.

50. Jill Johnston, *Lesbian Nation: The Feminist Solution* (New York: Simon and Schuster, 1973), 181–82.

51. On womyn's lands and lesbian separatism, see especially Dana R. Shugar, *Separatism and Women's Community* (Lincoln: University of Nebraska Press, 1995); Keridwen N. Luis, *Herlands: Exploring the Women's Land Movement in the United States* (Minneapolis: University of Minnesota Press, 2018); Joyce Cheney, *Lesbian Land* (Minneapolis: Word Weavers, 1985). On women's/lesbian periodicals and publishing, art and culture, and consumption, see Beins, *Liberation in Print*; Kristen Hogan, *The Feminist Bookstore Movement: Lesbian Antiracism and Feminist Accountability* (Durham, NC: Duke University Press, 2016); Finn Enke, *Finding the Movement: Sexuality, Contested Space, and Feminist Activism* (Durham, NC: Duke University Press, 2008); Heather Murray, "Free for All Lesbians: Lesbian Cultural Production and Consumption in the United States During the 1970s," *Journal of the History of Sexuality* 16, no. 2 (2007): 251–75.

52. See especially Luis's discussion of womyn's lands, racism, and transphobia in *Herlands*. On inclusion of transgender women in feminist organizing, see Heaney, "Women-Identified Women."

53. Warner, *Acts of Gaiety*, 110, 126, 107.

54. Birkby recorded a short message from Johnston, shortly after her original suspension from Woman's College. Letters to Birkby summary document ["From the girl . . .], n.d., Box 8, Folder 117, Birkby Papers. On "lesbian camp weekends," see Jill Johnston letter to Phyllis Birkby ["phisber bikber . . ."], n.d., Box 7, Folder 89, Birkby Papers.

55. Birkby letter to Bertha Harris ["OK Harris here I am . . ."], n.d. [c. 1972], Box 7, Folder 88, Birkby Papers. Johnston recalls this conversation as well in *Lesbian Nation*, 47, 57.

56. Phyllis Birkby, Letter to Bertha Harris ["and so maybe this isolation . . ."] n.d., Box 7, Folder 88, Birkby Papers.

57. *Amazon Weekend* (1973) and other films by Birkby have been preserved and digitized by the Sophia Smith Archives, available at https://media.smith.edu/departments/ssc/birkby/birkby_playlist.html. *Amazon Weekend* was featured in the film festival "Women by Women," organized by Amazon Media Project, January 16–20, 1974. See brochure in "Media: Amazon Media Project" subject folder, Lesbian Herstory Archive, Brooklyn, NY, retrieved from Gale's *Archives of Sexuality and Gender*.

58. Kate Millett, *Flying* (New York: Alfred A. Knopf, 1974), 156–57.

59. Workshop with Ann Pollon, Gail, and Bertha Harris, audio recording, n.d. [c. 1973], Box 76, Folder 65, Birkby Papers.

60. Joan, "My Block/Lavender Lane," n.d. [c. 1973/1974], Women and the Built Environment/Fantasy Drawings, Originals, Box 23, Folder 367, Birkby Papers.

61. Phyllis Birkby, "Amazon Architecture," *Cowrie: Lesbian/Feminist* 1, no. 2 (April 1974): 12–14.

62. Workshop with Liza [Cowan], Cheryl, and Mary, audio recording, March 1974, Box 75, Folder 63, Birkby Papers. Cowan's drawings appear in *Design & Environment* 5, no. 1 (1974), 38–39. Details about workshop confirmed, and drawings identified, by Liza Cowan, email correspondence with the author.

63. Ellen Perry Berkeley, "Women in Architecture," *Architectural Forum*, September 1972, 46–53.

64. Ada Louise Huxtable, "The Letterhead is Solidly Male," *New York Times*, May 19, 1974.

65. *Design & Environment* 5, no. 1 (1974), 38–39, accompanying article by Neil Kleinman, "The Middle-Class Minority."

66. Women in Architecture Symposium, 1974, program, https://openscholarship.wustl.edu/wia/1974/.

67. Birkby, "Some Personal Notes."

68. Phyllis Birkby, "After St. Louis Symposium on Women in Architecture," March 31, 1974, Box 21, Folder 310, Birkby Papers.

69. Leslie Kanes Weisman, Interview conducted by Lucille Goodman, June 2, 2004, for North Fork Women Archives Committee, https://www.youtube.com/watch?v=fAmSJCNzAwk.

70. Gay Academic Union Conference, New York University, "Negotiating Space: The Woman-Built Environment," Nov 30 1974, audio recording, Box 76, Folder 69, Birkby Papers; Workshop, "Women in Design: The Next Decade" conference, Women's Building, Los Angeles, CA, March 20–21 1975, audio recording, Box 76, Folder 70, Birkby Papers; Lecture and workshop, "Two Feminist Designers, Leslie Kanes Weisman and Noel Phyllis Birkby," University of Wisconsin—Green Bay, May 1–2, 1975, audio recording, Box 76, Folder 71–72, Birkby Papers; "Feminist Architects to Speak," *Kingston Daily Freeman*, October 16, 1975; Gloria Cole, "I Dreamt I Dwelt in Marble Halls," *Westport Fair Press*, January 21, 1976.

71. Weisman, *Discrimination by Design*, 169.

72. Noel Phyllis Birkby and Leslie Kanes Weisman, "A Woman-Built Environment: Constructive Fantasies," *Quest* 2, no. 1 (1975): 12, 15.

73. Birkby and Weisman, "Woman-Built Environment," 8.

74. Phyllis Birkby and Leslie Weisman, "Patritecture and Feminist Fantasies," *Liberation*, Spring 1976, 46, 52.

75. Weisman and Birkby, "Women's School of Planning and Architecture," 227. See also Harriet Stix, "They're Emerging: Women Architects: House that Jill Built," *Los Angeles Times*, August 19, 1976.

76. Gail, Letter to Birkby and Weisman, August 28, 1975, Box 23, Folder 360, Birkby Papers.

77. N. P. Birkby and L. K. Weisman, "Drawings of Women's Fantasies: An Environmental Investigation," Book Proposal, Box 23, Folder 371.

78. Weisman, *Discrimination by Design*, 169.

79. Noel Phyllis Birkby and Leslie Kanes Weisman, "Women's Fantasy Environments: Notes on a Projects in Process," *Heresies* 1, no. 2 (1977): 116.

80. Cole, "I Dreamt I Dwelt in Marble Halls."

81. Birkby and Weisman, "Patritecture and Feminist Fantasies," 51.

82. Anonymous fantasy drawing, copy, Box 23, Folder 368, Birkby Papers; Anonymous fantasy drawing, Box 9, Folder 67 [Oversize], Birkby Papers.

83. Cole, "I Dreamt I Dwelt in Marble Halls."

84. Anonymous fantasy drawings, originals, Box 23, Folder 367, Birkby Papers.

85. "Charleen's Place" drawing, Box 23, Folder 368, Birkby Papers. Birkby was friends with Whisnant and credits the drawing to a straight woman, married to an architect, in Gay Academic Union Conference, audio recording.

86. Anonymous fantasy drawings, originals, Box 23, Folder 367, Birkby Papers.

87. Bill Voyd, "Funk Architecture," in *Shelter and Society*, ed. Paul Oliver (New York: Praeger, 1969), 158, quoted in Simon Sadler, "The Dome and the Shack: The Dialects of Hippie Enlightenment," in *West of Eden: Communes and Utopia in Northern California*, ed. Iain A. Boal, Janferie Stone, Michael Watts, and Calvin Winslow (Oakland, CA: PM Press, 2012), 72–80.

88. Reproduced in Birkby and Weisman, "Patritecture and Feminist Fantasies." On the GAU Conference recording, Weisman identifies herself and two women who started a feminist credit union in Detroit as the creators of the drawings. See also audio recording of Val, Jo, and L, August 4, 1974, Box 75, Folder 60. On Angers and Parrent's creation of the feminist credit union, and their work with Feminist Women's Health Center, see Enke, *Finding the Movement*, 201–3.

89. GAU Conference recording, and "Quotes from Women on Their Environmental Fantasies," Box 24, Folder 379, Birkby Papers.

90. Reproduced in Birkby and Weisman, "Patritecture and Feminist Fantasies."

91. Birkby fantasy drawing, Box 23, Folder 367, Gay Academic Union Conference Recording.

92. Caroling [Caroling Constance Geary], Letter to Phyllis Birkby and Leslie Kanes Weisman, February 23, 1977, Box 25, Folder 399, Birkby Papers; Caroling, "Liberating the Handmaiden," *Glass Art Magazine*, April 1977, 18; Phyllis Birkby, Letter to Caroling, March 15, 1977, Box 25, Folder 399, Birkby Papers.

93. Frances Doughty, "Frances' Dome," n.d., Box 24, Folder 379, Birkby Papers.

94. Birkby's interest in women's vernacular architecture dovetailed with a growing social and cultural turn in architectural theory and history, and a growing interest in vernacular or "traditional" buildings—those buildings designed and constructed by untrained individuals and groups. See, for example, Bernard Rudofsky, *Architecture Without Architects: An Introduction to Nonpedigreed Architecture* (Garden City, NY: Doubleday, 1964), in conjunction with exhibition at the Museum of Modern Art; Paul Oliver, *Shelter and Society* (New York: Praeger, 1969); Amos Rapoport, *House Form and Culture* (Englewood Cliffs, NJ: Prentice-Hall, 1969). For overview, see Robert Brown and Daniel Maudlin, "Concepts of Vernacular Architecture," in *The SAGE Handbook of Architectural Theory*, ed. Greig Crysler, Stephen Cairns, and Hilde Heynen (London: SAGE, 2012).

95. Scott Herring, "Out of the Closets, into the Woods: *RFD*, *Country Women*, and the Post-Stonewall Emergence of Queer Anti-Urbanism," *American Quarterly* 59, no. 2 (2007): 341–72; Kate Coleman, "Country Women: The Feminists of Albion Ridge," *Mother Jones*, April 1978, 28.

96. Barbara of Covelo, "Shelter Meditation," *Country Women*, no. 9 (January 1974): 1. See also an account by another Albion feminist, River, *Dwelling: On Making Your Own* (Albion, CA: Freestone, 1974).

97. Birkby describes leaving Weisman after WSPA, and meeting Ena, in Problem solving diary, n.d., ["Fantasies, expectations, desires . . ."]. On anxieties about ownership of the fantasy project, see Problem solving diaries, n.d. ["The only time I felt 'happy' . . ."], and ["I was afraid

fo[r] myself more than anything . . ."], Box 21, Folder 311, and "Notes from 1978," and "Notes on Agreement," Box 24, Folder 379, Birkby Papers.

98. Barbara Hammer describes their visit, and the film, in the descriptive list she created of Birkby's films, appendix II, Birkby Papers Finding Aid. "Wholeo" film, Box 65, Folder 84, Birkby Papers. See also Birkby's letters to Hammer, Box 7, Folder 87.

99. Phyllis Birkby, Wholeo dome notes, Box 25, Folder 399, Birkby Papers.

100. Phyllis Birkby, Tye Farm notes, 1978, Box 25, Folder 398, Birkby Papers.

101. Phyllis Birkby, Notes ["piece about women as space makers"], n.d., Box 24, Folder 383, Birkby Papers. Punctuation added for clarity.

102. Phyllis Birkby, Anita Rodriguez interview notes, Box 25, Folder 395, Birkby Papers.

103. Phyllis Birkby, Marcia Oliver interview notes, 1979, Box 25, Folder 393, Birkby Papers.

104. Doris Cole, *From Tipi to Skyscraper: A History of Women in Architecture* (Boston: I Press, 1973). In a 1975 lecture on women in architecture, Birkby referenced Cole's book: "While the men were the ones who brought home the buffalo, as it were, it was the women who designed the tipis, selected the poles, tanned the hides, made the covers, sometimes communally with other women, much like a quilting bee. They learned to play with tipis as little girls and their architectural and construction skills were passed on from their mothers and other women of the tribe." Phyllis Birkby, "Women in Architecture" lecture notes, Detroit, 1975, Box 21, Folder 312, Birkby Papers.

105. Phyllis Birkby, "Herspace," *Heresies* 3, no. 3 (1981): 28–29.

106. Phyllis Birkby, "Designing for 'The Messiness of Life,'" *Ms.*, February 1981, 77.

107. Terry Wolverton, Feminist Perspectives on Pornography lecture, November 17–19, 1979, transcript by Phyllis Birkby, Box 33, Folder 558, Birkby Papers. On the feminist anti-pornography movement, see Echols, "Cultural Feminism"; and Carolyn Bronstein, *Battling Pornography: The American Feminist Anti-Pornography Movement, 1976–1986* (New York: Cambridge University Press, 2011).

108. Birkby, "Designing for 'The Messiness of Life,'" 77.

109. Birkby, "Designing for 'The Messiness of Life,'" 77.

110. Audre Lorde, "The Uses of the Erotic: The Erotic as Power," in *Sister Outsider: Essays and Speeches* (Berkeley, CA: Crossing Press, 1984), 53, 59. Lorde first presented the lecture on August 25, 1978, at the Fourth Berkshire Conference on the History of Women, Mount Holyoke College, and presented it again at the "Feminist Perspectives on Pornography" conference the following November, as recorded by Pacifica Radio Archives, https://archive.org/details/pacifica_radio_archives-KZ0884. Phyllis Birkby, *Ms.* essay draft, Box 21, Folder 323, Birkby Papers.

111. Echols, *Daring to Be Bad*. Essentialist frameworks of gender in lesbian/feminist culture paralleled work by psychologists and psychoanalysts including Carol Gilligan, *In a Different Voice: Psychological Theory and Women's Development* (Cambridge, MA: Harvard University Press, 1982), and Nancy J. Chodorow, *The Reproduction of Mothering: Psychoanalysis and the Sociology of Gender* (Berkeley: University of California Press, 1978).

112. Jane Gerhard, *Desiring Revolution: Second-Wave Feminism and the Rewriting of American Sexual Thought, 1920 to 1982* (New York: Columbia University Press, 2001), 186.

113. Birkby, "Designing for 'The Messiness of Life'"; and Birkby, *Ms.* essay draft.

114. Birkby met Jacobs through a mutual friend, photographer Hugh Rogers, when Jacobs was living in New York. The house took about a year to construct, from design to completion, and was built by James J. Famiglietti, Inc. of Glen Cove, NY. Interview with Joan Jacobs, June 19, 2020, and personal correspondence.

115. Birkby discusses designs for David Jacobs and Debra Lobel and Beverly Dash in

lecture for Southern California Institute of Art, https://channel.sciarc.edu/browse/alberto
-bertoli-phyllis-birkby-1980. See also Birkby's portfolio, c. 1990, Box 3, Folder 24, and project
folders, Box 12, Folder 199, and Box 13, Folders 206 and 207, Birkby Papers. For background on
Lobel and Dash, see "Donor Profile: Beverly Dash and Debra Lobel," *Impact* (Lambda Legal
magazine), Winter 2018, https://www.lambdalegal.org/impact-winter-2018/donor-profile.

116. Cardamon Lane Condominiums, Little Ferry, NJ, 1983–84, Box 12, Folder 190, Birkby
Papers; Anthony DePalma, "From Garage to Condominiums: Little Ferry Eyesore Yields 24
Units and Indoor Alley," *New York Times*, January 6, 1985.

117. Christopher Bascom Rawlins, *Fire Island Modernist: Horace Gifford and the Architecture
of Seduction* (New York: Metropolis Books, 2013).

118. Correspondence with Ann[e] Witten, 1983–84, Box 8, Folder 116, Birkby Papers; project folders on Watering Place Resort Hotel, Roatan, Honduras, 1984–1985, Box 16, Folder 258–
260, Birkby Papers.

119. For summary of Birkby's career in the 1980s, see her 1992 cv, Box 1, Folder 7, and her
professional portfolio.

120. On Spyer and Windsor, see Lillian Faderman, *The Gay Revolution: The Story of the
Struggle* (New York: Simon and Schuster, 2015), 622–29.

121. Spyer/Windsor home projects, Spyer, 2 Fifth Ave., New York, NY, 1991, Box 15, Folder
251; and 254 Tuckahoe Lane, South Hampton, NY, 1986–87, Box 15, Folder 252, Birkby Papers.

122. On disability, care, the built environment, and domesticity, see especially Robert
McRuer, "Capitalism and Disabled Identity," chap. 2 in *Crip Theory: Cultural Signs of Queerness
and Disability* (New York: New York University Press, 2006); Colin Barnes, "Understanding
the Social Model of Disability: Past, Present and Future," in *The Routledge Handbook of Disability Studies*, ed. Nick Watson, Alan Roulstone, and Carol Thomas (New York: Routledge,
2013), 12–29; and Rosemarie Garland-Thomas, "Integrating Disability, Transforming Feminist
Theory," *NWSA Journal* 14, no. 3 (2002): 1–32.

123. Letter from Alma Routsong to Sisters of Birkby, April 29, 1993, Box 1, Folder 5, Birkby
Papers. Birkby died a year later, on April 13, 1994, at age 61.

CHAPTER FIVE

1. F. E. Mitchell, "Emmaus House," and Mitch Mitchell, "What I Enjoy," *Gay Pride
Crusader*, June/July 1973; Lee M. Balan, "What is Emmaus House?" *Gay Times*, January 1972. In
his 1973 article on "Emmaus House," Mitchell says he has lived in San Francisco for three years,
which appears to be a mistake, as he was still attending Porterville College in the 1970/1971
academic year. Arriving in 1971 fits more clearly with other dates in his account of his early time
in San Francisco.

2. Joey Plaster, "Imagined Conversations and Activist Lineages: Public Histories of Queer
Homeless Youth Organizing and the Policing of Public Space in San Francisco's Tenderloin,
1960s and Present," *Radical History Review*, no. 113 (2012): 99–109; Jennifer Worley, "'Street
Power' and the Claiming of Public Space: San Francisco's *Vanguard* and Pre-Stonewall Queer
Radicalism," in *Captive Genders: Trans Embodiment and the Prison Industrial Complex*, ed. Eric A.
Stanley and Nat Smith (Oakland, CA: AK Press, 2011), 41–56; Christina B. Hanhardt, *Safe
Space: Gay Neighborhood History and the Politics of Violence* (Durham, NC: Duke University
Press, 2013).

3. On Compton's, see Susan Stryker, *Transgender History* (Berkeley, CA: Seal, 2008), and
the documentary *Screaming Queens: The Riot at Compton's Cafeteria* (2005), dir. Victor Silver-
man and Susan Stryker. On the role of queer and transgender youth in the Stonewall riots, see

Martin Duberman, *Stonewall* (New York: Dutton, 1993); and David Carter, *Stonewall: The Riots That Sparked the Gay Revolution* (New York: St. Martin's Press, 2004).

4. Donn Teal, *The Gay Militants* (New York: Stein and Day, 1971), 28.

5. "Page One," and "Spare Change, Pig!," *Bread Box* 1, no. 1 (1970): n.p.

6. Teal, *Gay Militants*, 33.

7. *Bread Box* 1, no. 1 (1970): n.p.

8. On gay health and social service activism in the 1970s, see Katie Batza, *Before AIDS: Gay Health Politics in the 1970s* (Philadelphia: University of Pennsylvania Press, 2018); Michael G. Lee, "Between Stonewall and AIDS: Initial Efforts to Establish Gay and Lesbian Social Services," *Journal of Sociology & Social Welfare* 40, no. 3 (2013): 163–86; and David S. Byers, Stephen Vider, and Amelia Smith, "Clinical Activism in Community-based Practice: The Case of LGBT Affirmative Care at the Eromin Center, Philadelphia, 1973–1984," *American Psychologist* 74, no. 8 (2019): 868–81. On responses to runaway and homeless youth in the 1960s and 1970s, see Karen M. Staller, *Runaways: How the Sixties Counterculture Shaped Today's Practices and Policies* (New York: Columbia University Press, 2006).

9. On gay liberation and gay culture in the 1970s, see especially David Eisenbach, *Gay Power: An American Revolution* (New York: Carroll and Graf, 2006); Martin P. Levine, *Gay Macho: The Life and Death of the Homosexual Clone* (New York: New York University Press, 1998); Alice Echols, *Hot Stuff: Disco and the Remaking of American Culture* (New York: W. W. Norton, 2010); and Brian J. Distelberg, "Mainstream Fiction, Gay Reviewers, and Gay Male Cultural Politics in the 1970s," *GLQ: A Journal of Lesbian and Gay Studies* 16, no. 3 (2010): 389–427.

10. On shifts in LGBTQ politics, see especially Robert Self, *All in the Family: The Realignment of American Democracy Since the 1960s* (New York: Hill and Wang, 2012).

11. On professionalization and nonprofitization of LGBTQ activism, see Myrl Beam, *Gay, Inc.: The Nonprofitization of Queer Politics* (Minneapolis: University of Minnesota Press, 2018).

12. On earlier forms of domestic reform as sites of social constraint, see especially Nayan Shah, *Contagious Divides: Epidemics and Race in San Francisco's Chinatown* (Berkeley: University of California Press, 2001); Shannon Jackson, *Lines of Activity: Performance, Historiography, Hull-House Domesticity* (Ann Arbor: University of Michigan Press, 2001); and Kevin P. Murphy, "Socrates in the Slums: Homoerotics, Gender, and Settlement House Reform," in *A Shared Experience: Men, Women, and the History of Gender*, ed. Laura McCall and Donald Yacovone (New York: New York University Press, 1998), 273–96.

13. On shifting conceptions of runaway youth, see Staller, *Runaways*; James S. Gordon, "Running Away in America: The History and the Hope," in *Uprooting and Development*, ed. George V. Coelho and Paul I. Ahmed (New York: Plenum Press, 1980), 249–66; David E. Suddick, "Runaways: A Review of the Literature," *Juvenile and Family Court Journal* 24, no. 2 (1973): 47–54; Robert Shellow et al., "Suburban Runaways of the 1960's," *Monographs of the Society for Research in Child Development* 32, no. 3 (1967): iii–51.

14. David Cole Gordon, "The Runaways," *Humanist*, January 1, 1968, 2.

15. "Runaway Kids," *Life*, November 3, 1967, 18–29.

16. Anne B. Moses, "The Runaway Youth Act: Paradoxes of Reform," *Social Service Review* 52, no. 2 (1978): 227–43.

17. On emergence of runaway houses, see Staller, *Runaways*, 97–121.

18. Staller, *Runaways*; Larry Beggs, *Huckleberry's for Runaways* (New York: Ballantine Books, 1969); *From Huckleberry's for Runaways to Youth Advocates: Our 1973 Report* (San Francisco: Youth Advocates, 1974); Jay Berlin, "Long-Term Placement at Huckleberry's," in *Reaching Troubled Youth: Runaways and Community Mental Health*, ed. James Samuel Gordon and Margaret Beyer (Washington, DC: U.S. Dept. of Health and Human Services, National Institute of Mental Health, 1981); Moses, "Runaway Youth Act."

19. Paul Gibson, "Developing Services to Lesbian and Gay Youth in a Runaway Shelter," in *Counseling Lesbian and Gay Male Youth: Their Special Lives, Special Needs*, ed. Sage Bergstrom and Lawrence Cruz (National Network of Runaway and Youth Services, 1983).

20. Edward Hansen, Mark Forrester, and Fred Bird, *The Tenderloin Ghetto: The Young Reject in Our Society* (San Francisco: Glide Urban Center, 1967), 1–3. For further analysis on the Tenderloin, the report, and efforts to secure government funding during the War on Poverty, see Hanhardt, *Safe Space*, chap. 1; and Martin Meeker, "The Queerly Disadvantaged and the Making of San Francisco's War on Poverty, 1964–1967," *Pacific Historical Review* 81, no. 1 (2012): 21–59.

21. Sister Betsy Hague, "In San Francisco's Tenderloin," *American Journal of Nursing* 69, no. 10 (1969): 2180–84.

22. The 1973 *Directory of Homosexual Organizations and Publications*, published by the Homosexual Information Center, listed gay switchboards in New York; San Francisco; Berkeley, CA; Washington, DC; Eugene, Oregon; and an additional lesbian switchboard in New York. See also Dan Healey, "Switchboards, Gay," in *Encyclopedia of Lesbian and Gay Histories and Cultures*, ed. George Haggarty and Bonnie Zimmerman (New York: Garland, 2000).

23. On collective in Louisville, Kentucky, for example, see James T. Sears, *Rebels, Rubyfruit, and Rhinestones Queering Space in the Stonewall South* (New Brunswick, NJ: Rutgers University Press, 2001), 62–63.

24. On Sylvia Rivera, Marsha P. Johnson, and STAR, see especially Stephan L. Cohen, *The Gay Liberation Youth Movement in New York: "An Army of Lovers Cannot Fail"* (New York: Routledge, 2008), 89–164; Duberman, *Stonewall*; Carter, *Stonewall*; Sylvia Rivera, "Queens in Exile, the Forgotten Ones," in *Genderqueer: Voices from Beyond the Binary*, ed. Joan Nestle, Clare Howell, and Riki Wilchins (Los Angeles: Alyson Books, 2002), 67–85; Jessi Gan, "'Still at the Back of the Bus': Sylvia Rivera's Struggle," *Centro Journal* 19, no. 1 (2007): 124–39; and a zine of collected interviews and writings, *Street Transvestite Action Revolutionaries: Survival, Revolt, and Queer Antagonist Struggle* (n.p.: Untorelli Press, 2013).

25. Steve Watson, "Sylvia Rivera, Founder of S.T.A.R. (Street Transvestite Action Revolutionaries)," in *Stonewall Romances: A Tenth Anniversary Celebration*, ed. Steve Watson, Ray Dobbins et al. (New York: Flower Beneath the Foot Press, 1979), quoted in Cohan, *Gay Liberation Youth Movement*, 131–32.

26. Arthur Bell, "STAR Trek: Transvestites in the Street," *Village Voice*, July 15, 1971. The group eventually moved to 640 East 12th Street, but it is not clear how long this home lasted. See transcript of Sylvia Rivera's speech from the 1973 Christopher Street Liberation Day celebration in Cohan, *Gay Liberation Youth Movement*, 158–59.

27. Donald Warman, "The Family at Liberation House: They Literally Have Nobody but Each Other," *Advocate*, August 4–17, 1971. See also "Gay Community Services Center L.A," *Gay Sunshine*, October/November 1971.

28. Warman, "Family at Liberation House."

29. Batza, *Before AIDS*, 25–26.

30. For more on the history of the early Liberation Houses, see Ian M. Baldwin, "Rethinking the 'Era of Limits': Equitable Housing, Gay Liberation, and the Opening of the American Family in Greater Los Angeles during the Long 1970s," *California History* 91, no. 3 (2014): 42–59.

31. "Liberation House #2 Opens; GCSC Picks Officers, Sets Course," *Advocate*, September 15–28, 1971.

32. "A Look at Sisters Liberation House," *Proud Woman*, March–April 1972. See also "Women Come Home!" *Lesbian Tide*, January 1972.

33. "Liberation House #2 Opens." See also narrative on housing program in *Outreach* 1, no. 1 (February 1973), Gay Community Center (Los Angeles), Phyllis Lyon and Del Martin Papers, Box 22, Folder 10, GLBT Historical Society, retrieved from Gale's *Archives of Sexuality*

and Gender. Van Ness Recovery House formed in 1973, see Van Ness Recovery House Records, Coll2011–096, ONE National Gay & Lesbian Archives, USC Libraries, University of Southern California. On Sisters Liberation House see "LA Collective Begins," *Lesbian Tide,* July 1972, 10. Estimate of 400 people served in the first year comes from a GCSC brochure on the Prisoner and Parole Program, mailed by Ken Bartley to Craig Thiersch in August 1972, William J. Canfield Papers, Box 2, Folder 73, Northeastern University Archives and Special Collections. Estimate of 4,308 people served by Housing Program in first four years from "The Gay Community Services Center: A Statement of Needs and Accomplishments," p. 21, submitted in March 1975 to the County of Los Angeles, L.A. Gay & Lesbian Center records, Coll2007–010, Box 11, Folder 34, ONE National Gay & Lesbian Archives.

34. L.A. Gay & Lesbian Center records, Box 11, Folders 37–41.

35. "The Gay Community Services Center: A Statement of Needs and Accomplishments," 15, L. A. Gay & Lesbian Center records, Box 11, Folder 34.

36. GCSC brochure, William J. Canfield Papers, Box 2, Folder 73.

37. Diane Trzcinski, "Herstory," *Lesbian Tide,* May 1972, 8.

38. On idea of cyclical service, see Grace Gallogly, "Transforming Gay Revolutionary Consciousness into Service to the People: The Gay Community Services Center and Gay Liberation Politics in Los Angeles, 1971–1975" (BA senior essay, Yale University, 2014).

39. Index cards, L.A. Gay & Lesbian Center records, Box 11, Folders 38–41; Liberation House intake forms, L.A. Gay & Lesbian Center records, Box 11, Folder 37.

40. Letter from Don Kilhefner Re: Redevelopment of the Van Ness Liberation House, March 26, 1973; and Van Ness Avenue Gay Collective to Ken Bartley, Morris Kight, and Don Kilhefner, March 27, 1973; in Van Ness House Correspondence, 1973–1975, L.A. Gay & Lesbian Center records, Box 10, Folder 21.

41. Warman, "Family at Liberation House."

42. General Revenue Sharing Funding Proposal, 1975, L.A. Gay and Lesbian Center Records, Box 11, Folder 34. For timeline of early government funding of GCSC, see Linda Marlene Poverny, "The Organizational Life Cycle and the Adaptation Process: A Case Study of the Los Angeles Gay and Lesbian Community Services Center" (PhD diss., University of Southern California, 1984), 220–28.

43. Batza, *Before AIDS,* 31.

44. "Fountain House Gives Gays a Second Chance," *Out! The Gay Newspaper,* May 12, 1977; "L.A. Housing Crisis Program Ends," *Gaysweek,* January 23, 1978.

45. On Hudson House and Pat Rocco, see Baldwin, "Rethinking the 'Era of Limits,'" and Whitney Strub, "Mondo Rocco: Mapping Gay Los Angeles Sexual Geography in the Late-1960s Films of Pat Rocco," *Radical History Review,* no. 113 (2012): 13–34.

46. *The Log,* Porterville College Yearbook, 1971. See also "Fantasticks Will be Porterville Offering," *Fresno Bee Republican,* November 8, 1970.

47. Mitchell, "Emmaus House." For additional early coverage, see John Grimbs, "Golden Gate Gay Liberation House: A Response," *Vector,* November 1974, 50–52.

48. "Reopening of the Emmaus Gay Switchboard," *Bay Area Reporter,* March 15, 1972.

49. Mitchell announced opening on October 1, 1973, in "Emmaus House Gay Switchboard," *Cross Currents,* Fall 1973. I have not been able to find any record of why they moved from Page Street, though it is likely they were evicted after an earlier attempt by the home's owner. "Two Gay Houses Refuse to Move," *Advocate,* April 24, 1974; and "A Change of Heart," *Advocate,* February 28, 1975.

50. Demographics of the house based on materials from Harvey Milk Archives—Scott Smith Collection, GLC 35, The James C. Hormel Gay and Lesbian Center, San Francisco Public

Library, San Francisco, CA, Box 9, Folders 3 and 15; and Golden Gate Liberation House, 1974–1977, Lyon and Martin Papers, Box 21, Folder 16.

51. A report to the Mayor's Office of Employment and Training, based on data from October 1977 to September 1978, does not list transgender people but states 88 percent of residents were men, 12 percent women (Golden Gate Liberation House, 1974–1977, Lyon and Martin Papers, Box 21, Folder 16). It is likely, however, a significant percentage of transgender women were categorized based on gender assigned at birth. A description of referrals to the city's Center for Special Problems listed six of thirty referrals between 1976 and 1977 as "transsexual."

52. Interview with Mitchell from "Survival House" documentary filmed by Bruce Pavlow, 1977, transcribed in Bruce Pavlow, *Survival House 1977, 758 Haight Street, San Francisco* (self-pub., 2011).

53. The film was screened at the Third Annual San Francisco Gay Film and Video Festival (now Frameline), in 1979. My thanks to Bruce Pavlow for sharing the original video footage with me and to Brian Meacham, Ron Gregg, and the Yale Film Study Center for preserving the original Portapak tapes.

54. Interviews with Tom and Jonathan, *Survival House* documentary, transcribed in Pavlow, *Survival House 1977*.

55. Interview with Fanny, *Survival House* documentary, transcribed in Pavlow, *Survival House 1977*.

56. Golden Gate Gay Liberation House, Lyon and Martin Papers, Box 21, Folder 16.

57. "General Revenue Sharing Proposal," March 14, 1975, L.A. Gay & Lesbian Center Records, Box 11, Folder 34.

58. Golden Gate Gay Liberation House Board Meeting, January 28, 1978, tape recording, Anson Reinhart Papers, GLBT Historical Society. On Dolan and Sexual Trauma Center, see Harriet Stix, "Sexual Attacks," *Los Angeles Times*, December 5, 1977. See also letter from Dolan, in support of Survival House, August 8, 1978, in Milk/Smith Collection, Box 9, Folder 3.

59. See grant applications in Golden Gate Gay Liberation House, Lyon and Martin Papers, and Milk/Smith Collection.

60. Steve Dansky, "Hey Man," *Come Out*, June/July 1970, 6. See also discussion of Dansky's article and advocacy around fatherhood in Daniel Winunwe Rivers, *Radical Relations: Lesbian Mothers, Gay Fathers, and Their Children in the United States Since World War II* (Chapel Hill: University of North Carolina Press, 2013), 114–17.

61. Counsel ruling quoted in Poverny, "Organizational Life Cycle," 235–36.

62. Lucinda Franks, "Homosexuals as Foster Parents: Is New Program an Advance or Peril?" *New York Times*, May 7, 1974. See also discussion of earlier debates at I House in New York, Randy Wicker, "Saddest of All: The Gay Kids Whom No One Wants," *Advocate*, January 3, 1973.

63. Michael Shernoff, "Gay Foster Homes," Paper for Hunter College School of Social Work, December 1974, National Gay and Lesbian Task Force Records, Box 139, Folder 40, Rare and Manuscript Collections, Cornell University Library.

64. Shernoff, "Gay Foster Homes."

65. Quoted in "Agency Reveals Kids Placed with Gay Couples," *Advocate*, August 15, 1973. There were later rumors of a ban, "Gay Ban Claimed in Chicago Child Placement," *Advocate*, August 29, 1973.

66. See chronology of documented placements in the 1970s in Wendell Ricketts and Roberta Achtenberg, "Adoption and Foster Parenting for Lesbians and Gay Men: Creating New Traditions in Family," *Marriage & Family Review* 14, no. 3–4 (1989): 83–118.

67. Marie-Amélie George, "Agency Nullification: Defying Bans on Gay and Lesbian Foster and Adoptive Parents," *Harvard Civil Rights-Civil Liberties Law Review* 51, no. 2 (2016): 363–422.

68. "New Row over Gay Foster Homes," *Advocate*, July 3, 1974; David Sindt, "Exorcising Homophobia," *Workforce*, September–October 1974, 33–39.

69. Randy Shilts, "Foster Homes for Gay Children—Justice or Prejudice?" *Advocate*, December 17, 1975.

70. Oral history with Bruce Pennington by Mark Meinke, January 27, 2001, Rainbow History Project. Shernoff reports on a similar case where the judge ruled in favor of a gay foster parent, "Gay Foster Homes."

71. On history of bans and their overturning, see George, "Agency Nullification."

72. Joseph DeMarco, "Philadelphia's Eromin Center Serving Sexual Minorities for 10 Years," *Advocate*, April 28, 1983; Tacie L. Vergara, "Meeting the Needs of Sexual Minority Youth: One Program's Response," *Homosexuality & Social Work* 2, no. 2/3 (1984): 19–38. On broader history of Eromin, see Byers, Vider, and Smith, "Clinical Activism in Community-based Practice."

73. "Foster Parents," Eromin Center (Philadelphia, Pa.) Records, Accession 573, Box 7, Folder 55, Special Collections Research Center, Temple University Libraries, Philadelphia, PA.

74. Vergara, "Meeting the Needs of Sexual Minority Youth."

75. Susana Peña, "'Obvious Gays' and the State Gaze: Cuban Gay Visibility and U.S. Immigration Policy during the 1980 Mariel Boatlift," *Journal of the History of Sexuality* 16, no. 3 (2007): 482–514; Julio Capó Jr., "Queering Mariel: Mediating Cold War Foreign Policy and U.S. Citizenship among Cuba's Homosexual Exile Community, 1978–1994," *Journal of American Ethnic History* 29, no. 4 (2010): 78–106.

76. James S. Gordon, "Group Foster Homes: Alternatives to Institutions," in Gordon and Beyer, *Reaching Troubled Youth*, 67–78.

77. In 1980, the *Los Angeles Times* reported on a group home for six boys operated in West Hollywood. Ann Japenga, "Foster Homes for Young Gay Runaways," *Los Angeles Times*, May 14, 1980.

78. On the complexity of confidentiality with Eromin case records, see David Weinberg, "The Other Side of the Human Experience: Providing Access to Social Service Case Files," *American Archivist* 53, no. 1 (1990): 122–29.

79. Sofia Novoa, "A Description of the Eromin Gay Cuban Program," c. 1981, Eromin Center Records, Box 7, Folder 24.

80. Eromin House, Cuban Program/Cuban Refugees Program/Cuban Refugees Program Correspondence, Eromin Center Records, Box 7, Folders 21–25.

81. Monthly Progress Report, December 1980, January 1981, and Discharge Report, April 1981, Eromin Center Records, Box 7, Folder 21.

82. Progress Report, December 1980, Eromin Center Records, Box 7, Folder 21. Mateo is a pseudonym.

83. Capó, "Queering Mariel," 79–80.

84. Discharge Report, Eromin Center Records, Box 7, Folder 21.

85. Mark Blair, Letter to Ann Noonan, Pennsylvania Council on Voluntary Child Care Agencies, March 7, 1981, Eromin Center Records, Box 7, Folder 25.

86. "Eromin House Rules," Eromin Center Records, Box 9, Folder 3.

87. Administrative Policies, 1982–83, Eromin Center Records, Box 5, Folder 3.

88. Untitled (Rules), August 1981, Eromin Center Records, Box 9, Folder 55.

89. Jeff Keith diary about work at Eromin House, January to May 1981, private collection, courtesy of Jeff Keith, with thanks to John Anderies. For background on Jeff Keith, see Scott A. Drake, "Jeff Keith: Turning the Pages of LGBT History," *Philadelphia Gay News*, April 2, 2015.

90. "Notes for House Meeting," June 24, 1982, Eromin Center Records, Box 8, Folder 26.

91. "Eromin House Rules," Eromin Center Records, Box 9, Folder 3.

92. Quoted in Japenga, "Foster Homes for Young Gay Runaways."

93. Individual Treatment Plans, Box 9, Folder 20. Denise is a pseudonym.

94. On the history of gender identity disorder diagnoses, see especially Jack Drescher, "Queer Diagnoses: Parallels and Contrasts in the History of Homosexuality, Gender Variance, and the Diagnostic and Statistical Manual," *Archives of Sexual Behavior* 39, no. 2 (2010): 427–60.

95. House Logs, November 1982, Eromin Center Records, Box 8, Folder 10.

96. House Logs, September 1982, Eromin Center Records, Box 8, Folder 8; Progress Contract, December 30, 1982, Eromin Center Records, Box 8, Folder 11. Michael is a pseudonym.

97. "City Suspends Contract with Youth Care Center," *Philadelphia Tribune*, November 8, 1983; Stanley Ward, "Eromin Controversy Heats Up," *Philadelphia Gay News*, September 22, 1983; "Philadelphia Gay Center Closes Forever," *Update*, March 7, 1984. See also Byers, Vider, and Smith, "Clinical Activism in Community-based Practice."

98. On LGBTQ homeless youth today, see Rachel Aviv, "Netherland: Homeless in New York, a Young Gay Woman Learns to Survive," *New Yorker*, December 10, 2012; and Stephen Vider and David S. Byers, "Queer Homeless Youth, Queer Activism in Transition," *Slate*, December 10, 2015.

CHAPTER SIX

1. Liliana Fasanella interview with the author, May 3, 2017, for the exhibition *AIDS at Home: Art and Everyday Activism*, presented at the Museum of the City of New York, 2017.

2. *Buddies for Life: GMHC Volunteers*, dir. Liliana Fasanella, 1996, Gay Men's Health Crisis (GMHC) Records, 217001.mp4, New York Public Library. Thank you to Carolina Hausmann-Stabile and Rosi Song for consultation on Spanish transcription and translation. Juan uses the term "infestada," which would typically be reserved for parasitic infections.

3. On early history of GMHC, see Susan M. Chambré, "Managing the Madness," chap. 1 in *Fighting for Our Lives: New York's AIDS Community and the Politics of Disease* (New Brunswick, NJ: Rutgers University Press, 2006).

4. On history of ACT UP, see especially Deborah B. Gould, *Moving Politics: Emotion and ACT UP's Fight Against AIDS* (Chicago: University of Chicago Press, 2009); Jennifer Brier, *Infectious Ideas: U.S. Political Responses to the AIDS Crisis* (Chapel Hill: University of North Carolina Press, 2009); Douglas Crimp, "Mourning and Militancy," *October* 51 (1989): 3–18; Benita Roth, *The Life and Death of ACT UP/LA: Anti-AIDS Activism in Los Angeles from the 1980s to the 2000s* (New York: Cambridge University Press, 2017); Tamar W. Carroll, *Mobilizing New York: AIDS, Antipoverty, and Feminist Activism* (Chapel Hill: University of North Carolina Press Books, 2015); the documentaries *United in Anger*, dir. Jim Hubbard, 2012, and *How to Survive a Plague*, dir. David France, 2012; and the film *120 battements par minute*, dir. Robin Campillo, 2017.

5. Gould, *Moving Politics*, see esp. chap. 1.

6. Larry Kramer, *The Normal Heart* (New York: New American Library, 1985), 79. See also Kramer's writing on GMHC in *Reports from the Holocaust: The Making of an AIDS Activist*, rev. ed. (New York: St. Martin's Press, 1994).

7. David W. Dunlap, "Three Black Members Quit AIDS Organization Board," *New York Times*, January 11, 1996. The case is discussed by Cathy J. Cohen, "Punks, Bulldaggers, and Welfare Queens: The Radical Potential of Queer Politics?" *GLQ: A Journal of Lesbian and Gay Studies* 3, no. 4 (1997): 437.

8. The term "counterpublic" was coined by feminist scholar Rita Felski in *Beyond Feminist Aesthetics: Feminist Literature and Social Change* (Cambridge, MA: Harvard University Press,

1989), and elaborated by Nancy Fraser in "Rethinking the Public Sphere: A Contribution to the Critique of Actually Existing Democracy," *Social Text* 25/26 (1990): 56–80. On queer counterpublics, see Lauren Berlant and Michael Warner, "Sex in Public," *Critical Inquiry* 24, no. 2 (1998): 547–66; and Michael Warner, *Publics and Counterpublics* (New York: Zone Books, 2002).

9. Cohen, "Punks, Bulldaggers, and Welfare Queens."

10. Gould, *Moving Politics*; and Ann Cvetkovich, *An Archive of Feelings: Trauma, Sexuality, and Lesbian Public Cultures* (Durham, NC: Duke University Press, 2003). See also Heather Love, *Feeling Backward: Loss and the Politics of Queer History* (Cambridge, MA: Harvard University Press, 2007), and José Esteban Muñoz's conceptualization of "belonging-in-difference," in "Queerness as Horizon: Utopian Hermeneutics in the Face of Gay Pragmatism," chap. 1 in *Cruising Utopia: The Then and There of Queer Futurity* (New York: New York University Press, 2009).

11. Lauren Berlant, "Intimacy: A Special Issue," *Critical Inquiry* 24, no. 2 (1998): 283.

12. For more on the exhibition *AIDS at Home: Art and Everyday Activism*, see Stephen Vider, "Public Disclosures of Private Realities: HIV/AIDS and the Domestic Archive," *Public Historian* 41, no. 2 (2019): 163–89. See also Frederick Weston's discussion of *Searching and Fearless Moral Inventory* in a 2017 tour of the exhibition, cosponsored by the museum and Visual AIDS, archived at https://vimeo.com/240906533. The title of the collage is a reference to the fourth step of twelve-step programs.

13. Thank you to Eric Rhein, who used this phrasing at an opening event for *AIDS at Home* in May 2017.

14. For overview and interpretation of a buddy program in Vancouver, see Michael P. Brown, *RePlacing Citizenship: AIDS Activism and Radical Democracy* (New York: Guilford Press, 1997). On GMHC volunteerism, see Philip M. Kayal, *Bearing Witness: Gay Men's Health Crisis and the Politics of AIDS* (Boulder, CO: Westview, 1993). Thank you also to Lena Eckert-Erdheim for sharing her undergraduate thesis, "Taking Care: Women, Gay Men, and AIDS in New York City, 1981–1992" (BA thesis, Smith College, 2011).

15. On AIDS and home care, see, for example, Helen Schietinger, "A Home Care Plan for AIDS," *American Journal of Nursing* 86, no. 9 (1986): 1021–28; Jeannee Parker Martin, "Hospice and Home Care for Persons with AIDS/ARC: Meeting the Challenges and Ensuring Quality," *Death Studies* 12, no. 5–6 (1988): 463–80; and M. Y. Smith and B. D. Rapkin, "Unmet Needs for Help Among Persons with AIDS," *AIDS Care* 7, no. 3 (1995): 353–64.

16. Steve Gendel, "Issues in Home Health Care for People with AIDS," *Issues: An AIDS Forum* 1, no. 1 (1987): 1.

17. See UCLA/UCSF Caregiver Study, Allen J. Leblanc, Andrew S. London, and Carol S. Aneshensel, "The Physical Costs of AIDS Caregiving," *Social Science & Medicine* 45, no. 6 (1997): 915–23. On parents' responses to HIV/AIDS, see Heather Murray, *Not in This Family: Gays and the Meaning of Kinship in Postwar North America* (Philadelphia: University of Pennsylvania Press, 2010), 136–78.

18. E. Alex Jung, "Writer and Activist Sarah Schulman on *The Normal Heart*, Being Friends with Larry Kramer, and the Whitewashing of AIDS History," *Vulture*, June 1, 2014, https://www.vulture.com/2014/06/writer-sarah-schulman-on-the-normal-heart-larry-kramer.html. See also Sarah Schulman, *The Gentrification of the Mind: Witness to a Lost Imagination* (Berkeley, CA: University of California Press, 2013), 37.

19. Joseph Interrante, "To Have Without Holding: Memories of Life with a Person with AIDS," *Radical America* 20, no. 6 (1986): 60.

20. "The Backroom" printouts: Frank and Serge, August—December 1987, David Charnow Upper Westsider Papers, Coll2013–004, Box 1, Folder 11, ONE National Gay & Lesbian Archives, USC Libraries, University of Southern California.

21. Interview with Mitchell Cutler by Paula Berg, May 5, 1988, GMHC Records, 204018. mp4 and 204019.mp4. Interview with Stash Santoro, media ID 231.0683, Gay Cable Network Archives, Fales Library and Special Collections, New York University Libraries. See also Maureen Dowd, "For Victims of AIDS, Support in a Lonely Siege," *New York Times*, December 5, 1983.

22. Team Leaders/Captains Meeting Minutes, April 5, 1985, GMHC Records, Box 408, Folder 1.

23. Team 1 Meeting Minutes, August 26, 1985, GMHC Records, Box 105, Folder 3.

24. Team 1 Meeting Minutes, various, 1984, GMHC Records, Box 105, Folder 2.

25. Team 1 Meeting Minutes, May 29, 1984, GMHC Records, Box 105, Folder 2.

26. *GMHC Buddy Support Program Training Handbook*, 1983, GMHC Records, Box 96, Folder 10.

27. Bruce Ross, Team 1, Meeting Minutes, November 2, 1985, GMHC Records, Box 105, Folder 3. Ross had returned to the program after a leave and reread his anniversary statement from November 2, 1984.

28. Team 1 Meeting Minutes, various, 1983–1984, GMHC Records, Box 105, Folder 2.

29. AIDS service organizations with buddy programs listed in National AIDS Network Directory, 1988. See also Bea Hanson, "Resources," in ACT UP/NY Women and AIDS Book Group, *Women, AIDS, and Activism* (Boston: South End Press, 1990).

30. Michael J. Sieradzki, *Buddy Programs: Volunteer Peer Support Programs for People with HIV-Related Illness* (Washington, DC: National AIDS Network, 1988).

31. Stephanie Saul, "Comparing the Efforts of New York and San Francisco," *Newsday*, June 8, 1986; Peter S. Arno, "The Nonprofit Sector's Response to the AIDS Epidemic: Community-based Services in San Francisco," *American Journal of Public Health* 76, no. 11 (1986): 1325–30. On the Shanti Project, see *Shanti Projects: Histories of Shanti Project and the AIDS Crisis*, digital exhibit curated by Brendan McHugh, 2020, https://shantiprojects.dash.umn.edu/biography/.

32. Ian K. Lekus, "Health Care, the AIDS Crisis, and the Politics of Community: The North Carolina Lesbian and Gay Health Project, 1982–1996," in *Modern American Queer History*, ed. Allida M. Black (Philadelphia: Temple University Press, 2001), 227–52; Stephen Inrig, *North Carolina and the Problem of AIDS: Advocacy, Politics, and Race in the South* (Chapel Hill: University of North Carolina Press, 2011).

33. Art Cohen, "Creating Family Feelings: Companions for Men with AIDS," *Gay Community News*, November 24, 1984.

34. R. Frank Warner, "Buddy Program Celebrates Successes," *Update*, May 1, 1991.

35. Devron Kelly Huber, "Finding New Strength, Thanks to an AIDS 'Buddy System,'" *Orange County Register*, November 11, 1985.

36. Glenn Dale, "Love, Growth, and Friendship: Being an AIDS Buddy Helps the Helper," *Advocate*, June 10, 1986, 8.

37. Team 1 Meeting Minutes, May 1984, GMHC Records, Box 105, Folder 2.

38. Team 7 Meeting Minutes, December 14, 1986, GMHC Records, Box 108, Folder 3.

39. Michael J. Williams, "Gay Men as 'Buddies' to Persons Living with AIDS and ARC," *Smith College Studies in Social Work* 59, no. 1 (1988), 47. Alison Ann Leaney, "An Evaluation of the Buddy/Home Care Program, A Palliative Care Program Operated by AIDS Vancouver" (MSW thesis, University of British Columbia, 1990), 107.

40. Team 7 Meeting Minutes, August 20, 1987, GMHC Records, Box 108, Folder 3.

41. Team 1 Meeting Minutes, GMHC Records, Box 105, Folder 2.

42. *Buddies*, dir. Arthur Bressan, 1985. For background on film, see Steve Warren, "Artie Bressan: Keeping AIDS in the Gay Family," *Montrose Voice*, November 15, 1985.

43. 1986 client demographics from GMHC Team Leaders and Buddy Captains Monthly

Meeting Minutes, November 3, 1986, GMHC Records, Box 408, Folder 2; 1993 demographics from Mireya Navarro, "Diversity but Conflict Under Wider AIDS Umbrella," *New York Times,* May 28, 1993.

44. Client demographics from GMHC Annual Report for 1987/1988, and Navarro, "Diversity but Conflict." In 1987/1988, 15 percent of clients were recorded as Hispanic, 12 percent as African American, 1 percent Asian American, 0.3 percent Native American, 0.1 percent Indian, 0.1 percent Eurasian.

45. 1986 volunteer demographics from Kayal, *Bearing Witness,* 102; 1988–90 demographics from J. Brian Cassel, "Altruism Is Only Part of the Story: A Longitudinal Study of AIDS Volunteers" (PhD diss., City University of New York, 1995).

46. On house ballroom culture, see Tim Lawrence, "'Listen, and You Will Hear All the Houses that Walked There Before': A History of Drag Balls, Houses, and the Culture of Voguing," in *Voguing and the House Ballroom Scene of New York City, 1989–92,* photographs by Chantal Regnault (London: Soul Jazz, 2011); and Marlon M. Bailey, *Butch Queens Up in Pumps: Gender, Performance, and Ballroom Culture in Detroit* (Ann Arbor: University of Michigan Press, 2013), 3–10. On the House of Latex, see "Having Fun Never Has to End," dir. Chas B. Brack, 1994, posted on *The Luna Show,* https://www.youtube.com/watch?v=O-CG9cN4Ibw.

47. Team Leaders Meeting, December 5, 1985, GMHC Records, Box 408, Folder 1.

48. Team Leaders Meeting, June 5, 1986, GMHC Records, Box 408, Folder 2.

49. Cassel, "Altruism Is Only Part of the Story."

50. Susan Kuklin, *Fighting Back: What Some People Are Doing About AIDS* (New York: Putnam, 1989). Buddy Team 7 Meeting Minutes, Box 108, Folders 3–9. I refer to all buddy volunteers by first and last name, but only refer to buddy clients by first name, to preserve confidentiality, following the model of Kuklin's book and the meeting minutes.

51. Team 7 Meeting Minutes, August 20, 1986, GMHC Records, Box 108, Folder 3; January 13, 1987, GMHC Records, Box 108, Folder 4.

52. Team 7 Meeting Minutes, April 28, 1987, GMHC Records, Box 108, Folder 4.

53. Team 7 Meeting Minutes, October 21, 1986, GMHC Records, Box 108, Folder 3.

54. Team 7 Meeting Minutes, GMHC Records, Box 108, Folder 4.

55. Team 7 Meeting Minutes, July 14, 1987, GMHC Records, Box 108, Folder 4.

56. Kuklin, "Dennis," chap. 9 in *Fighting Back.*

57. Team 7 Meeting Minutes, various, from November 18, 1986 to February 17, 1987, GMHC Records, Box 108, Folders 3 and 4.

58. Kuklin, *Fighting Back,* 46.

59. Team 7 Meeting Minutes, various beginning April 28, 1987, GMHC Records, Box 108, Folder 4; and Kuklin, *Fighting Back.*

60. Alison Luterman, "Buddies for Life," *Boston Sunday Herald Magazine,* December 6, 1987, 4, 20.

61. Beth Gillin, "Buddies 'Give of Their Hearts,'" *Philadelphia Inquirer,* July 27, 1987.

62. Alexandra Juhasz, *AIDS TV: Identity, Community, and Alternative Video* (Durham, NC: Duke University Press, 1995); *We Care: A Video for Care Providers of People Affected by AIDS,* dir. WAVE (Women's AIDS Video Enterprise), 1990.

63. Alexandra Juhasz, "A Political Sense of Being at Home with HIV and Video," *Drain Magazine* 13, no. 2 (2016), http://drainmag.com/a-political-sense-of-being-at-home-with-hiv-and-video/. Juhasz's book, *AIDS TV,* also touches on *Living With AIDS*: before forming WAVE, Juhasz had collaborated on segments for the show, and the series was still airing when the book was completed.

64. Roger Hallas, *Reframing Bodies: AIDS, Bearing Witness, and the Queer Moving Image*

(Durham, NC: Duke University Press, 2009). On revisiting and reusing 1980s footage by Testing the Limits, DIVA, and other video collectives, see Lucas Hilderbrand, "Retroactivism," *GLQ: A Journal of Lesbian and Gay Studies* 12, no. 2 (2006) 303–17; and Jih-Fei Cheng, "How to Survive: AIDS and Its Afterlives in Popular Media," *Women's Studies Quarterly* 44, no. 1/2 (2016): 73–92. On division between ACT UP and other forms of activism, see also Alexandra Juhasz, "Forgetting ACT UP," *Quarterly Journal of Speech* 98, no. 1 (2012): 69–74.

65. Kelly Anderson and Annie Goldson, "Alternating Currents: Alternative Television Inside and Outside of the Academy," *Social Text* 35 (1993): 56–71; James C. McKinley, "Judge Blocks Scrambling of Cable Fare," *New York Times*, September 21, 1995.

66. Episodes of *Pride and Progress*, including "Healthline" and "Outreach" segments, are archived and digitized as part of Gay Cable Network Archives, MSS 231, Fales Library and Special Collections, New York University Libraries. Episodes of *AIDS Network* and *Living With AIDS* (as well as original, unedited footage) are archived as part of the GMHC Records.

67. Jean Carlomusto oral history interview by Sarah Schulman, ACT UP Oral History Project, December 19, 2002, http://www.actuporalhistory.org/interviews/images/carlomusto .pdf.

68. Scott Jordan/GMHC public service announcement, dir. Jean Carlomusto, 1987, https://vimeo.com/119779491.

69. Gregg Bordowitz, introduction to *The AIDS Crisis Is Not Over* video program catalog (New York: Artists Space, 1988).

70. On People With AIDS Coalition and Michael Callen, see Chambré, "Fighting the Victim Label," chap. 2 in *Fighting for Our Lives*; and Martin B. Duberman, *Hold Tight Gently: Michael Callen, Essex Hemphill, and the Battlefield of AIDS* (New York: New Press, 2014).

71. See also Max Navarre, "Fighting the Victim Label," *October* 43 (1987): 143–46.

72. "A Kaposi's Sarcoma Makeup Session," dir. Jean Carlomusto, 1987, https://vimeo.com/226840960.

73. People With AIDS Coalition, "Summary of Programs," 1986, Published and near Print Material, Newsline PWAC/NY, 1987–1989, ACT UP New York Records, Box 185, Folder 14, NYPL. Retrieved from Gale's *Archives of Sexuality & Gender*.

74. Carlomusto oral history interview.

75. "Shop and Cook," dir. Juanita Mohammed, c. 1994, 7528.mp4, GMHC Records; "Mission: Nutrition: The Meals Program at GMHC," dir. Chas B. Brack, 1995, 216994.mp4, GMHC Records.

76. "Video Portrait: Nora Molina," c. 1994, 204390.mp4, GMHC Records.

77. "GotsToBeADrag," dir. David Bronstein, prod. Junior Vasquez, 1990, https://vimeo .com/366262012; "Having Fun Never Has to End," dir. Chas B. Brack, 1994.

78. See discussion of *PWA Power* in Jean Carlomusto, "Interview," *Square Peg*, no. 23 (1988): 38.

79. Gregg Bordowitz, "Picture a Coalition," *October* 43 (1987): 195.

80. Gregg Bordowitz, "Operative Assumptions" in *Resolutions: Contemporary Video Practices*, ed. Michael Renov and Erika Suderburg (Minneapolis: University of Minnesota Press, 1996), 178–79.

81. *Living With AIDS* TV show survey, all quotes from surveys in GMHC Records, Box 292, Folder 5.

82. *Living With AIDS* TV show survey, GMHC Records, Box 292, Folder 6; Box 293, Folder 2; Box 292, Folder 6.

83. "Juanita Mohammed," in *Women of Vision: Histories in Feminist Film and Video*, ed. Alexandra Juhasz (Minneapolis: University of Minnesota Press, 2001), 211–22; Juanita Mohammed,

"WAVE in the Media Environment: Camcorder Activism in AIDS Education," *Camera Obscura: Feminism, Culture, and Media Studies* 10, no. 1 (1992): 152–55.

84. Juanita Szczepanski oral history interview with the author, April 21, 2018.

85. "Caring: Bruce-Michael Gelbert," dir. Juanita Mohammed, segment in *Living With AIDS #7*, originally aired 1991, 216997.mp4, GMHC Records.

86. "Caring: Marilyn Kach," dir. Juanita Mohammed, segment in *Living With AIDS #4*, originally aired 1993, 8116.mp4, GMHC Records.

87. "Caring: Florence Rush," dir. Juanita Mohammed, segment in *Living With AIDS #8*, originally aired 1992, 9068.mp4, GMHC Records; "Caring: Iris De La Cruz," dir. Juanita Mohammed, c. 1994, 7752.mp4, GMHC Records.

88. "Two Men and a Baby," dir. Juanita Mohammed, in *Living With AIDS #1*, originally aired 1992, 204071.mp4, GMHC Records; and unedited video footage for interview with John Harrington, case worker at Brooklyn AIDS Task Force, 7919.mp4 and 7694.mp, GMHC Records.

89. "Part of Me," dir. Alisa Lebow and Juanita Mohammed, segment in *Living With AIDS #6*, originally aired 1993, 8028.mp4, GMHC Records.

EPILOGUE

1. To protect confidentiality, I refer here only to residents who participated in student interviews who have also spoken in the past with the media. My summary is a composite of oral history interviews conducted by students on April 12, 2019, as well as published articles and audio including Michael Winerip, "Rainbow-Hued Housing for Gays in Golden Years," *New York Times*, March 13, 2014, and "A Beautiful Gray in the Gayborhood," *Storycorps* Podcast, July 23, 2019, https://storycorps.org/podcast/a-beautiful-gray-in-the-gayborhood/.

2. On "normalization" and legitimation, see Michael Warner, *The Trouble with Normal: Sex, Politics, and the Ethics of Queer Life* (New York: Free Press, 1999); Judith Butler, "Is Kinship Always Already Heterosexual?," *differences* 13, no. 1 (2002): 14–44. See also Jaye Cee Whitehead's sociological study of a marriage rights organization, *The Nuptial Deal: Same-Sex Marriage and Neo-Liberal Governance* (Chicago: University of Chicago Press, 2011); and Kathleen Hull's discussion of the "cultural power of law," in *Same-Sex Marriage: The Cultural Politics of Love and Law* (New York: Cambridge University Press, 2006). On the limits of inclusion as a legal strategy, see Dean Spade, *Normal Life: Administrative Violence, Critical Trans Politics, and the Limits of Law*, rev. ed. (Durham, NC: Duke University Press, 2015).

3. Douglas NeJaime, "Before Marriage: The Unexplored History of Nonmarital Recognition and Its Relationship to Marriage," *California Law Review* 102, no. 1 (2014): 87–172. For a longer history on the prioritization of the romantic couple in US culture, see Elizabeth Freeman, *The Wedding Complex: Forms of Belonging in Modern American Culture* (Durham, NC: Duke University Press, 2002).

4. On changing households, see "Households and Families: 2010," 2010 Census Briefs, United States Census Bureau, issued April 2012, http://www.census.gov/prod/cen2010/briefs/c2010br-14.pdf; "Households by Type, 1940 to the present," United States Census Bureau's Families and Living Arrangements webpage, Historical Table HH-1, released November 2019, https://www2.census.gov/programs-surveys/demo/tables/families/time-series/households/hh1.xls. See also Nancy D. Polikoff, *Beyond (Straight and Gay) Marriage: Valuing All Families Under the Law* (Boston: Beacon Press, 2008); Elizabeth H. Pleck, *Not Just Roommates: Cohabitation after the Sexual Revolution* (Chicago: University of Chicago Press, 2012); Eric Klinenberg, *Going Solo: The Extraordinary Rise and Surprising Appeal of Living Alone* (New York: Penguin Books, 2012).

5. On domestic partnership, see Pleck, *Not Just Roommates*, 209–28; Ryan Patrick Murphy, "United Airlines Is For Lovers?: Flight Attendant Activism and the Family Values Economy in the 1990s," *Radical History Review*, no. 112 (2012): 100–12. See also Carlos A. Ball's discussion of *Braschi v. Stahl Associates Co.*, 74 N.Y.2d 201 (1989) in *From the Closet to the Courtroom: Five LGBT Rights Lawsuits That Have Changed Our Nation* (Boston: Beacon Press, 2011), 21–66. On adoption and custody battles, see Daniel Rivers, "'In the Best Interests of the Child': Lesbian and Gay Parenting Custody Cases, 1967–1985," *Journal of Social History* 43, no. 4 (2010): 917–43; and Carlos A. Ball, *The Right to Be Parents: LGBT Families and the Transformation of Parenthood* (New York: New York University Press, 2012). On sodomy laws, see William N. Eskridge, *Dishonorable Passions: Sodomy Laws in America, 1861–2003* (New York: Viking, 2008). On same-sex marriage, see George Chauncey, *Why Marriage?: The History Shaping Today's Debate Over Gay Equality* (New York: Basic Books, 2004). On lesbian and gay household and family law, see also Nancy D. Polikoff, "Equality and Justice for Lesbian and Gay Families and Relationships," *Rutgers Law Review* 61, no. 3 (2009): 529–65; and Polikoff, *Beyond (Straight and Gay) Marriage*.

6. On the impact of AIDS and the lesbian baby boom, see Chauncey, *Why Marriage?*, 96–111. On gay and lesbian child custody, see Marie-Amélie George, "The Custody Crucible: The Development of Scientific Authority about Gay and Lesbian Parents," *Law and History Review* 34, no. 2 (2016): 487–529; Elizabeth A. Harris, "Same-Sex Parents' Hurdles," *New York Times*, June 20, 2017. On trans parents and child custody, see Leslie Cooper, *Protecting the Rights of Transgender Parents and Their Children: A Guide for Parents and Lawyers* (New York: American Civil Liberties Union; Washington, DC: National Center for Transgender Equality, 2013).

7. Brief for respondent, *Bowers v. Hardwick*, 478 U.S. 186 (1986); *Payton v. New York*, 445 U.S. 573 (1980). For an overview of *Bowers*, see David A. J. Richards, *The Sodomy Cases: Bowers v. Hardwick and Lawrence v. Texas* (Lawrence: University Press of Kansas, 2009).

8. Transcript of oral argument, Michael E. Hobbs for petitioner, March 31, 1986, *Bowers v. Hardwick*.

9. *Lawrence v. Texas*, 539 U.S. 558 (2003). For summary, see Richards, *The Sodomy Cases*, 122–56; Ball, *From the Closet*, 199–247; and Dale Carpenter, *Flagrant Conduct: The Story of Lawrence v. Texas: How a Bedroom Arrest Decriminalized Gay Americans* (New York: W. W. Norton, 2012). Arrest report, and longer investigative narrative, reprinted in Carpenter, *Flagrant Conduct*, 83–85.

10. "Mainstream presentation" is a phrase from Carpenter's interview with William M. Hohengarten, one of the attorneys at Jenner & Block, hired by Lambda Legal as co-counsel for the petitioners, quoted in *Flagrant Conduct*, 188.

11. Brief of petitioners, *Lawrence v. Texas*. See Carpenter's discussion in *Flagrant Conduct*, 192–98. Number of households with same-sex partners, and number of children with one or more gay or lesbian parents, are from the petitioners' brief, based, respectively, on data from the 2000 United States Census and estimates from Ellen C. Perrin, "Technical Report: Coparent or Second-Parent Adoption by Same-Sex Parents," *Pediatrics* 109, no. 2 (February 2002): 341–44, in turn derived from Edward O. Laumann, *National Health and Social Life Survey* (Chicago: University of Chicago and National Opinion Research Center, 1995).

12. *Lawrence v. Texas*, 539 U.S. at 567. See also George Chauncey, "'What Gay Studies Taught the Court': The Historians' Amicus Brief in *Lawrence v. Texas*," *GLQ: A Journal of Lesbian and Gay Studies* 10, no. 3 (2004): 509–538, on the court's reconception of sodomy.

13. See, for example, Chris Bull, "Justice Served," *Advocate*, August 19, 2003, 35; Joseph Landau, "Ripple Effect," *New Republic*, June 23, 2003, 12–16. See also Diana Hassel, "The Use of Criminal Sodomy Laws in Civil Litigation," *Texas Law Review* 79, no. 4 (2001): 813–48.

14. Katherine M. Franke, "The Domesticated Liberty of *Lawrence v. Texas*," *Columbia Law Review* 104, no. 5 (2004): 1414. For critiques of the *Lawrence v. Texas* decision, see also Teemu

Ruskola, "Gay Rights Versus Queer Theory: What Is Left of Sodomy after *Lawrence v. Texas?*," *Social Text* 23, no. 3–4 (2005): 235–50; Nayan Shah, "Policing Privacy, Migrants, and the Limits of Freedom," *Social Text* 23, no. 3–4 (2005): 275–84; Siobhan B Somerville, "Queer Loving," *GLQ: A Journal of Lesbian and Gay Studies* 11, no. 3 (2005): 335–70; Jasbir K. Puar, *Terrorist Assemblages: Homonationalism in Queer Times* (Durham, NC: Duke University Press, 2007), 114–38; David L. Eng, *The Feeling of Kinship: Queer Liberalism and the Racialization of Intimacy* (Durham, NC: Duke University Press, 2010), 23–57.

15. Carpenter, *Flagrant Conduct*, 41–45.

16. For critiques of Lambda Legal's "mainstream" approach, see especially Dahlia Lithwick, "Extreme Makeover," *New Yorker*, March 12, 2012, 76–79; and a response by Lambda Legal Executive Director Kevin M. Cathcart, "*Lawrence v. Texas*: Extreme Truth," *Lambda Legal* (blog) (cross-posted on *Huffington Post*), March 7, 2012, https://www.lambdalegal.org/blog/lawrence-texas-extreme-truth.

17. *United States v. Windsor*, 570 U.S. 744 (2013); *Obergefell v. Hodges*, 576 U.S. 644 (2015). On language of dignity, see Kenji Yoshino, "The Anti-Humiliation Principle and Same-Sex Marriage," *Yale Law Journal* 123 (2013): 3076–3103; Kenji Yoshino, "A New Birth of Freedom? *Obergefell v. Hodges*," *Harvard Law Review* 129 (2015): 147–79; and Jeffrey Rosen, "The Dangers of a Constitutional 'Right to Dignity'" *Atlantic*, April 29, 2015, https://www.theatlantic.com/politics/archive/2015/04/the-dangerous-doctrine-of-dignity/391796/.

18. Melissa Murray, "*Obergefell v. Hodges* and Nonmarriage Inequality," *California Law Review* 104 (2016): 1207–58; Melissa Murray, "One Is the Loneliest Number: The Complicated Legacy of *Obergefell v. Hodges*," *Hastings Law Journal* 70, no. 5 (2019): 1263–72; William B. Rubenstein, "We Are Family: A Reflection on the Search for Legal Recognition of Lesbian and Gay Relationships," *Journal of Law & Politics* 8 (1991): 89–105; Stephen Vider, "What Happened to the Functional Family? Defining and Defending Alternative Households Before and Beyond Same-Sex Marriage," in *Intimate States: Gender, Sexuality, and Governance in Modern US History*, ed. Margot Canaday, Nancy F. Cott, and Robert O. Self (Chicago: University of Chicago Press, 2021); Melissa Murray, "Family Law's Doctrine," *University of Pennsylvania Law Review* 163 (2014): 1985–2018; Serena Mayeri, "The Functions of Family Law," *University of Pennsylvania Law Review Online* 163 (2015): 377–82.

19. For a range of queer critiques of same-sex marriage, see *Against Equality: Queer Revolution, Not Mere Inclusion*, ed. Ryan Conrad (Oakland, CA: AK Press, 2014). For calls to reform family law to recognize more diverse household forms, see especially Polikoff, *Beyond (Straight and Gay) Marriage*.

20. Gretchen Livingston and Anna Brown, "Intermarriage in the U.S. 50 Years After *Loving v. Virginia*," Pew Research Center, May 2017; "Fact Sheet: Attitudes on Same-Sex Marriage" Pew Research Center, May 14, 2019, https://www.pewforum.org/fact-sheet/changing-attitudes-on-gay-marriage.

21. Shawn Shimpach, "Realty Reality: HGTV and the Subprime Crisis," *American Quarterly* 64, no. 3 (2012): 515–42. On housing inequality and instability, see Matthew Desmond, *Evicted: Poverty and Profit in the American City* (New York: Broadway Books, 2016). On residential segregation, see Richard D. Kahlenberg and Kimberly Quick, "The Government Created Housing Segregation. Here's How the Government Can End It," *American Prospect*, July 2, 2019, https://prospect.org/civil-rights/government-created-housing-segregation.-government-can-end-it./.

22. Melinda Cooper, *Family Values: Between Neoliberalism and the New Social Conservatism* (Brooklyn, NY: Zone Books, 2017), 67. For example, see Todd S. Purdum, "Clinton Sets New Rules on Deadbeat Parents," *New York Times*, September 29, 1996. On neoliberalism, welfare,

and the family, see also Laura Briggs, *How All Politics Became Reproductive Politics: From Welfare Reform to Foreclosure to Trump* (Oakland: University of California Press, 2017).

23. Preston L. Morgan, "Public Assistance for the Price of Privacy: Leaving the Door Open on Welfare Home Searches," *McGeorge Law Review* 40, no. 1 (2009): 227–60; Michele E. Gilman, "The Class Differential in Privacy Law," *Brooklyn Law Review* 77, no. 4 (2012): 1389–1445; Peter Micek, "A Genealogy of Home Visits: Explaining the Relentless Search for Individualized Information Without Individual Suspicion," *University of San Francisco Law Review* 44, no. 4 (2010): 1007–32.

24. Elaine Tyler May, *Fortress America: How We Embraced Fear and Abandoned Democracy* (New York: Basic Books, 2017); Joshua Reeves, *Citizen Spies: The Long Rise of America's Surveillance Society* (New York: New York University Press, 2017); Caroline E. Light, *Stand Your Ground: A History of America's Love Affair with Lethal Self-Defense* (Boston: Beacon Press, 2017); Ben Zimmer, "Where Does Trump's 'Invasion' Rhetoric Come From?," *Atlantic*, August 6, 2019, https://www.theatlantic.com/entertainment/archive/2019/08/trump-immigrant-invasion -language-origins/595579/; Adam Harris, "When ICE Raids Homes," *Atlantic*, July 17, 2019, https://www.theatlantic.com/family/archive/2019/07/when-ice-raids-homes-immigration/ 594112/.

25. Lisa Duggan, *The Twilight of Equality? Neoliberalism, Cultural Politics, and the Attack on Democracy* (Boston: Beacon Press, 2003).

26. See Andrew Stein, "Sick and No Place to Go: 5000 Homeless People with AIDS and AIDS-Related Illness" (New York City Council, 1988); Gay Men's Health Crisis, Citizens Commission on AIDS, Brooklyn AIDS Task Force, et al., Amicus Curiae Brief, *Braschi v. Stahl*; "AIDS and Homelessness: Personal Accounts," *Yale Journal of Law & Liberation* 2, no. 1 (1991): 85–93; Anne-Christine D'Adesky, "Lives on the Edge," *Advocate*, March 10, 1992, 40–44; "Housing Needs of Persons with Acquired Immune Deficiency Syndrome (AIDS)," Hearing Before the Subcommittee on Housing and Community Development of the Committee on Banking, Finance, and Urban Affairs, House of Representatives, March 21, 1990.

27. Sarah Schulman, *The Gentrification of the Mind: Witness to a Lost Imagination* (Berkeley: University of California Press, 2013).

28. On Trump Tower protest, see Stephen Vider, "Surrender Donald! A Queer Call to Action Since 1989," *Slate*, December 1, 2016. On ACT UP New York's housing activism more broadly, see Tamar W. Carroll, "Turn Anger, Fear, Grief into Action: ACT UP New York," chap. 5 in *Mobilizing New York: AIDS, Antipoverty, and Feminist Activism* (Chapel Hill: University of North Carolina Press, 2015).

29. See *Housing Works History*, interactive timeline written, edited, and produced by Gavin Browning, 2017, http://housingworkshistory.com.

30. Greg Greeley, "Service Organizations for Gay and Lesbian Youth," *Journal of Gay & Lesbian Social Services* 1, no. 3–4 (1994): 111–30; Gerald P. Mallon, "Serving the Needs of Gay and Lesbian Youth in Residential Treatment Centers," *Residential Treatment for Children & Youth* 10, no. 2 (1992): 47–61; Liz Galst, "Throwaway Kids," *Advocate*, December 29, 1992, 54–57; Karen M. Goulart, "The Attic Readies for Its New Home," *Philadelphia Gay News*, May 26–June 1, 2000; Victoria Scanlan Stefanakos, "The Death of a Legend," *Advocate*, November 21, 2000, 16; Christopher Daikos, "No Place Like Home," *Advocate*, June 25, 2002, 74–82; Frank Mok, "A Haven for Homeless Youths" *Advocate*, August 29, 2006, 26–27.

31. Stephen Vider and David S. Byers, "Queer Homeless Youth, Queer Activism in Transition," *Slate*, December 10, 2015. For recent data on homelessness among LGBTQ+ youth, see the report *At the Intersection: A Collaborative Resource on LGBTQ Youth Homelessness*, True Colors United in collaboration with the National LGBTQ Task Force, 2019. On Casa Ruby, see "Giving

Homeless Transgender Youth a Safe Haven from the Streets," *PBS Newshour*, May 22, 2015.
On host home programs, see Katy Read, "Suburban Host Homes Let Homeless Youth Stay in
Their Communities," *Star Tribune*, April 27, 2019, http://www.startribune.com/suburban-host
-homes-let-homeless-youth-stay-in-their-communities/508623252/; and Laura Symthe, "Philly
'Host Home' Program Aims to Slash LGBTQ Youth Homelessness, Shelter Costs," *WHYY*,
July 27, 2019, https://whyy.org/articles/philly-host-home-program-aims-to-slash-lgbtq-youth
-homelessness-shelter-costs/.

32. On the early history of SAGE, see Lauren Jae Gutterman, "'Caring for Our Own': The
Founding of Senior Action in a Gay Environment, 1977–1985," *Radical History Review*, no. 139
(2021): 178–99. See also Arlene Kochman, "Gay and Lesbian Elderly: Historical Overview
and Implications for Social Work Practice," *Journal of Gay & Lesbian Social Services* 6, no. 1
(1997): 1–10.

33. On GALAXY, see Carolyn Said, "Gay-Friendly Senior Housing, Half-Century-Old
Idea," *San Francisco Chronicle*, June 26, 2011; Sue Hyde, "Galaxy Grays," *Gay Community News*,
December 22, 1984.

34. "Gay Retirement Village under Way," *Womyn's Words*, November 1998, 9; "The Florida
Palms First Gay Retirement," *Networker*, Fall 2000, 1, 7; "Emerging Retirement Options for
Older Lesbians Gays," *Networker*, Fall 2000, 1, 11; Deborah Baker, "For Gay Retirees, a Place to
Feel at Home," *Washington Post*, January 18, 2004; Claire Wilson, "Gay Retirement Communities
Are Growing in Popularity," *New York Times*, November 20, 2005; Dan Frosch, "Hard Times for
Gay Retirement Homes," *New York Times*, October 28, 2011; Matthew Wilkinson, "What It's Re-
ally Like at an LGBTI-Inclusive Assisted Living Retirement Facility in Palm Springs," *Gay Star
News*, September 28, 2018, https://www.gaystarnews.com/article/what-its-really-like-at-an-lgbti
-inclusive-assisted-living-retirement-facility-in-palm-springs/. On discrimination in retirement
communities and nursing homes, see *Gen Silent*, dir. Stu Maddox, 2010.

35. Mark Segal, *And Then I Danced: Traveling the Road to LGBT Equality* (Brooklyn, NY:
Akashic Books, 2015); Emily Wax-Thibodeaux, "Philadelphia Apartment Building May Be a
National Model for Low-Income LGBT Seniors," *Washington Post*, September 12, 2014.

36. Winnie Hu, "Creating a Home for L.G.B.T. Seniors in New York City," *New York
Times*, July 3, 2017; Tim Teeman, "'We Want to Live, Not Hide': Inside New York City's First
LGBT Elder Housing Project," *Daily Beast*, March 8, 2019, https://www.thedailybeast.com/
we-want-to-live-not-hide-inside-new-york-citys-first-lgbt-elder-housing-project; Hailey
Branson-Potts, "For LGBT Seniors, Affordable Housing is Scarce and Often Unwelcoming," *Los
Angeles Times*, April 19, 2014; Catherine Fusillo, "Affordable LGBTQ-Affirming Senior Living
Center Breaks Ground in the Third Ward," *Houston Public Media*, August 6, 2019, https://www
.houstonpublicmedia.org/articles/news/local/2019/08/06/341956/affordable-lgbtq-affirming
-senior-living-center-breaks-ground-in-the-third-ward/; Robert Weisman, "Boston Selects De-
veloper for Region's First LGBTQ-Friendly Senior Housing Complex," *Boston Globe*, November 13, 2019, https://www.bostonglobe.com/metro/2019/11/13/boston-selects-developer-for
-region-first-lgbtq-friendly-senior-housing-complex/fL6wuPXYoR5ObwsyDBUijN/story.html.

INDEX

(television program), 201–9, 213; public
access television, 204; queer community,
expanded vision of, 183–84; structural
racism, 182; substance abuse, 194–95, 198;
support, forms of, 187–88; transgender
clients, 194; video, use of, 201; volunteers,
demographics of, 193–94
Gay Militants, The (Teal), 144
Gay New York (Chauncey), 4–5
gay rights movement, 73
gay space, 90, 162
Gay Sunshine (newspaper), 75–76, 83
Gay Women's Service Center, 154–55
Gelbert, Bruce-Michael, 209
gender, 9, 108, 140; as kind of script, 8; as styl-
ized repetition of acts, 8
gender dysphoria, 176–77
gender essentialism, 99, 109
gender identity disorder, 177
gender nonconformity, 73
gender separatism, 99
George, Marie-Amélie, 170
Georgia, 216–17
Gerhard, Jane, 135
Germany, 91
Giard, Luce, 9
GI Bill, 14, 45. *See also* Servicemen's Readjust-
ment Act
Gifford, Horace, 137–38
Giuliani, Rudy, 6
Glide Methodist Church, 148
Goffman, Erving, 8, 54
"Golden Age of Queens, The" (Hogan), 62, 78
Golden Gate Gay Liberation House, 159, *160*.
See also Survival House
Gonzalez, Alida "Lilly," 211–12, *212*, 213
Gonzalez, Federico, 204
Goodman, Paul, 87
Good News (musical), 62, 252n15
Goodstein, David, 255n69
Goodyear, Carmen, 131
Gordon, David Cole, 147
Gould, Deborah, 181, 184
Gray, Beverly, 198
Gray, Virginia, 133
Grayson, Howard, *95*
Great Barrington (Massachusetts), 140
Great Depression, 14
Greenberg, Anne, 200, *201*

Green Chimneys, 225
Greenhouse, 148
Grier, Barbara, 39, 41, 48
Grinker, Lori, 184
group marriage, 85
Growing Up Absurd (Goodman), 87
Gruzen & Partners, 138
Guild Book Service, 59
Guild Press, 73
Gund, Catherine, 207
Gutterman, Lauren, 7, 17, 20

Hague, Betsy, 149, *150*, 151
Haldane, Mark, 56–57, *57*
Hallas, Roger, 203
Hammer, Barbara, 132, *132*, 133, 135; essential-
ism of, 110
Hanhardt, Christina, 143–44
Hanson, Craig Alfred, 75–76
Hardwick, Michael, 216–17
Harrad Experiment, The (Rimmer), 85
Harrad West, 85
Harris, Bertha, 106, 117, 119
Hawaii, 155
Hay, Harry, 18, 103–4
Hayden, Dolores, 111
Haynes, Reggie, 95, *95*, 96
Heresies (journal), 135
Herring, Scott, 131
Herrle, June, 155
"Herspace" (Birkby), 133
Hesford, Victoria, 109–10
heteronormativity, 5
heterosexual home: as less typical today, 215;
as oppressive, 51–52
heterosexual marriage: as mark of maturity,
45; as repressive institution, 89. *See also*
marriage
HGTV, vision of domestic citizenship, 221
Highland Park Collective, 100
Hill, Robert, 20
Hillmer, Jack, 43
hippie communes, 84–85
hippies, 84
HIV/AIDS, 3, 25, 179–80, 182–84, 188–90,
192, 197–98, 201–4, 207, 209, 211, 213, 223,
225–26; activism, 26; buddy programs, 185;
demographics of, 193–94; domestic history,
as overlooked, 181; home, as critical space

HIV/AIDS (*continued*)
of care, 185; and isolation, sense of, 186–87, 208; women of color, as overlooked, 2
HIV Housing (Dzubilo), 184–85
Hobbs, Michael E., 217
Hogan, Lou Rand, 24, 59, 64–65, 75, 89, 253n21; background of, 62–63; camp, version of, 60–61, 67; camp humor, 61, 68, 76, 78; cosmopolitan cookery of, 74; gay domesticity, representation of, 71, 73, 79; humor, and affluence, 74; "Mother" persona of, 78; respectability, as pragmatic approach, 73. *See also* Randall, Louis
Hogan, Lucille, 62
Hoganson, Kristin, 74
Hohengarten, William M., 281n10
Holmes, Elsie, 43
Holmes, Mark, 185–86
home, 3, 19, 106, 108; adaptation, as site of, 177–78; AIDS activism, 184, 213; AIDS epidemic, 185; American idealization of, 12–13; communal belonging, and kinship, 213; and conformity, 18; and connection, 227; as contradiction, site of, 108; cultural ideal of, 221; housing justice, 227; ideas, as realization of, 8; isolation, as space of, 186; kinship, sense of, 21; LGBTQ shelter activism, 177; marginalization, site of, 214; middle-class values, adoption of, 8; parlor, presence of, 8–9; personal comfort, as site of, 43–44; picture window, 57–58; politics of exclusion, 222; as portal to public, 10; privacy of, 20, 31; as private space, 10, 12; queering of, 222; as refuge, 12, 185–86; regularity of, 8; resistance, as site of, 10; as retreat, 58; same-sex sexual intimacy, 217; as sanctuary, 12; sense of self, 21; social conservatism, as site of, 10; as space of care, 25; stability, projection of, 8; as stage, 58; state intrusion, as shield against, 216, 227; and subversive repetition, 8; and surveillance, 10, 177–78; zone of privacy, 216
homelessness, 156; among LGBTQ, 25, 143, 223; oppression, as symptom of, 144; police harassment, 143; among youth, 151, 158
homemaking, 8, 227; belonging, boundaries of, 223; communal and national belonging, expression of, 3; and conformity, 87; cultural citizenship, as form of, 7; and

domesticity, performance of, 3; normative, 15–16; redefining of, 131; social performance, as mode of, 7; subversive potential of, 10–11. *See also* household
homeownership, rise in, 13
homonormativity, 6, 10, 31–32
homophile movement, 43, 54, 71, 105, 149; adjustment, reframing language of, 46–47; bill of rights, 245n11; domestic citizenship, 31–32; and home, as site of adaptation, 177–78; homosexual marriage, support for, 31, 56; and integration, 61, 178; marriage, prioritization of, 30; and middle-class life, 31; privacy, prioritizing of, 61, 146; in psychological terms, 49; queer people of color in, 52; romantic adjustment, as path toward integration, 58; swishing, distancing from, 61; as white and middle class, 52, 84
homophobia, 42, 118, 185–86, 195–96, 198, 221
homosexuality, 59, 88; conformist stance toward, challenging of, 71, 73; as defense mechanism, 45; as "dread disease," 55; happy homosexual, notion of, 67; integration of, 47; maladjustment, as symptom of, 45, 51, 67, 69; mental illness, as sign of, 47; as neurosis, 45; normative ideals, rejection of, 73; public space, and visibility, 78; racial, class, and gender privilege, 78; vs. transgender identities, 177
Homosexuality and Citizenship in Florida (report), 55
homosexual marriage, 24, 36, 48, 52, 54; acceptance of, by parents, 39, 41; as adjustment, form of, 31; as alternative to "immature" sexual expression, 30; anxiety in, 56; as aspirational model for citizenship, 30; average length of, 32; as double-bind, 58; gay male couples, male and female lines of responsibility, 34–35; heterosexual marriages, mimicking of, 34; lesbian couples and butch/femme roles, 34; and loneliness, 33; maturity, step toward, 47; and monogamy, 49; police encounters, 42–43; and privacy, 30, 35, 42, 56, 58, 220; psychological adjustment, link between, 49; and psychology, 43; public disapproval, 35; and respectability, 31; social disapproval, fear of, 30; wedding ceremonies, 33. *See also* same-sex marriage

and bound by CPI Group (UK) Ltd, Croydon, CR0 4YY